D1519997

THE MATERIAL WORD

RICHARD W. F. KROLL

The Material Word

Literate Culture in
the Restoration and
Early Eighteenth Century

The Johns Hopkins University Press
Baltimore and London

The Johns Hopkins University Press
701 West 40th Street, Baltimore, Maryland 21211
The Johns Hopkins Press Ltd., London

The paper used in this publication meets the minimum requirements of American National Standard for Information Sciences—Permanence of Paper for Printed Library Materials, ANSI Z39.48–1984.

LIBRARY OF CONGRESS CATALOGING-IN-PUBLICATION DATA

Kroll, Richard W. F.
  The material word: literate culture in the Restoration and early eighteenth century / Richard W. F. Kroll
      p.   cm.
  Includes bibliographical references.
  ISBN 0-8018-4002-3 (alk. paper)
    1. English literature—Early modern, 1500–1700—History and criticism—Theory, etc. 2. English literature—18th century—History and criticism—Theory, etc. 3. Great Britain—Intellectual life—17th century. 4. Great Britain—Intellectual life—18th century. 5. Neoclassicism (Literature) 6. Classicism—Great Britain. 7. Epicurus—Influence. I. Title.
PR437.K7 1990   820.9′004—dc20   90-30586 CIP

In Memoriam Philip Wilhelm Ulrich Kroll
To my Mother

So much delights me as those graceful acts,
Those thousand decencies that daily flow
From all her words and actions mixed with love
And sweet compliance, which declare unfeigned
Union of mind, or in us both one soul.

John Milton, *Paradise Lost*, 8:600–604

And this I well remember, and afterwards observed, how I first learn'd to speake. For my elders did not teach me this abilitie, by giving of me words in any certaine order of teaching, (as they did letters afterwards) but by that minde which thou my God gavest me, I myself with gruntings, varieties of voyces, and various motions of my body, strove to express the conceits of mine own heart, that my desire might be obeyed; but could not bring it out, either what I would have, or to whom I desired. Then I settled in my memory when they named anything; and when at that name they moved their bodies towards that thing, I observed it, and gathered thereby, that that word, which they then pronounced, was the very name of the thing which they shewed me.

And that they meant this (or that) *thing, was discovered to me by the motion of their bodies, even by that naturall language (as it were) of all nations; which expressed by the countenance and cast of the eye, by the action of other parts, and the sound of the voice; discovers the affections of the mind, either to desire, enjoy, refuse, or to do any thing. And thus words in divers sentences, set in their due places, and heard often over, I by little and little collected, of what things they were the signes; and having broken my mouth to the pronunciation of them, I by them expressed mine owne purposes. Thus (with those whom I conversed withall) did I communicate the expressions of mine owne desires; and ventured thereby upon the troublesome societie of humane business, depending all this while upon the authoritie of my parents, and being at the beck of my Elders.*

William Wats, D.D., *Saint Augustine's Confessions Translated* (1650)

Our Business here is not to know all things, but those which concern our Conduct.

John Locke, *An Essay concerning Human Understanding* (1690)

Contents

Illustrations

Preface

In this book I describe the peculiar conditions that gave rise to English neoclassical culture. I also trace the ways in which that culture saw itself as coherent, though it expressed that coherence less by a series of thematic connections or tropes, and more by a commitment to method as an idea and as a way of seeing things. Even if these aims are only partially realized, I hope at least to show how English culture alternately exploited and distinguished itself from Continental, especially French, culture. For example, I attend to the sceptical-empirical strain of English thought from the mid-seventeenth century on. And I would argue (without, I hope, seeming merely parochial) that we should not treat Restoration and early-eighteenth-century England as representative of a wider European 'enlightenment.' Indeed, it is relatively rare for English neoclassical authors to apply that term to themselves, especially with the valencies it achieves across the channel.

My own training and inclinations as a literary critic foster a determination to revive and extend our general expectations of how English texts (of all kinds) from the period I discuss do and should behave. This desire is born partly out of the belief that the eighteenth century as a literary field labors under two main disadvantages, by contrast to the Renaissance and Romantics—those periods that traditionally bracket it. The first is a product of a Romantic, then a Victorian, and yet later an Eliotic assault on the aesthetic that the eighteenth century was thought or said to embody. In a brilliant and damning formulation, Matthew Arnold praised the eighteenth century as an age of "prose and reason," with Dryden as its high priest. Whereas T. S. Eliot added Milton to that genealogy, Milton has been quicker to recover than his poetic contemporary. These prejudices are fast eroding—I can even persuade my undergraduates of Dryden's virtues—but this attitude still manifests itself in the way that literature is anthologized for college teaching in the United States, and it has oddly achieved a late life in the literary landscape depicted by Harold Bloom's highly influential book *The Anxiety of Influence*.

More significantly (though for related reasons), the Renaissance and Romantic fields can assume an established and broadly descriptive historiography from which to depart or, as commonly, with which to quarrel. By contrast, the eighteenth century—a shorthand for the century and half after 1660—has no Rosamund Tuve or M. H. Abrams to present a series of useful generalities about an entire literary period which we can later refine or discard. This is not to say that books such as Paul Fussell's *The Rhetorical World of Augustan Humanism* or Martin Price's *To the Palace of Wisdom* cannot be described as seminal. It is just that in the range or manner of their enquiry, they either describe a narrow strain of neoclassical literature or comprise a series of provocative essays on individual texts spanning the period. Outside introductory surveys, some of which are admirable, perhaps the most general account of this kind is still W. J. Bate's *The Burden of the Past and the English Poet;* but again, this appears more in the form of a sketch than a comprehensive description.

My own response to the difficulty has been to extend the most fruitful line of enquiry to be applied to Restoration comedy into the wider arena of this book. Modern criticism of that drama experienced a revival in the 1950s, by virtue of a flexible application of intellectual history to the problems it posed. Following Thomas H. Fujimura's *The Restoration Comedy of Wit,* Norman N. Holland's *The First Modern Comedies* elegantly exemplified how intellectual-historical method could provide a tool for the interpretation of literary texts. Similar methods were also being elaborated in Earl Wasserman's strenuous readings of individual neoclassical poems (as in *The Subtler Language*) and, supremely, in his brilliant article on the poetics of eighteenth-century landscape literature, "Nature Moralized: The Divine Analogy in the Eighteenth Century." If I have any ambition for myself, it is that this book should manifest something of the regard I hold for Wasserman's work, which in its way has never been surpassed.

By a similar token, for me the most useful *general* models for understanding the seventeenth and eighteenth centuries remain two books of intellectual history: Ernst Cassirer's *The Philosophy of the Enlightenment* and Richard H. Popkin's *The History of Scepticism from Erasmus to Spinoza.* Beginning with these works, I have asked how the 'ideas' they treat thematically could be applied to a more *rhetorical* understanding of the texts they discuss. Something of this revision is, obviously, embodied in Michel Foucault's *The Order of Things*. And it is also one effect of a slew of studies on seventeenth- and eighteenth-century forms of probability, such as Henry van Leeuwen's *The Problem of Certainty in Seventeenth-Century England*, Ian Hacking's *The Emergence of Probability*, Barbara Shapiro's *Probability and Certainty in Seventeenth-Century England*, and Douglas Lane Patey's *Probability and Literary Form*.

Once we have seen how ideas are embedded in rhetorical forms, conditions, and motives, the next step is to introduce intellectual history—as traditionally practiced—to the realm of what is currently called cultural studies. Loosely conceived, cultural studies hold that we can only interpret the workings of a given culture, displaced from us in either space or time, by reading it as a complex matrix of symbols and rhetorical devices, most of which are inevident to the actors within that culture. Although cultural studies as currently conceived often present themselves with a Marxist patina, their genealogies are more various than that. Two sources that have influenced me here are Ludwig Wittgenstein's *Philosophical Investigations* and Kenneth Burke's *Language as Symbolic Action*. The former proposes that language is indistinguishable from all other forms of human behavior, which together weave that fabric of human meanings Wittgenstein denominates a "form of life"; the latter similarly proposes that culture is constituted of a network of symbols that must be understood rhetorically. Burke's theory of symbolic action quite understandably influences the symbolic anthropology of Clifford Geertz's *The Interpretation of Cultures*.

Finally, I have drawn upon the post-Kuhnian historiography of science, which concentrates on the social conditions and uses of ideas, whether or not we value these as 'scientific.' For example, both Paul Feyerabend's *Against Method* and David Bloor's *Knowledge and Social Imagery*—which also draws on Wittgenstein—attempt to reduce the status of the scientific to the social. I do not accept the more extreme consequences of Feyerabend's or Bloor's arguments (for example, I do not think that we should admit a simple ratio between interest and rationality), but I view important elements in mid-seventeenth-century natural philosophy through the filter provided by the neo-Epicurean revival because neo-Epicureanism was able—unlike much modern science, and the positivism in much history of science—to admit and examine its ethical and political motives. In this, I am influenced by Steven Shapin and Simon Schaffer's study of the success of Restoration experimentalism as an ideology of natural as well as social knowledge and behavior (*Leviathan and the Air Pump*).

Although indebted to Shapin and Schaffer, I depart from them in two ways: first, I argue more insistently for a notion of reading that, by attending to neoclassical philosophies of language, can show where historical forces are detectable in Restoration texts. Second, I use the neo-Epicurean revival to examine how the appropriation of ancient cultural models served the English at a moment of cultural crisis. I thus owe a great deal to R. H. Kargon's excellent *Atomism in England from Hariot to Newton*, but again wish to extend its narrower interests in physics to the broader ethical and aesthetic consequences of the neo-Epicurean revival. Kargon does, however, show how the importation of atomism to England from France after the 1640s is a matter of group commitments, and the implications of this recognition are more fully described in Robert Frank, Jr.'s *Harvey and the Oxford Physiologists*.

By thus reworking this line of inquiry in the history of science, I wish, like Brian Vickers, to lay to rest the tradition of 'plain-style' criticism, which owes its origin to R. F. Jones's numerous utterances and has its most comprehensive expression in Robert Adolph's *The Rise of Modern Prose Style*. Jones's notion of science is visibly influenced by the progressivism of his era. When applied to the notion of scientific conduct as rhetorical and cultural—which, I argue, informs not only Restoration natural philosophy but also neoclassical discourse in general—it reveals itself as an anachronism. This is also to take issue with another means of describing the changes in literary protocols that emerged at midcentury—namely, George Williamson's argument that prose writers self-consciously adopted a Senecan, curt style, as a means to displace a Ciceronian stylistic model (see *The Senecan Amble*). Cicero's own theory of the rhetorical nature of culture provided a rationale by which the Restoration could prescribe 'plain style' as itself a highly artificial, rhetorical vehicle of expression.

My interest in the philosophy of language and the history of linguistics is abundantly served by Hans Aarsleff's *From Locke to Saussure*, whose main theses about intellectual history I confirm. Again, my departure occurs when I discuss texts that precede Locke, and when I urge that we must attend specifically to the texts' own methods of representing their arguments—that is, their rhetoric—and that their philosophies of language represent clear institutional motives. I also disagree with M. M. Slaughter's *Universal Languages and Scientific Taxonomy in the Seven-*

teenth Century because I do not see the shift from essentialist to nominal epistemologies taking place first in the middle of the Restoration, or as suddenly as Slaughter's Foucauldian methodology would suggest. The period of gestation, I argue throughout, is 1640–1660. I bring similar criticisms to Murray Cohen's *Sensible Words*. As regards theology, I gratefully use and then depart from H. R. McAdoo's luminous *The Spirit of Anglicanism,* Gerard Reedy's *The Bible and Reason,* and Hans Frei's *The Eclipse of Biblical Narrative.*

In sum, I hope to explore the limitations placed on our understanding of neoclassical culture by academic constraints. And I hope to locate and describe some of those manifold criteria that the culture itself acknowledged. Only the reader can determine how fruitful that ambition is.

Acknowledgments

Like most authors, I have a host of debts. I owe a keen intellectual debt to Alan Roper, who comes closest in my experience to what Matthew Arnold describes as "disinterestedness." He exemplifies what I have come to value most about the academy. John Wallace's deep and elegant articles on seventeenth-century reading serve appropriately as some original points of inspiration for what follows. Those of us gathered at the William Andrews Clark Memorial Library during 1981–82 still celebrate "the readers of the lost Clark," a group animated and refreshed almost hourly by Richard Popkin's fecundity. I count among those Paul Alkon, Jim Force, Jan Golinski, John Rogers, Simon Varey, and Bob Westman. The Clark later introduced me to Brean Hammond and Rose Zimbardo. I also thank Chris Grose and Max Novak, my teachers at UCLA, for their assistance with this book.

At Princeton, I had two years of leave, a luxury few can enjoy. I have also been fortunate in my colleagues and my students. Hans Aarsleff, Margaret Doody, and Earl Miner are undoubtedly better equipped to address aspects of my thesis than I. Vicky Kahn, a friend and an exemplary colleague, valiantly slogged through much prose that no longer appears here. Seth Lerer has been a model reader, providing the ideal balance of praise and criticism. Fraser Easton, Bill Edinger, David Furley, Lynn Joy, Uli Knoepflmacher, Jayne Lewis, Michael McKeon, Eric Rothstein, Simon Varey, and Margaret Wilson read and commented on parts of the book at different stages and undoubtedly improved it. Cyrus Hoy and Russell Peck extended their hospitality at the University of Rochester during my first leave. I have also benefited from conversations with Richard Ashcraft, Ian Balfour and Deborah Esch, Jim Buickerood, Aileen Douglas, Aline Fairweather, Anne Barbeau Gardiner, Mark Kipperman, Jules Law, Deborah Payne, Tom Roche, David Sewell, and Harvey Teres. I learned much from the members of my Spring 1988 graduate seminar on neoclassical discourse: Christoph Holländer, Laura

Kellogg, Sheila Newbery, and Sarah Zimmerman. And Laura, Sarah, and Peter McCulloch, as well as Jane Warth at the Johns Hopkins University Press, all patiently worked with me to check and refine the manuscript. Any mistakes are, of course, mine.

Princeton University provided me with generous grants and fellowships, including the Surdna Foundation Grant, the Frank D. Graham Research Grant, and the John E. Annan Preceptorship. I am grateful to the American Council of Learned Societies for a fellowship and the National Endowment for the Humanities for a travel grant. The William Andrews Clark Memorial Library provided a dissertation fellowship, as well as a host of friends: apart from those already mentioned, John Bidwell, Carol Briggs, Susan and Larry Green, and Carol Sommer deserve thanks. I have also received assistance from the staffs of the Bibliothèque Nationale; the Bodleian Library; the Henry E. Huntington Library; the Princeton University Library; and the University of Rochester Library.

Finally, I have been blessed in my wife, Victoria, who has been the ideal partner in every way. Those who know her know her rare capacity to combine moral passion with intellectual integrity. She has brought with her a family whose support and assistance I could never repay.

THE MATERIAL WORD

Introduction: Atoms, Bodies, and Words

In 1936 R. F. Jones published *Ancients and Moderns,* his influential study of the scientific revolution in England. Jones celebrated the emergence of a 'scientific' attitude from the mid-seventeenth century on, in which an earlier, ancient, and nonscientific mentality gave way before the advances of a new, modern, and utilitarian conception of the world and of language. Supplemented by a series of articles on language change in the late-seventeenth century, Jones's thesis appeared in the world with all the force of scholarly range and prestige;[1] so that in 1938, in an equally influential monograph "Science, Technology and Society in Seventeenth-Century England," Robert K. Merton could write with perfect confidence that "toward the middle of the century, science, as a social value, rose conspicuously in the scale of estimation" and that, as an aesthetic value, "realism, in the sense of concrete empiricism, permeated all fields. The realistic genre and landscape painting predominated; in music the realistic opera was introduced; in literature, the realistic drama and concretely descriptive essay."[2] Jones's and Merton's view that the enlightenment cultivated 'scientific,' 'realistic,' or 'utilitarian' desiderata for literary expression still informs much modern criticism of the period. Thus Timothy Reiss has written (apparently without irony) that the perfect referentiality of the Houyhnhnms's language in *Gulliver's Travels* is "very close to that ideal transparent mediator which [became] the ideal expressive instrument of European rationalism."[3]

No scholar challenges the view that something that we might now call 'science' emerged as a coherent and recognizable series of practices and attitudes in the mid-seventeenth century. But relatively few have investigated the language that figures from that period used to describe their own practices. Even fewer have sought to ask whether Jones's and Merton's portrayal of aesthetic norms after roughly 1650 could be defended either as characterizations of what the historical agents themselves sought, or as providing a useful descriptive language for modern

1

criticism. The study that follows proceeds with the following assumptions: that the Jones-Merton thesis has distorted our view of literary history in the second half of the seventeenth century (in which I include *Paradise Lost*); that this distortion is only corrigible by challenging it squarely on the methodological grounds it established; that the literary community has subscribed to the Jones-Merton thesis (often without knowing it) because it has served to reinforce a Romantic characterization of the limitations of the neoclassical aesthetic, an aesthetic that many college undergraduates find somewhat elusive; that even the developments in poststructuralist theory have been so determined by their own (post-Romantic) genealogies that they also have contributed to the misappropriation of the eighteenth century as a cultural fiction, treating it as the locus of an 'enlightenment' that exaggerated the powers of the mind; and that finally such misprision is neither inevitable nor desirable.[4]

Like others, I argue first that Jones was right to attach his interest in science to his interest in language. If 'science' emerged in the later seventeenth century, we also see an accompanying revision in attitudes to language and to literary practice. Changes in ideas about knowledge involved changes in ideas about language as the vehicle of knowledge. Second, I believe that intellectual history (including those studies focussing on seventeenth-century ideas about language) is limited when it fails to recognize that the very rhetoric of the materials that supply its evidence constitutes for us a substantive claim in itself, and it was so seen by neoclassical authors. This is true not least because seventeenth-century schooling was heavily indebted to Cicero's arguments about the rhetorical grounds of all knowledge, especially as they intersected with the public sphere.[5] Without examining this tradition at length, I show that the cultural theories encouraged by that rhetorical tradition developed a distinctive vocabulary from the mid-seventeenth century on. Certainly, style did not shift from some 'Ciceronian' model to a 'Senecan' equivalent, which is what Morris Croll and George Williamson proposed to explain the shift in prose styles that occurred in the period I describe. The Croll-Williamson thesis finally requires too simple a notion of how literary styles are imitated in any age, and it ignores the extent to which the later seventeenth century adapted any ancient models only by first distancing and reexamining them from a methodical perspective: the focus on 'style' is simply too precious. Thus, the way a text such as *Leviathan* or *Paradise Lost* behaves can become the main subject matter of that text, or can qualify the assertions it makes in other ways.

Third, I hold that the significance of the methodical claim embedded in the rhetoric of a text depends on the values with which the culture locally endows that method. The way a text behaves came to assume specific symbolic and ideological importance for a culture acutely sensitive to reading at such a level: Roy Porter has properly suggested that the eighteenth century anticipates 'modernity' in its capacity for "auto-analysis."[6] Further, the ability to read for method and to understand its implied claims was itself the product of the series of cultural and epistemological revisions that the rise of experimental science typifies.

Finally, I argue that the method implied by textual behavior or performance achieves a value that simultaneously affects not only one but many different cultural arenas, whether we now label those arenas 'science,' 'literature,' 'theology,' or 'linguistics.' The story of the rise of science in the later seventeenth century thus belongs inexorably to an entire set of narratives of which 'science' is both beneficiary and stimulus. To see Newton as important only as a scientist who wrote the *Principia* is to neglect the extent to which (biographically) the major energies of his life were given over to other decidedly 'unscientific' things and the degree to which he treated all his intellectual activities as mutually reinforcing.

My historical argument uses a starting date of 1640, though at points refers to earlier historical moments. It ends around 1720, a date of convenience suggested by the death of Queen Anne in 1714 and by the establishment of political stability by the Whig hegemony that arose after the South Sea Bubble.[7] Ronald Hutton points out in his history of the Restoration that the crucial period immediately preceding the Restoration represents something of a historiographical lacuna.[8] The interval between the death of Oliver Cromwell and the formal reestablishment of the Church of England has not received major treatment by historians. However, the middle years of the seventeenth century seem to me undeniably the crucible in which the chief features of what I call neoclassical culture were under formation. I therefore confirm a long-held view that the Restoration of King Charles II coincided with a determination to revise and police an entire panoply of cultural norms, which included the practice of experimental natural philosophy and new protocols for literary expression. But I question the Jonesian thesis that the scientific world view produced an ideology that treated language as transparent or referential—as an instrument, that is, to an unmediated cognitive and experimental grasp of objects in the world. When neoclassical authors talk about the 'plain style,' they do not advertise what Jones and later scholars in his tradition associate with 'scientific' neutrality or self-evidence.

As Michel Foucault intuits, neoclassical discourse is conscious of its own artificiality. The empiricism that informs this culture is neither naïve nor absolutist, but is consistently sceptical about the powers of the mind. When applied to language, it argues that words always intervene between our desires and what we seek to apprehend. Viewed from one perspective, this recognition might suggest that we can dispose of language, or that we can convert it into some stable referential system of signs. Viewed, however, from the perspective I stress below, the limits of language are the necessary limits within which human cognition can and must operate: there is no 'outside' language. In this latter interpretation, cognition itself is understood to represent a universe of signs already displaced from objects in the world, and words constitute a second series of displacements from what they supposedly might signify. Moreover, arguments about cognition in this period also entail attitudes to representation by another route, because they often use a vocabulary that has obvious applications to language itself.

Like the mind's merely contingent access to physical bodies, language does not provide a transparent medium of knowledge, but composes a series of opaque verbal cues that reinforce the external symbolism of cultural behavior. The palpable quality of words—commonly illustrated by metaphors of writing and printing, a consciousness of typography, and an interest in hieroglyphics—approximates something of the palpable quality of the discourse of manners executed in three-dimensional social spaces. As Milton suggests in my opening epigraph from *Paradise Lost,* words and actions are coterminous insofar as, in the context of linguistic use, they reinforce each other. Words appear as constituent elements of a mode of verbal behavior and are not imagined as readily disposable utilitarian vehicles of knowledge: Kenneth Burke might say that they perform "dramatistically." They come endowed with almost tactile properties in their own right, so language is like action where it performs as a mode of social knowledge, along with all the other means by which we function as human and civilized beings. The argument is, for example, familiar to readers of Wittgenstein's later philosophy—Lockean and Wittgenstinian notions of linguistic "use" are not unrelated; but the route by which neoclassical theories of language arrive at this position is peculiar. It finds something of an equivalent in

Burke's view that human beings are "bodies that learn language," the implication being that all features of the human world assume symbolic properties. Just as bodies moving in space constitute one focus of the uniquely human determination to convert all the materials of our environment into elements of a cultural grammar, so language, the most distinctive feature of human behavior, epitomizes a parallel tendency. This argument assumes not that words refer to objects in any simple sense, but that, because the universal human motive is to convert all objects in the world into a language—that is, into rhetorical instruments of communication—words prove merely to be the most economical means to the same end.

Because so much focus has been given to the relationship between science and language in order to propound the view I would like to question, it seems to me unavoidable that we reexamine what was at stake in the historiographical union of science and language. The very determination to move *from* 'science' *to* 'language' in Jones's argument assumed a historically continuous stability of meaning for the categories involved and constructed 'science' as the prior and privileged category of the two. This seems to have guaranteed, in Jones's mind, the kind of narrative of progress in which Americans of his generation believed; it also seems to have provided him with the view that because science was scientific, it supplied a firm ground from which to survey the much more marshy territory of rhetoric. Jones's assumptions contrast markedly with a more recent tradition within the history of science that treats scientific texts as implicated in rhetoric and ideology, which the sociological thrust of Merton's study anticipates. Thomas Kuhn's revolutionary *The Structure of Scientific Revolutions,* as well as his subsequent debates with Karl Popper and Imre Lakatos, reveal how distressing for its opponents the conjunction between language and science could be.[9] Because Kuhn's argument shows that scientific knowledge could not escape its current linguistic and thus ideological condition, Lakatos accused Kuhn of—in almost as many words—inviting mob rule into the sacred halls of scientific inquiry. I do not believe, however, that to argue for the linguistic and rhetorical condition of science necessarily precludes an appeal to rationality, but the story I tell below argues that such appeals also involve clear ideological and political motives. For Jones, for example, as well as for a Church historian such as G. R. Cragg, we may have lost Magic to the change that occurred during and after the Civil War, but we have at least retained Science. For Christopher Hill, this transformation constitutes only a loss, because his claim that literature declined at this point is premised on the decline of the radical tradition he admires.

Ironically, many recent works of eighteenth-century criticism have inadvertently reinforced this version of neoclassical linguistics. Their strong commitment to the novel as a special genre (a value accorded it not by eighteenth-century views of language or genre, but most recently by Mikhail Bakhtin's belief that the novel enjoys special access to reality) still assumes that this genre operates as a special ontological category and that its chief motives are to mirror real life in ways that other modes of representation will not or cannot do. The argument is compounded by those kinds of Marxist analysis that hold that the notion of transparency allegedly recommended by neoclassical views of knowledge accompanies the emergence of the bourgeois consciousness; thus socially responsible criticism implicitly depends on accepting a post-Romantic picture of eighteenth-century forms of representation. Without taking issue with the political motives of these studies, many of which are admirable, I am nonetheless uncomfortable with the ahistorical nature of their seemingly historical claims. In hypothesizing the 'novel' as the site of most intense political and social activity (whether as a means of policing knowledge or of freeing the reader to question the cultural norms), such studies often overlook the depth of linguistic, social, and political analysis at work in the culture at large, which (as Carol Kay has forcefully demonstrated) the 'novel' exploits as much as invents.[10] For the Restoration and eighteenth century, genre (whether poetry, prose, or drama) constitutes no fixed category, but what I prefer to call an "experimental space," or what Eric Rothstein has dubbed "systems of inquiry," which enact the conditions of other kinds of socially symbolic spaces, whether we think of the Lockean space of the mind, texts, or landscapes.

One response to these problems is to see that the period I discuss did not ascribe epistemological or political priority to any discursive field. What happened in natural philosophy is always part of some other movement, and, as we shall see, is defined in large part by 'nonscientific' motives. The same is true for the 'novel,' which (apart from the preceding comments) I do not discuss: my main contribution to the current interest in the eighteenth-century novel is to show that numerous other discursive modes developed in the late-seventeenth century into a remarkably sophisticated defense of narrative. They argued that narrative (along with other rhetorical strategies) signifies and confirms the condition of all human ways of apprehending the world, none of which, in the examples that occur below, necessarily requires the resort to the literary form we now call the novel.

A consequence of the argument as I conduct it is that I must address two different audiences. Although some recent studies within the history of science have begun to demonstrate the rhetorical conditions under which natural philosophy during the Interregnum was practiced, for the most part their authors are demonstrably undertrained in the language and concerns of literary criticism, for which I believe their arguments have profound consequences. I appeal consistently to Steven Shapin and Simon Schaffer's excellent book on the conflict between a Hobbesian and Boyleian conception of scientific, social, and literary conduct.[11] But the weakness of that study is, precisely, its failure to admit that Hobbes's rhetoric is by no means diametrically opposed to the contingent and provisional manner of Boyle's scientific attitudes and texts: viewed from another set of perspectives (in my book, symbolized by an opposition to Aristotle, the Stoics, and Descartes), Hobbes, Boyle, Milton, and others cooperate in constructing a distinctively neoclassical method within their literary practices. As several recent literary critics with intellectual-historical training have pointed out,[12] Hobbes's rhetorical practice in *Leviathan* reveals a Hobbes whose geometrical and demonstrative urge is belied by his assumption that the reader's assent to the entire edifice of his argument is itself provisional. Because Hobbes treats as unique the workings of his own mind evinced in his treatise, they can only achieve suasive force when the reader provisionally accepts the analogy between his own and Hobbes's mental fictions. At the end of *Leviathan,* indeed, Hobbes releases the reader from absolute submission to his argument, just as he sees himself as now free to continue with other, and different, projects. To look solely at the geometrical rhetoric of (for the most part) books one and two is to ignore its boundary conditions, and the way that Hobbes himself becomes a contingent reader of texts (the Scriptures) in book four. Close attention to the rhetoric of *Leviathan* shows how the strategies of a text can materially alter the substantive assertions we make about its thesis: when we practice intellectual history or political science, we are still too comfortable with trading lapidary paraphrases of Hobbes's position.

To bring more rigorously rhetorical concerns to intellectual history is only one part of my project. I contend that a similar readjustment of assumptions must occur in the way that literary critics and theorists read neoclassical literature by learning to scrutinize more patiently the local intellectual conditions under which discursive attitudes are forged. (We must know why it is specifically *neoclassical*.) To execute this multiple maneuver, I have divided my book into three sections, and then close with a reading of John Dryden's *Absalom and Achitophel*. Part one ("The Neoclassical Turn at the Restoration") expounds in greater length the thesis I have paraphrased above. Chapter one depicts the Restoration as a psycho-historical fulcrum in English history, which experienced a transformation in the ways the culture imagined and represented itself. I argue that English society strenuously reconstructed a new cultural rhetoric, forging a system of symbols by which to define itself and creating a comprehensive mechanism by which individuals could navigate within that society. Chapter two involves a general exposition of those codes of reading. Without arguing that it universally defines our experience of Restoration and eighteenth-century discourse, I believe that the hermeneutic I describe persists throughout the eighteenth century and still determines the peculiar confluence of arguments about knowledge, reading, and ethics that drives, variously, Samuel Johnson's *Rasselas* and Jane Austen's *Northanger Abbey* or *Pride and Prejudice*. Indeed, introducing his famous edition of Plato (1804), Thomas Taylor sees this hermeneutic as still so coherent and visible at the beginning of the nineteenth century that it constitutes his chief object of attack: for Taylor's transcendental epistemology, the particulars of the "experimentalists" operate as insufficiently transparent principles. Defending his view of Platonic 'science,' he writes that "the particulars . . . of which an induction is made in order to produce science, must be so simple that they may be immediately apprehended, and that the universal may be predicated of them without hesitation. The particulars of the experimentalists are not of this kind, and therefore never can be sources of science truly so called."[13]

My general argument requires part two of my book ("Plotting Neo-Epicureanism: The Transmission of Method and Cultural Imagery"), even though I risk making some of my readers impatient. Here I show one of the great attractions of the period I describe, namely the detail with which neoclassical writers questioned and strategically revised the inherited grounds of their cultural practices. I am not alone in arguing that the Restoration represents a moment of extraordinary fluidity that seemed to require a redefinition of the myths by which English culture might function. The chief architects of the social and literary scene after the Restoration reimagined those terms by envisaging their knowledge of the ancient world as a map of their present circumstances: unlike one earlier Renaissance habit that tended to treat the ancients as a unitary font of allusion and appropriation, the neoclassical habit sought rather to contextualize and discriminate consistently among its ancient sources. By contrast to Jones's assumption that Restoration and eighteenth-century culture finally cultivated the moderns over the ancients, J. W. Johnson and Howard Weinbrot have shown how far neoclassical culture used and mythologized those ancient sources for its modern purposes;[14] I show that this attitude also applies to experimental natural philosophy. By visibly preferring one philosophical or cultural model to another, neoclassical writers demonstrated what in their own culture they desired to replace, and how they wanted to replace it. It is important to recognize that individuals often drew on a number of different sources, such as the Stoic vocabulary of obligation. But they also found in ancient Epicureanism a highly sophisticated view of how the physical world was constructed from atoms and the void; a unique (in ancient culture) expression of a hypothetical method that followed from and reinforced its cosmology, as well as a self-conscious cultural ethic that dissented from the surrounding Hellenistic culture, made important departures from Scepticism and Stoicism, its Hellenistic cousins, and incidentally proposed the bonding of all, even women and slaves, by a friendship carried out within the confines of Epicurus's famous garden. Thus I hope to demonstrate that, for an influential group of English thinkers and writers, Epicureanism articulated a cultural model that they felt to symbolize a resistance to cultural fragmentation (associated with the Civil War) on the one hand, and tyranny (associated with the radical sects or Louis XIV's France) on the other. This is not, of course, to claim that Epicureanism offered the only such model. But in many cases in which it was not explicitly or consciously adopted, its network of values seems to provide the modern observer with an extraordinarily apt metaphor for the intellectual and ethical needs of a generation that was coming to terms with a period of national crisis.

I label this section of the book "Plotting Neo-Epicureanism" both because the story ('plot') of the neo-Epicurean revival is itself significant for my thesis and because I want to stress the deliberation with which neo-Epicureanism appears to have been cultivated and advertised ('plotted'). I emphasize a historical narrative to show how Epicurus came to England and to localize the formation of attitudes that later became general. Despite the prominence I give this account, I do not wish to imply that every author I discuss was somehow a neo-Epicurean. I char-

acterize neoclassical linguistics, for example, as 'Lucretian' because it
supposes language to derive from minimal elements in ways that recall
the Epicurean account of language. Nevertheless, to understand why
Epicurus appealed to the writers I discuss in part two more powerfully
than Aristotle or the Stoics (whose models of knowledge, physics, and
language they found inhospitable), I conduct the reader through some
fairly detailed discussions of Epicurus, Gassendi, and the early English
neo-Epicureans. To the actors involved, the details are what counted: it
was crucial, for example, that they saw the difference between Stoic and
Epicurean theories of knowledge and matter. The Stoics harbored a
conception that a rare form of knowledge was available to the initiate, a
view that caused the Epicurean in Horace to satirize the resulting social
elitism, because the Epicureans treated the capacities of all minds as
similar, and as similarly incapable of perceiving the essences of things.
The Stoics thought of matter as being continuous; the Epicureans
wanted to distinguish between the atoms and the void. Each cosmology
implies different views, for example, of human will: the Epicurean void
exists in large part to preserve the capacity for discrete particles to move,
a physical expression of a democratizing commitment to individual
choice.

My separate discussions of Epicurus and then Gassendi articulate an
argument that the elements of Epicurean and neo-Epicurean thought
achieve an extraordinary mutuality. Together, these elements cohere in
their attitudes to knowledge, the physical world, to method, to cognition, and finally not only to language in general but also a particular idea
of how representation, viewed as an imagery, comes to have cultural and
exemplary significance. In this I follow Bernard Frischer's book *The
Sculpted Word: Epicureanism and Philosophical Recruitment in Ancient
Greece.*[15] Like a detective novel, and like Gassendi's own fascination with
this object, my argument pursues the elusive idea of Epicurus's image. In
the inscribed image of Epicurus, the bookish equivalent to the statues of
Epicurus revered by his followers, I find a concentrated emblem of a
series of Epicurean attitudes to cognition that have consequences for
how we should see language. That Epicureanism could result in a poetic
is constantly attested to by Lucretius's masterpiece, *De Rerum Natura,*
which was first translated into English in 1656—that is, the very period of
English history with which we are concerned.

The Epicurean poetic deserves some careful explanation. It presupposes the Lucretian axiom that matter derives from atoms and the void.

It is important to recognize that Lucretius's almost obsessive punning on the parallel between atoms and letters elegantly collapses a series of arguments that relate language to the world. The world is a comprehensive and complicated concourse of invisible atoms, which, though they combine to construct gross bodies, still retain their particulate integrity. Thus Lucretius derives two related principles that will also apply to cognition and language: atoms are atomic—completely discrete—even though Lucretius imagines them coming in all kinds of shapes; they compose larger wholes precisely by becoming mutually articulated. The physical indivisibility of the *minima* of the cosmos is one principle that Gassendi, for example, constantly stressed. With this principle, Epicurus was attempting to solve a problem within much ancient philosophy, namely the need to account both for physical stability and change. The singular integrity of atoms guaranteed that there were limits to chaos or entropy; the provisional relationship of atoms within gross bodies accounted for the observable fact of change. What we can see or know is an expression of what we cannot see or know, inasmuch as invisible particles are the building blocks of things around us; yet what we see or know only retains a provisional quality because it is the construct of *relations* among the atoms that go into its making. The architecture of the cosmos is the total sum of its constituent parts.

When Epicurus discusses cognition, a similar architectonic principle operates. The building blocks of cognition are for him individual contacts between the world and the mind, because it is atoms thrown off the superficies of gross bodies that strike the organs of sensation, so producing an image. It is possible to see Epicurus's sensationalism as dogmatic, because he never questions the fact of the sensations we experience. But he seems to suppose that knowledge in the ordinary sense is a conglomerate of such individual contacts, the mind's role being to compare and combine them after having judged them inferentially. Epicurus resists the Stoics precisely by arguing against their view that a special, gnostic form of knowledge could at points dramatically bypass our common need to infer knowledge from what we observe. Thus, though the atomic grounds of knowledge can be thought of as natural, the sum total of knowledge is, echoing the complex fabric of the universe, a result of multiple mental juxtapositions (to use Locke's word), and thus artificial.

Once again, the same double structure seems to apply to language. If the atoms of language are individual letters, representing some irreducible facticity in its very nature, language as we know it is a highly sophisticated aggregation of letters, syllables, words, and so forth: hence Lucretius's and Boyle's fascination with the homology between the world and language. Although, as far as I know, Epicureanism gives no clear causal explanation of the rise or existence of letters as such, Lucretius's famous passage in *De Rerum Natura*, 5: ll. 1093–1155 does suggest some parallel between the distinct but curiously related fabrics of the cosmos, knowledge, and language. Here, Lucretius postulates that human beings share with animals a set of minimal physical needs and responses to external stimuli. Human beings manipulate and represent their experience and, like the animals, cry out or gesture whenever they experience passion or desire, in response to an economy of pleasure and pain. These articulations are in part onomatopoeic, in part mere sonic reflexes; and whether one or the other, they constitute the atoms of what is to become language proper. Because, unlike animals, humans are invested with a primal need to organize themselves into societies—that is, to become civilized—they convert those originary, particular signs into arbitrary and general signs, so repeating in their movements the rise of the complex world from simple atoms, and general knowledge from the particular elements of cognition.

It remains unclear how the parallels between language, mind, and world operate. Certainly, they operate by analogy: language is like the mind is like the cosmos. The relation between mind and world is also causal, because the cognitive process is set in motion by the arrival of atomic films from objects outside the mind; though, as we have seen, the beginnings of the cognitive process do not of themselves produce knowledge as such. But the relation between the elements of cognition and the elements of language is less clear, and yet it seems connected by more than analogy. Some scholars have suggested that at moments such as this in his argument, Epicurus resorts to *isonomia,* namely the principle that the laws which internally govern language or the mind reenact the laws of the physical cosmos, without necessarily being mechanically related.

The isonomic relations among world, mind, and language produce (at least for the Restoration) one view of the ethical properties of language. Atoms within Epicurus's cosmology are the irreducible *minima* of things, guaranteeing the stability of matter in the final analysis; so in cognition, the *minima* of knowledge are the equally indivisible images or icons produced by contacts with the world. In both cases, the atom and the image seem to retain their own discrete and palpable nature, however fully they might become submerged into some larger, more abstract construct or conception. Moreover, because (descriptively) the mind gains knowledge by such an incremental process, the implication is that a resort to the imagistic powers of language is our best means of persuasion and exemplification. The icon of Epicurus thus achieves cultural force precisely because it is such an image: like the fragmentary and often epistolary Epicurean texts transmitted to posterity, it recognizes the necessarily rhetorical and positional nature of any cultural artifact, which is to say that it invites (rather than coerces) an inferential act of judgment by the viewer or reader. False knowledge can be thought of as the unwarranted collapse or compression of discrete particles into one another, like an act of prestidigitation that deludes an audience into seeing two things as one: this is what Johnson, in an unjustly maligned moment, meant when he accused the metaphysical poets of yoking ideas by "violence" together.

Johnson's dictum assumes that the mechanism I have described becomes a model for reading when it concerns language, one that also receives support from the way Epicurus thought of the mind obtaining experimental knowledge of the world. Epicurus proposed the use of an empirical method, namely the application of inference and analogy as instruments for knowing the properties of bodies. Although atoms and the void are invisible facts, we can know whether they exist only by inferring their existence from our experience of gross bodies and by comparing their relative natures.[16] Whether we think of Epicurus's isonomic argument for language, or his view of how we know the world, the consequences for language are similar: what we know, we know only superficially. Language can never legitimately claim to refer to some prelinguistic or essential entity, because what is beyond appearances or representation is simply hidden from us. Epicureanism perfectly matches the widespread distrust, voiced during the seventeenth century, of the Aristotelian view that we can catalogue the essences of bodies. Similarly, like the scientific observer, the reader of a text can never do more than make entirely provisional discriminations in view of what is presented and must be ready at any moment to discard one postulate in favor of some revised, equally provisional, intuition. John Bender contrasts the inferential mechanisms of Defoe's novels and *The Beggar's Opera* with Pope's hermeneutic; but because they share a neoclassical commitment to readerly inference I would maintain, rather, that Defoe, Gay, and Pope are profoundly related.[17]

The hermeneutic involves a carefully calibrated politics of apprehension. The Lucretian model of reading presupposes that the individual elements represented to the mind maintain their own integrity, resisting the mind's desire to appropriate them and digest them into its own system. To the degree that it is antisystematic, it also presupposes that they do serve some model of mental (and, by implication, social) conduct by responding to the mind's capacities for mutually arranging them into relations. The almost-plastic nature of atoms, images, and letters guarantees to them a quality of resistance, but one that invites rather than prohibits the act of inference, that stimulates the mind to discriminate and choose. I talk from time to time about the "negotiable" nature of Lucretian elements of all sorts to signal precisely this unstable symbiosis between resistance and assent: these elements behave as items of public coinage, open to trade, yet available as the materials on which the mind can exercise its method. I accordingly stress at points the neoclassical use of numismatic metaphors for the circulation of knowledge and language, not least in John Evelyn's *Numismata* (1697).

Thus the cries of pain and pleasure registered on the bodies and faces of animals and men in the Lucretian account do not denote some oral— as it were invisible—purview of knowledge. Instead, they exist to show that all human sign systems, however 'natural' in origin, occur as visible, tactile, and somatic (hence *material*) forms of behavior. Neoclassical linguists were fascinated by the phenomenon by which words occur as the physiognomic maneuverings of the mouth, tongue, palate, and lips. The Restoration frequently resorted to the metaphor of printing to emphasize this plastic quality in language: the age seems to have delighted in the concreteness of the page impressed by visible marks, ascending atomically from letters to words, to sentences, to entire discourses. It is no accident that Evelyn's *Numismata* closes with a chapter on physiognomy. Moreover, when the Restoration described the natural grounds of language, it did so not in the belief that we could actually recover such a state, but as a means to imagine the essentially metaphorical nature of language as it presently functions. Baxter quite properly characterized the changing view of knowledge in the mid-seventeenth century as "somatic"; when Hobbes wrote that all we conceive is body, he was in this not far from many of his critics. It has recently become fashionable to observe that the body, though natural in some sense, is a site of cultural construction, revealing the artifice embedded in all cultural metaphors. In the "somatic" culture I describe, the discourse about bodies (physics, gestures, physiognomy) becomes the means to displace some competing, less self-consciously embodied form of cultural imagination, to discuss its own assumptions about knowledge and language, and to insist that language, like bodies, must perform within social spaces.

The chapter on Pierre Gassendi (1592–1655) places the Epicurean argument in the seventeenth century. Gassendi was one of the chief, and presently most neglected, figures of his time, as well as the age's single most important catalyst in the neo-Epicurean revival. To argue for Gassendi's importance is to endorse his contemporaries' view of him. This also implies that we should revise the history of philosophy. Even within the Anglo-American tradition, many intellectual historians simply assume the preeminence of Descartes and a continental philosophical tradition established by a Victorian historiography. To point to the contemporary importance accorded Gassendi and Hobbes as anti-Cartesians is both to redefine Descartes's significance for the mid-seventeenth century and to argue that the so-called British empirical tradition arises largely out of a self-conscious criticism of Descartes. This tradition is not of course purely indigenous, confined to the English, since Gassendi plays a crucial role in its formation. (In a similar context, Hans Aarsleff argues for the importance of Mersenne.) I therefore show that Gassendi's response to Descartes focuses on Descartes's confidence in his system's defining moment of certainty, with what it implies for a reading of language and social relations. Although Descartes is a great rhetorician, he is impatient with language because it obstructs the transparent apprehension of certainty on which his mind is so forcefully set. Gassendi wants to assert the conditioning of the mind by representation and to defend a contingent and cooperative vision of social relations. Gassendi mobilizes his probabilism against Cartesian certainty. Without questioning Descartes's importance, which is undeniable, I do want to challenge the assumption that the period after 1640 was in some definitive sense post-Cartesian.

This adjustment of the map of mid-seventeenth-century philosophy does not have merely antiquarian consequences, because the preeminence of the Cartesian and a certain Continental genealogy is more or less required as a foil for the conduct of poststructuralist linguistics. Although it often appears as an ahistorical or antihistorical view, the poststructuralist critique of language is deeply determined by a philosophical canon that establishes the questions it asks. Poststructuralist linguistics, that is, are very finely tuned to a series of family arguments within the Continental tradition, of which Ferdinand de Saussure is a perfect example: they have so far had little interesting to say about Hobbes or Locke (as opposed to Rousseau or Condillac). In many ways, my own argument constitutes an appreciation of the climate established by poststructuralism, because it supposes the virtue of moving from an analysis of epistemology, to an analysis of language, to an analysis of the politics implied by that conjunction. This is one reason for referring to "culture" in my title. But in two major ways, I feel uncomfortable with the route by which poststructuralism has often established its claims. First, my book shows that the eighteenth century did not cultivate the rule of reason, where reason stands for a trust in our mental capacities that seeks to ignore or suppress the metaphorical constraints of language. What I show at length is the historical emergence of an argument that, for exact epistemological and social motives, more or less states the opposite: the mind operates within narrow confines, which language largely defines, and beyond which we cannot and should not venture. Second, I also show that this defense of contingency, premised on a sceptical empiricism, becomes not the chief discourse of dissent but, again, its opposite: the language of the most visible institutions returned to power after the Restoration. I therefore resist a common assumption in the poststructuralist slide from epistemology and language to politics, which usually holds that epistemological totalizing (the attempt to establish stable grounds of knowledge) acts in direct positive ratio to the hegemonic motives of power. I resist, that is, the view that the demand for certain knowledge and transparent language invariably serves the political purposes of centralized and authoritarian institutions.

However, like a newer line of reasoning within poststructuralist circles, my argument would be that politics is not a matter of who subscribes to what view of language and knowledge, but what individual parties do and say they are doing in local social and political circumstances. As Locke keeps stating, knowledge is a matter of "use" and "end": it is social and positional. (This is one reason why Locke's journals and notebooks are filled with comments on travel narratives, representing to Locke different forms of cultural symbolism.) So my study shows the deployment of a contingent epistemology to serve the motives of instituted organs of power, of which a typical case is the Royal Society. This is not to say that all attempts at opposition required a more dogmatic view of knowledge; but in many cases they did. I think here of Richard Baxter and John Owen, whose acts of dissent from Restoration Anglicanism are explicitly supported by appealing to secure sources of knowledge: Owen defends Scriptural language as a transparent vehicle of religious apprehension. It is also possible to argue that the use of a contingent epistemology is most frequently the prerogative of the establishment: scepticism can rather neatly deflate the justification of political action, because that often requires some recourse to a stable epistemology. (However, I would argue that dissenters such as John Bunyan and John Locke seek to construct dissent within the constraints established by the newer epistemology I describe; but this is a subject for another study on the nature of neoclassical dissent.)

My argument about politics and language parallels a similar view of politics articulated by important actors within my historical narrative, a view they used to powerful effect against their rivals. If knowledge is merely contingent, then various ethical or political positions can be made known or be realized only by juxtaposing a series of figures in the political landscape. This has two consequences: no individual can claim to map the entire political territory: such a claim itself implies a false epistemology. And because on this view political claims can be established only by marking a position within that territory, those claims that pretend to some traffic with noumenal (so private or gnostic) grounds of knowledge become impotent, because their premises cannot be opened to public trade. Hobbes is, of course, the perfect case in point, because he effectively argues that valid power is the visible product of convention: he mocks the hermetic quality of Catholic infallibility as having the same cognitive substance as the Kingdom of Fairies.

Although, for precise reasons, I talk throughout of "neoclassical" culture or (less precisely) of "the Restoration" or "the eighteenth century," I am referring to what we might call the dominant discourse of the age. I believe we still do not fully understand its governing assumptions, which also define the parameters of neoclassical dissent. Neoclassical culture is not the product of a single Foucauldian rupture, but a series of dramatic epistemological and linguistic revisions in response to the Civil War and Interregnum. Those revisions, which together produce a powerful orthodoxy, occurred as a sequence of tectonic shifts in the culture between 1640 and 1680, often in strategic debates between promoters of the preferred discourse of contingency and those espousing alternative models of knowledge and language. Accordingly, my book stages a number of exemplary clashes between such alternatives, in every case involving a conflict between seeing language as transparent and seeing language as a fully mediated vehicle of knowledge. So we observe Dryden (and many others besides) criticizing Aristotle; Baxter, as a neo-Aristotelian, assaulting the rise of the "somatists"; Gassendi attacking Descartes; Ward attacking Webster; Owen attacking Grotius and Walton; Leibniz attacking Locke; Locke attacking Malebranche; and so on.

Chapter five, which closes my discussion of neo-Epicureanism, outlines the transportation of Gassendist neo-Epicureanism from mid-seventeenth-century France to England. Like their modern English counterparts, the propagandists for official culture were few and powerful; individuals such as Robert Boyle and John Evelyn played an important role in the transmission of culture, with significant consequences for the texture of Restoration life. For my description of the neo-Epicurean revival in England, I draw on earlier studies by Robert Kargon *(Atomism in England from Hariot to Newton)* and Thomas Mayo *(Epicurus in England)*, but I extend Kargon's excellent study from its focus on atomism as a physical hypothesis to considering neo-Epicureanism as a cultural model; I take issue with Mayo's view that the political significance of neo-Epicureanism is primarily royalist and libertine.[18] (Lucy Hutchinson, who translated Lucretius at midcentury, was wife to one of the regicides, who died in prison in 1664.) We could treat the 1650s (especially 1656, when Walter Charleton published *Epicurus's Morals,* and John Evelyn his pioneering translation of Lucretius) as a watershed in the fortunes of English neo-Epicureanism; but I begin that narrative with the émigré group gathered in Paris in the early 1640s, whose experiences and attitudes proved to have general importance for the texture of English Restoration culture.

Exiled to France as a result of the Civil War and its aftermath, the members of the Cavendish circle (amongst others) sought models of philosophical conduct that coincided with their sense of how a less contentious society should behave; it examined and commented on the activities of the most distinguished philosophical circle in Europe, which included Mersenne, Descartes, Gassendi, and Hobbes. Chiefly by re-reading the letters between Sir Charles Cavendish and Dr. John Pell, I argue that the English émigrés developed a preference for Gassendi's neo-Epicurean philosophical conduct over Descartes's dictatorial manner and demonstrative systematizing. Evelyn perfectly embodies the literal transposition of ideas from France to England in the mid-seventeenth century, as well as their subsequent translation into something recognizably native. Evelyn's garden at Sayes Court could be said to found definitively the tradition of the English garden, because it was attached to an entire reading of cultural behavior that, inspired by the classics, was later to become commonplace and to govern the neoclassical literary aesthetic. (I also talk about Samuel Hartlib, William Petty, and the young Robert Boyle to offset the impression that the aesthetic decides party-political and royalist affiliations.) Because the aesthetic very self-consciously derived from complicated acts of translation and domestication—from ancient to modern culture, from France to England—I stress in some detail how the neo-Epicurean revival was conditioned by a series of important exchanges of letters. The individuals I discuss seem to believe that, like Epicurus's image (the frontispiece of Gassendi's *De Vita et Moribus Epicuri,* his *Animadversiones,* and Charleton's *Epicurus's Morals,* where an identical engraving is reproduced but in reverse), and like books, medals, and bodies in space, letters provide ideal artificial devices for the propagation of new epistemic, scientific, and social motives.

The neo-Epicurean revival was not the sole impetus in the reorganization of cultural attitudes I describe. Part three of my book ("Activating the Word: Language, Theology, and Criticism") places the discourse of neoclassical linguistics, theology, and literary criticism in parallel to show, first, the similarities among their views of knowledge and language (like Barbara Shapiro, I do not believe that they are specialized discourses in our modern sense); and second, the breadth of the attitudes adumbrated and focussed in part by the arrival of neo-Epicureanism. My reader can then pass from the details of the neo-Epicurean revival to synoptic discussions that connect the history of science, language, and rhetoric, so preparing the ground for my exposition of Dryden's *Absalom and Achitophel.* Much of the material present here belongs only tangentially to the neo-Epicurean story. For example, John Bulwer's writings on gesture from the early 1640s, before the neo-Epicurean revival had registered in England, seem already to feel their way toward a linguistic position I have characterized as Lucretian.

My chapter on linguistics deals with a number of texts that discuss language explicitly or supply theories of language. Their authors all seem to think of language first as a series of discrete tactile or peculiarly plastic moments (whether originary gestures, letters, pictures, or words), and subsequently viewing language-as-we-have-it as a tissue of such almost-concrete elements, just as Evelyn is capable of imagining history as the rendering linear of an atomic series of moments condensed in the medals populating his *Numismata.* At work within these arguments about language are two views I would reemphasize: that the plastic quality of the elements of language ensures that any argument cast in linguistic terms cannot escape some form of public, institutional accountability or scrutiny, because these elements are imagined as incapable of escaping the conditions that define any phenomenal object. So when I refer to language as "phenomenal," I mean not to allude to recent phenomenological philosophies of language but to the means by which language participates in the phenomenal world and resists mystification from being treated as a purely private or hidden property. I have already argued that this idea supports a view that language, because it operates as a public artifact, is *negotiable,* resisting appropriation from the perspective of some supreme Cartesian observer or puppeteer; but, by the same token, the argument also secures language as the possession of visible, public institutions, such as the Anglican church or the Royal Society. So in one tract ("Dr. Hooke's Method of Making Experiments"), Robert Hooke takes pains to ensure that the cooperative and forensic conditions of experimental science achieve a rhetorical equivalent in reporting the experiment to the assembled fellow-scientists, inscribing the entire process (or "History") of debate and proof, and guaranteeing its public value by a list of the witnesses' names, which seals both the experiment and the public conditions under which it is deemed valid. Similarly, a signed document such as a contract emphasizes the artifice of language; it guarantees the contracting parties a measure of discrimination or assent, yet defines the visible and institutional arena within which socially effective activities can occur.

The neoclassical linguists (as well as theologians and literary critics) I describe seem possessed of a fear that if we treat language as anything less than material, it will slip away from the public forum and offer itself as the secret and insidious instrument of radical or tyrannical control; they often resorted to metaphors of print to emphasize the materiality of words. Their theory does not force us to choose between the need to police society, which it accepts as inevitable, and the recognition that individuals still require persuasion and can experience a meaningful measure of choice. It perfectly serves the requirements of the institutions that symbolize the Restored monarchy; but it is by no means limited to them. For example, like other neoclassical language texts, Daniel Defoe's *An Essay upon Literature* (1726) emphasizes first that (but not how) language by its very nature must operate as a condition of human institutions (like writing itself). Defoe does not prescribe which specific political institutions should benefit, though he assumes that the visibility of writing (as opposed to orality, a disturbingly impalpable quality of speech) subjects the claims of power to public scrutiny, which allows for the emergence of political opposition. Thus N. H. Keeble has misleadingly implied that the resort to print culture is a special tactic of the dissenters; he fails to see how the printing trope is pandemic, serving both the language of hegemony and of dissent.[19] Both Anglicans and dissenters hated and vilified the Catholics in terms that had common implications for language. A dissenter such as Bunyan distrusted the Quakers as deeply as his Anglican persecutors precisely because the Quakers claimed a gnostic ground of knowledge that rendered the Scriptures redundant, thus destroying all media of negotiation and scrutiny.

My chapters on biblical and literary criticism elaborate a similar argument in slightly different terms. I focus primarily on Anglican hermeneutics and do not, for example, discuss the Deists, though I would maintain that the hermeneutic I describe applies to Locke. I also include references to Continental critics whose arguments paralleled or influenced the English tradition: primarily Isaac Casaubon, Hugo Grotius, Richard Simon, and Jean Le Clerc. Biblical criticism began to emphasize the textual, mediated nature of biblical events well before the neo-Epicurean revival occurred, though I show that the reorganization of knowledge in the second half of the seventeenth century methodizes that recognition. Knowledge of the crucial events recorded in the Bible now comes not by some direct apprehension, but through the process of examining them in the forensic light presented by the accounts themselves, and necessitated by the historical and fragmentary condition of the manuscript sources. The activity of historically informed inference parallels the individual's act of faith or assent to the propositions of the Gospel. The historical, linear terms by which the original witnesses experienced Mosaic prophecy or the ministry of Christ are symbolically reinforced by the textual, graphic, and linear nature of the Scriptures we have inherited.

Similarly, neoclassical literary criticism, which I propose was virtually initiated in the famous exchange between Davenant and Hobbes in 1650, attacks the aural as inscrutable and improbable and defends the visual as approximating our need to know and to judge represented experience on probable grounds. In linguistics, theology, and criticism alike, the atomic and visual terms in which the elements of language are imagined first ensure the discrete integrity of individual signs and, second, assist their combination into series of spatial and narrative articulations. Knowledge is thought of as derived from individual instances of inference and judgment from a world that, because always represented, we cannot know in any essential sense; so I also argue that the preferred figure of neoclassical discourse is synecdoche or metonymy, denoting the reader's responsibility to educe general principles from partial but suggestive signs. Like a certain version of poststructural criticism, neoclassical criticism held that metaphor as a figure entails the attempt to identify and collapse two discrete terms, or to make the sign partake of the signified; and so it sought to expose this figural claim as a cognitive chimera, connoting some politically motivated attempt to coerce the reader by aesthetic means, and so to deny him or her true liberty of readerly judgment.

One major theme of this book is, of course, reading itself. I am concerned not so much with a literary culture, in which 'literature' is the presumed locus of special knowledge, but a *literate* culture, in which all forms of knowledge (including natural philosophy) were commonly known and confessed to be rhetorical. So the mid-seventeenth century could comprehensively revise its view of itself by rereading classical culture; it subsequently adapted a method—in part from ancient culture—that could reveal and discuss that very process of rereading; it argued for a general practice of reading governed by such methodical self-consciousness; and (as I have several times intimated) it treated as tantamount to an ethical or political failure the failure to read with sufficient empirical rigor.

This mechanism is revealed rather neatly in the frontispiece of Jean Le Clerc's *Ars Critica* (1697) (p. 23), whose movements are also enacted in an earlier portrait of Brian Walton, the chief editor of the massive *Biblia Polyglotta* (1653–57) (p. 24). We find ourselves in a library, a space consisting of many books, each clearly and distinctly set on the shelves that line this cabinet. The library acts as a theater intensifying the perspective where the drapery at the top and right recalls the proscenium, a feature of the London theater introduced only at the Restoration. The woman scrutinizing a book rehearses our activity of scrutinizing the frontispiece. Like the woman, the reader comes to knowledge under the tutelage of Hermes, the god of interpretation, who stands to one side to illuminate the pages of the book. The scene reminds us that the process of interpretation is analogical: like the open pages of the book, the walls of the library comment on one another and in the transition of the woman from

ARS
CRITICA
CLERICI

Frontispiece to Le Clerc, *Ars Critica* (1697)

Brian Walton, editor of the *Biblia Polyglotta* (1653–57)

reader to writer, it appears that she has substantially completed two lines of writing, as if imitating Dryden's neoclassical prose or the outlines of a Popean couplet in which the terms of knowledge are always comparatively weighted.

In this scene it is evident that reading and writing are visible, tactile, and corporal activities. If experience is structured as a series of comparative judgments, the reader's hitherto uninformed mind will become stocked with knowledge. The contents of the library and the Lockean figure of the informed mind manifest themselves as historical, because books (like medals) are the atomized repositories of a past inviting interpretation, a point symbolized by the sphinx in the lower left corner. The clutter of items casually disposed opposite the sphinx on the chamber floor reveals that every interpretive motion is part of a general cultural activity and thus embraces the world of arts and arms.

It is obviously significant that the reader in the scene is a woman. On the one hand, like the child's, the feminine mind could represent some blank precultural space waiting to be inscribed, to be passively molded into a cultural and ideological entity. But alternatively, as Mary Evelyn seems to recognize, the very idea of inference governing such interpretive activity offers the reader a certain moment of discrimination within the act of judgment. I have suggested above that such moments imply the possibility of distancing and ironizing what is offered for our consumption, however provisionally: by visibly exercising her prerogative of interpretation, the reader here secures the play of readerly assent within the larger necessities of culture, represented by the public world inscribed in books and monuments. (And I am suggesting here that preserving the prerogatives of assent has particular force for those communities that do not experience cultural protocols as transparent and natural.) As the figure of interpretation, Hermes stands tactfully to the side, assisting, rather than governing, the act of reading. So, unlike the frontispiece of Joseph-François Lafitau's *La Vie et les Moeurs des Sauvages Ameriquains* (1724–32) (p. 26), Le Clerc's model of interpretation and knowledge does not reduce observed particulars into some homogenized allegory, but rather treats general knowledge as the local and contingent result of forensic method.

Against an implication in James Clifford's *Predicament of Culture,* I do not believe that Lafitau summarizes 'enlightenment' attitudes to ethnography or cultural interpretation.[20] Although Le Clerc also finally subordinates all knowledge to Christian truth, Le Clerc's frontispiece

Frontispiece to Lafitau, *La Vie et les Moeurs des Sauvages Ameriquaines* (1724–32)

presents an altogether different mechanism resisting the instant and self-evident translation of local particulars into the general and controlling truths of Scripture. In Lafitau's frontispiece, the master story for all interpretation—the spatialized details of biblical history—appears as a tableau set in the walls of the researcher's room and dictating a single controlling model for interpreting the details of Iroquois culture, whose artifacts lie randomly scattered on the floor. In Lafitau, illumination occurs as a Cartesian fiat interrupting the fabric of daily life, one characteristically issuing from on high, even though, as Clifford points out, the frontispiece does not disguise how far anthropology operates from the objects it describes. Both Lafitau and Le Clerc show that ethnography and history require the intervention of an interpretive agent, in both cases symbolized by a scene of writing. But in Le Clerc, illumination comes by the single candle delicately held up to the pages of a book, within ordinary space and time, so if we create general knowledge, it arrives by a more strenuous, less clearly transcendental route.

I have, finally, introduced the question of dissent in this introduction more than once because I recognize that a study such as mine, if only by range of sources to which it appeals, will invite criticism for having failed to account sufficiently for exceptions. For example, I do not fully discuss the role and place of women in the neo-Epicurean revival, though Lucy Hutchinson almost certainly made the first complete translation of Lucretius into English,[21] though the Duchess of Newcastle was an important figure within the émigré community, and though I show that Katherine Philips and Mary Evelyn also played a part in the construction of the cultural ideals I describe. This is a job for further studies. But my claims operate at a certain level of generalization, because I believe that societies at any given time operate by certain broadly accepted codes, such as the British caste system, or the anticommunism that defines the parameters of American political rhetoric. It is not as easy to determine when and how those rules change; but I argue that the period immediately after the Civil War and Interregnum provides a signal instance of just such a change. For the purposes of this study, the challenge is to draw the cultural rules against which the pattern of exceptions and activity of dissent may acquire meaning.

PART 1

The Neoclassical Turn at the Restoration

In Effgiem & ... borum ... Dr Charlton

Imago pulcra Est picta ... oris manu.
At pulcrioem dat libris ... utor suis.
Hic Corpus_Illis ipsa ... ens depingitur
Imo Vniuersi Men ... Ipsius simul

C.B.

Frontispiece to Charleton, *The Darkness of Atheism Dispelled by the Light of Nature* (1652)

To My Honored Friend, Dr. Charleton

The longest Tyranny that ever sway'd,
Was that wherein our Ancestors betray'd
Their free-born *Reason* to the *Stagirite*,
And made his Torch their universal Light.
So *Truth*, while onely one suppli'd the State,
Grew scarce, and dear, and yet sophisticate,
Until 'twas bought, like Emp'rique Wares, or Charms,
Hard words seal'd up with *Aristotle*'s Armes.
Columbus was the first that shook his Throne;
And found a *Temp'rate* in a *Torrid* Zone:
The fevrish aire fann'd by a cooling breez,
The fruitful Vales set round with shady Trees;
And guiltless *Men*, who danc'd away their time,
Fresh as their *Groves*, and *Happy* as their *Clime*.
Had we still paid that homage to a *Name*,
Which onely *God* and *Nature* justly claim;
The *Western* Seas had been our utmost bound,
Where *Poets* still might dream the *Sun* was drown'd:
And all the *Starrs*, that shine in *Southern* Skies,
Had been admir'd by none but *Salvage* Eyes.

Among th' *Assertors* of free Reason's claim,
Th' *English* are not the least in Worth, or Fame.
The World to *Bacon* does not onely owe
Its *present* Knowledge, but its *future* too.
Gilbert shall live, till *Load-stones* cease to draw,
Or *British* Fleets the boundless Ocean awe;
And noble *Boyle*, not less in *Nature* seen,
Than his great *Brother* read in *States* and *Men*.
The *Circling* steams, once thought but pools, of blood
(Whether Life's fewel, or the Bodie's food)
From dark Oblivion *Harvey*'s name shall save;
While *Ent* keeps all the honour that he gave.
Nor are *You,* Learned Friend, the least renown'd;
Whose Fame, not circumscrib'd with *English* ground,
Flies like the nimble journeys of the Light;
And is, like that, unspent too in its flight.
What ever *Truths* have been, by *Art* or *Chance*,
Redeem'd from *Error*, or from *Ignorance*,

Thin in their *Authors*, (like rich veins of Ore)
Your Works unite, and still discover more.
Such is the healing virtue of Your Pen,
To perfect Cures on *Books*, as well as *Men*.
Nor is This Work the least: You well may give
To *Men* new vigour, who make *Stones* to live.
Through You, the *DANES* (their short Dominion lost)
A longer Conquest than the *Saxons* boast.
STONE-HENG, once thought a *Temple,* You have found
A *Throne,* where Kings, our Earthly Gods, were Crown'd,
Where by their wondring Subjects They were seen,
Joy'd with their Stature, and their Princely meen.
Our *Soveraign,* here above the rest might stand;
And here be chose again to rule the Land.

These Ruines sheltred once *His* Sacred Head,
Then when from *Wor'sters* fatal Field *He* fled;
Watch'd by the Genius of this Royal place,
And mighty Visions of the Danish Race.
His *Refuge* then was for a *Temple* shown:
But, *He* Restor'd, 'tis now become a *Throne*.

1. The Restoration as Cultural Moment

A revolution is . . . a special sort of change involving a certain sort of reconstruction of group commitments.

Thomas S. Kuhn, *The Structure of Scientific Revolutions*

Yet the most I can find, that the contending learned Men of different Parties do, in their Arguings one with another, is, that they speak different Languages.

John Locke, *An Essay concerning Human Understanding* (1690)

Dryden's Epistle to Charleton: Reading, Difference, and the Resistance to Tyranny

John Dryden's early verse epistle "To My Honored Friend, Dr. Charleton" is a work of genius, not because it conveniently describes Dryden's acquaintance with members of the Royal Society, but because it prescribes for the Restoration a new model of linguistic and ethical conduct.[1] That is, it describes the construction of a new ideal of science, a new scientific community, and the terms under which the reader's activity in Dryden's text becomes a corollary to participating in this new cultural milieu. Falling into three verse paragraphs, the poem begins by describing the "longest Tyranny" (l. 1) of Aristotle, whose rule is first interrupted by Columbus's voyages of discovery (Dryden here introduces visions of an exotic New World paradise), and concludes with a homage to King Charles II, recently restored to the English throne. The second, longest verse paragraph (ll. 21–52) involves two movements: it first celebrates "Th'*English*" (l. 22) contributors to the new knowledge—Bacon, Gilbert, Robert and Roger Boyle, Harvey, Ent, and, finally, Dryden's addressee—Walter Charleton.[2] Charleton then becomes the focus of the second movement (ll. 33–52): he contributes to knowledge not only as a doctor or natural philosopher but also as an antiquarian.

Charleton's *Chorea Gigantum* (1662) to which the poem is a dedication, revises Inigo Jones's earlier thesis about Stonehenge and argues that it was a Danish coronation site, not a Roman temple. The royalist resonances of Charleton's argument occasion the third paragraph of the poem (ll. 53–58), which recalls King Charles II sheltering at Stonehenge after the battle of Worcester, and, by a deft inversion, inscribes the king's ultimate victory in the Restoration:

> His *Refuge* then was for a *Temple* shown:
> But, *He* Restor'd, 'tis now become a *Throne*.

The poem's discursive community is realized—rendered phenomenal before our eyes—by a complex spatial conception that is at the most obvious level quite literal. Just as Charleton has reinvented or restored a mythic origin in order to legitimize King Charles II's monarchy, the poem is conscious of its original status as a text, its position in a book, which then leads to increasingly metaphorical ramifications. With the reader in 1662, we begin at the poem's *literal* location—its typographical place at the beginning of Charleton's *Chorea Gigantum* and, as that work was reissued in 1725,[3] intervening between it and Inigo Jones's *The Most Notable Antiquity of Great Britain,* posthumously published by John Webb in 1655.[4] This very physical position in turn suggests Dryden's (and by implication Charleton's) invocations of other kinds of spatial conception. Most obviously, the poem connects figures in an exotic, then domestic, western landscape (America, then Stonehenge) to the figure of eastern domestic power (the Stuart *"Throne"*), a space swiftly traversed by the poem's final couplet, which also reflects the secularization of sacred authority.

The poem can also marry the authority of King Charles II's restored throne—the locus of monarchical power—to an ideal of "free-born *Reason*" (l. 3), whose incipient individualism could potentially collapse that legal authority. This can happen because, paradoxically, the poem recommends the atomic dispersion of knowledge back into history, a form of historicizing the past that fractures the centralizing tendencies of political or philosophical tyranny, yet works toward an ideal of modified coherence, which arises from mythologizing what we have inherited. Dryden's epistle constitutes, precisely, a critical meditation on those motives by which a literate culture can differentiate among, revise, and translate older sources of authority. Again at the most literal typographical level, the interposition of Dryden's text between Inigo Jones's and

Charleton's works helps to disrupt monolithic and undifferentiated claims to power symbolized by the contrary tendency to conflate and stabilize texts. Those urges are signalled by Aristotle's "longest Tyranny" (l. 1), whose absolute and "universal Light" (l. 4) also implicates sectarian inspirationalists—in Dryden's eyes, the fomenters of the late civil upheaval.[5] Nor is the Stuart monarchy exempt from criticism, because Charleton's considered revision of Inigo Jones's mythology of Stonehenge suggests that the earlier, unmediated claims to Stuart power also contributed to that conflict. This is why for Dryden there must exist no univocal or universal relation between past and present, no necessary preference for the ancients or moderns. The poem invokes in order not to identify or conflate, but to differentiate the terms of knowledge—for example, in the roll of scientific and political worthies—and this becomes a textual or hermeneutical anticipation to a Restoration insistence on the exclusion of tyranny from society, politics, and science.

While, for analytical purposes, the modern critic (and even Dryden himself) might treat as distinct the activities of 'science,' 'politics,' 'philosophy,' 'history,' 'literature,' and so forth, they become entirely equivalent discursive activities within the world of the poem. Witness how the two Boyles come to represent the new discursive mode: whereas Robert confronts "Nature" (l. 7), Roger confronts "*States* and *Men*" (l. 8). But—this is significant—the two become equivalent not in the *objects* of their knowledge, but in their *methods*, in the activity of reading. Robert reads Nature; Roger reads Politics. Although we quite properly impute interpretive activity to the two Boyles, the action of the poem pointedly renders that activity to us in the passive voice, so the poem converts us into spectators observing the two Boyles operating within their respective spheres of natural philosophy and politics. The reader's moderation is accordingly recommended and constructed not only by the poem's physical presence mediating between Jones's and Charleton's texts, but also by its figural activities of spatial and historical discrimination. The society to which the reader finally assents is just that—a society created by assent, because it discriminates among the varied and constituent elements of our social, historical, philosophical, and even visual knowledge, not to force, but to create or enable the recognition of King Charles II's "*Throne*" (l. 58). The addressee of the poem is, after all, a healer, not a tyrant.

It is easy and doubtless correct to object that the order Dryden postulates is as *interested,* as invested in its own urge to cultural hegemony as Aristotle's "Tyranny." On this criticism, the rhetoric of moderation is a form of mystification, because to exclude Aristotle is to make an exception fatal to the claims of moderation, and Dryden becomes as much of a tyrant as his "Aristotle," a wielder of centralized power. Dryden's strategy clearly adumbrates the epistemological and political exclusion of Catholics and dissenters throughout the Restoration, which I shall later discuss. But the focus for the present is on how Dryden's poem asserts its own cultural superiority to other texts embodying different epistemological and social motives, and that it seeks to silence.

Dryden's epistle to Charleton participates in what Alexandre Koyré, in another connection, so eloquently called "the materialization of space."[6] Dryden makes his poem 'material' by virtue of its acts of, first, rendering its objects of description concrete, and second, enforcing the necessity of discriminating among them. And these acts are rendered tropological within the poem by organizing its argument around a specific and concrete, though mythologized, origin—Stonehenge, a physical point on the Salisbury plain. That moment or locus of specification is intensified by the poet's energetic epideictic gestures in the closing lines of the poem ("here . . . here . . . These Ruines . . . this Royal place" [ll. 51–55]). Because Stonehenge stolidly remains a fact inscribed on the English landscape, preceding and resisting the desires of different interpreters, it frustrates the (supposedly) Scholastic tendency to collapse distinctions by mere verbal juggling, by the magic of "Emp'rique Wares, or Charms, / Hard words seal'd up with *Aristotle*'s Armes" (ll. 7–8). The poem carefully distinguishes between *mythologizing* and *mystifying* the past. The first authorizes its own activity of selecting and claiming authority from disparate figures in history and the landscape; the second, by contrast, Dryden equates with violence and tyranny.

Dryden's criticism of such violence by mystification occurs at one level as a commentary on figuration itself. Dryden focuses on an elision and the resultant pun to capture the sense in which Aristotle's mysterious and preternatural "Charms" overwhelm or subvert the category of the empirical: in the acts of elision or punning the reader is never given mental space to weigh the discrete terms of the proposition. The pun on "Emp'rique" is significantly a primarily aural trick, rather than a visual or intellectual device, so Aristotle's conjuration appears to have taken effect almost unawares and has colonized (or imperialized) the empirical before we have had time to contemplate it. Where the poem's wider 'empirical' motive seeks to render its own machinery explicit, to distribute the figures in the landscape, Aristotle's tautological and occult charms secure and preserve secrecy ("Hard words seal'd up . . . " [l. 8]).[7] Dryden implies that the epistemology of Aristotelian syllogistic and physics inculcates a purely circular, hermetic logic; whereas the epistemology of his own poem is linear and thus open-ended, in that the figures that lend authority to King Charles II's throne (Stonehenge, Columbus, Bacon, Boyle, Charleton) do so by association, juxtaposition, and analogy.[8]

    Finally, if the poem celebrates a notion of the 'natural' (for example, in the figures of Bacon, Boyle, Charleton, and in King Charles II's patronage of the Royal Society), it is a 'nature' to which access is effortful and to that extent artificial or mediated, just as Roger Boyle's reading of "*States* and *Men*" in these highly unsettled times is hazardous and contingent. The postulate of direct access to God and Nature in the first verse paragraph of the poem is couched in terms of an exotic prelapsarian paradise from which we have inevitably fallen. As I have already indicated, the alternative, contingent kind of knowledge finds its corollary not only in Bacon's experimentalism but also in the associative and analogical activity of interpretation the poem offers us as readers. If the discourse of Dryden's poem is 'naturalized,' it is 'naturalized' in a world as far removed from the intuitive and universal certainties of Aristotle's philosophical tyranny as from a world of "guiltless *Men*" dancing away their time "*Fresh* as their *Groves,* and *Happy* as their *Clime*" (ll. 13–14). In this new world, Nature is implacably an artifice to be read.

Cultural Transformation and the Restoration

Dryden's great early poem signals a moment in the establishment of what we should properly call neoclassical culture.[9] As Dryden's readers in 1662 were meant to assume, the founding practitioners of this culture, whatever the spectrum of their own commitments within the new political order, reacted almost universally and monolithically to that distinctive series of national traumas—the Civil War, the king's execution, and the Interregnum, which (even in Christopher Hill's otherwise sympathetic allegory)[10] had degenerated into a military oligarchy. For example, J.G.A. Pocock writes that "seventeenth-century men were still premodern creatures for whom authority and magistracy were part of a natural cosmic order, and . . . the starting point of much of their most radical thinking was the unimaginable fact that, between 1642 and 1649, authority in England had simply collapsed."[11] The Cromwellian inheritance rankled so deeply in the English mind that the cry of "no standing army" still had great political force in the early eighteenth century. Marlborough's demand that Queen Anne make him captain general for life recalled memories of the army rule almost fifty years before, and deliberate comparisons were made between Marlborough's ambitions and Cromwell's.[12] Despite Hobbes's institutional containment after the Restoration,[13] his *Leviathan*, inasmuch as it presented a vision of the agonies of civil strife, captured and predicted the mood of that era nine years before King Charles II's return. In his dedication to *Seven Philosophical Problems and Two Propositions of Geometry*, addressed to the king and, like *Chorea Gigantum*, published in 1662, Hobbes attempts to mollify the critics of his great work, protesting that "it was written in a time when the pretense of Christ's kingdom was made use of for the most horrid actions that can be imagined."[14]

It would greatly simplify our understanding of the Restoration if we thought of it as a single and decisive reaction against the Interregnum. However, we are dealing not only with sudden cultural change but also the terms by which a society must revise the pressures of the immediate past. This is one of my central concerns here, and it defines my choice of the neo-Epicurean revival as a narrative within which both potentially contrary tendencies coexist. The difficulty of arriving at an accurate description of this moment of transition is revealed by the historiography of the "puritan" inheritance.[15] It would be foolish to deny the sectarian origins of what became central features of Restoration orthodoxy, or what Pocock has more widely typified as "the conservative enlightenment in England."[16] But in an influential account, Charles Webster discovers, in the "puritan" revival of learning and the commitment to a millenarian eschatology, two origins of the strongly irenic strain of British natural philosophy. According to Webster, a consensus within 'scientific' circles served as a type of the Second Coming of Christ and could be assisted by tools such as a universal language or the conversion of the Jews. Thus the traumas of the Thirty Years War, followed by the English Civil War, portended the millennium that natural philosophy could assist.[17] J. R. Jacob particularizes this confluence by tracing the early influence of Dury and the Hartlib circle on Robert Boyle.[18]

However, because he treats 'puritanism' as a stable intellectual and social category,[19] Webster damages his capacity to describe the sublimation of 'puritan' experience in the Restoration, for example in the question of how the instituted Royal Society was at once indebted to and distinct from the London and Oxford groups that had anticipated it.[20]

Only by divorcing the political behavior of and constraints on the Royal Society from its purely intellectual inheritance can Webster suppress the difficulty and thus seamlessly achieve an argumentative continuity between them.[21] Admitting the importance of what some historians have identified as a "latitudinarian group" to the establishment of the Royal Society, Webster ultimately identifies it with "the puritan movement," whether we interpret his latitudinarians as representing a defined intellectual stance, or as consisting of a group of separate thinkers.[22] That is, Webster tends toward a thematic rather than a methodological approach to notions of 'science' and 'religion' as historical categories. When he approaches the Restoration, Webster seems to compromise his own founding definition of English 'puritanism,' which depends on a primary opposition between the puritans and Laud's Arminian party in the pre–Civil War church.[23] However, the 'latitudinarians,' whom Webster treats as the natural products of puritan commitments to science, have—ironically—some intellectual ties to certain elements of the Laudian church; for example, all sides appeal to *The Religion of Protestants a Safe Way to Salvation* (1638), written by Laud's celebrated godson, William Chillingworth.

Some of these interpretive difficulties disappear if we hypothesize that the Restoration marks a multiple discursive reorientation, responding to a series of pressures that focuses and encourages a new constellation of discursive activities. Earlier forms of discourse and inherited vocabularies remain visible but assume different connotations and alliances; we witness the invention of new discourses to serve the needs of revived or new institutions. Dryden is one of many who both encourage and report on this shift from within, which explains, among other things, his interest in translation. Whatever the difficulties involved in using the rather vague notion of 'discourse' in this way, I speak of 'multiple' discourses in order to suggest that we can, from an analytical standpoint, legitimately and fruitfully treat discourse from many points of view—institutional, generational, technological, linguistic, and so forth. But because discourse at the Restoration resists precisely those specialized modern terms of analysis we bring to it, the vocabulary of Restoration texts perplexes the very attempt to legislate differences among discourses. This is one reason why—contrary to received wisdom—the Restoration habitually treats literary genre less as a question of some fixed ontological or epistemological hierarchy than as a heuristic device, an experimental space within to test wider discursive issues, a habit that explains the neoclassical tendency to treat linguistic forms not as fixed but as plastic and contingent. I shall argue that this is also one motive for the appeal of Hellenistic models of philosophic conduct, because they also deny simple demarcations between logic, physics, and ethics. Admittedly, if we treat a certain group of texts from the Restoration as in some way 'scientific' in their leanings, we can usefully illuminate some of their central historical concerns. As I hope to demonstrate in later pages, provisionally to imagine these texts as 'scientific' can help focus their substantial concern with questions of method. But because 'science' is such an ideologically loaded postindustrial term, a device of exclusion and limitation, it must necessarily ignore or suppress the play of vocabularies within what the Restoration very deliberately termed "natural philosophy," an integral branch of "science," which by contrast embraced all human knowledge.[24] Even Johnson's dictionary definition of "science" in 1755 shows how far that term denoted a catholic view of knowledge at a relatively late date. To describe a more precise way for engaging with texts so procedurally remote from us, I find useful Pocock's notion of "multivalent paradigms" by which we register as far as possible the complex of linguistic forces, claims, and actions within any given historical matrix, involving what he also describes as a *"migration"* of vocabularies and significances.[25] Historical utterances habitually spill over into one another in ways quite foreign to our generic expectations, and in so doing they assert their historical specificity.

I would argue, then, that the dominant rhetoric of Restoration discourse, of which (Dryden recognizes) natural philosophy is a central feature, entails a distinct epistemology, which in turn necessitates an equally distinct will to knowledge and representation.[26] Although *coherent,* this reorientation is not rational or 'scientific' (in the sense assumed by many historians of science, intellectual historians, and critics of the 'plain style'). For heuristic purposes, I would therefore propose a distinction between an inherited *vocabulary* and its articulation within a *method,* so to speak of a 'reorientation' would be to show that even though Webster's puritans may have provided a vocabulary for Restoration science, the specific configuration of Restoration scientific discourse—the rhetoric of its texts, experimental practices, ideology of social behavior, in sum, its encompassing method—is nevertheless distinctive.[27]

My own argument involves an appeal to various methods articulated by several different, though related, theoretical models. The problem is to describe or define the coherence of a set of cultural attitudes without treating the object of study monolithically. The focus on method as a concern within neoclassical culture highlights the emergence of epistemological attitudes at a given historical juncture that revise attitudes to language and representation. But this reorganization of attitudes involves political choices, because it occurs in a contestatory cultural arena where philosophical preferences are deemed to reinforce or criticize alternative models of social and political conduct. An expressed preference for a given set of attitudes to knowledge and method (contemporary actors thought) must not only reveal political and ethical preferences but also do so at the cost of alternatives. Especially within the historiography of science, we have seen the expression of general theoretical models that register the cultural and political implications of different methods and cosmologies, though none has resolved the intrinsic tension between attending to the formal integrity of intellectual arguments and their sociological force: I do not believe that either aspect of the analysis can be reduced to the other. Within all these theoretical models, what is significant for the conduct of my argument is the shift in emphasis from a traditional intellectual-historical focus on ideas (entities protected from their textual, linguistic, and even sociological circumstances) to some view that the cultural *position* of a given utterance, embodying an idea or set of ideas, structurally alters our access to those ideas. Kuhn's *The Structure of Scientific Revolutions* presents a thesis about cultural change and cultural practice, for example, that none can safely ignore: in the movement between what he calls "normal science" and revolutionary changes in scientific paradigms, Kuhn quite properly emphasizes the conservative (self-propagating) nature of all institutions, including that of science, and the degree to which scientific models and metaphors change, becoming quite alien imaginative constructs to later generations of practitioners.[28] Kuhn has been criticized for overemphasizing the monolithic nature of 'normal' scientific practice, and he himself is ambivalent about seeing scientific hypotheses solely as metaphors, such that scientific revolutions might occur as a kind of change in conceptions about language.[29] That language is an issue, however, is suggested by Kuhn's anxiety to disclaim any influence of the later Wittgenstein upon his thesis; nevertheless, there are remarkable similarities between Kuhn's paradigms stressing the pedagogical conditions that tell scientists what is deemed 'scientific' and Wittgenstein's notion of language games and "forms of life."

It is significantly to Wittgenstein that Shapin and Schaffer recently turned as a model for their argument that Boyle (representing the Royal Society) established a set of behavioral, linguistic, and ideological codes under the banner of experimentalism to displace the implications of Hobbes's plenist physics, geometrical method, and absolutist politics. In Shapin and Schaffer's view, Boyle strategically deployed textual, experimental, and social spaces to constitute an encompassing and coherent symbolic form of life, a mode of exemplifying the desiderata of participating in the new institution.[30] The positive recommendation of textual, experimental, and philosophical behavior by one group becomes the means to marginalize an alternative form of behavior represented here by Hobbes.[31] Although I do not accept Shapin and Schaffer's characterization of Hobbes, theirs is an important model for my own argument that the Restoration marked the success of certain modes of textual and linguistic conduct, which codified very real ethical and political directives and that did so in competition with alternative cosmologies, epistemologies, and methods.

In *Against Method*, Paul Feyerabend effectively extends Kuhn's point about the ideological and theoretical constitution of 'facts' by the second-order languages in which 'science' is conducted. Like Pocock, Feyerabend criticizes the tendency "to approach problems of knowledge *sub specie aeternitatis*," in which "statements are compared with each other without regard to their history and without considering that they might belong to different historical strata."[32] He argues that we should rather conceive science, or any social practice, as a "complex and heterogeneous *historical process* which contains vague and incoherent anticipations of future ideologies side by side with highly sophisticated theoretical systems and ancient and petrified forms of thought."[33] Feyerabend wants the researcher to describe the delicate balance between culture as a total system, and the fact that alternative modes of thought and language still inhabit it as remnants of some past system, or as the material for some future cultural construct.

Finally, like all the above, Foucault wishes to create a conceptual instrument that can preserve both the rhetorical and linguistic multiplicity and the historical and political specificity of cultural analysis. Thus, in *The Archeology of Knowledge* he presents his rather cryptic concept of "discursive formations." A discursive formation "is not an a-temporal form, but a schema of correspondence between several temporal series."[34] It is also the site of cultural authority—which in Foucault's

terms denotes its historical particularity—and that authority is determined by (among other things) *"the rules and processes of appropriation* of
discourse" and "the *possible positions of desire in relation to discourse."*[35]
Without reference to Foucault, the art historian Jonathan Brown provides a particularly elegant example of Foucault's principle of power and
desire in his essay "On the Meaning of *Las Meninas."*[36] Brown shows
how Velázquez's masterpiece, although retaining the decorums of the
Spanish court by refusing to represent the king and queen directly, subtly
challenges the kinds of conventions that systematically excluded painters
from full participation in the practices of the Spanish nobility. Velázquez
himself aspired to be accepted as a member of the Order of Santiago, an
elite aristocratic military order;[37] his painting attempts to reinterpret
and subvert the prevailing rules of exclusion. By an apparently unprece-
dented act—representing in the same space a living monarch and a painter at work—Velázquez seeks, in effect, to alter the rules of discursive
appropriation.[38]

Whatever the conceptual differences between the "paradigm" and
the "discursive formation," these phenomena manifest themselves not as
directly competing logical structures, but as forms of oppositional and
exclusionary rhetoric. (This is not to say that the eduction of logical and
factual arguments cannot play a role in acts of persuasion; nonetheless,
they cannot escape the rhetorical contexts in which they are embedded.
The force of logic varies in different communities.) The group of relations composing the discursive formation, Foucault writes, "forms a
principle of determination that permits or excludes, within a given discourse, a certain number of statements";[39] even "exchange and communication are positive forces at play within complex but restrictive
systems," though "it is probable that they cannot operate independently
of these."[40] Foucault postulates that there are governing rules for admission into a given culture and that these rules are attached by implication
to the construction of desire in relation to language—are constituted, in
short, as a cultural rhetoric. My own argument seeks to show how a new
notion of the cognitive image provided the Restoration with its own
means to discuss a similar relation between desire (or assent) and language (or propositions). One generation of thinkers succeeded in re-
defining the chief rules for obtaining cultural authority by attacking
alternative linguistic models; the linguistic model they preferred also
allowed them to reflect on the comparative methods by which they could
displace and marginalize competitors.

Because I am defending a remarkably coherent if plural cultural reorganization at the Restoration, there are particular arenas in which the terms of that shift are most immediately evident. I would risk the proposition that for the first time English culture becomes curiously organized and concrete (London after the Great Fire is an obvious example), and I have already referred to the ways in which we might speak of that fact. They are primarily institutional and generational. As institutional features of this reorientation, we could cite, variously, the frontispiece of Sprat's *History of the Royal Society,* depicting King Charles II in alliance with Bacon and Boyle's totemic air pump, or the establishment of the publication industry as a distinct subculture, or the reorganization of university publishing, the architecture of the Royal Naval College at Greenwich, Wren's London churches, the Royal Society Charter, the granting of theatrical monopolies to Davenant and Killigrew, the introduction of women players on the stage, the institutionalization of royal mistresses, the development of a strikingly homogeneous portrait-painting style influenced by Lely and Kneller, and the beginning of tea-drinking as a characteristically English habit.[41] Such a catalogue is less whimsical than it may at first appear, because its items signal features of what must have been part of any post-Restoration person's experience of the phenomenal world.

Second, without unduly emphasizing it, Dryden's epistle to Charleton associates conceptual change (symbolized by Columbus) with the way a new generation seeks to adopt, revise, or translate what it inherits. Apart from Boyle, an astonishingly high proportion of the luminaries of Restoration and early-eighteenth-century culture were born between 1630 and 1636. Boyle was born in 1627, King Charles II and Tillotson in 1630, Dryden in 1631, Locke and Wren in 1632, Pepys in 1633, Hooke and Stillingfleet in 1635, and Glanvill in 1636. Of these ten figures, four (Dryden, Hooke, Locke, and Wren) were educated at Westminster School under the fabled Dr. Busby. The immediately preceding generation of important natural philosophers (which had had to formulate the terms by which to cope with a national crisis), Wilkins, Wallis, Ward, and Charleton, was born within a space of six years (1614, 1616, 1617, and 1620, respectively). Pearson was born in 1613, Baxter was born in 1615, and Evelyn, like Charleton, in 1620.

Although it is probably too easy to make much of what is, after all, a certain coincidence, the pressure and turmoil of political events in mid-century seem to have dictated even the rhetoric by which men in the same generation could disagree. Dryden died in 1700 a fervent Tory and Catholic, and Locke in 1704, the ideological conscript of the new Whig order (as well as a man implicated, we now know, in the Rye House plot).[42] But both men nevertheless helped to advertise those distinctive methods of discourse by which figures within the Restored order could achieve visibility and wield power. And the same truth applies to Stillingfleet, who on two famous occasions entered into public debate with first Locke, then Dryden.

But there is also a sense that, as the memory of the Civil War and Interregnum faded, the sheer urgency (if not the terms) of the desire to maintain the new order declined. Thus, like those famous moments of *Leviathan,* earlier visions of dissent vigorously, even violently, reimagine the force of civil conflict. Writing before the Restoration of cupidity in *Epicurus's Morals,* Charleton declares that "cupidities are insatiable, subverting not only single persons, but also numerous and opulent Families, yea somtimes the most potent and flourishing Common-wealths. From Cupidities arise Hatred, Dissentions, Seditions, Warrs; nor do they only diffuse themselves abroad, or invade others with blind fury: but being included in private breasts, they cause intestine mutinies therein, and totally evert the oeconomy and peace thereof."[43]

Charleton's Christianized, Epicurean text deliberately echoes the epistle to James, but his vocabulary is also meant to invoke the remembrance of the late intestine mutinies. Glanvill's attack on Aristotelian (and Stoic) dogmatism evinces a similar urgency to indict social and political diffraction.[44] Glanvill compares the epistemological presumption of scholastic "*Philosophy,* that makes most accurate Inspections into the *Creatures* of the *Brain;* and gives the exactest *Topography* of the *Extramundane spaces*" to "our late *Politicians,*" who make "discoveries, and to their objects also; and deals in beings, that are nothing beholden to the *Primitive Fiat.*"[45] He later comments: "'Tis zeal for *opinions* that hath fill'd our *Hemisphear* with smoke and darkness, and by a dear experience we know the fury of those *flames* it hath kindled."[46]

The same need to exclude and suppress figures of dissent occurs in an astonishingly violent outburst in Hooke's diary entry for 11 January 1676/77: "To Bedlam, Mr. Chase, Whistler, Pillington, Crisp, Spires, Goald, Stanly, and Ducane, 2 presbiterian dogs, Botteler, (Haines absent), Mr. Fitch."[47] As a measure of the social change that must have occurred in his life, Hooke got his start as Boyle's most outstanding research assistant in Interregnum Oxford, surrounded by "presbiterian dogs."

The energy of Hooke's outburst should show that the coherence of such attitudes at the Restoration does not necessarily imply uniformity, because behind it lurks a threat to its cherished images of stability and hegemony. The case of Richard Baxter is especially instructive, and it nicely exemplifies both Feyerabend's and Foucault's sense that a cultural formation must involve competing rhetorics. I therefore will use Baxter throughout my argument as a foil to the dominant model I describe. Baxter's highly detailed critique of "Somatists or Epicureans" in *The Reasons of the Christian Religion* (1667) is most often viewed as a concerted attack against Hobbesian materialism,[48] but it connotes something more subtle and more interesting. It offers a highly intelligent, deeply informed but unsympathetic appraisal of midcentury natural philosophy, a criticism not only of Hobbes but also of the two other greatest figures on the Anglo-French intellectual scene, Gassendi and Descartes.[49] As we shall see, the "somatic" position, particularly the version represented by Gassendi, proved an essential feature in the formation of British natural philosophical discourse. When writing *The Reasons of the Christian Religion,* Baxter was in the process of being completely excluded from the establishment, though he was known and respected as one of the great Presbyterian moderates in political matters (he was appointed a royal chaplain at the Restoration and was offered a see, which he refused).[50] Baxter's moderation produces a highly equivocal rhetoric because he displays obvious sympathies with the ethical consequences of the moderate (or academic) scepticism in Cicero, Glanvill, Parker, Willis, and Gassendi.[51] Yet, ultimately, his prior and explicit alliances with a scholastic epistemology and physics cannot admit the preparatory scepticism of the new empiricism. Not only does he reject the reduction of soul to matter, with its attendant determinism (as do Glanvill, Parker, Willis, and Gassendi), but he is also seeking to abolish the empirical methodology that postulates or requires intermediate, secondary causes in physics.[52] God is the one immediate and efficient cause in motion, and "all motion . . . would cease, if the first cause continued not his powerful efficacy." Rather than admitting observed physical laws inferred via secondary causes, Baxter still employs the scholastic notion that orderliness in the universe is the immediate product of *entelechē,* the movement of beings toward their own perfection in a preordained hierarchy.[53] Thus the reason a horse "can move more than a man" proves to be the perfectly tautological fact that it possesses equine qualities: "He hath more strength or moving power; but he moveth not so regularly, nor to such intended ends, because he hath not wisdom and benignity or goodness as man hath."[54] In short, the attack on Hobbes camouflages an attack on the new empirical epistemology; Baxter cannot even allow that Gassendi's admission of the divine origin of atoms accommodates orthodoxy.[55]

Because a mediated, contingent epistemology and physics are central features of the increasingly dominant vocabulary of the Restoration, Baxter is in effect reporting from *outside* the establishment. As Kuhn hypothesizes about one aspect of scientific revolutions, Baxter explicitly dramatizes this discursive reorientation both in terms of generational change and a shift in the sources and purveyors of authority:

> I find . . . that the most who in this age adhere to the Epicurean or Cartesian hypothesis, are *the younger sort of ingenious men,* who have received prejudice against the peripatetics, Platonists, and stoics, before they did ever thoroughly study them; but, *reverencing more some person noted for much ingenuity, by his authority,* have been drawn to defend what they scarce understand themselves; and that there is the mere novelty of some of these new-started notions, which maketh them so much followed; as novelties in religion are with some young and wanton wits: and, accordingly, I expect that, ere long, they will grow out of fashion, and die again, before ever they come to have such supporters as the other philosophy hath had.[56]

Baxter's peevish rejection of the "somatic" view, in short, echoes his banishment or self-exclusion from the institutional church.

The establishment commitment to social order was also capable of a more confident rhetoric. Although a survivor from a more radical and transcendental tradition seeking universal harmony, Johann Amos Comenius dedicated the 1668 edition of his *Via Lucis* to the members of the Royal Society, in the belief that their researches could assist "that golden age which has ever been longed for, the age of Light and peace and religion."[57] The success of the reestablished church in recruiting the ideology of natural philosophy against "radicals, enthusiasts, and atheists," and thus to "Christianize social relations in a market society" and "provide for religious peace," is the central theme of Margaret C. Jacob's *The Newtonians and the English Revolution*.[58] Certainly, Samuel Clarke's dedication of his published correspondence with Leibniz (1717) jubilantly aligns Christianity, "the truth of natural religion" and "the true and certain consequences of experimental and mathematical philosophy" with "the Protestant Succession in that illustrious house of Hanover."[59] What in Dryden is strenuously in formation has in Clarke already achieved the status of a self-congratulary vocabulary.

2. "Moments of Verisimility": The Neoclassical Discourse of Contingency

One of the fundamental techniques by which members of a group, whether an entire culture or a specialists' sub-community within it, learn to see the same things when confronted with the same stimuli is by being shown examples of situations that their predecessors in the group have already learned to see as like each other and as different from other sorts of situations.

Thomas S. Kuhn, *The Structure of Scientific Revolutions*

The Imagination is the first internall beginning of all Voluntary Motion

Thomas Hobbes, *Leviathan* (1651)

It is true, wordes serve to expresse thinges: but if you observe the matter well; you will perceive they do so, onely according to the pictures we make of them in our owne thoughts, and not according as the things are in their proper natures.

Sir Kenelm Digby, *A Treatise of Bodies* (1644)

Probability, Method, and Reading in the Restoration

In *The Emergence of Probability,* Ian Hacking writes that "probability began about 1660."[1] Although Douglas Patey and Barbara Shapiro have qualified this view, they have not undermined it.[2] More than Hacking, Patey and Shapiro emphasize that ancient rhetoric and its Renaissance inheritors had already developed highly elaborate notions of *probabilitas* or verisimilitude.[3] But, like Hacking, they still see empirical probability as a marked departure from that tradition, denoting a newly focussed constellation of ideas about the nature of evidence, symptomology, prognosis, and inference.[4] And again, like Hacking, they see the twenty years before the Restoration as a period when notions of empirical probability were being defined and, less clearly, the Restoration as a point where they became visible. Shapiro accordingly depicts a distinctively English appropriation of probability during the seventeenth century, and Patey takes probability to define the central tenets of "Augustan" literary practice.[5] Shapiro argues, further, that it is their shared attitudes to knowledge that bound the disciplines after the Restoration more profoundly than before.

I therefore take the emergence of probability (broadly defined) as a given, in order to highlight several strategic assumptions within my argument. First, that we can indeed detect a coherent (if not universal) set of epistemological pressures in formation and operation between 1640 and 1660. Second, that the articulation of these pressures by English society is distinctive (if not unique) because the development and adoption of probability—or at least the language associated with it— constituted a reaction to the psycho-historical conditions of the Civil War and Interregnum, which came to be symbolized by all forms of epistemological dogmatism, including—and later especially—Catholic infallibilism. The demand for probability also suited a more constructive desire to fix the stabilizing rules or boundaries of a newly reinstituted social fabric and to exclude all those perceived as a threat to its stability, most specifically in the form of Catholics and dissenters.[6]

The alliance between probability and certain requisites for social and political behavior appears, for example, in Shaftesbury's "A Letter concerning Enthusiasm" (dated 1707). The economy of the mind, we learn, operates by the criterion of probability, for the passions are best represented by the "appearance of reality" and move us most persuasively only "upon some probable grounds."[7] This mental economy, which Shaftesbury associates with the twin figures of health and liberty, depends upon public regulation, or a facsimile of it, which we artificially cultivate in private. Enthusiasm assumes the form of disease and a disruption of social liberties, which Shaftesbury elegantly distills from the conventional etymological myth about the origin of "*a panick*":

> We read in history that PAN, when he accompany'd BACCHUS in an expedition to the *Indies,* found means to stike a terror thro' a host of enemies, by the help of a small company, whose clamors he manag'd to good advantage among the echoing rocks and caverns of a woody vale. The hoarse bellowing of the caves, join'd to the hideous aspect of such dark and desart places, rais'd such a horror in the enemy, that in this state their imagination help'd 'em to hear voices, and doubtless to see forms too, which were more than human: whilst the uncertainty of what they fear'd made their fear yet greater, and spread it faster by implicit looks than any narration cou'd convey it.[8]

This passage most obviously mocks the grotesque consequences of fears stimulated by superstition, significantly symbolized not so much by concrete, domestic, and visually negotiable signs as by the fantasies evoked by "voices" echoing in a claustrophobic and exotic landscape, such as the caves of Malabar. But in the process, Shaftesbury also wishes to equate superstition with enthusiasm. It is true that he specifically denies to the magistrate the use of force to quell enthusiasm and panic as "a most unnatural method."[9] But he nevertheless desires to sustain the public quality of social and political exchange—in effect, to *police* it—by deflating through his myth of panic the numinous and so elusive authority of mere "voice" as a means of social representation. He adds to the effect by exploiting the notion of the enclosed space to symbolize an entire society scrutinized jointly by the philosopher and his reader.[10] Shaftesbury's own fear is, obviously, that things will get out of hand, but equally that they will do so because they might escape his or his reader's controlling gaze. Shaftesbury argues that control should nevertheless occur, but by an act of magisterial sympathy, not force; the disease of enthusiasm is thus purged, not by radical surgery but by diverting and healing it "by chearful ways."[11]

This does not mean that Shaftesbury recommends active political and religious toleration, because he does not. He actually agrees with Harrington's view that "'tis necessary a people shou'd have a *publick leading* in religion":[12] we should guarantee publicly sanctioned and authorized forms of public behavior, which all the same cannot and need not directly control the individual conscience by force. By analogy with the self-regulating mental economy, whose defining epithet is "balance," and sustained by the criteria of probability whose activities occur visibly, the historical and political economies[13] can also become self-regulating, serving to eliminate the effect of enthusiasm, and eventually to silence it. The images of the Civil War sectarians and the vigorous forms of Scottish dissent that the Duke of York (James II) had earlier violently crushed supply Shaftesbury with a vocabulary for mocking the fantastic and irresponsible forms of romance, which his ideal literary economy will also manage to contain and absorb. In this world of potentially subversive fantasy, "old people and young wou'd be seiz'd with a versifying spirit: we shou'd have field-conventicles of lovers and poets: forests wou'd be fill'd with romantick shepherds and shepherdesses; and rocks resound with echos of hymns and praises offer'd to the powers of love."[14] If not perhaps by the direct application of violence, Shaftesbury nevertheless demands the exclusion and extinction of radical dissent from his ideal community by a magisterial action he paradoxically imagines as a form of cheerfulness or "raillery."

A third assumption informing my entire argument is that, by inquiring further into neoclassical probability, we can understand the alliance between a confluence of fairly distinct ideological demands and a rhetoric invented to serve and recommend it. Patey and Shapiro refer to rhetoric as a classical discipline from which notions of empirical probability emerge, and they catalogue references to probability in a multitude of texts, but neither satisfactorily discusses how probability translates into an entire symbolic cultural mode. My brief analysis of Shaftesbury can at least introduce the claim that a more revealing way of speaking about probability is to see it at once as an epistemology, a method, and a rhetoric; that is, as formulating a coherent and decisive attitude to representation.

For the sake of clarification, we should perhaps rehearse before proceeding further the seemingly inextricable, circular relation between epistemology and representation. The quality and scope of our knowledge of the world determines the quality and scope of our descriptions of the world; because to describe a thing is to appropriate, to *know* it, the quality and scope of our descriptions must also determine the quality and scope of our knowledge. Taken as a contingent epistemology, probability must entail a merely contingent physics, ethics, and form of representation. If it also involves a critical mode—a second-order language designed to reflect on its own utterances—it may also permit a theory or critique of contingency.

The threat of being thus circumscribed typically produces one of two responses: either a rebellion treating the contingent as a form of imprisonment frustrating the search for certain, absolute, or transcendental categories; or a submission to contingency, as describing the inevitable and necessary condition of human and historical experience. When, in this instance, the latter view transforms (consciously or otherwise) into a description of human experience and subsequently a social desideratum, it achieves the force of ideology.[15] And if to propagate that ideology, a culture desires to recommend it to its participants, it must cultivate a form of representation that signals, by a range of devices, that the experience of contingency is inevitable and desirable.[16] We might expect a complex encompassing rhetoric—involving theme, allusion, textual behavior, typography, and so forth—that enacts its own failures to achieve epistemological certainty and allies that failure to a defined social ethic. In its critical mood, such a rhetoric might also depict or dramatize the rules for appropriating discourse, showing how it can respond in varying relations to desire, and the cost to those communities (such as Shaftesbury's field-conventicles) that fail to obey its terms of appropriation. We must recognize, finally, that under such cultural and discursive conditions a text (however defined) becomes in itself a concrete image or example of what it recommends.

Although this model places rhetoric and ideology into a mutually constitutive relationship, I believe that—contrary to a largely unstated assumption in many current Anglo-American discussions of language, discourse, and ideology—there exists no necessary logic that binds a certain critique or form of representation to a certain set of ethical and political points of view.[17] A rhetoric promoting contingency, which I shall argue seeks to expose the machinery of its own figural devices, does not automatically entail the exposure of those covert forms of rhetoric exploited by institutional forms of power. For it is conceivable that such a contingent rhetoric (as one could indeed argue about certain forms of Anglo-American criticism) could equally serve as a means to a new political orthodoxy. As the Restoration knew, what makes a particular rhetoric political is not its epistemological orientation but its social condition, its position within the institutions that promote it.[18] Politics is not a question of how symbols are constructed in themselves, but how they are used.

If neoclassical texts, then, habitually reveal and examine the terms under which they construct themselves, perhaps their most distinctive device is to allude to and dramatize the reader's necessarily contingent activity when faced with the text. A double purpose is thereby achieved. The topos serves directly to reiterate those distinctions among constituent textual elements, features, or signs, which only the reader's judgment and sagacity can provisionally reassemble and articulate.[19] So in an entire vocabulary of attention, focus, habit, wit, and sagacity is inscribed the reader's progress from interpreting individual signs, to repeated articulation, to his or her constitution within and by the appropriate linguistic and social virtues.

But by thus postulating the reader as a figure in the text, the text also invites the reader into its interpretive activity or hermeneutical model under two related conditions: first, that the reader *assent* to that activity. The notion of assent recognizes that in practice it is always possible to stop reading, that the reader cannot be coerced, an option characteristically underscored by multiple neoclassical devices for emphasizing the strain and artifice of inference, for atomizing the text: the discrete letters composing the epistolary novel; journals assembled as collections of varied styles and genres; Swift's and Sterne's calculated interruptions and hesitancies; the discontinuous experience of neoclassical landscape poetry; digressions; the printing of parallel texts, typographical breaks, hiatuses, lacunae, and so forth.

Moreover, when the reader assents to this activity, it is by implication an activity shared by other, similar readers, for the knowledge gained is exchangeable because inessential and contingent. That is, the comparative habits it cultivates and that cause us to admit a neoclassical text's persuasive powers are already inscribed in its own processes of forging mere analogies among its constituent elements, which thus resist a private, gnostic, or enthusiastic identification between reader and text.[20] Moreover, the characteristic open-endedness and fondness for digression produce a double, almost contradictory, effect, both of inviting the reader to engage and of training him or her into a purely methodical posture toward its propositions, which, like the ha-ha at Stowe, projects our habits of reading out from this particular text and into the landscape of our common life.

For instance, different as they are, both Hobbes and Shaftesbury emphasize that *Leviathan* and "A Letter concerning Enthusiasm" are representational analogues of their private opinions and thus analogues at a double remove to the reader's cognitive experience. Thus, whereas Hobbes, stressing the epistemological difficulty of access to other minds, still hopes that "when I shall have set down my own reading orderly, and perspicuously, the pains left another, will be onely to consider, if he also find not the same in himself,"[21] Shaftesbury tentatively reserves to himself "the privilege of imagining you read all, with particular notice, as a friend, and one whom I may justifiably treat with the intimacy and freedom which follows."[22] Their respective and equally powerful prescriptions for social and political behavior only follow after Hobbes and Shaftesbury have requested the reader's purely analogical and contingent assent to what they will propound.[23]

Textual and social knowledge thus come to assume a dialectical force, a congruence perhaps most concretely realized in the cognitive mechanism of the English landscape garden: in his or her progress through the syntax of the landscape, and led in sequence to particular spots that mark junctures within it, the individual is trained in habits of association and analogy, which act as corollaries to highly defined social and political forms of engagement. Like the library in the frontispiece of Le Clerc's *Ars Critica*, the literary text presents a three-sided cabinet waiting completion in the presence of the reader. The landscape garden similarly postulates the reader as a constant: a potential though unexpressed figure in whom alone its disparate elements are provisionally organized and converted into a grammar representing social and civilized behavior.[24]

In sum, as applied to its development between roughly 1640 and 1660, we can imagine the culture and ideology of contingency as defined by a nexus of linguistic and behavioral cues awaiting constant reenactment by its participants or readers. One peculiarity of the age is that it could imagine this complex of relations as a kind of philosophical narrative, effectively determining the logic of a number of major English texts published after 1650. The narrative begins with the postulate of some primal sceptical catastrophe, which is capable equally of figuring the postlapsarian condition, the trauma of the English Revolution, or *la crise Pyrrhonienne*, each of which denotes a simultaneous condition of crisis and possibility. As the narrative continues, the possibility is realized by the reader's gradual, arduous reconstruction of knowledge, which becomes the corollary to an entire social fabric. Here it is important to recognize that, though the argument demands the exercise of reason, it is a prudential reason breathing a certain sceptical air that propounds in turn a distinctive ethic. The limitations accordingly placed on the reader's activity are best symbolized by the difficulties of narrative itself: temporality here enacts a sceptical resistance to the self-evident, the instantaneous. So, as Milton, Boyle, Locke, and others insist, what we do *not* know, and what we know only uncertainly, primarily circumscribe our claims for what we know, how we know it, and how we communicate it to others.[25] By contrast with Cartesian, Malebranchian, and Leibnizian claims to knowledge, the English develop a peculiar critique of knowledge after midcentury, which is not demonstrative but rhetorical.[26]

The philosophical narrative I describe is itself premised on the historical triumph of Pyrrhonian scepticism in the Reformation and Renaissance, especially in Montaigne's hugely influential *Essais*. (Charles Schmitt has also shown that academic scepticism, conveyed by Cicero's *Academica*, enjoyed a rather different and more ancient vogue, which partly yielded to the triumph of Sextus Empiricus.[27]) The most famous midcentury exponent of this narrative is probably Descartes, whose *Meditations* (1641) seek to reconstitute knowledge only after invoking the purgative power of Pyrrhonian doubt. Nevertheless, Henry van Leeuwen's work suggests that we can also see a distinctively English version of the same epistemological myth, which incorporated the same essential movement from a preliminary scene of chaos or crisis to a methodical (though rarely systematic) reconstruction of knowledge. Whatever the status of their ultimate epistemological claims (Hobbes being the most complicated case), this pattern equally distinguishes *Leviathan, Paradise Lost, The Vanity of Dogmatizing, Pilgrim's Progress, The Sceptical Chymist, Absalom and Achitophel,* and *An Essay concerning Human Understanding.*[28] One might legitimately object that these works obey generic dictates, that they simply reveal archetypical and inherited tropes, but that would be to neglect their specific responses to the sceptical critique of knowledge and language as formulated from midcentury on.

If we can thus imagine scepticism creating the conditions for certain narrative possibilities, it also encouraged the Restoration to speak of knowledge as inhabiting a *scene,* which is really a different metaphor for a similar combination of effects.[29] Such a metaphor reflects the age's predominantly spatial and visual characterization of knowledge; knowledge-as-we-have-it is frequently represented as occupying or creating a space, an architectonic fabric composed of discrete, atomic components (such as the library, the laboratory, the landscape garden).[30] As in its narrative equivalent, this model, which is also sceptical in its assumptions, imagines the possibility of anatomizing and analyzing the constituent elements of knowledge, prior to reassembling them either logically or temporally into some desired edifice, whether projected as a mode of knowledge, language, or society.[31]

All of these activities, which only meet in the reader or onlooker, necessitate and constitute a *method* of analysis and combination, not defined by a single context or argument, but applied globally to different expressions of thought, belief, or knowledge, or many different modes of discourse. As we shall see, method in this sense represents a kind of dispassionate critical, ironic stance toward natural philosophy, language theory, biblical criticism, and literary discourse; by this token, it characterizes writers as distinct as Hobbes, Charleton, Boyle, Evelyn, Hooke, Dryden, Stillingfleet, and Locke, in whom most of these tendencies are epitomized.[32] The neoclassical privileging of method over the mere contents of knowledge is distinct from a much less decisively critical approach to method in the Renaissance[33] and occurs, for example, in the Lockean view that true knowledge consists not of the individual units of experience given to us by the world, but by our perception of the relations among them: "*Knowledge* . . . seems to me to be nothing but *the perception of the connexion and agreement, or disagreement and repugnancy of any of our Ideas.*"[34] As Shapiro suggests, the structure or method of neoclassical knowledge is (in theory) infinitely transferable from subject to subject, which thus converts it into a flexible and universal instrument of discovery and criticism.[35]

The flexibility and pervasiveness of neoclassical method can be seen in three major effects. First, we find that neoclassical texts, regardless of subject matter, constantly signal their own attitudes to knowledge and language, not least by talking directly about knowledge, interpretation, or method.[36] Second, because the critical possibilities of method disregard generic and disciplinary boundaries, individual texts frequently escape or defy our specialized categories of analysis. Here I would point to what Pocock calls the semantic "migration" of terms: a term that to us might denote a localized, technical application or realm of activity, we find to escape that localization in a Restoration text, and not uncommonly to invoke a much wider cultural resonance.[37] Terms culled from economics, law, or theology wander in and among utterances we no longer associate with those activities. But by thus connoting areas of thought and practice that transcend our frequently restrictive demands for how a given historical text should behave, that text evinces a much greater methodological and epistemological coherence, when faced with the assorted objects of its knowledge, than we often expect.

Once we agree, for example, that Locke's *Essay* is a 'philosophical' classic, no one would assign it a central place in the history of economics, but, nevertheless, two of its chief operating terms are "commerce" and "economy." "Commerce" offers an excellent example of semantic, and by implication paradigmatic, migration. As a metaphor for language or communication—its primary and ostensible purpose in the *Essay*—it evokes not only the act of communication but also a continuous series of actions akin to commercial processes. Its economic sense reveals the immanence of Locke's assumptions about the priority of economic individualism in maintaining liberty and society. (The growth of the *Essay* historically parallels the development of the national debt.[38]) And "commerce" describes the processive and developmental nature of the *Essay* as a literary artifact, its mentalism, and its rhetorical development of the relationship between the figure of 'Locke' and his reader: in the exchanges permitted by "commerce," the activities of writing, thought, and social intercourse are fused. The development of the relationship between 'Locke' and the reader, moreover, enacts Locke's general method of inductive enquiry, which certainly derives in part from natural philosophy.[39] But the social dimension of the *Essay* can never be expunged from its purely 'philosophical' concerns. Indeed, it could be said to be one of its conditions; for the particularities of the reader's apprehension of the author allow the text to approach some of the more logical consequences of his scepticism without calling down a total collapse of knowledge and society. Locke's abiding ethical presence constantly reiterates the constructive social demands to which philosophy is an handmaiden, whatever threats scepticism might pose. By pursuing the multiple values of "commerce" in the *Essay,* then, we can see how the work's implicit features (its method and rhetoric) serve and condition its explicit arguments and intentions.

Third, that method can be transferred equally among natural philosophy, theology, literature, and textual scholarship without compromising its integrity is manifested concretely in the careers of authors such as John Pearson, Robert Boyle, and John Locke. With equal authority, each presumed that he could write on a very wide range of topics and in very different modes. John Pearson—whom Gilbert Burnet judged "in all respects the greatest divine of the age"[40]—was revered as a great textual scholar by none other than Richard Bentley, and he edited the *Golden Remains of . . . Mr. J. H[ales]* (1659), as well as the vast critical anthology *Critici Sacri* (1660) to accompany Brian Walton's distinguished *Biblia Sacra Polyglotta* (1653–57).[41] Pearson also published an important edition of Diogenes Laertius (1664), as well as assisting Thomas Stanley, the author of *The History of Philosophy* (4 vols., 1655–62), and whom we have already met in Hooke's company, with his spectacular edition of Aeschylus (1664). Stanley himself was one of the original signatories of the Royal Society charter (along with Dryden, Sprat, Aubrey, Digby, and Evelyn) and became a fellow in 1663.[42] Pearson's election followed in 1667, though he was never active. Stanley's *History of Philosophy,* which was at least partly modelled on Diogenes Laertius, included a translation of Sextus Empiricus and—significantly—a translation of Pierre Gassendi's smaller and earlier synthesis of Epicureanism, his *Philosophiae Epicuri Syntagma* (originally published in 1649 and partially republished in volume three of Gassendi's important *Opera Omnia* of 1658).[43]

Boyle's publishing career, as J. R. Jacob has shown at length, disregards modern discursive and disciplinary boundaries with equal ease. For example, the methods adumbrated by *Origin of Forms and Qualities* (1666), *The Sceptical Chymist* (1661), and *Some Considerations Touching the Style of the H. Scriptures* (1661) are essentially interchangeable; they all combine Boyle's peculiar epistemological diffidence with those rhetorical stances that condone it as an inevitable fruit of inquiring into any subject, whether the nature of matter or the Scriptures. As Boyle puts it in "Some Considerations Touching Experimental Essays in General," an epistolary text that echoes the rhetoric of Luke and prefacing *Certain Physiological Essays* (1661),[44] he finds "many things, of which I could give myself no one probable cause, and some things, of which several causes may be assigned so differing, as not to agree in any thing unless in their being all of them probable enough"; he accordingly resolves that because "I have often found such difficulties in searching into the cause and manner of things, and I am so sensible of my own disability to surmount those difficulties, that I dare speak confidently and positively of very few things, except of matters of fact."[45] Thus he eschews a "succinct way of writing" in favor of "a more free and uncircumscribed way of discoursing, a greater liberty to insist on and manifest the reasonableness of such animadversions, as I thought seasonable for . . . a beginner in experimental learning."[46] Likewise, in *Some Considerations Touching the Style of the H. Scriptures,* Boyle defines literary style not as a catalogue of schemes and tropes but as a writer's "method, his lofty or humbler character (as orators speak) his pathetical or languid, his close or incoherent way of writing; and in a word, almost all the whole manner of an author's expressing himself."[47] So Boyle defends his own seemingly unsystematic mode of presentation and insists that "much of the seeming desultoriness of my method, and frequency of my rambling excursions, have been but intentional and charitable digressions out of my way, to bring some wandering friends into theirs."[48]

Mediated Signs: Etiology and Cognition

The neoclassical obsession with method accompanies a fascination with the constituent elements or particles of knowledge and with their origins. In all cases, the motive is to ensure that we never lose sight either of the elements of knowledge or their mutual relations, that they do not slip away into some nonnegotiable realm of knowledge. The etiological urge finds its most interesting application in three closely related areas of discussion: the question of the origins of human knowledge, of which a major part is a debate over the mechanics of cognition; the question of the origins of language, both imagined as an event occurring in the individual mind (ontogenetically) and as some hypothetical cultural moment (phylogenetically); and the question of the origins of texts, particularly, in my discussion, biblical texts.[49] These discussions jointly constitute a profound if unsystematic series of meditations on the nature of human knowledge, human language, and human history.[50]

The idea of origins—whether of knowledge or language—signaled by Locke's troupe of savages, children, and idiots, appears first to describe the rise of general ideas and linguistic universals from the raw materials of knowledge, particulars founded in experience, which provide the grounds of our inferential and analogical abstractions. But, as Hans Aarsleff repeatedly insists, it also effectively seeks to ensure that we respond to the way knowledge and language actually work, not to some abstract or historically remote conception of them. That is, neoclassical descriptions or myths of origin usually serve a doubly descriptive and prescriptive purpose: the qualities apparently projected back to that moment of origin, the first glimmerings of knowledge, the first attempts at speech, often apply directly to how we should now conduct ourselves mentally, verbally, and socially.[51] Although, since the poststructuralist assaults on them, all etiological myths are permanently under suspicion, neoclassical thinkers exploited the language used to describe the original scene of knowledge or language not as some actual historical occurrence but as a means of projecting it into the arena of social behavior, and thus revealing the requirements for acceptable, civilized social forms.

In the neoclassical scheme, as we shall see, cognitive and linguistic origins are thought of as material, somatic, and particular, and they thus serve the reconstructive motives I have described, because they resist that numinous mass of abstractions, linguistic universals, and general ideas that Bacon, Hobbes, and Locke severally and powerfully indict.[52] The hypothesis of origins offers a means to reanchor knowledge and language in particulars gained from experience, from which we infer general ideas and linguistic universals. The edifice of knowledge is accordingly often imagined as a structure like the tower of Babel, where the higher we build from its foundations in particular sensible signs, the more we risk toppling the fabric of knowledge, language, and society.[53] The guarantee against a potential collapse is not to raze the entire edifice but to ensure that, however complicated it becomes, it is evenly built from particles that uniformly respect the quality and nature of its foundations.

This is not to say that we witness a naïve trust in the ability to recuperate those foundations, because the mythic or hypothetical cast of neoclassical fictions of origins responds to an epistemological climate that denies unmediated access to any definite originary point or moment. Even a mitigated scepticism frustrates a trust in human capacities unequivocally to grasp the origins and nature of our physical, historical, and mental experience. But where the tropes of Pyrrhonian scepticism deny access to meaningful knowledge, forcing us to suspend all judgment in the face of multiple, shifting, and unstable evidences, mitigated scepticism argues that, for the contingent requirements of daily living, we possess all that is sufficient (if not proven) for our social and religious existence. Apparently echoing Carneades,[54] Locke writes in an exemplary moment:

> For though the *Comprehension* of our Understandings, comes ex-
> ceeding short of the vast Extent of Things; yet, we shall have Cause
> enough to magnify the bountiful Author of our Being, for that
> Portion and Degree of Knowledge, he has bestowed on us, so far
> above the rest of the Inhabitants of this our Mansion. . . . And we
> shall then use our Understandings right, when we entertain all
> Objects in that Way and Proportion, that they are suited to our
> Faculties; and upon these Grounds, they are capable of being pro-
> pos'd to us; and not peremptorily, or intemperately require Dem-
> onstration, and demand Certainty, where Probability only is to be
> had, and which is sufficient to govern all our Concernments.[55]

Locke implies that acceptable knowledge is merely knowledge of our present mansion, phenomenal rather than transcendental, probable rather than demonstrative. This is the only kind of knowledge that God has deemed suitable to our natures: we would be crushed by the weight of microscopic, occult, or gnostic perception.[56] The origins of language and society, therefore, are themselves imagined as a display of palpable, external signs, because in so respecting the circumscribed conditions of all human knowledge, they act as a means of hypothesizing and validating its irreducible and indivisible atomic constituents. Neoclassical etiology thus serves as only one aspect of a general discussion about the nature and requirements for neoclassical representation, of which descriptions of human cognition are another.

If the protocols of neoclassical representation are being formed and revised during the mid-seventeenth century, this occurs in terms that derive from concurrent debates over epistemology (method, logic, cognition), physics, and ethics. The move from discussing knowledge in general to describing the nature of representation requires that, to obtain any knowledge of the world and of others, we require a theory or method for apprehending and interpreting Nature or human beings. As we shall see, Hellenistic philosophy, crucially, conceived of philosophy as falling into logic or method, physics, and ethics and thus formalized the intuition that, without a coherent philosophy of mind or hermeneutic, we can propound no coherent physics or ethics.

The implication is that the qualities that we assign to cognition will signify our theories of matter and society, and vice versa. Our perceptual acquaintance with the world can be either *immediate* or *mediate,* each alternative betokening, respectively, a dogmatic or sceptical epistemology. Notions of unmediated knowledge seem to evoke some intuitive, gnostic, mystical communion between the knower and the known, and they eventually betray an impatience with the very idea of representation as such, because a sign necessarily denotes an intervention between two privileged realities: the figure of pure mystical communion between the worshiper and the divine is silence.[57] To re-present is, precisely, to operate at a remove from the present, the immediate. At least according to the neoclassical critique, on this model the unmediated knowledge of bodies is a knowledge of their essential, ontic, inward natures; similarly, true human bonds are forged by means of some infallible, gnostic process or point of recognition.[58] The necessities of scientific, social, or political negotiation are swept aside because knowledge occurs in effect purely arbitrarily and definitionally: it either is or is not the truth; one either does or does not belong to a defined society.[59] In Stanley's *History of Philosophy,* Zeno points out that "things which are certain require no sign, for they are comprehended of themselves; neither those which are wholly uncertain, for they can no way be comprehended; but those only which are uncertain in time, or by nature, may be comprehended by signs."[60] Dryden realizes that a dogmatic epistemology such as Aristotle's could become the grounds for a nonnegotiable, arbitrary, even predestinarian dispensation in physics and ethics.[61] Dryden's attack on Aristotelian tyranny in the Epistle to Charleton is not mere polemic.

The development of a distinctively neoclassical ideology of contingency,[62] by contrast, accompanies a remarkably coherent theory of *mediation, accommodation,* or *incarnationalism.*[63] A sceptical epistemology not only admits but also welcomes the infusion of signs into our mental economy. It may deny an immaculate access to spirit, the mind of God, other minds, the individual conscience, and the essential properties of bodies, but it does not dismiss any of these as working postulates if supported on sufficient evidentiary grounds.[64] Signs, in short, mediate between us, the world, God, and others, and even our own cognitive processes.[65] Seen from another angle, for us to know any of these things, representation must accommodate itself to our partial ways of knowing.[66] Thus the neoclassical use of the term "proportion" (which Hooke significantly calls "appropriation"[67]) most frequently denotes the ways that evidences available to us must by nature be accommodated proportionately to our limited means of perception;[68] it rarely implies Platonic or Neoplatonic realism, because that is fundamentally at odds with the epistemology that necessitates neoclassical "proportion."[69] Glanvill writes that "another reason of our *ignorance* and the *narrowness* of our *apprehensions* may arise hence; That we cannot perceive the manner of any of Natures operations, but by proportion to our *senses,* and a return to *material phantasms.*"[70] Neoclassical notions of proportion derive from a distinct emphasis on the uniformly hemeneutical condition of all human experience: the limits on the human capacity to apprehend the world operate in some ratio or proportion to the total sum of possibilities the world represents.

Baxter properly calls the emerging theory of mediation "somatic" because signs are emphatically conceived of in terms paralleling Glanvill's *"material phantasms."*[71] This embodied (or incarnated) sense of the sign is not always immediately evident, if we fail to distinguish between individual descriptive words used to refer to mental signs and their place in the larger argumentative and epistemological framework. The age could not invent a stable vocabulary for signs out of whole cloth, and it consequently struggled with terms borrowed from inherited vocabularies.[72] The most obvious and pertinent example is the originally Aristotelian term "species" to denote mental representations. When Charleton writes that "all Sensation is performed by the Mediation of certain Images or Species,"[73] his sceptical and cognitive assumptions knowingly defy Aristotle's essentialist view that "sensations are not an insurmountable barrier between the intellect and the world, but are rather the natural vehicle by which the intelligible structure of the world is brought into *nous,* and made accessible to it: they furnish a vision, a kind of natural revelation of the world to intellect."[74] Because "cognitive awareness for Aristotle is transparent; it is simply the actualization of the object of the experience,"[75] Aristotelian *logos* imports a greater immediacy than neoclassical representation, for "the structure of the Greek language and the structure of the world are ultimately the same because the Greek language is a natural instrument for knowing and expressing the world's structure."[76] Furthermore, though Locke's argumentative uses of the word "idea" are increasingly defended as internally consistent,[77] his uncertainty about what local vocabularies to apply at any particular moment has nourished an entire branch of Locke criticism. Despite some shared vocabularies applied to cognition and mental representation, then, for Aristotle science is certain,[78] whereas it is merely probable for Glanvill or Locke.[79]

The prevailing consideration in the discussion of signs, including mental ones, is (within sceptical constraints) to fix and stabilize the components of knowledge by rendering them at once *discrete* and *apparent*. Aristotelian *species* now tend to serve a pervasively pictorial or visual description of the primary constituents of knowledge, those that logically or historically precede and thus ground the abstractions and generalities of knowledge-as-we-have-it. Accordingly, Hooke's decision to begin his *Micrographia* with a chapter on *"the Point of a sharp small Needle"* is entirely methodical. He explains:

> As in *Geometry,* the most natural way of beginning is from a Mathematical *point;* so is the same method in Observations and *Natural history* the most genuine, simple, and instructive. We must first endevour to make *letters,* and draw *single* strokes true, before we venture to write whole *Sentences,* or to draw large *Pictures.* And in *Physical* Enquiries, we must endevour to follow Nature in the more *plain* and *easie* ways she treads in the most *simple* and *uncompounded bodies,* to trace her steps, and be acquainted with her manner of walking there, before we venture our selves into the multitude of *meanders* she has in *bodies of a more complicated* nature; lest, being unable to distinguish and judge of our way, we quickly lose both *Nature* our Guide, and *our selves* too and are left to wander in the *labyrinth* of groundless opinions; wanting both *judgment,* that *light,* and *experience,* that *clew,* which should direct our proceedings.[80]

As for Milton, the labyrinth of serpentine complexities and *"meanders"* confining and misleading human knowledge denotes our postlapsarian condition.[81] The attempt to clarify the particular concrete components of our knowledge perfectly describes the narrower project of the *Micrographia,* which literally enlists the aid of ocular devices, as well as the wider project of rendering all knowledge accountable to particulars, in Hooke's case symbolized by "a *Physical point.*"[82] If only notionally, thus to endow originary signs with a kind of atomic, ontic weight or density is to propose a dual theory of accountability. First, the atomic elements of mind and language are derivable by inference from equivalent features in the world, a notion of mediated reference that even Glanvill's highly sceptical form of conceptualism presupposes.[83] This demand for a peculiarly weighted mental representation also assists Locke's desire that ideas be defined exclusively as actual objects of awareness.[84]

Second, the same atomic elements of mind and representation posit the indirect but nevertheless real accountability of one mind to another by virtue of analogy. We have already seen how this model informs a neoclassical theory of reading.[85] Where Ian Hacking contends that seventeenth-century "ideas" philosophy could develop no adequate public theory of meaning[86]—something W. V. Quine also evidently believes[87]—I would argue that if mental signs could at root be described as phenomenal (whatever their subsequent status), they could theoretically be converted into counters for exchange, contract, and assent.[88] Mind and language are thus accountable first to the world by virtue of inference, and then to other individuals by virtue of analogy.[89]

It must be stressed that the politics of accountability deliberately subverts the politics of immediate and direct supervision, if still to establish its own form of hegemony. Whereas Catholic infallibilism,[90] Sectarian and Quaker inspirationalism, and some implications of Cartesianism[91] were understandably thought to claim unmediated access to the individual conscience or the mind of God,[92] and thus to vitiate the power of the individual will, we are now theoretically encouraged to exercise our individual wills in the act of assenting to another's purely contingent assertions of knowledge and authority. By the same token, political coercion is associated with the power arbitrarily to force identifications among the discontinuous figures of experience (such as Satanic "force" in *Paradise Lost*); whereas theories of assent resist coercion precisely by preserving and vindicating the atomic nature of experience, to reflect its original accountability to the world.[93] Locke expresses this correlation, in attacking the enthusiasts' demand to force assent, by a purely circular, self-regarding logic: "they are sure, because they are sure: and their Persuasions are right, only because they are strong in them. For, when what they say is strip'd of the Metaphor of seeing and feeling, this is all it amounts to: and yet these Similes so impose on them, that they serve them for certainty in themselves, and demonstration to others."[94] We inevitably create structures, but they are now bound by mere relations, rather than identifications, among their constituent parts; those relations are represented and exposed as artificial, as invented, and not essential, occult, or metaphysical.[95]

I have already remarked that if cognitive and linguistic mediation appears thus epistemologically inescapable and politically desirable, Restoration notions of 'plain style' can have little to do with the still lamentably familiar critical interpretations of Restoration prose. In brief, modern—and almost exclusively American—criticism characteristically assumes that the Restoration naïvely sought to purge metaphor from language, seeking a transparently referential, "utilitarian" form of representation.[96] The Restoration not only propounded an argument for language-as-use as an aspect of mediation but also developed a critique of representation that, in sum, authorized some figural devices (notably synecdoche) over others,[97] fully aware that to excise figuration from representation altogether amounts to abolishing language itself. Viewed from one angle, synecdoche attaches itself to our cognitive engagements with the world, because it symbolizes a partial effect of some unknown cause, just as we infer physical laws by attending to partial physical appearances; but viewed from another angle, it enacts by the same token the inevitable displacements embedded in any form of representation. And whereas theories of radical metaphor can suppress the mechanism by which one sign is provisionally borrowed or derived from another, synecdoche must expose it, because its very structure (part-for-whole) embeds the contingent and artificial structure of inference itself. Language, then, follows Nature, not because it provides a transparent window on the world, but because its symbolic devices are made to echo and enforce our partial means of access to it, one construed by inference and analogy.

Image and Symbolic Action

By an extraordinary historical confluence, the ideology of contingency that I describe could exploit models of mind, language, society, and physical matter that came to stand for one another. This is in large part because its emergence parallels the development and success of corpuscularian physics in England. This theory of matter entailed two closely related strategies, which provided enduring metaphors for the mind and a causal explanation for the origins and grounds of human knowledge. By contrast to scholastic and hermetic physics, it first offered itself as a merely hypothetical explanatory device, which thus entailed an entire and contingent critique of method: because atoms and the void escape inspection by ordinary means, they operate as an hypothesis provable only by recourse to inferences and comparisons from what we observe. Second, by postulating atoms as the prime and (usually) irreducible *minima* of nature, it endowed this theory of matter with a concrete and literal form. Where atoms were imagined as indivisible, concrete, physical properties, they guaranteed the minimal stability of the physical cosmos. And because their actions on the mind occasioned the individual, originary particles of perception, they satisfied a much more general cultural urge to ensure that the discrete elements of experience could, despite the flux of experience, enjoy a similar palpable stability.[98] The epithet "solid philosophy" to denote mid-seventeenth-century natural philosophy thus resounds with multiple cultural and rhetorical possibilities, because the solidity of atoms underwrote the solidity of things, and the solidity of things, within this physical hypothesis, underwrote the solidity of the new cultural enterprise.

The attempt to preserve the atomic, solid elements of knowledge and language and the world is undoubtedly one motive for the etiological obsessions noted earlier. It also helps to explain why the origins and constituents of knowledge and representation should be conceived of first as a kind of *image* and then as a form of *action*. The urge to bolster knowledge against epistemological scepticism, on the one hand, and social collapse, on the other, tends to privilege vision as the most reliable of the senses, as best exemplifying and responding to the conditions of mediation and assent. Moreover, graphs and diagrams are assumed to approximate most nearly the individual moments by which the world represents itself to our minds:[99] both Hobbes's and Locke's versions of conceptualism presuppose that the original elements of experience are the literal and kinematic effects of atomic particles striking the eye to create a representation of the object perceived. Although they both obscure the question of how these mental representations are converted into and by our common mental activity, they neither resort to Descartes's bald reliance on the pineal gland nor do they once question the primacy of kinematic perceptions.[100]

Image translates into *action* when we consider the origin and rise of language either in terms dictated by the dynamic action of the world upon our senses or, more significantly, in the terms established by two great Western myths of the origin of language: book five of Lucretius's *De Rerum Natura,* and Augustine's *Confessions.* On the one hand, we entertain the postulate that in some cultural past language originally denoted passions (the atomic elements of feeling) by the same unreflexive gestures by which we cry out when in pain, laugh when pleased, and so forth. Alternatively, in some personal past, we learned the meanings of words by observing an adult, perhaps a teacher, gesture toward an object denoted by a particular noun, rightly thought of as an arbitrary sound. In the first case, the putatively 'natural' bond between the abstract concept or arbitrary collection of sounds "I am in pain" and the actual pain it describes is supposedly forged by an ejaculation ("Ow!" "Damn!") or a symbolic gesture. Knowledge of others is accordingly derived, over time, from the signs of their affections, which rapidly assume an entirely arbitrary status. The second instance provides an enduring myth about language acquisition both in high and popular culture.[101] The physical act or gesture of pointing appears to forge a link between the utterance "bread" and that edible object on the table. Ostension—pointing to an object—can be thought of both as a means of particularizing a referent ("that package of Wonderbread" or "E.T. phone home") and as itself symptomatic of the desire to render all language accountable to particulars.

We might ask how the poststructuralist critique of the philosophy of language could affect this historical description. Almost any positive assertion can be accused, especially if engaged with Derrida's densely ironic mode, of reinscribing the fallacies that that critique reveals. But in the Anglo-American academy we have arguably witnessed the success of at least a pedagogical version of poststructuralism: inasmuch as history is conscripted to reinforce the argument, its allegory of the history of linguistic philosophy tends to ascribe to the German Romantics the "idea that language is radically metaphorical in character," the founding recognition of Nietzsche's seminal critique of Western metaphysics.[102] That language is always already metaphorical, a highly sophisticated, artificial, and conventional medium of social exchange, quite properly mocks the very intention of questions such as "How did I first learn words?" or "What is the origin of language?" Such questions, and the manner in which they are cast, can be shown to reveal the covert ideology of the individuals, cultures, or texts that put them.

But in contrast to a frequent poststructuralist implication that we can somehow expose from a privileged vantage the ideological and rhetorical delusions of logocentrism, the neoclassical mythology of origins was offered, precisely, as a fiction serving overtly ideological and cultural purposes, as an admitted means of circumscribing current linguistic rules. Like its origins, language is phenomenal, an instrument made culturally significant not by its nature, but by what its signs are contracted to mean at a given point and time. We may not necessarily like the politics thus propounded; but the neoclassical philosophy of language was quite unsentimental about the inevitability of locating power in some groups or discourses at the expense of others, even as it exploited a perennial nostalgia for the origins of language.[103] As in so much, Hobbes predicted the necessity of commitment to some form of discursive authority, and the Restoration did not ignore his lesson. The widespread attacks on "words" and "metaphor" do not mean that neoclassical etiology, as one influential expositor of poststructuralism would suggest, opposed "reason . . . to the opaque materiality not only of inanimate nature but of writing as an alien and obtrusive medium."[104] Rather, the language of ideas, with its talk of image and action, signals an entire theory of representation, which, in response to a sceptical model of perception, prescribed the necessity of the mediating function of writing (among other things), denoting a language serving a defined version of social behavior.[105] As I have argued elsewhere, it is no accident that Locke's primary figures for the mediated action of the world upon the mind and for the traffic of ideas are drawn from printing and architecture, as if to express their plastic nature.[106]

A certain accepted reading of the published versions of Locke's *Essay* (1690) is, incidentally, partly responsible for a misreading of neoclassical 'plain style' and the notion that Locke stumbled upon the necessity of language late in his philosophical argument, in book three.[107] But Draft A of the *Essay*, completed in 1671,[108] conveniently highlights the true proportions of Locke's assumptions. Locke opens with the language of ideas, but his strategic argumentative hesitancies anticipate his admitting the entanglement of ideas and representation (here, "Images"). Locke begins: "I imagin that all knowledg is founded on and ultimately derives its self from sense, or something analogous to it and may be calld sensation which is donne by our senses conversant about particular objects which give us the simple Ideas or Images of things."[109] A contrastive conjunction ("or") appears twice, in both cases converting the proposition from an attempt to discuss mind *tout court* into the proposition that mind and representation are one ("Ideas or Images") and that in order to talk of mind we have already conceived of it by analogy and thus *as* language ("sense, or something analogous to it"). This perplexity becomes the occasion of Locke's second paragraph or movement, where he attempts in vain to separate talk about mind from talk about words,[110] chiefly because originary ideas are already representations, for the world is at best indirectly available to us: "The Idea of matter is as remote from our understandings and apprehensions as that of spirit."[111] In attacking "words" as provoking "great errors and disputes," Locke desires not so much to demolish figuration as finally to prescribe its behavior according to certain authorized mental and social categories, symbolized by "the knowledg of things."[112]

The actions of the world upon our minds, then, are what produce the 'naturalized' grounds of neoclassical knowledge, its raw material of (variously) ideas, notions, species, images, conceptions. The fabric of knowledge-as-we-have-it is, by contrast, the workmanship of the mind (in Locke's phrase), forged from those elements. Similarly, significative actions or gestures constitute the raw and unrefined moments of passionate response to the world. But because we experience life as a succession of such moments, it becomes difficult, if not impossible, to extricate those atoms of significative action from the view that language as a whole is constituted as a series of actions played out in space and time—as a symbolic mode of life. If, for example, the knowledge of human beings is conveyed by a kind of symptomology of action, then human behavior over time and taken as a whole can be described as gestural, a sophistication of the individual actions which compose it.[113] Ordinary language can then appear 'naturalized' and thus exemplary not only by echoing its origins in ideas and actions but also by dramatizing the rules of human behavior. An illocutionary symbolism can thus prescribe the natural, desirable, and responsible social forms.

In brief, our knowledge of others is inessential, contingent, and behavioral, a special, externalized restriction on the definition of character, which drives the neoclassical obsession with physiognomy.[114] The epistemological restriction then becomes a social desideratum, which fosters the characteristic irenist rhetoric of neoclassical discourse. Barred from the essential constitution of matter, the ineffable mind of God, and the workings of the individual conscience, we prohibit claims to such knowledge as epistemologically absolutist and as arrogating to themselves the arbitrary privilege to manipulate and revise social forms. Although merely contingent and phenomenal, such forms are *cognitively* prior to assertions of special knowledge, whether issuing from the mouths of Catholics or dissenters. The Anglican attack on Catholic infallibilism and enthusiastic inspirationalism was not mere polemic inasmuch as it argued, against their common "fanaticism" and "idolatry," that a formal and instituted church was a necessary and contingent social phenomenon, which their absolutist epistemologies sought to fragment.[115] Idolatry is associated with the claim that language or form is not so much representational or symbolic as capable itself of mysterious, instrumental, and incantatory powers.[116] The attack could be made equally on astrology,[117] the notion of the infinite divisibility of atoms, or the occult process of transubstantiation:[118] giving way to hyperbole, Charleton writes that we conceive the indivisibility of atoms, suggested by analogy with gross bodies, as

> so clearly comprobated by Reasons of evidence and certitude equal to that of the most perfect Demonstration in Geometry, that to suspect its admission for an impraegnable Verity, by all, who have not, by a sacramental subscription of *Aristotles* Infallibility, abjured the ingenious Liberty of estimating Philosophical Fundaments more by the moments of Verisimility, then the specious Commendums of Authority; were no less then implicitly to disparage the Capacity of our Reader, by supposing Him an incompetent judge of their importance and validity.[119]

The infallible, sacramental appeal to authority (again Aristotle) does violence upon the reader's liberty of assent to probable evidences, those precious "moments of Verisimility" Charleton wants to protect. The rhetoric is irenic or apparently socially permissive because it claims to accommodate all forms of knowledge that preclude epistemological supremacy. For Charleton and Stillingfleet (especially as the latter grew more institutionally entrenched), this supports a conservative politics; for Locke, it supports a more radical social vision, but one that, on identical grounds, excludes Catholics and Quakers. If probable knowledge is permissive, there are logically no grounds of appeal to the single authority of the Anglican church or the Crown. Locke realized that to question the authority of such institutions one needed less to employ an alternative epistemology than to push the phenomenalist argument to its logical conclusion. And because the authors' epistemological and rhetorical modes of representation share similar commitments, Locke's *Essay* (if not the *Two Treatises*) could be appropriated both by Addison's conservative Whig ideology in the *Spectator* and Pope's description of the true lady's intellectual equipment, and thus conscripted as the philosophical imprimatur of a social rhetoric for which society was itself sacramental because formal and phenomenal.[120]

The illocutionary rhetoric of neoclassical representation—language as social action—occurs in a context that underlines its social purposes both by treating textual behavior as paralleling other forms of social behavior and, more directly, by appropriating metaphors of social bonding to its activities and subject matter and thus propagating a rhetoric of cooperation. Thus for both Charleton and Boyle, one obvious appeal of the atomic hypothesis is that atoms could be described as if capable of accommodating themselves into a larger, coherent body without sacrificing their individual integrity. Charleton writes

> that, though polite and orbicular Atoms, cannot by mutual apprehension and revinction of each other, compact themselves into a Mass; yet may they be apprehended and retained by the Hooks, and accommodated to the Creeks and Angles of other Atoms, of Hamous [*sic*] and Angular figures, and so conspire to the Coagmentation of a Mass, that needs no other Caement besides the mutual dependence of its component particles, to maintain its Tenacity and Compingence.[121]

Boyle echoes the sentiment: "Oftentimes corpuscles of very differing natures, if they be but fitted to convene or to be put together after certain manners which yet require no radical change to be made in their essential structures, but only a certain juxtaposition or peculiar kind of composition."[122]

Most importantly, this social vocabulary is served by a theory of linguistic action that frames individual moments of conversation, debate, discussion, dialogue, exchange, or "commerce" and converts them into miniature dramas or tableaux of social intercourse.[123] What is said is not as important as its social context and how things are expressed; because the nature of our social knowledge cannot definitively judge the final truth of individual assertions, we make judgment dependent upon a performative and contextual criterion. Once again, knowledge issues from action, in this case a tissue of locutions treated as a single illocutionary act. And again, this knowledge is comparative, contingent: as in

Restoration comedy, we judge the relative social weight of individuals by observing the acuity of their (contingent) forms of judgment, as evidenced by the internal integrity of their utterances and by that integrity relative to other speakers.

The model derives at least in part from the *Cratylus,* a dialogue precisely about linguistic origins. The dialogue logically fails to resolve the question of whether language is divinely, naturally, or institutionally ordained; but its activities are resolved in a double and different sense— first, by endowing significance on its having exemplified language-in-action (the dialogue form), and, second, by Socrates' culminating gesture, which disperses the speakers into the Greek landscape.[124] This is Plato the sceptic in action, bestowing on social action a contingent political authority.[125] Boyle likewise uses dialogue both as a miniature of his ideal for social exchange and as the corollary to his epistemological scepticism: indeed, his mouthpiece in his most famous dialogue, *The Sceptical Chymist* (1661), is that late Platonist, the academic sceptic Carneades. Dryden's great literary critical statement, "Of Dramatic Poesy" (1668), is billed as "An Essay"[126] and prescribes the exemplary power of literary and social forms not by presenting a ready-made system of rules, but by modifying and domesticating recognizable precepts by a range of exemplary techniques. Like the *Cratylus,* "Of Dramatic Poesy" occurs as a dialogue among friends and, more so than the *Cratylus,* invokes a particular social and political landscape: the friends take a barge down the Thames, while the sounds of the naval battle of Lowestoft (in which the Duke of York beat the Dutch on 3 June 1665) "reached our ears about the City" and die away toward Greenwich, betokening the English victory and permitting the friends to engage in literary discourse.[127] The promise of the ensuing dialogue can only be fulfilled, Dryden implies, when it is returned into the world of social activity: the friends part unwillingly at the foot of Somerset stairs, pass through an empty-headed crowd of dancing French people, and thus reengage the wider world of social intercourse.[128] This habit of dramatizing dialogue as the primary context for linguistic action, as well as a model of linguistic significance, also informs the beginning of Locke's *Essay,* in which, precisely, the origins of his enterprise are embedded in a similar discussion among friends, a fiction that introduces neither Draft A nor B.

This effect is further amplified by a familiar neoclassical adoption of an older trope: the figure of a spectator or observer capable of operating within the represented space and of standing apart from and examining those emblems of social action depicted by complete linguistic utterances or exchanges. The social scene is made known as a single illocutionary act. Michael Ketcham argues persuasively that this figure is a founding strategic premise of the appropriately named *Spectator,*[129] but it is a trope that saturates Restoration comedy and numerous novels and paint-ings.[130] It is also an assumption informing the creation of the terrace above Riveaux Abbey as a concrete means of contemplating the figure of an entire bygone society. And it is an important symbolic device in Defoe's *A Journal of the Plague Year.* The reader can also experience neoclassical authors in the act of constructing texts: while performing within the represented space, the author can also comment on the perfor-mance. This is an essential Lockean device, but it is also one of the most common tropes of the ubiquitous neoclassical preface.[131] Even knowl-edge of the authorial self is phenomenal, and thus performative; the criteria are always whether linguistic performance is appropriate to and expressive of the contingent relations between world, mind, and repre-sentation, and thus depict wit, judgment, or sagacity.[132]

In the broadest terms, we witness the transformation of the inherited Renaissance vocabulary of exemplification and its cognates into some-thing servicing new cognitive and epistemological categories. Like os-tension, which only inadequately pictures what it points to, example is a mere fragment, a partial indication of some larger idea or linguistic universal, which we are asked to infer. To endow example with its ideal exemplary force, we must therefore preserve and clarify the distinction between what is and what is not known. On the one hand, it is of utmost importance to preserve the unknown as a postulate signifying the limita-tions on our direct knowledge, as well as the realm of general precepts we induce from examples. On the other hand, we must sustain the curious integrity of the "solid," phenomenal, yet merely fragmentary nature of the sign available to us, which we thus value as exemplary or indicative. Whether in biblical hermeneutics or in literary criticism, this produces a neoclassical doctrine I call the *necessity of obscurity,* arising from a dual necessity Wittgenstein also exposes in the *Philosophical Investigations.*

First, obscurity is an inevitable consequence of our sceptical condi-tion. We see through a glass darkly—almost everything we deem to be highest in our aspirations is hidden from us, and the reified or quasi-material nature of what we treat as originary ideas or signs obscures as much as it reveals. Thus we might begin with Augustine's account of ostension, but, as Wittgenstein shows, pointing at an object tells us astonishingly little about what is meant, and the more we explore the gesture, the more it degenerates into ambiguity, an ambiguity only resolvable by treating the gesture as one sign within a previously constituted fabric of symbolic forms. Second, the particular nature of mitigated scepticism nevertheless requires the conversion of the exemplary into our primary cognitive access to knowledge. Even though ostension might prove an inadequate logical means by which to capture and pin down knowledge and language, it represents our inescapable and partial condition; if the act of ostension tells us little about what is meant or intended, it nevertheless does propose the actual existence of the object signified.

The Ethics of Probability

I have already emphasized that the probabilist argument about representation converts into political grounds for excluding those communities whose claims to knowledge resist its particular sceptical configuration. This is, for example, an important implication of Shapin and Schaffer's argument about Boyle's determination to exclude Hobbes from the Royal Society. Applied more widely, the necessity of obscurity provides the grounds for an attack on all *systems* (as distinct from methods), a term associated with absolute, arbitrary, and frequently foreign forms of knowledge and power, especially those issuing from Versailles or the Vatican.[133] In Locke's *Essay, method* is allied to *use* and *end,* both denoting the contingent and social condition of knowledge, whereas *system* stems from inflexible and antisocial dogmatism, symbolized by Scholasticism, and also intended as a rebuke to Descartes's rigid axiomatic habits.[134] The peculiar nexus of politico-epistemological pressures partly explains why we still have inadequate—or merely conflicting—views of Hobbes's and Descartes's influence on late-seventeenth-century England. I suspect that their purely philosophical importance was immense, and both are consummate prose masters; but inasmuch as either appeared to perpetuate the kinds of absolutism associated with unmediated and totalizing forms of knowledge and representation, they were contained, reinterpreted, and reinscribed into an epistemological, ideological, and rhetorical fabric they may not have recognized.[135]

A coherent critique of dogmatism to create an ideology of contingency unites some very different projects and authors, among them Charleton, Locke, and Boyle. Charleton attacks "*Teutonick* (rather, *Fanatique*) Philosophers" for their absolutist categories, because "they frequently adscribe a *Dark,* and a *Light* side to God; determining the Essence of *Hell* in the one, and that of *Heaven* in the other." And he concludes that "whether the expression be proper and decent enough to be tolerated; requires the arbitration of only a mean and vulgar judgment. We shall only affirm, that had they accommodated the same to the shadow, or Vicegerent General of God, to *Nature;* their Dialect had been, as more familiar to our capacity, so more worthy our imitation."[136] Locke finds in Malebranche's occasionalism a form of gnostic communion between mind and God, an unmediated form of knowledge or "idea of intimate union," which cannot also accommodate representations of the world to the mind.[137] Locke's argument is, precisely, that Malebranche uses no perceptual model of "accommodation" or "proportion," whereas the atomic account of perception allows the revision of the Aristotelian *species.*[138] The mind is struck by synecdochic elements of the world ("perhaps the 1/1000 or 1/10000 part coming to the eye"), producing sensations painted on "the bottom of the eye or retina." Locke admits as "incomprehensible" the means of conversion from physical impact to ideas; but he insists that "we see the figures and magnitudes of things rather in the bottom of our eyes than in God," because the "eye, accommodated to all the rules of refraction and dioptrics, that so visible objects might be exactly and regularly painted on the bottom of the eye," the representations of the sizes and shapes of objects being "proportioned to the bigness of the area, on the bottom of our eyes."[139]

Boyle is similarly disturbed by the implicit politics of an essentialist theory of substantial forms, because it is patently an attempt to police matter directly by an appeal to a nonevident law: "some late learned men," he objects, have urged the view "that, matter being indifferent to one sort of accidents as well as to another, it is necessary there should be a substantial form to keep those accidents which are said to constitute it, united to the matter they belong to."[140] Against the implicit metaphor of compulsion, Boyle legitimizes political assent, on the view that the corpuscularian distinction between primary and secondary qualities— foundational for Locke—frees the individual mind to infer the complex properties of bodies, which cannot be decreed by demonstrative fiat.

A rhetoric of empiricism, then, can be said to support an ideology of contingency, by undercutting one model of rational authority by another. Alchemists, enthusiasts, Stoics, Aristotelians, Cartesians, and Catholics are in different ways associated with unmediated claims to knowledge, loosely typified by the epistemology and language of the mystical, the occult, absolute, universal, preternatural, systematic, intuitionist, innatist, or inspirationalist, and often parodied by diffuse and grotesque pneumatic metaphors. Against the negotiable, externalized, visual forms of contingency are set the numinous, gastric, internalized, and mysterious movements of enthusiasts and dogmatists: because the gnostic and oral/aural are tropes for hidden and nonnegotiable forms of knowledge and communication, they stand for the monolithic exercise of power and the forceful subjection of individual will and judgment.[141] (Charleton describes Descartes's philosophy as a form of logical rape or violence.[142]) In neoclassical texts, this sometimes manifests itself in the form of a highly psychologized terror of subsumption into the whole, which reacts against metaphorical equations between terms, as a figure of collapse or uncontrollable identity between the terms of experience.[143]

The sceptical premises of a contingent rhetoric insist on the combined necessity and limitations of mediated forms of knowledge—informed by a primary regard for the particular sensible sign, the concrete image, the discrete originary moment of action—and are characteristically visual in their origins and manifestation. Because the single sensible sign portrays knowledge and language as atomic, and constituted not by identities among its elements, but by an analogical dispersion across the face of experience, it authorizes the metaphor of a social construction realized by negotiations among particulars to denote assent rather than force. Assent also assumes a central role because of the cognitive power of the neoclassical example: the spectator is willingly drawn to the image or text because it proposes an analogy to his or her experience.[144] Unlike an a priori figure of identity (a form of determinism), the neoclassical example achieves only a modified authority or power, because analogy is as much *unlike* as *like* what the perceiver already knows, so his or her movement across the gap this difference creates respects the reader's individual integrity because it can only be made willingly.

Rhetoric and the Neo-Epicurean Revival

I bring this chapter to a close by emphasizing rhetoric, because it is in the very nature of rhetoric to escape a simple equation or ratio between the possessors of political, military, or clerical power and those individuals or groups capable of adopting it. This book cannot become a direct exercise in political history, even as it reflects on political realities, because linguistic behavior and political action are not identical. Moreover, a rhetoric serving broadly defined institutional purposes is still capable of considerable individual variations. Boyle is clearly an important figure in the establishment of a distinct ideology that goes beyond his personal preferences and that, despite his own affiliations during the Interregnum, sought authority at the expense of certain minorities and figures of dissent. But even as Boyle vigorously circumscribes and muffles the voices of the alchemical and scholastic traditions, he is also deeply aware of his debts to them. That is, as in the case of Aristotelian *species,* the language by which discourses are excluded is partly of their invention. By contrast, Bunyan was a direct victim of the Clarendon Code; but for all his debts to sectarian and dissenting traditions of autobiography, it seems he could not help substantially adopting the new rhetoric of contingency, which informs the entire hermeneutic of the proem to *Pilgrim's Progress.* If Bunyan is thematically constructing a critique of the hegemonic institutions of the Restoration, he shares a common Restoration vocabulary for describing the means by which his reader is thought to come to knowledge. He was not above attacking the Quakers, who represent a willingness to dispose of the mediations of Scripture as the vehicle of Christian knowledge, as well as a popular target of attacks on the same grounds by his captors. Similarly, Locke is arguably one of the greatest propagators of the founding assumptions of neoclassical discourse; but that in no way prevented his entertaining one of the more violent acts of dissent during the Restoration.

In their different ways, Hobbes, Smollett, Radcliffe, and Austen argue that, because language is the possession of none, a chief device for dissent to make its claims is to reorganize the terms of an authoritative and centralized discourse.[145] Access to discursive power is rarely (probably never) forged by the wholesale manufacture of an alternative discourse clinically protected from prevailing epistemological and linguistic conditions—a position Smollett argues in *Roderick Random.* Rather, communities establish their special claims to discursive authority by exploiting possibilities of choice provided by the accepted discourse, though in the process they risk compromising their peculiar and alienated vision, as one could argue happens with Defoe. If neoclassical discourse fragmented the claims of dissent by appealing to sceptical modes, its own magisterial claims to authority were instantly threatened by an identical sceptical move, a strategy Catholic apologists were quick to exploit. When Anglicans attacked Catholics and inspirationalists for their dogmatic attitudes to knowledge, they were subtly but surely undermining a secure basis for their own need to ensure conformity to their position.

To conclude with rhetoric is, finally, to remember that natural philosophers, as fully as other educated members of Restoration society,
were products of a deeply literate training and mode of apprehending
and representing experience. Neoclassical culture is, precisely, *neoclassical*, not because it arbitrarily adopted the contents of the Augustan myth,
or because it indulged in local imitations of classical styles; but because
by a coherent method it also owed to an incisive reading of ancient
philosophy, it mythologized for its own purposes the most fruitful models it could choose from the most widely documented ancient culture
available to it. This act of mythologizing imported a genuinely historical
consciousness inasmuch as it urged the discontinuities between the patterns of its experience and ancient history on the one hand, and earlier
seventeenth-century English history on the other; but later seventeenth-
century culture also sought to actualize and negotiate with its own emerging aspirations by rereading and domesticating classical culture. The
neo-Epicurean revival, which occurred between roughly 1640 and 1660,
richly exemplifies the neoclassical turn I describe and localizes the argument outlined above. In short, we shall see that, because (with Christianized refinements) it provided a strikingly coherent analogue for a
desirable epistemology, method, theory of cognition and matter, an irenist and domestic morality, and powerful myth of the origin of language,
all supremely expounded by Lucretius's poetic masterpiece, neo-Epicureanism arrived in the mid–1650s with a sudden and startling impact on
the English imagination. In the subsequent three chapters, I shall turn to
the narrative of the neo-Epicurean revival and show how it could lead, in
the exemplary case of John Evelyn, to the promotion of those ideals of
neoclassical cultural knowledge that I have just described.

PART 2

Plotting Neo-Epicureanism

The Transmission of Method and the Making of Cultural Imagery in the Late-Seventeenth Century

Portrait of Epicurus (from Stanley's *History of Philosophy* [1655–60; 3d ed., 1701])

EPICURÉISME ou EPICURISME, subst. m. (Hist. de la Philosophie.) *La Secte éléatique donna naissance à la* secte épicurienne. *Jamais philosophie ne fut moins entendue & plus calomniée que celle d'*Epicure. *On accusa ce philosophe d'athéisme, quoiqu'il admît l'existence des dieux, qu'il fréquentât les temples, & qu'il n'eût aucune répugnance à se prosterner auz pies des autels. On le regarda comme l'apologiste de la débauche, lui dont la vie étoit une pratique continuelle de toutes les vertus, & surtout de la tempérance. Le préjugé fut si général, qu'il faut avoüer, à la honte des Stoiciens qui mirent tout en oeuvre pour le répandre, que les* Epicuriens *ont été de très honnêtes gens qui ont eu la plus mauvaise réputation. Mais afin qu'on puisse porter un jugement éclairé de la doctrine d'*Epicure, *nous introduirons ce philosophe même, entouré de ses disciples, & leur dictant ses leçons à l'ombre des arbres qu'il avait plantés*

Denis Diderot, Encyclopédie (1751–65)

Their fortune has been much like that of Epicurus, in the retirement of his gardens: to live almost unknown, and to be celebrated after their decease.

John Dryden, Defence of the Epilogue: Or an Essay on the Dramatic Poetry of the Last Age (1672)

If [a] solid and resisting substance, without moving out of its place, should admit into the same place another solid and resisting substance, it would from that moment, in our apprehension, cease to be a solid and resisting substance, and would no longer appear to possess that quality, by which alone it is made known to us, and which we therefore consider as constituting its nature and essence, and as altogether inseparable from it. Hence our notion of what has been called impenetrability of matter; or of the absolute impossibility that two resisting substances should occupy the same place at the same time.

This doctrine, which is as old as Leucippus, Democritus, and Epicurus, was in the last century revived by Gassendi, and has since been adopted by Newton and the far greater part of his followers. It may at present be considered as the established system, or as the system that is most in fashion, and most approved of by the greater part of the philosophers of Europe. Though it has been opposed by several puzzling arguments, drawn from that species of metaphysics which confounds every thing and explains nothing, it seems upon the whole to be the most simple, the most distinct, and the most comprehensible account that has yet been given of the phaenomena which are meant to be explained by it.

Adam Smith, Essays on Philosophical Subjects (1795)

3. The Neo-Epicurean Revival: Method, Atomism, and the Palpable Image

The theory of natural history cannot be dissociated from that of language.
Michel Foucault, *The Order of Things*

A wise man, if he happen to have the images or statues of his Ancestors or other persons, will be far from taking pride in them, or showing them as badges of honour; yet on the other side, he will not neglect them, but place and keep them carefully in his gallery.
Thomas Stanley, "Epicurus," in *The History of Philosophy* (1659)

Cultural Transmission in Late-Seventeenth-Century England

The last chapter articulated my model for reading neoclassical culture and showed that the notion of contingent reading informs its founding metaphors of apprehension. I closed by proposing the neo-Epicurean revival as one crucible within which those distinctive protocols were formulated. Chapters four and five shall discuss in detail the adaptation of Epicurean method, physics, and ethics first by Gassendi and later by the English community. At this point I want to focus on Epicureanism as the object of rereading or an act of cultural appropriation that marks the neoclassical turn as distinctively 'neoclassical.' The content of Epicureanism is also relevant here, because it validates a view of contingent historical interpretation that finds a remarkable corollary in the midcentury capacity to observe itself in the act of mythologizing cultural models. For mid- to late-seventeenth-century English authors, Epicureanism thus provided a new means to discuss cultural and historiographical issues.

More to the point, Epicureanism also supplied a precedent and justification for a newer culture to displace an older one. In so doing, it stimulated an attitude that probably marks a new phase in late-Renaissance appropriations of ancient texts: the notion that because historical knowledge is the contingent reconstruction of very different texts scattered by the corruptions of time, we must reinforce not only their mutual distinctions but also our difference from them. Like physics and language, history becomes atomistic. To mythologize the past is not to homogenize past texts for our local historical consumption, but to recognize their resistance to our desires. An ancient cultural model such as Epicureanism may provide us with a useful cultural metaphor, but it does so at a remove, and in so doing inescapably displaces a series of alternative claims. It is crucial to recognize that for two reasons this strategy is part of Epicureanism's self-conception: first, Epicurus set out to compete with older systems of authority; second, if all knowledge now derives its main metaphors from the atomistic model, and if we create coherence from cultural atoms (such as texts) by acts of inference and analogy, then we must be especially conscious of the artificiality, the contingency, of the final result. The neo-Epicurean revival happened fortuitously to coincide with a changing set of cultural requirements, which, because the age needed to purge itself of a series of embarrassments, reached their apogee in the Restoration.

To clarify how the neoclassical activity of translation is carried out, and to show that it is often self-consciously dramatized by the rhetoric of neoclassical texts, I return briefly to Dryden's epistle to Charleton. In this poem, *translation* and *revision* are the governing devices by which Aristotle is dethroned and finally banished from Dryden's new discursive community. Having displaced scholastic tyranny, Columbus the foreigner is translated and—significantly—domesticated at the hands of Bacon, Gilbert, and Harvey, an earlier English generation that awaits adoption and revision at the modern hands of Charleton, Boyle, and the Royal Society. The poem exploits its governing metaphors of temporal and physical space for parallel motives: its acts of historical discrimination are paralleled by a spatial form of differentiation, as if the Romans and Danes might physically compete within the poem for title to Stonehenge. Bacon's crucial role is to render knowledge native and reformed, after Columbus, a Catholic, has opened up alluring (and morally somewhat suspect?) visions of exotic and paradisical lands, and so displaced Aristotle's myopic tyranny. As an antiquarian, Charleton reenacts Bacon's reinterpretive activity (along with Dryden, who records it) by revising Inigo Jones's mythology of Roman religion into a northern European monarchical trope. Curiously, however, as Charles E. Ward points out, Charleton's place in the poem is as much 'philosophical' as 'antiquarian': the poem concerns the philosophical map as fully as the English landscape.[1] The inevitable suggestion is that the final and liberating revision of Aristotle has occurred by means of an instrument Charleton has invented and that Dryden approves. This is, I would propose, Charleton's vital contribution to the neo-Epicurean revival in England via a series of texts published in the 1650s.[2] Admittedly, the poem appears to focus on Charleton's antiquarianism, and Dryden never directly mentions Epicurus. But the poem celebrates the transition to a new philosophical era, epitomized in Charleton himself. So I take Dryden to be alluding in part to Epicurus as a figure who has helped his generation to exorcize scholastic tyranny from the republic of letters.

Dryden's subtle conscription of Charleton's Epicurus signals that moment of cultural translation which occurs at the Restoration, and which, as I have described, serves a matrix of epistemological, linguistic, and political motives. Translation is a provocative and typical neoclassical figure, because fundamentally, as Dryden indicates, translation involves global and double-edged acts of displacement and recuperation. In doing so, it again brings into focus the entire question of method. Translation is both act and criticism: to operate at all, it necessitates a method, but almost inevitably at some historical or logical point it encourages a discussion of its own method.[3] Consequently, method or translation incorporates a complex nexus of pressures that focuses the informing considerations of Restoration discourse, namely: (1) the origins and grounds of our knowledge; (2) whether and how we can assemble the components of knowledge into a coherent (though usually anti-systematic) body, or facsimile thereof; (3) how we can represent the elements of knowledge to ourselves; (4) how we can begin to communicate those elements to others—to make them public; (5) how we can guarantee the public nature of knowledge, once achieved, a feat involving its circulation or reproducibility in a given society; (6) how the problematics of public knowledge (the urge to maintain stable rules of exchange and interpretation, the desire to *police* it) necessitate a coherent hermeneutic; and (7) how we transform these rules of reading into social and political ethic, rhetoric, or myth.

I have so far been arguing that, by the Restoration, we can detect a historically particular articulation of these questions, taking articulation to denote both the vocabulary in which they are cast and their articulation into a comprehensible grammar. And we shall see how both Epicurus and Gassendi deal with these issues. We also witness at the Restoration the institutionalization of criticism, the cultivation of a global second-order discourse that seeks to reflect on the culture. At the most general level, this is to admit no more than a post-Cartesian and post-Hobbesian condition, which attempts to clarify the irreducible founding elements of human knowledge by means of a strategic sceptical device, then to determine how they are articulated into the complex relations and structures of knowledge-as-we-have-it. From Hobbes on, E. A. Burtt writes, "it is a settled assumption for modern thought in practically every field, that to explain anything is to reduce it to its elementary parts, whose relations, where temporal in character, are conceived in terms of efficient causality solely."[4]

But at another level, as I have indicated, we are discussing a peculiar adaptation of the possibilities of critical method, tailored at least in part to English politics. In miniature, Dryden's epistle to Charleton enacts the new cultural conditions. In so doing, it also anticipates Dryden's meditations on translation, which serve to comment on his own poetic method and to reflect critically on the nature of cultural transmission. Thus in his famous essay on translation, Dryden distinguishes among three kinds of translation, what he calls "metaphrase," "paraphrase," and "imitation." "Metaphrase" denotes, first, the ontic fact of a prior text (Horace's *Ars Poetica,* Ovid's epistles), as well as the politics of submission to textual and linguistic authority—Dryden amplifies the language of entanglement, containment, and capture.[5] Ben Jonson's metaphrase slavishly turns the *Ars Poetica* "word by word, and line by line, from one language into another." Second, "paraphrase" denotes the politics of "latitude" (a word we have seen Richard Baxter apply to Cicero's moderate scepticism): the original author's words "are not so strictly followed," though never entirely lost sight of. Third, "imitation . . . assumes the liberty not only to vary from words and sense, but to forsake them both as he sees occasion," a liberty that Dryden implies is very close to license and always in danger of erasing the original.

Jonson's "servile, literal translation" (with its attendant "obscurity") and Denham and Cowley's "libertine way of rendering authors" equally constitute failures of historical imagination:[6] the former falsely imagines that it can transport its method, claims, and desires *back,* the latter *forward,* in history, to treat English and Latin as culturally equivalent or identical artifacts. By contrast, Dryden's method recognizes the insuperable division between the languages of individuals as well as whole cultures, and the complex personal and cultural desires informing the act of translation: this attitude also informs the competitive atmosphere of Dryden's poem "To the Earl of Roscommon, on His Excellent Essay on

Translated Verse." In no case can the ancient text finally escape the act of appropriation, but the translator's exercise of power can vary between on the one hand, outright subordination (Jonson) or suppression (Cowley, Denham) and, on the other, a more tactful negotiation (Dryden), which remembers that the original author's "particular turn of thoughts and of expression . . . are the characters that distinguish, and, as it were, individuate him from all other writers."[7] It is important to see that, on this theory of translation, the final, published translation—such as Dryden's epistle to Charleton—exemplifies or enacts the historical and textual mediations that have made it possible, mediations with which first the translator and later the reader must negotiate. And Dryden imagines those mediations to connote a particular kind of textual politics, which atomizes and frustrates the desires of more absolute epistemologies than his own.

The Coherence of Neoclassical Mythologizing

Both Charleton and Dryden commit themselves, then, to an atomized view of the grounds of knowledge, whether the antiquarian contemplates the ruins of Stonehenge or the poet orchestrates dispersed texts from the past.[8] The negotiations of Dryden's poem reflect a wider realignment of epistemological possibilities in the early Restoration. Moreover, by implication Dryden connects the neo-Epicureanism that has promoted the new atomistic hypothesis in physics, both to its role as a vehicle of cultural interpretation and to the rhetorical strategies of his poem that signal a new philosophic climate. At first, this might strike the reader as an improbable or overly elaborate connection; but two features of neoclassical method help to explain it. The simultaneously historical and critical nature of neoclassical method allowed it to make fine distinctions between its immediate circumstances and those it perceived in historical patterns, as well as to distinguish among the different historical models it inherited. Second, it treated the history of ancient philosophy as one element in the history of civilized societies and refused to see philosophy as a discrete form of intellectual analysis: like ancient philosophy in general, and Hellenistic philosophy in particular, it could not divorce method from physics, or physics and method from ethics. And again, the content of Epicureanism provided one myth by which philosophy could be treated as culturally coherent in precisely this way. Indeed, Dryden's poem to Roscommon on the subject of translation treats the Epicurean and Academic gardens as metaphors not of the narrow exercise of philosophy, but of communities that learned to absorb and transmute the cultural models they inherited.[9]

In a series of important articles, John Wallace has demonstrated how Restoration reading and interpretation involved the appropriation of "parallels" between historical or mythical narratives and their "application" to the present shapes of personal and political experience.[10] This profoundly analogical habit—like Dryden's "paraphrase"—inculcates a consciousness of how a given pattern in the past or in a text is both like and, crucially, *unlike* what we bring to it. It is not a matter of allegorizing wholesale some former literary or historical plot. As Dryden, Baxter, and Glanvill have already shown quite explicitly, one such pattern derives from the history of ancient philosophy (especially as digested by Diogenes Laertius), which they read with the same mythologizing cast of mind as they read any other ancient sequence of texts. The implication is that Restoration readers could exactly situate themselves in relation to what they read.

This special mythologizing habit can view itself as a moment in the history of philosophy from Thales to the present, a device to scrutinize the alternatives posed by Anaxagoras, Plato, Aristotle, Sextus Empiricus, Bacon, Hobbes, Descartes, Gassendi, and so on. It also views the history of ancient philosophy as a coherent and almost three-dimensional drama in which struggles for philosophical authority are played out and decided. In turn, these struggles become a myth by which to understand contemporary claims to philosophical authority. We shall see in chapter five how the English conscription of neo-Epicureanism becomes an instrument by which the claims of Descartes, Aristotle, and other putative epistemological absolutists are displaced in favor of a more contingent model of philosophic—and thus social—practice. In this sense, the neo-classical ability to mythologize the history of philosophy creates a method of criticism that is both particular and precise.

Furthermore, as a number of modern historians of philosophy have urged,[11] to conceive of 'philosophy' here as a simple corollary to our modern, institutionalized, and almost entirely academic practice—that is, as a *speciality*—fatally damages the power of the critical model I describe. We have already noted how historians similarly tend to treat 'science' as a reified, stable analytical category, even as applied within a mid-seventeenth-century context. There are, it is true, hints of early forms of specialization—as we now conceive it—in 'philosophical' texts of the period. For example, in the *Discourse on the Method,* Descartes depicts his life "as solitary and withdrawn as if I were in the most remote desert," though surrounded by "this great mass of busy people who are more concerned with their own affairs than curious about those of others."[12] He thus offers a three-dimensional correlative to his philosophical strategies, which ultimately radically divorce the certainties of true philosophy from the contingencies of mundane existence. Although, as far as I know, he never directly addresses the problem of specialization as such, he is in his own eyes saving the purity of philosophical enquiry from the contingencies of ethics, which are mere matters of probability. It is not without regret, it seems, that he writes that "it is sometimes necessary to act upon opinions which one knows to be quite uncertain just as if they were indubitable."[13] However, he begins his *Rules for the Direction of the Mind* with the much more conventional view that "the sciences are nothing other than human wisdom, which always remains one and the same, however different the subjects to which it is applied, it being no more altered by them than sunlight is by the variety of things it shines on."[14] Moreover, as if in recognition of his own rhetorical facility, he recommends first reading his *Principles of Philosophy* as a *literary* text, an exhortation that, if taken as seriously as he intends, would undoubtedly create horror or derision among those for whom the *Meditations,* for one, are assumed to guarantee the logical purity of the philosophical enterprise: "I should like the reader first of all to go quickly through the whole book like a novel, without straining the attention too much or stopping at the difficulties which may be encountered."[15]

Inasmuch as Descartes is trying to divorce philosophic axioms from the judgments of everyday life, he disturbs the English search for a style of philosophical conduct that can provide coherent ethical models for a new society. But inasmuch as Descartes conflates what to us are the distinct activities of literary and philosophical apprehension, he exemplifies precisely the erosion of disciplinary boundaries that is essential to that very demand. The practice of the reader in Descartes's text, a literary activity, must surely, like the rhetoric of Dryden's epistle to Charleton, objectify the founding assumptions of Descartes's argument.

The final chapter of Locke's *Essay,* "Of the Division of the Sciences," is often similarly taken to create or endorse modern notions of specialization. In his *New Essays on Human Understanding* (completed in 1704, though published in 1769, in time to influence Kant's critique of empiricism), Leibniz, probably Locke's most intelligent contemporary reader, brilliantly distinguishes between the *analytical* and *institutional* implications of a "Division of the Sciences." He says that an ancient division obtains between logic, physics, and ethics, "but the chief problem about that division of sciences is that each of the branches appears to engulf the others."[16] Analytically, that is, logic, physics, and ethics ultimately entail one another, and they do so precisely because they are already linguistic in nature. Thus "one cannot explain words without making incursions into the sciences themselves . . . and, conversely, one cannot present a science without at the same time defining its terms."[17] Boundaries appear first, if, like the medieval nominalists, we see knowledge *only as* discrete particulars; second, if we see the divisions, such as the names of different seas and oceans arbitrarily dividing the truly "uninterrupted ocean," as purely conventional and artificial; and third, if we treat the divisions as the product of institutional development, as in the so-called disciplines of "Theology, Jurisprudence, Medicine, and Philosophy."[18] We only invent disciplinary boundaries for institutional, heuristic purposes. If we treat them as having some ontological status, we falsely suppress their common cultural origins and their common linguistic constitution. This is precisely the force of Gassendi's dictum in the *Institutio Logica* that "our way of proceeding in the sciences, then, is the same as in the arts."[19]

I make the point partly because a fully equipped history of the subject of specialization has yet to appear.[20] But Leibniz focuses the most relevant issue by citing, precisely, the ancient division of the sciences, in which logic, physics, and ethics are seen as integral parts of one single project. Because this describes the neoclassical attitude to knowledge, the finely calibrated neoclassical reading of history for its own purposes has often escaped our partial, because specialized, treatments. For example, Lynn Joy has definitively shown how Gassendi constructs his positive philosophical positions by placing them into the history of philosophy, so manifesting a late debt to humanist historiography. Joy argues, further, that Gassendi's ability to reveal scientific views as themselves culturally constructed indicates an attitude toward knowledge that was, by the Restoration, outdated. Figures such as Locke and Newton inhabited a world in which science was the purview of 'nature,' not 'culture.' Science now operated, in short, as a speciality, one increasingly freed from the contingencies of history. This is an assumption that allows Joy to distinguish—even in her title—between Gassendi's historical mode and an "age of science." But I argue that what seemingly divides Gassendi from late-seventeenth-century natural philosophy is, though with some changes in emphasis, what shows their affinities: a historical mode of mythologizing their situation, whether cast in the terms of logic, physics, or ethics. The difference then between Gassendi and Boyle or Locke must lie less in some fundamental difference in content or strategy than in the local resonances of their positions: the adoption of Epicureanism achieves different symbolic effects for each.[21] Admittedly, there is a sense in which any individual's philosophical debts are inevitably syncretic and heterogeneous—we are, after all, products of an entire, cumulative history. But, as Jackson Cope argues, for instance, to see Glanvill as primarily synthetic in his philosophical debts is to overlook how his contemporaries treated him as occupying a particular philosophical place, conceived of as a place within the history of philosophy.[22]

The neoclassical distribution of philosophical possibilities relative to its own acts of appropriation is, I would urge, more precise than even Cope will allow. For his thesis that Lucretius is less implicated in an attack on the Stoics than modern critics have thought, D. J. Furley recruits the subtlety of Lucretius's seventeenth- and eighteenth-century interpreters. Here Furley is impressed by a singular clarity in the neoclassical reading of Lucretius. He assumes that because seventeenth-century thinkers employed a less cumbersome "apparatus of learning," and because they had developed a sophisticated and informed opposition to Aristotelianism, "the position of Lucretius was properly appreciated at the beginning of the scientific renaissance, and has been obscured by the mistakes of the last hundred years."[23] Even if Furley were only partly correct, we would do well to take seriously the implications of his view. For Furley's response to the late-seventeenth century reintroduces from another perspective the pivotal question as to *why* Lucretius (and Epicureanism) should have symbolized the emergence of a powerful epistemological, physical, and ethical orthodoxy between 1640 and 1660.

Scholars have long recognized that neo-Epicureanism played an important intellectual role in the Restoration. But they have usually construed its effects narrowly. In consequence, Epicureanism has stood either for a physical or an ethical postulate, constituting an element in the success of atomism, or part of the history of seventeenth-century libertinism. Recent work on Gassendi has begun to consider his importance within seventeenth-century historiography and ethics.[24] But we still have no account of how neo-Epicureanism provides the means and the occasion of a methodological revolution in England, which accom-

panied a revolution in attitudes to language and culture, dictating—
among other things—what was possible and desirable for literary representation. For—to reiterate my main point—the neo-Epicurean revival
served as one of the chief vehicles of the multiple discursive reorientation
I have already described. Interpreted specifically as a Hellenistic philosophy, Epicureanism could be made to serve as a rejection or refinement of
earlier philosophies (especially as a means to displace Aristotle); it could
be posited as a legitimate and informed alternative to Scepticism and
Stoicism, the two rival Hellenistic philosophies; and, because the Hellenistic period is deemed to end with Octavian's victory over Mark Antony
at the battle of Actium in 31 B.C.,[25] it could be conceived of as a herald of
Augustan culture (especially because vital knowledge about Epicureanism comes to us through Cicero). Again, when Epicureanism is interpreted as a Hellenistic philosophy, its concern with ethics as the focus of
the philosophical enterprise was properly recognized by its mid-
seventeenth-century adaptors to govern its logical, methodological, linguistic, and physical speculations. Epicureanism represents the possibility of creating a discrete and alternative society from what preceded it,
one maintained by special techniques of what Bernard Frischer calls
"philosophical recruitment."[26] Finally, among ancient philosophies,
Epicureanism uniquely offers a comprehensive second-order critique of
method (the use of inference and analogy as cognitive and scientific
tools). Its promoters could advertise it as a superior explanatory mechanism in physics and a model that could also reflect on the methods by
which it establishes its claims against other philosophical systems. It
constitutes not only, in Wittgenstein's evocative phrase, an entire form of
life, but also a device for discussing the language games involved.

It is important to see what value, by contrast, intellectual historians
have usually placed on the neo-Epicurean revival. Most commonly, Epicurean physics is seen to have assisted atomism to become the ruling
physical hypothesis of the next century or so.[27] According to this narrative, the age was faced with four major competing theories of matter.
These were, in summary:

1. The peripatetic doctrine of the four elements, in which, however, the
    originally essential feature of homogeneity of the *minima naturalia*
    was already beginning to lose ground to the conception that the
    smallest particles of a chemical compound are aggregates of inde-
    pendently subsisting particles.

2. The doctrine of the three *principia* or *tria prima* (salt, sulfur, mercury), originating from Paracelsus and referred to as the Spagyristic doctrine.
3. The Cartesian doctrine that matter is identical with extension, but that it exists in three degrees of fineness.
4. The Democritic-Epicurean theory of atoms revived by Gassendi.[28]

Although E. J. Dijksterhuis sees these traditions merging in the work of Boyle and Newton, the arrival of the Democritean-Epicurean hypothesis in midcentury undeniably served as a revolutionary and decisive stage in the development of modern physics, chemistry, and physiology.[29] Historians of science have also discussed at length the theoretical implications of the Epicurean postulates that (a) submicroscopic, physically indivisible atoms and the void compose the primary, constituent elements of matter, and that (b) we should conceive bodies through the distinction between their primary and secondary qualities.[30] These hypotheses serve, it is generally admitted, as founding assumptions for the work of Boyle, Locke, and Newton.[31] Nevertheless, scholars have rarely asked what political and ethical pressures might have dictated the specific choice of Epicurean over, say, Cartesian atomism, or, to put it another way, what metaphors of social action and representation within Epicurean atomism could make it congenial to the physical and social requirements of post–Civil War natural philosophy.[32]

The second standard view of Epicureanism stresses its sensationalism. This produces an equation between Epicureanism, ethical libertinism, and Hobbes's 'atheism,' materialism, and determinism. Again, late-seventeenth-century figures undeniably enlisted Epicurus for their different versions of libertinism, particularly in France, as J. S. Spink's and Ira O. Wade's judicious histories show.[33] But the English fortunes of Epicureanism as an ethic are still represented largely by Thomas F. Mayo's *Epicurus in England,* originating in 1934. This book, a commentary on Lucretian and Epicurean texts between 1650 and 1725, is almost entirely vitiated by its explanatory model, an unwitting parody of Whig history. Mayo unswervingly equates the "hedonistic,"[34] "sceptical and frequently downright atheistic" Restoration with the royalist proponents of the Epicurean revival, whom the "semi-republican Whigs"— who had "usually been anti-Epicurean," and aided by the combined forces of Rational Theology and the New Science—swept out of power in 1688. A number of figures perplex such a characterization: Lucy

Hutchinson, wife of the regicide, who probably made the first complete translation of Lucretius in English; Newton, deeply indebted to Charleton in his earliest formulations of the mechanical philosophy, and later a member of the Convention parliament; and Boyle, a lifelong friend of Evelyn's, both of whom were public and sincere Christians. It is no part of my intention here to enter into a calculus of attacks on or defenses of Epicurus, but several things are clear. In his book on the attack on Hobbesian materialism, Samuel I. Mintz only mentions Epicurus once.[35] Baxter, who does attack the Epicurean threat to orthodox religion, as we have seen, assaults not so much Hobbes (which we would expect) as Descartes, and, above all, Gassendi, whose deliberately Christianized Epicureanism was rapidly achieving respectability. And M. A. Stewart, introducing his edition of selections from Boyle, takes Richard Westfall and R. H. Kargon to task for starting and propagating a "romantic fiction . . . that Boyle wanted to burn [his early papers on atomism] because he was nervous of being accused of atheism."[36] The implication here is that Epicurus did not automatically invoke visions of atheism and corruption to Boyle. Finally, the Restoration, we must remember, was a late stage in what is a long and respectable Renaissance tradition of rehabilitating Epicurus: for example, both Erasmus and Valla show that a true philological interpretation of Epicurean *hēdonē* is compatible with orthodox ethics, such as Christian joy.[37]

Whatever the importance of neo-Epicureanism for physics and ethics, if we restrict it to those realms of knowledge, we disturb its subtle orchestration of method, physics, and ethics and hinder our capacity to reimagine the peculiar fascination it exercised for mid-seventeenth-century English authors. As we shall see in chapter five, this is not to claim that its power was monolithic, or that its materialist implications did not cause discomfort, but it is as common to see neo-Epicureanism absorbed silently or the hypothesis of atoms ascribed to Moses (and thus legitimized)[38] as to see it directly attacked.[39] Because Epicureanism provides a model for a contingent critique of method, cognition, language, society, and even physics (if not the basic propositions of the atomic theory), the Restoration found in it a powerful vehicle for realizing and representing its ideological motives.

Epicurean Epistemology, Cognition, and Method

The remainder of this chapter discusses ancient Epicureanism, though the syntax of my argument anticipates the terms in which the Restoration mythologized Epicurus. (I therefore omit reference to Philodemus, because his semiotic discussion, though confirming the sophistication of Epicurean hermeneutics, is a twentieth-century discovery.) Partly following Frischer, I propose that Epicurus must be taken as a *cultural* figure and that every element of his scheme—the epistemology, physics, view of language, and, above all, the idea of the cultural icon, or inscribed example—is systematically prejudiced in favor of certain ethical inclinations. I therefore begin and end with ethics. And I conclude with the central concern of this book—namely, the various means by which literary strategies encouraged by Epicurus both enforce a contingent method and align it with very clear ethical expectations. Like Diderot, we must remember throughout the haunting figure of Epicurus presiding over his community within the confines of his garden. Epicurus's garden is a physical projection of his organic vision of method, knowledge, and ethics; it anticipates John Evelyn constructing a new ethical ideal in the English landscape from the 1650s on. So, in moving from physics to cognition to ethics, I hope to show why the image of the master in his garden came to have the significance it did.

Because I shall examine how philosophic styles compete with one another for cultural authority, I shall use the Stoics as a foil for the Epicureans, for they help to highlight Epicurus's determination to construct a new ethic within Hellenistic culture, a determination that the Restoration reenacted in its preference for Gassendi's model of philosophic and social conduct over Descartes's. The metaphors informing both Epicurus's and Gassendi's physical and cognitive speculations serve to iterate their ethical aims and, in doing so, to distinguish them from other philosophical systems. Both cling to the physical irreducibility of atoms and the postulate of the void in order (a) to secure the physical (and, by implication, the social) cosmos against complete entropy; (b) to allow matter free movement, by analogy with gross bodies; and (c) to allow the mind (by analogy with the free movement with physical bodies) a free choice in response to what is proposed to it. The view obviously treats the atoms of the physical world as metaphors for the atoms of cognition and language, such that physical space and freedom become ways of executing mental and ethical forms of liberty; the atoms of language are likewise both irreducible and negotiable. This voluntarist ethic also entails the refusal to validate philosophic systems as such. Against the ethical and epistemological metaphors suggested by the Stoic plenum and Cartesian vortex—which imply the impossibility of individual dissent from certain absolute assertions of knowledge—the inferential methods proposed by Epicurus and elaborated by Gassendi retain throughout a commitment to merely probable formulae.

We cannot, then, appreciate the peculiar fascination Epicureanism exercised as a model of cultural knowledge unless we grasp two defining facts. The first is that its complex machinery of scientific methods, its propositions about the nature of matter, and its views of cognition and language jointly serve an ethical teleology, a purpose that also governs Stoicism and Scepticism, its Hellenistic cousins.[40] Responding to a prevailing if not unique sense of cultural fragmentation and dispersion during the Hellenistic period,[41] all three philosophies inculcated the ideal of *ataraxia,* a quietist and irenist ethic that withdraws from the earlier, more public assumptions about the relationship between the individual and the *polis,* which inform Plato and Aristotle.[42] Indeed, Festugière interprets Hellenistic philosophy as harvesting the fruits of an ethical crisis—namely, a conflict between civic and personal religion, which had been brewing since the last third of the fifth century. Contrary to the populist misrepresentations of Epicureanism, Epicurus's own vision of *ataraxia* was actualized in the modest and moderate ideals of his famous garden, an influential figure for Horace's notions of the *vir bonus* in ideal retirement, and the context of a new ethic, which encompassed women and slaves within the bonds of private friendship. The garden symbolizes the distinct claims by which the Epicureans sought to distance themselves from inherited and alternative forms of cultural knowledge.

Second, Epicureanism can quite legitimately be taken to offer one of the most coherent models of ancient philosophy. Long, for one, admits that this coherence is purchased at the expense of a certain narrow and dogmatic cast.[43] But by contrast, the brilliance of the Platonic or even Aristotelian achievements cannot be said to have been quite as systematic or coherent. As Ernst Zeller characterizes it, "Aristotle had not succeeded in blending into one harmonious whole all the elements out of which his system was composed."[44] However, it is not only Epicureanism's internal coherence that is significant, because Stoicism could rival this claim. The fundamental, startling, and decisive fact remains that, for all the particular analytical problems we can detect, only Epicurus, in adopting atomism, went beyond the Stoics by developing a critique of general principles or *kanōn,* which marks "one of the rare cases in Greek science where conceptual development can be studied in a well-defined theory, worked out in detail right from the beginning."[45] The implication for a neoclassical mythology of Greek philosophy should be clear: the most effective means by which Epicurus could be used to displace the authority of Aristotle in the seventeenth century is not by appealing to his range of inquiry or depth of insight, but to his second-order critique of method, which neither Plato nor Aristotle ever comprehensively provides.[46] Thus, as we shall see, Gassendi treats the Epicurean canonic as fundamental to his view of Epicurus and a version of the Epicurean canonic as foundational for his final philosophic enterprise. And it is this very canonic that finds its way into Locke's early views of probable knowledge.[47]

The Epicurean community also achieved a remarkable continuity between its philosophical concerns (a central part of which was occupied by physics) and the realization of a practical, working community embodied in the image of the garden.[48] Whereas the wider context of Hellenistic science, especially in Alexandria, advertised the public and institutional achievement of kingly patronage and power, the modest and irenist ethic of Epicurus converted the garden into a living, "charismatic" example of the marriage of physics and ethics.[49] The two movements agree in their common urge to propagate ideals of social behavior; but whereas the Ptolemies could simply erect public monuments to declare their own glory,[50] the Epicureans were confronted by a dilemma, namely the need to broadcast publicly a private and intimate ethic.[51] Its desire to proselytize rendered the Epicurean dilemma more intense, but, as we shall see, this was resolved by an appeal to the Epicurean *kanōn*, which, in its theory of cognition, fosters a notion of the exemplary image *(eikon),* to which potential disciples can assent, especially when this image appears in the form of representations of the revered master, Epicurus himself.[52]

It is thus by the development of a distinct ideology of the *image* that Epicureanism learns to mediate between its desire to reject public participation and its need to accommodate its private ethic to some form of public representation, however modified.[53] This Epicurean ideal receives support from its historical context, in which the nature of signs was being hotly debated. G.E.R. Lloyd points out that "most of the famous anatomists and physiologists in the ancient world were also, and often primarily, medical practitioners,"[54] which provides one reason why the Hellenistic discussion of signs and symptomology should have been at once so prominent and so sophisticated.[55] Not least among the contributors to the debate were the Empirical physicians,[56] who argued (against the Dogmatic physicians) that hidden causes could not be known and that the doctor should be guided by manifest symptoms in the treatment of disease.[57]

Like the art of medical symptomology, Epicurus's entire scheme is predicated on the mediating function of signs. And his *kanōn*, or revolutionary statement of method, serves to judge the relative value of those signs and thus to articulate individual signs into a larger fabric of knowledge. Commentators from Gassendi on have therefore begun with Epicurus's *kanōn*. Epicurus's canonic is distilled in the assertion that "our sensations *(aisthēseis)* and preconceptions *(prolēpseis)* and our feelings *(pathē)* are the standards *(kritēria)* of truth."[58] Epicurus's ancient reputation as a dogmatist derives from his assertions about the submicroscopic constitution of bodies[59] and from his peculiar sensationalism, summed up in the view that "every sensation *(aisthēsis)* . . . is devoid of reason and incapable of memory. . . . Nor is there anything that can refute sensations or convict them of error."[60] Some interpreters tend to favor this dogmatic interpretation of Epicurean sensationalism,[61] but others treat Epicurus as somewhat more sceptical about the content and stability of sensations, a view much closer to that of the Restoration.[62] As in Locke, both Epicurus's atomic description of matter and his reliance on sense impressions denote a certainty about the actual existence of world on the one hand, and mind on the other. But these ontic presumptions are in part the grounds for a merely hypothetical or probable knowledge of things. Sensations are the given, the raw material of mental experience, and by introducing the idea of preconceptions *(prolēpseis)*—which the Restoration often called *"Anticipation"* or "Praenotion"[63]—and admitting the necessity of criteria by which to judge the reliability of sense impressions, Epicurus assumes all along the possibility of cognitive disjunction. That is, though Epicurus remains certain that atoms and void make up the cosmos, the need for criteria of judgment implies that we can also experience difficulty in obtaining a clear and certain view of objects in the world. The view can be supported by fragments of Epicurus's biography, in which he is said to have admired Pyrrho:[64] rather than rejecting Pyrrhonianism outright, Epicurus modifies it for the purposes of an empirical critique of social and scientific knowledge.[65]

According to Epicurus, the atomic and dynamic constitution of bodies causes them continually to throw off microscopically thin representations of themselves *(eidōla)*, which almost instantaneously strike the eye or another sense organ, producing a presentation *(phantasia)*. The mind can then take hold of the image by an act *(epibolē)*. Thus the entire basis of Epicurus's mental economy presumes the mediating function of the *phantasia*. The atomic constitution of bodies also permits Epicurus to forge the distinction between primary and secondary qualities: size and shape are actual properties of bodies, a corollary of the indestructible nature of atoms, whereas the other qualities are the effects of the distinctive configuration of the atoms and thus do not have an irreducible, ontic value.[66] Preconceptions *(prolēpseis,* or "praenotions") denote simultaneously those paradigms we apply to particular sense impressions, and the general notions (or "complex ideas") we abstract from cumulated experiences of particulars.[67] Epicurus implies quite clearly that the complex ideas or general notions and abstract terms or universals grow together, or by equivalent processes, such that "we should not have given anything a name, if we had not first learnt its form by way of preconception."[68]

As with Locke, the further we build from the origins of knowledge in simple unreflective experience, the more the edifice of knowledge or language totters. So, because "sensation is devoid of reason and incapable of memory" *(aithēsis alogos esti kai mnēmēs oudemias dektikē)*,[69] it cannot in itself denote ordinary knowledge, which must create propositions, and with them judgments that introduce the possibility of falsehood and error.[70] The mind is also, by analogy with its experiences of raw sensation, capable of an "image-making contact" *(phantastikē epibolē tēs dianoias)*; but, as Rist suggests, though such images are "true" in the sense of having existence, they no more guarantee an exact reference to the actual nature of things than preconceptions.[71]

Raw sensation provides the basis of all mental activity; but any thinking being is automatically a long way from that intuitive moment. So it is at this point that Epicurus invokes a mechanism for giving the structure of knowledge-as-we-have-it some contingent stability, for making our general notions and linguistic universals accountable to unfiltered individual sensations. Much to the disgust of Cicero's stoic mouthpiece in *De Finibus,* Epicurus replaces the traditional disciplines of syllogistic and dialectic by a hermeneutic or *kanōn* for interpreting the relative reliability of mental and material signs.[72] He proposes a contingent, inferential, and analogical method for organizing all human knowledge. By contrast with this hermeneutic commitment, Stoic dialectic is only sporadically sceptical about perception, such that under particular circumstances denoted by the Stoic "grasp," language, mind, and world suddenly become exact and purely rational templates for one another.[73] As Thomas Stanley paraphrases it, "Comprehension [*katalēp-sis*] made by the Senses is true and faithful, (according to *Zeno*) for as much as Nature hath given it as a rule for Science, and principle of her self."[74]

Epicurus, however, distributes signs along a single epistemological continuum, not (apparently) arbitrarily selecting some parts of knowledge as absolutely true, others as absolutely false. All signs partake of relative degrees of probability, and they force on the individual the necessity of inference. (Thus Richard Baxter correctly treats the new "somatists" as "levellers" of the epistemological hierarchy he wishes to preserve.) The *eidōla* themselves only represent the superficies of bodies, incapable of indicating their essential natures; even if they survive their flight to the perceptual organs intact (which is itself not always certain),[75] once they become *phantasia* and the objects of the mental processes of judgment, comparison, and combination,[76] their existence becomes increasingly artificial and nominal. Questions of the truth and falsity of propositions, then, belong to the realm of "opinion" (*prosdoxazomenos*), which operates by evidentiary rules. Evidence must then in some logical or temporal space await confirmation, fail to be confirmed or denied, or positively denied by the arrival of other evidence.[77] This forensic model is more hypothetical and probabilistic than dogmatic because Epicurus makes clear that it operates as a means to contain error, not rigidly to guarantee truth: "Error would not have occurred, if we had not experienced some other movement in ourselves, conjoined with, but distinct from, the perception of what is presented. And from this movement, if it be not confirmed or be contradicted, falsehood results; while, if it be confirmed or not contradicted, truth results."[78]

Epicurean physics also remains merely contingent in its views about our access to the essential natures of bodies and in its analogical defense of its views about the construction of matter. Epicurus insists on the obscure (*adēlon*)[79] properties of bodies, what the Restoration described as their *occult* properties. Our originary knowledge of bodies may arrive by the mechanical action of *eidōla* upon our senses; but because complex ideas are the abstracted and artificial consequences of mental operations, Epicurus anticipates the distinction that Boyle and Locke elaborated, between the real and nominal essences of bodies. What we call things cannot decide their hidden natures, and this in turn gives rise to a conventionalist and contractualist theory of language, to which Cicero objects in *De Finibus,* where he indicts Epicurus's conceptualism for its denial of any intrinsic meaning in the notion of *"honestum,"* or moral worth.[80]

Lucretius devotes a long section to the problem of optical weaknesses and illusions[81] and, in a famous moment, discusses the difficulty of knowing whether towers seen at a distance are round or square.[82] As in the case of an oar apparently bent when partially submerged in water,[83] the *kanōn* seeks to offer a model for a hypothetical means to resolve such phenomena. But Epicurus insists that perceptual difficulties in no way undermine sensation as such, and this seems the motive behind his notorious assertion that the sun is actually as large as it appears.[84] Uncertainty about the true causes of phenomena belongs rather to the realm of opinion and judgment, such that we can not only offer some, but *multiple,* hypotheses to explain what we see. This "method of plural explanation" preserves the integrity of phenomena, but emphasizes the obscurity of their causes: a phenomenon "may happen in any of the ways which facts within our experience suggest such an appearance to be explicable." But, Epicurus warns, "one must be not so much in love with the explanation by a single way as wrongly to reject all the others from ignorance of what can, and what cannot, be within human knowledge."[85] Diogenes Laertius provides, in the form of an imagined sequence of alternative postulates that could explain phenomena, a rare but extended rhetorical correlative to Epicurus's method of multiple hypotheses,[86] one that clearly predicates some of Lucretius's (and later Milton's) most sustained descriptive tableaux and epitomizes the distinction between a *system* and a *method* of knowledge. A sequence of alternative explanations may maintain a consistent stance toward the way certain physical appearances demand inferences, but it can nevertheless refuse to validate a single, stable interpretation as true.

Although Epicurus quite confidently describes the submicroscopic properties of bodies, he frequently emphasizes how far those descriptions derive from two kinds of analogies with what we can see and know.[87] First, microscopic particles are endowed with properties by analogy with gross bodies. Thus Epicurus defends the minimal proposition that matter is constituted of atoms and void, because "beyond bodies and space there is nothing which by mental apprehension or on its analogy we can conceive to exist."[88] For example, because we observe that the free movement of a gross body presumes a space into which it can move, mobile atoms also must require a void.

It is also on inferential and analogical grounds that Epicurus clings

The true Magnitude of the S∪n compar'd with the E A R T H.

The S∪n's contains according to the following Authours.	True Diameter.	Circumference.	Area of itsgreatest Circle.	Convex Superficies.	Solidity.
	Simple Diam. of the Earth.	Simple Diam. of the Earth.	Square Diam. of the Earth.	Square Diam. of the Earth.	Solidity of the Earth.
Ptolomæus, Maurolycus, Clavius, and Barocius.	5 $\frac{3}{7}$	17 $\frac{3}{7}$	24 0	134 0	166 $\frac{1}{4}$
Aristar- more than / chus less than	6 $\frac{1}{3}$ / 7 $\frac{1}{6}$	20 $\frac{1}{7}$ / 22 $\frac{3}{7}$	30 $\frac{3}{7}$ / 38 0	127 0 / 155 0	254 $\frac{1}{11}$ / 368 $\frac{1}{11}$
Albategnius	5 $\frac{7}{10}$	18 $\frac{1}{7}$	26 0	108 0	186 0
Copernicus	5 $\frac{27}{60}$	16 $\frac{1}{2}$	22 0	91 0	161 $\frac{1}{4}$
Tycho and Blancanus	5 $\frac{44}{75}$	16 $\frac{3}{7}$	22 0	85 0	140 0
Longomontanus	5 $\frac{8}{7.10}$	18 $\frac{1}{14}$	26 0	95 0	196 0
Keplerus	15 0	47 $\frac{1}{15}$	176 0	705 0	3375 0
Lansbergius	7 $\frac{13}{17}$	24 0	46 0	176 0	434 0
Galilæus	7 0	22 $\frac{2}{7}$	39 0	156 0	343 0
Wendelinus	64 0	203 $\frac{7.1}{1.1}$	3216 0	12864 0	262144 0
Kircherus	5	16 0	21 0	83 0	140 0
Rheita	10 0	31 $\frac{1}{7}$	78 0	314 0	1000 0
Ricciolus	33 $\frac{1}{4}$	106 $\frac{11}{14}$	885 0	30056 0	38600 0

Table of Calculations of the Size of the Sun
(from Creech's translation of *De Rerum Natura* [1682; 6th ed., 1715])

to his argument that atoms cannot be infinitely divided.[89] Epicurus's guiding assumption about the ontology of gross bodies is radically at odds with Aristotle's: for Aristotle, gross bodies aspire to realize their essential forms within a continuous and organic hierarchy; for Epicurus, gross bodies belong on a discontinuous but ontologically undifferentiated plane. They are marked not by their essential ontological form, but by their appearances as represented to us. In other words, they now compete as equally weighted signs within a unified hermeneutic field.[90] Distinctions for Aristotle are vertical, marked differences or signatures within a preordained hierarchy, which creates an ontological divorce between the lunary and sublunary spheres. For Epicurus, the primary divorce occurs between what is and what is not known, and what binds measurable signs are solely our acts of inference.[91] It is thus possible to imagine unknown and plural worlds such as ours because what we infer about this world could theoretically be applied ad infinitum to others.[92] In this connection, Epicurus can be seen as the inheritor of Platonic and Pythagorean physics, which subjects all phenomena to the possibility of uniform geometrical description.[93] Aristotelian taxonomy is essentialist; Epicurean taxonomy is largely nominal.[94]

The second pressure on the motives of Epicurean physics is again simply ethical. Because the bond between Epicurean physics and ethics is a curious mixture of causality and similitude, they are more a *corollary* to each other than a simple analogy writ large.[95] Crucially for the Restoration, it is at this point that the differences with Stoicism (which had adapted Aristotelian physics) are most marked. The conflict is fundamental: Diogenes Laertius significantly reports violent attacks on Epicurus by Diotimus the Stoic.[96] The Stoics offer a plenist and continuist model of matter, where no spaces intervene between the elements of matter, and that seems to support a fatalist and determinist ethic.[97] In response the Epicureans, seeking at all points to undermine superstition, arm themselves with a consistent voluntarism. The disinterested nature of the gods, the existence of void to permit atomic movement,[98] and the famous Epicurean doctrine of the *klinamen,* or atomic swerve,[99] all seek to vindicate the instrumental power of individual will in the conduct of ordinary life, exemplified in the calm, virtuous society of the garden. There is freedom of movement within the system and no danger of arbitrary intervention from without. Cotta, Cicero's spokesman in *De Natura Deorum,* insists that "all space is filled with material bodies" and consequently rejects the hypothesis of atoms and void, as well as the indivisibility of bodies.[100] Gaius Velleis, his Epicurean opponent, properly associates Stoic plenism with a "doctrine of Necessity or Fate, *heimarmenē* . . . the theory that every event is the result of an eternal truth and an unbroken sequence of causation";[101] he attacks the Stoic notion of "*mantikē*, or Divination," as tending to superstition, which Epicurean method exists to eradicate by treating true knowledge as a question of scrutiny and judgment.[102] It brings all things into the open.

Language and Ethics: Epicurus's Icon and *Suggrammata*

A trust in the facticity of sense impressions and the irreducible quality of atoms helps to support the Epicurean search for psychological and ethical stability. The ethical imperative in Epicurus's language, as reported by Diogenes Laertius, is evident: "These elements are indivisible and unchangeable, and necessarily so, if things are not all to be destroyed and pass into non-existence, but are to be strong enough to endure when the composite bodies are broken up, because they possess a solid nature and are incapable of being anywhere or anyhow dissolved."[103] At two critical points, then, the Epicureans offer models of matter to counter the Stoics: they propose figures of discontinuity (the *klinamen*, the "void") to vindicate the will and attack the determinist implications of the Stoic plenum; they also endow the individual elements of discontinuity with an inherent minimal resistance to physical and psychological decay or instability.

When Epicurus announces that "there are two kinds of inquiry, the one concerned with things, the other with nothing but words," he desires not to abolish language in the face of things, but to make language minimally accountable to his models of physics and perception. But Epicurus and Lucretius (in his myth of the emergence of civilization, which clearly anticipates Hobbes's)[104] assume that ordinary language operates by contract. Epicurus writes that "there never was an absolute justice, but only an agreement made in reciprocal intercourse in whatever localities now and again from time to time, providing against the infliction or suffering of harm."[105] This conventionalism in no way precludes a founding belief in the natural origins of language, just as the complex Epicurean economy of pain and pleasure is grounded in the primitive elements of feeling, our passions *(pathē)*.[106] The *eidōlon, aisthesis,* and *phantasia* represent the originary, irreducible atoms of linguistic experience, an intimate connection between world and mind reflected in Lucretius's extended punning on *elementa,* which denotes at once the elements of matter and language: the analogy between atoms and letters is arguably Robert Boyle's most pervasive simile.[107] The units of consciousness are unequivocally single images, which leads Epicurus to represent mental experience through time as a kinematic sequence of images, certainly a single image repeatedly impressed on the mind,[108] and potentially a succession of images such as Muybridge's photographs of a horse in motion.[109] There is some critical debate about whether "thinking" as such requires an act of attention,[110] but it seems that the *phantasia* is the point at which will and representation meet. What is imaged to the mind becomes the grounds of its acts of will, a version once again of voluntary assent.[111]

Admittedly Cicero reports that Zeno also believes in mental assent to *phantasia* or presentation *(visum)*. But it cannot be true knowledge for the Stoic unless assent accords with an ineffable "manifestation" mysteriously linking the presentation with the objects presented.[112] This sporadic and calculated intervention is linked to the Stoic view that the *pneuma* is an undifferentiated and essentially unrepresented locus of reason, the logos, or the divine:[113] we can apprehend no particular or localized images of the divine with which to negotiate. Epicurus's sensationalism effectively erodes the privileged epistemology implied by Stoic gnosticism,[114] because the images we obtain (including those of the gods) are continuously available to all, even in the state of sleep. Once again, the Epicurean *kanōn* offers a universal—because contingent—ethic of interpretation.

The Stoic restriction of knowledge to a certain special class of knower, which implies an attitude of social privilege, begs the question of whether Epicurus's more liberal attitudes to knowledge have different political implications.[115] Certainly, there are moments when Horace treats the Stoic élite as a definite form of tyranny. Of course, it is anachronistic to think of Epicurus's forms of epistemological and ethical egalitarianism as a herald of modern socialism or democracy, as Benjamin Farrington asks us to.[116] But within the limits of an essentially aristocratic culture,[117] Epicurus's unprejudiced distribution of knowledge to all minds equally echoes the refined but real egalitarianism that could extend to women and slaves within the confines of the garden. Bernard Frischer emphasizes that the inclusion of women on the basis of interest and free will was an especially marked departure from prevailing cultural expectations,[118] one also underscored by the myth attached to Epicurus's self-education,[119] as if further to represent a distinct form of dissent from sources of authority. Moreover, in criticizing Farrington's notorious celebration of Epicurus's radical "socialism," Arnoldo Momigliano develops some intriguing meditations on the later, Roman, fate of a politics predicated on Epicurean belief.[120] He determines that, though no socialists, Roman Epicureans in the late republic and early empire tended to become associated with the republican criticism of the Caesars, which of course included the assassination of Julius Caesar.[121] Cassius is a particularly notable example of a "double conversion to Epicureanism and *libertas.*"[122]

Whatever form of *libertas* it cultivated, the Epicurean view of society necessitated some method of representing and focussing Epicurean claims to authority, if only authority contained within the bounds of the garden. Frischer argues that this was the role of the cult of Epicurus's image or icon.[123] A unique and intense ethic of friendship[124] bound Epicurus with his original disciples, but later Epicureans regarded their master primarily with admiration and awe, and they cultivated those sentiments by preserving images of Epicurus. Frischer argues that these iconic habits are best interpreted by the anthropology of fetishism.[125] But if we recall the Epicurean analogy between the mental operation of *aisthēsis* and the social function of the *eikonas,* it is easy to interpret the social power of the Epicurean image from a less sacramental perspective, one that harmonizes with the Epicurean dislike of superstition.[126] Thus Charleton writes in *Epicurus's Morals* that "if a Wise man chance to have the Statues, or Images of his Ancestors, or other Renowned Persons of Former Ages; he will be very far from being proud of them, from shewing them as Badges of Honour, from affecting a Glory from the Generosity of their Actions and Atchievements: and as far from wholly neglecting them, but will place them (as Memorialls of Virtue) indifferently either in his Porch, or Gallery, or elsewhere."[127]

The Epicurean image *(phantasia)* inculcated by Epicurus's mentalism predicates a suspicion of eloquence per se, a requirement that we stick to the common uses of terms.[128] If only by analogy to the passions, where sensation is necessary in order to create natural representations as corollaries and objects of pleasure and pain,[129] Epicurus evidently proposed his criterion of clarity to remind us of the universal origins of language in the primary elements of cognition.[130] But the view also helps to develop a special notion of literary exemplification, because by implication Epicurus's own notion of clarity allows "Epicurus himself" to speak throughout his prolific writings.[131] Epicurus's reputation as an author executes two of his prescriptions for the wise man, neither of which encourages an unmediated access to his intentions: that he will "set up votive images" *(eikonas)* and that "he will leave written words *[suggrammata]* behind him."[132] The succeeding injunction to avoid panegyric assumes that the wise man can succeed in textualizing himself in his own writings, such that his *oeuvre* can form the epitaph to his life: the life becomes biography or a bundle of writings, even graphic fragments. This epitaph ensures the continuation and renewal of the practices of Epicureanism inasmuch as the writings continue to exemplify their author, an exemplification incarnated in the propagation of his icon by a "charismatic community."[133] It is apt that we possess Epicurus's will, because, like the Christian testament, it marks the inevitable transition from the focus on the master as an example of his own teachings to the focus on textualized and communal social practices.

Yet if, like his garden, Epicurus himself constitutes an inscribed and exemplary object of desire, he is not simply manifested as a unifying *voice*, a formal organizing ethos. That is, the multiple representations of Epicurus by which we know of him obscure as much as they reveal: they occur largely by report, and reports of his disciples' attitudes to him. The further historical fragmentation and dispersion of evidences and identity (which characterizes many ancient texts) become for a later generation a positive ethic, because it represents a potential object for Epicurus's unsystematic method, which requires interpretation by using multiple hypotheses and the analogical and inferential instruments of the *kanōn*.[134] Diogenes Laertius goes to some pains to stress Epicurus's prolific habits as a writer,[135] as well as the quantity of his writings now lost; we now only possess occasional, epistolary, and fragmentary Epicurean texts.[136] As if to epitomize the textual situation, book ten of the *Lives* closes with a series of quotations from the Sovran Maxims, a collection of extracts from Epicurus's writings possibly anthologized by a disciple.[137] Although accidental, the sheer dispersal of such modes and evidences emphasizes that any historical and biographical knowledge of others echoes our limited means of access to physical phenomena, to texts and the history they compose, and is as equally contingent and mediated by representation. We cannot know whether Diogenes Laertius's strategy is intentional, or whether it is so intended to symbolize Epicurean modes of knowledge. Certainly, the ordering of the *Lives*, as well as the evident care lavished on book ten as its culminating statement, has fostered a convenient myth of Diogenes Laertius's own Epicureanism, one that the Restoration is likely to have enjoyed. The form and rhetoric of the *Lives* can thus be taken to parallel and necessitate Epicurus's peculiar hypotheticalism, because, like Epicurus's icon, they present a memorial image, a textualized example of Epicurus's missionary empiricism. The Epicurean *suggrammata*[138] thus discover a curious and contingent existence in Diogenes Laertius's historical vehicle.

Laertius's *Lives* is only one of many texts from which a knowledge of Epicurus is derived. Not all of them are sympathetic to Epicureanism, but, like the *Lives,* the major texts all reenact the contingent terms of knowledge to which Epicureanism is committed. So Lucretius metamorphoses Epicurus's scheme by an act of mythopoeia, such that the conduct of philosophy cannot occur demonstratively; he presents his entire text as an occasional epistle addressed to Gaius Memmius, which frames it as a momentary utterance situated in place and time, not as a definitive transhistorical view of knowledge. Moreover, like Diogenes Laertius's *Lives* and so many neoclassical texts, its ending is notoriously inconclusive or open-ended, moving from a discussion of epidemics into its famous and extended description of the plague of Athens (6:1090–1286).[139] Lucretius's final image of bodies strewn about the streets enacts, at a grotesque level, the methodological and physical premises of Epicureanism, because both predicate their mechanisms on the atomic dispersion and analysis of the particular elements of knowledge and matter.

Similarly, Cicero's important treatment of Epicureanism in *De Finibus* and *De Natura Deorum* occurs by way of dialogues. Again, the form of the dialogue, like the essay and like history, dramatizes an epistemological universe in which nothing is known for sure and forces on the reader the responsibility of inference and judgment. Cicero's personal sympathies lie more with the Stoics than Epicureans, but the method of Epicurean hypotheticalism can operate as an ideal supplement to the academic scepticism of the *Academica.* This, I shall argue, is Gassendi's view of the relation between Ciceronian and Epicurean forms of probability. Cicero himself admittedly treats Epicureanism as incurably dogmatic in content. But again, his dialogues are evidently the literary corollary to his own form of probabilism, which, like Epicurean method, offers conjectural or hypothetical positions for the reader's judgment.[140] Thus the Restoration language of probabilism draws from both sources and tends to blend them. In his letter to Varro that prefaces the *Academica,* Cicero anticipates Locke's opening gesture in the *Essay* by insisting that what was once private and conditional is now public and indicative, but that the dialogue form (like the essay) can nevertheless preserve the tentative quality of the original speculations: "I have been unable to keep myself from making public, in such literary form as was within my powers, the community of studies and of affection that unites us. I have accordingly composed a dialogue, held between us at my place at Cumae, with Pomponius as one of the party."[141] As in Plato's *Cratylus* and Dryden's *Of Dramatic Poesy,* in the *Academia* the crisis and possibilities of mitigated scepticism are deflected into the contingencies of communal life, themselves betokening a due apprehension of the frailty of the human lot. Like those two great dialogues, the *Academica* concludes with a logical hiatus resolved not by further discussion (significantly concerning the reliability of perception), but by a communal return to social activity. Catulus is inclined to assent to the view that "nothing exists that can be perceived," whereupon: "'I have your view,' said I, 'and I do not think it quite negligible; but pray, Hortensius, what do you think?' 'Away with it!' he replied with a laugh. 'I take you,' said I, 'for that is the true Academic verdict.' The conversation thus concluded, Catulus stayed behind, while we went down to our boats."[142]

For all Cicero's strictures against Epicureanism, his own dialogues, interpreted from a particular epistemological vantage, could still be read by the Restoration as one more mode of exemplification, whose methodical and ethical power paradoxically reinscribes the conditions of the Epicurean *suggrammata.* The action of the dialogue translates Cicero's epistemological scepticism into local symbolic negotiations, which, however tenuously, construct a community. The wisdom of Epicurus was to propose the textualization of his "self" in his *suggrammata* to construct and maintain a new society, one that was based on the act of assent as the best response to a universe of merely probable knowledge, and one that consciously established itself as different from what had hitherto been possible or desirable.

PETRVS GASSENDVS DINIENSIS.
Hic est Ille, dedit cui se Natura videndam,
Et Sophia æternas cui reserauit opes:
Inuida non totum rapuistis Sidera Vultum
Nantolius, Mentem pagina docta refert.

Portrait of Gassendi (from Gassendi's *Opera Omnia* [1658])

4. Gassendi's Architectonic Method and the Quest for Epicurus's Image

Surely a distinguished public service has been rendered by those who have protected from envy the noble achievements of men who have excelled in virtue, and have thus preserved from oblivion and neglect those names which have deserved immortality. In this way images sculptured in marble or cast in bronze have been handed down to posterity; to this we owe our statues, both pedestrian and equestrian; thus we have those columns and pyramids whose expense (as the poet says) reaches to the stars; finally, thus cities have been built to bear the names of men deemed worthy by posterity of commendation to all the ages. For the nature of the human mind is such that unless it is stimulated by images of things acting upon it from without, all remembrance of them passes easily away.

Galileo Galilei, Starry Messenger (1610)

For by one means or the other we form in our mind ideas of things heard or read about just as we do of things we have ourselves perceived; and the more so if the account includes a demonstration or picture or something to make the object even clearer to us.

Pierre Gassendi, Institutio Logica (1658)

The Grand Base on which the whole Fabrick of the Atomists, i.e. our Physiology is supported, confesseth it self to be this; that Nature cannot extend her Dissolution of Bodies beyond [ti stereon kai adialuzon], *somewhat that is* Firm *and* Inexsoluble.

Walter Charleton, Physiologia Epicuro-Gassendo-Charletoniana (1654)

Gassendi's Epistemology and Method

In his *New Essays on Human Understanding*, Leibniz accords Descartes and Gassendi equivalent intellectual authority. But his description of the European intellectual scene also pits Locke, Gassendi, and Foucher against Descartes: Locke's epistemology,[1] Foucher's use of academic scepticism,[2] and Gassendi's reintroduction of Epicureanism "onto the stage"[3] give them comparable roles in this drama. Modern historians agree that Gassendi is the chief single vehicle by which Epicurus was rehabilitated in the mid-seventeenth century.[4] But although modern critics know of Gassendi's contemporary reputation as one of the greatest intellectual figures of his age, they are still puzzled by it.[5] Even attempts to proclaim Gassendi a major architect in the construction of British empiricism have failed to account for his enormous cultural importance in the seventeenth century.[6] Lynn Joy's *Gassendi the Atomist* has happily extended the kinds of questions we should ask. Joy argues that Gassendi's "advocacy of various Epicurean principles in logic, physics, and ethics . . . became inseparable from his efforts to devise a genre of historical writing that would supplant the humanists' conception of universal history."[7] Joy stresses how Gassendi's historical method inherits an outworn humanist historiography yet, paradoxically, anticipates the emergence of specialized discourses roughly after the Restoration and certainly by Newton's *Principia*.[8] But this view tends to consign Gassendi to a kind of historical cul-de-sac; Joy denies, for example, that we can find persuasive connections between Gassendi and Locke.[9] Yet Joy still illuminates the extent of Gassendi's critical reworking of Epicureanism as a model for the sciences; she also explicates the relationship between Epicurus's *kanōn* and Gassendi's historiography. In embedding his positive views within an objectified imagining of the history of ancient philosophy, Gassendi proves one of the first great neoclassicists: he translates and mythologizes the entire Epicurean scheme by a method not only indebted to Epicurus but also itself similarly subject to a second-order critique.

Gassendi Christianized Epicurean physics and theology as an essential overture to the acceptance of Epicureanism by an age demanding Christian orthodoxy. In brief, Gassendi simply jettisoned Epicurus's materialist views that the gods and the soul are composed of extremely fine particles; he rejected the atomic swerve as signifying the rule of chance rather than providence in the construction of an orderly universe; and he denied that the atoms were "eternal and uncreated" and that "they are infinite in number and occur in any sort of shape."[10] Rather, "atoms are the primary form of matter, which God created finite from the beginning, which he formed into this visible world, which, finally, he ordained and permitted to undergo transformations out of which, in short, all the bodies which exist in the universe are composed."[11] Finally, denying to atoms any "power to move themselves," he suggested that though atoms are indeed "mobile and active *(actuosas),*" they derive these qualities "from the power of moving and acting which God instilled in them at their very creation, and which functions with his assent."[12] Gassendi thus sought to reconcile atomistic physics with divine agency.

It was not, however, the content of Gassendi's physics that proved revolutionary, but, as in Epicurus, its construction within the scope of an explicit union of epistemology and method, which coheres with a distinctive ethical stance. Atomism as such—even the postulate of atoms and void—was already available for adoption as a physical hypothesis. What had *not* been available much before the mid-seventeenth century was the articulation of a cohesive method applied globally to the sciences. Gassendi proposed a method that sought not (like Descartes) to resist or truncate the sceptical critique of knowledge in order to propound some demonstratively certain system, but that rather allowed its sceptical premises to inform its final attitudes to the world, language, and society. In some sense, both Descartes and Hobbes behave as hostages to their founding sceptical strategies, whereas Gassendi converts a potential prison into a unique arena for social intercourse.[13]

Some debate has surrounded the development of Gassendi's epistemological views, but Howard Jones has argued that Gassendi's entire career is informed by a commitment to mitigated scepticism.[14] As early as 1624, in his important *Exercitationes Paradoxicae adversus Aristoteleos,* when Gassendi introduces the sceptical postulate, he almost invariably assumes the impossibility of sustaining the complete suspension of judgment within the conduct of ordinary life.[15] Even Pyrrhonians, he implies, must behave *as if* appearances were sufficiently reliable in order minimally to function.[16] Conversely, Gassendi tends to treat many ancient philosophers as sceptics, though of this moderate kind.[17] Used as a polemical device against Scholasticism, his own scepticism can both undermine Aristotelian essentialism and sustain an explicitly probabilist tenor: Gassendi's preface to the *Exercitationes* presents Cicero as a kind of presiding genius of the enterprise,[18] whose probabilism infuses Gassendi's entire method and ethic with a kind of cohesive epistemological decorum. Appropriately, the rhetoric of the *Academica* reappears as a leitmotif throughout Gassendi's work.[19]

Although Gassendi never abandoned the premises of mitigated scepticism, his career did evince two closely related kinds of intellectual shifts that had powerful consequences for the mid-seventeenth century. First, the shift from classical notions of verisimilitude to recognizably modern notions of hypothetical, probable method is vaguely assumed to occur at midcentury, but no one has demonstrated exactly where or how.[20] However, volume one of Gassendi's posthumous *Opera Omnia* (1658), which anthologizes his life's work, provides a single point where precisely this transformation occurs.[21]

In the prefatory material to the *Syntagma Philosophicum* (1658) (not to be confused with his earlier *Philosophiae Epicuri Syntagma* [1649]), the conversion is achieved, significantly, by a rhetorical device, for Gassendi's proemial statement, "De Philosophia Universe," places his *Syntagma Philosophicum* within the history of Western philosophy.[22] The following section, "De Logicae Origine," first describes the Mosaic, then the classical account of the origins of philosophy, then describes the development of first ancient, then modern method.[23] The history of classical logic thus begins with the Eleatics and culminates in Epicurus's *kanōn;* the history of modern logic runs from Lull to Ramus, Bacon, and Descartes. Gassendi preserves a significant silence about himself, which is designed to force us to imagine his claims for ourselves. Especially given that the *Syntagma* is later introduced by Gassendi's important methodological statement, the *Institutio Logica,* Gassendi's view of his own project is clear: just as Epicurus has brought ancient method to maturation, so Gassendi will complete the development of modern method. The next section, "De Logicae Fine," applies the same narrative and the same implied claims to the history of interpretation.[24] Although, in Gassendi's description of the ancients, Academic probabilism now assumes much of the focus, it is again Epicurus who most nearly anticipates true interpretive method. And again Gassendi pointedly absents himself from the history of modern interpretation.

This series of fables from the history of philosophy creates a double effect: in its content, it discusses the translation of ancient into modern philosophical ideas; and by its very rhetoric Gassendi also seeks to translate his readers from conventional students of classical *paideia* into embodiments of modern interpretive method, because his claim can only be understood by attending to the implied parallels his narratives construct. The boldness of Gassendi's implicit but revolutionary claims for himself emerges solely from our observed distinctions among the series of disjunctive narratives we read. Like the mechanism of Dryden's epistle to Charleton, our introduction into a new world of reading must occur by submitting to the analogical and inferential mechanisms of Gassendi's text.

In the same pages of the *Syntagma*, Gassendi describes another kind of shift, one that can occur because at some point in his personal history (possibly the mid–1620s) Gassendi had chosen to adopt the method derived from the Epicurean canonic in order to supplement and articulate his generic commitment to mitigated scepticism. This decision marked a strategic but not a substantive shift in Gassendi's epistemology, for it is possible to see Epicurus's method as an extension (for example) of Ciceronian probabilism, where it supplies a fully articulated discussion of method and criteria of judgment lacking in Cicero.

The lifelong consistency of Gassendi's probabilism is also evinced by the consistency of his philosophic targets. When, at various stages of his career, he confronts Stoic,[25] Scholastic,[26] or Cartesian[27] systems or, alternatively, the mystical enthusiasms of Fludd[28] and Herbert of Cherbury,[29] Gassendi displays a similar discomfort, because, like the Stoics, his targets share a predilection to arbitrary suspensions or modulations of the sceptical critique of perception.[30] Of course, Gassendi never questions the minimal existence of God or the occult properties of bodies. But whereas the nature of the world is perhaps theoretically distinct from the nature of God, Gassendi attacks Descartes's attempt to preserve each realm as a discrete space for the operation of different kinds of knowledge.[31] Gassendi wishes to sustain the inferential capacities of the mind across all planes of experience,[32] such that *propositions* about God, essences, and the mind must equally submit to the same implicitly linguistic rules of interpretation.[33] He imputes to Descartes's assertion about God an implied claim to divine knowledge, which arrogantly disposes of our chief means to understanding—namely, second causes[34]—and he explicitly links God's accommodations to the frail human intellect with the strenuous medical discipline of symptomology.[35] From the human perspective, Gassendi wants to show that God and Nature are equally mediated.

Because they pretend to penetrate into the essences of things, the Scholastic prescriptions for the machinery of transubstantiation accordingly come under vigorous scrutiny both earlier and later in Gassendi's career.[36] For prudential reasons—significantly, the formal harmony of the Catholic church[37]—Gassendi maintains the doctrine itself, but he rejects the official Scholastic interpretation as internally self-contradictory and accordingly intellectually oppressive. If, by a miracle, God is going to suspend the ordinary operations of matter, Gassendi implies that he shall do so under conditions in accord with "natural inference."[38]

If the elements were transformed in essence, God would ensure that we could somehow test that fact.

Gassendi is clearly not as irritated by the claims of induction as he is by Descartes's solipsistic and "completely random" deductive method.[39] Nevertheless, Baconian induction fares little better than Cartesian method, because Gassendi finds induction per se, like other forms of essentialism, an inadequate means to knowledge, incapable of propounding contingent models of universal propositions as a means to construct universals from particulars. Induction does not present a coherent theory of scientific interpretation.

Significantly, for Gassendi the political implications of deductivist and inductivist strategies are alike: the one denotes the tyranny of the mind, spinning out ready-made fictions by its own unfettered energies; the other, the tyranny of an accumulated mass of self-evident and self-regulating particulars ascending into totalizing and irresistible universal propositions. Inductivism is a mirage, because it is impossible for the mind "to pass under review beforehand and enumerate every individual case, by reason of which the proposition may be called universal."[40] Similarly, though Gassendi applauds Bacon's experimentalism, he unerringly intuits the fatal weakness of Baconian science in Bacon's failure to provide a "general treatment of method."[41] The Aristotelian traces in Bacon predispose him to discover "to what extent general propositions subject to no exceptions exist."[42] But Gassendi is arguing that without an articulated and sustained hypotheticalism, which denies the possibility of such absolute generalities, some individuals will inevitably secure an arbitrary, privileged authority. Like Peiresc, Gassendi's mentor, we would also be threatened with paralysis by detail.[43] And we can add that neither Bacon's "anticipations"—which are more millennial than instrumental in character—nor his elaborate and endlessly self-qualifying prose sufficiently displays the hypothetical posture Gassendi really wants.[44]

Like Locke, Gassendi insists on the a posteriori condition of knowledge[45] because he still wishes to preserve the dispositional powers of the mind,[46] which include the capacity to distinguish similarity and difference, the fundamental features of "internal discourse."[47] But Gassendi's lifelong attack on all forms of essentialism[48] nevertheless denies the existence of a priori or essential mental contents before the mind is informed by the operations of the senses. Contrary to what Descartes appears to claim,[49] we cannot know what things *are*;[50] we can only know what they

are *like,* because objects appear to us only sporadically and merely phe-
nomenally,[51] resulting in a profusion of signs we must catalogue and
compare. We must again be content with inference and analogy. Even in
maturity, Gassendi proclaims the primacy of sense experience[52] and, in
his reply to Descartes, echoes the Epicurean maxim that no "deception,
or falsity, is . . . to be found in the senses themselves, which merely
behave passively and only report things as they appear and as they must
appear given their causes."[53] Although *limited,* sensory knowledge is
sufficient, because it is tailored to human perception.[54] And God has
ensured that the senses are the sole and humbling means by which all
knowledge is accommodated to human needs.[55] The senses are reliable,
then, inasmuch as they minimally refer to objects, a reference (as we shall
see) emphatically guaranteed by the mediation of discrete images impressed upon the mind.[56]

Predictably, the moment the world is represented by those mental
images is the very moment at which it begins to elude our grasp. The
incursion of discrete images—as in Epicurus reflecting the mechanical
effects of irreducible and indivisible material atoms[57]—catalyzes the activity of judgment by which we abstract ordinary knowledge in the form
of propositions. Thus as knowing creatures, we inescapably operate at an
epistemological and perceptual remove from unfiltered sensation.[58] Gassendi celebrates this condition, though he recognizes that this is the
critical point at which we need to invoke some overarching method,
which can regulate and describe the traffic between individual, relatively
stable sensations and abstract ideas or linguistic universals.

Gassendi is rightly thought of as broadly "empirical" because, in
offering a refined version of Epicurean canonic as his instrument, he
commits himself to a hypothetical and experimental attitude to knowledge. Already in 1624, even before he explicitly recruits Epicureanism for
this purpose, he emphasizes the necessity of supplementing a practical
experimental method—which Aristotle clearly developed[59]—with a
second-order discussion of method as a universal tool—something Aristotelian logic patently failed to do.[60] Like Epicurus, Gassendi wants to
displace Aristotle by harmonizing the *conduct* with the *theory* of knowledge: we may spend time gathering facts and having experiences, but we
also need some way of discussing (a) how we can consistently reach some
general conclusions and develop workable scientific or ethical hypotheses, and (b) when and how the arrival of new or different facts or ideas
requires an adjustment in those hypotheses. Gassendi's stance is perva-

sively probabilistic. For example, whereas it is common in the seventeenth century to argue for the self-evidence of geometrical figures, Gassendi argues that such figures are empirically derived by a process of analogy to common experience and are the products of our pedagogical and ideological contexts, serving as purely contingent descriptive models, to be discarded if falsified.[61] Gassendi's search for a consistent hermeneutic, entailing explicit criteria for judging and manipulating signs, begins in the *Exercitationes* (1624) and culminates in the sequence of essays on logic that introduces the posthumous *Syntagma Philosophicum* (1658), and thus Samuel Sorbière's entire edition of the *Opera Omnia*, of which the *Syntagma* occupies the first two volumes.[62]

Gassendi retains a deep respect for the syllogism, by which we can dissect the propositions of ordinary language, and which he uses against Descartes's *Meditations* with considerable force.[63] But he rejects the claims of dialectic to fill the role of genuine method.[64] Gassendi writes in the *Institutio Logica* that true method serves three main ends—namely, "sound enquiry and investigation; judicious analysis and assessment of what has been discovered; and the formulation of the material in a manner appropriate for teaching it to someone else."[65] Method thus functions both as a means of describing and representing the inherited structures of knowledge, and as a means of arriving at such complex structures by "the particular kind of resolution and composition employed by geometricians," which Hobbes also adopted from Galileo.[66] In the *Institutio Logica*, the resoluto-compositive method is useful not only as a means of analyzing knowledge but also of communicating it, which leads to a political point of view that Gassendi anticipated in the *Exercitationes*. Because the new method reflects universal and common mental operations, the attack on dialectic amounts to an attack on the mystifications of knowledge by an élite. Even children, rustics, Indians, and practical men of affairs can adequately interpret and communicate experience without resorting to the rarefied instruments of Scholastic logic (and, by implication, Cartesian essentialism).[67]

Gassendi uses the clock metaphor as an image of how knowledge consists of a symbiosis between a whole and its parts.[68] This image presumes that we must either logically or temporally begin with focussing and fixing concrete particulars before we can begin to discuss the fabric of knowledge as a whole—that is, their relations. Although method acts as a way to discuss the inherited *terms* of knowledge, it also serves as a means to supervise the intrinsically obscure *grounds* or *origins* of knowledge, because it continually discriminates between the founding elements of knowledge and what they produce. The importance of this second application provokes Gassendi to a sudden flurry of similitudes in the *Institutio Logica:* he compares the pursuit for the *minima* of knowledge to a hunting dog who, "if he cannot see his prey, seizes on its track and sniffs along it until the prey is uncovered";[69] then to the construction of a genealogy "to establish that someone was born from a particular family";[70] and, finally, to Theseus tracking Ariadne's clue in the maze.[71]

If these analogies are introduced to illustrate the process of the purely abstract, analytical discovery of terms within a proposition, they also release a somewhat different forensic energy, which anticipates Gassendi's fervent appreciation of the Epicurean method of inference and analogy from natural signs.[72] Here, Gassendi uses familiar examples drawn appropriately from medicine (are there pores in the skin?) and physics (can we postulate a void?), which allude to Sextus Empiricus's discussion of signs[73] and remind us that knowledge can only productively operate by inferential and analogical criteria supplied first by the senses and then by reason.[74]

This is not to say, finally, that Gassendi underrates the potential difficulties of perceptual disjunction or illusion, and he frequently educes Epicurus's examples of whether we can distinguish between round and square towers at a distance, or how we are to judge the true shape of an object partially submerged in water.[75] Gassendi reminds us that interpretation is constrained by "surface explanations," because "the true reason for the phenomenon appearing to the senses as it does" remains hidden.[76] Nevertheless, we still may infer the existence of pores by observing a person sweat; and, by analogy with the free movement of bodies in space, we can support the existence of void.[77] So, once again, as in Epicurus, the *kanōn* provides a working boundary within which the degree and quality of misinterpretation can occur.[78] A proper application of method through inference and analogy can at least save the appearances.

The Architectural Trope and the Cognitive Image

One of Gassendi's final and most striking analogies in the *Institutio Logica* provides a crucial figure for his hypothetical neo-Epicurean method. In comparing knowledge to a building, Gassendi draws a parallel between the act of constructing workable hypotheses within natural philosophy, and his own rhetoric, which presents a specific analogy to assist his argument.[79] Clarifying analogies occurring in philosophical prose serve as atomic building blocks for some larger and more abstract argument in the making: just as the reader's apprehension of a single comparison only provisionally illuminates a juncture, a single articulation of a wider discourse subject to its own independent (as yet unrealized) laws, so Gassendi emphasizes the proleptic use of explanatory models extrapolated from adjacent but nonetheless distinct realms of enquiry.[80] Further, the reader's progress through an argumentative universe implies the preliminary assent to, then discarding of, such incremental moments of discovery (which promotes a series of mental adjustments). And this progress consequently parallels an empirical use, then rejection, of a series of increasingly useful or elegant approximations to a perfect grasp of the physical universe.

Like many of his contemporaries, Gassendi frequently resorts to the architectural trope.[81] He finds it useful because it echoes the atomic construction of nature and serves as a convenient image of his conceptualism. As in Epicurus, the building blocks of knowledge are the mental images that result from the atomic action of the world upon the mind. And as in Epicurus, this architectonic notion of the origins and processes of mental activity creates very specific metaphorical and ethical resonances. The architectural metaphor most obviously emphasizes the *spatial* quality of the world, mind, language, and subsequently all human structures, such as history, texts, and buildings. As a metaphor for the resoluto-compositive method, the architectural trope preserves a sense of the atomic foundations and building blocks of experience, even as it assumes that the mind binds and abstracts them into workable structures of knowledge. Like the pervasive Lucretian analogy between atoms and letters,[82] the *elementa* help first to secure sensations as the universal grounds of knowledge and, second, to vindicate their discrete and particular quality in order to reflect their mechanical origins.[83] Because cognition is a question of atoms literally striking the mind, the architectural trope, like the trope of printing that infuses Locke's *Essay,* tries to indicate the physiological, somatic origins of human knowledge. For Gassendi, the originary and irreducible atoms of cognition are exclusively *images,* which mediate between the world and the mind.[84] Dismissing Descartes's lurking a priorism, which on occasion impatiently discards or penetrates external phenomena, Gassendi insists that the mind cannot think without images, as representing the phenomenal grounds of all knowledge.[85] Gassendi's subsequent account of cognition and language is rigorously conceptualist, because images having entered the mind by the mechanical, atomic action of the world upon our senses, the mind's faculties of selection, comparison, and combination produce increasingly complex and abstract concepts, which words seek to bind and signify.[86] In an architectural image anticipating Locke, Gassendi speaks of the mind as a storehouse of judgments.[87]

Especially in his replies to Descartes, Gassendi stresses the purely *representational* character of our ideas: ideas inevitably intervene between us and the world, which is itself only partially known by indicative signs. Because this view of cognition has distinct ethical implications, Gassendi distrusts the Cartesian implication that an idea can be unmediated in character, operating perfectly as the unified content and form of knowledge. Although referential in one regard, our access to propositions about the existence of any object is already mediated by the kinematic habits of cognition. Gassendi occasionally speaks as if direct sensory apprehension invoked the "presence" of an object more immediately than the reports of a witness, but he assumes that the sensory view of an object is already represented because it is synecdochic.[88] We only know an object by some partial, external indication of its nature, whose totality or essence is hidden from us. Although Gassendi states that some representations are more probable than others, they are all already partial and arbitrarily selected phenomenal features of an object (its smoothness, roughness, etc.) serving as a sign for that object, as a means of distinguishing it from other objects, but in no way capturing its essence. It follows that linguistic universals are purely arbitrary assemblages and generalizations abstracted from a series of such originary and partial representations: if ideas are already represented, then words, which represent complex conjunctions of ideas, do so at a double remove.[89] In some respects, Gassendi is more consistent than Hobbes or Locke in following through the consequences of his conventionalist reading of language, because he refuses to grant mathematical representation any greater epistemological authority than ordinary language: as conventional symbols for actual quantities and objects in the world, numbers and words are equally displaced from what they signify.[90]

In his attack on Descartes, Gassendi aggressively puns on the etymology of *realitas* in order to implode Descartes's claim that an idea can have a "reality of its own,"[91] as if reality were *in* the mind, not represented to it. Because *res* is a thing, it must denote some postulate preceding representation, and therefore an idea must only be a representation of a *res*. Ideas *mediate,* precisely, between things and the mind; though ideas may enjoy a certain phenomenal status, they cannot have *realitas* in the sense in which Gassendi interprets Descartes's ambition for the term. Thus Gassendi writes that "the likeness or representation of the seal in . . . wax is merely a relation and not a being at all, so the likeness or representation of an external thing in the mind which you call an 'objective' reality, is merely a relation, and will never be a being."[92] We cannot permit ideas to enjoy their own self-sustaining ontic status; Gassendi's argument for the representative value of ideas helps to ensure their empirical traffic with the world.

For Gassendi, as opposed to Descartes or Arnauld,[93] the idea is conceived not only in spatial terms but also in consistently corporeal and visual ones. The purpose is to regulate the distinction between mind and world, because to see ideas as phenomenal is to erode the linguistic nostalgia for unmediated identity. Ideas intervene between the world and the knowing subject and thus frustrate the mind's ambition to imperialize the world. Because only God's Word can unite speech and pure being, Descartes, like Milton's Satan, can be seen to aspire to the divine by treating his utterances as if they bring about what they invoke. The insidious danger of linguistic universals and the allurements of ideation constitute a common tendency to collapse the distinction between being and representation and to nourish misleading and disturbing fantasies of universal, transcendental, or totalizing forms of knowledge and discourse.[94] To Gassendi, the Cartesian predicate "I am" subverts the human condition by arrogating to a mortal those absolute terms by which God describes himself: to speak in human language is not to create but to re-create; not to fashion new beings, but to represent and reinscribe the limited and humbling circumstances of human cognition. The architect's idea does not build a house; it merely offers a conjecture, a prognosis of what might be.[95]

Echoing Epicurus's curious mixture of causal and isonomic explanations, Gassendi wishes to preserve not only the *indivisibility* of physical atoms but also the 'solid,' corporeal quality of images. Described in this way, images best approximate the phenomenal, sensational grounds of knowledge. Their fragmentary and partial, if discrete, natures stimulate a kind of centripetal effect in the mind, an action that serves to subvert Aristotelian and Cartesian metaphors of epistemological control. Appropriately, Gassendi depicts this activity as the sapping of the foundations of the Aristotelian edifice of knowledge, in preparation for a new and different structure.[96] Whereas Aristotle and Descartes pretend to locate, penetrate, and catalogue the essential properties of bodies or the mind, Gassendi proposes an entirely different taxonomic ideal, which substitutes sufficient tokens for absolute signs.[97] Things are now only known by arbitrarily selected and artificially combined ideas, by which we are made aware of the degree to which those ideas are as much removed from the nature of the object they symbolize as they differ from one another. Their discrete and corporeal quality enforces their merely contingent relations and resists arbitrary yokings or conflations of ideas.[98] Thus we can only create taxonomies by taking partial and phenomenal signs as a means of standing in for the object designated and as a way of distinguishing between objects within the resulting taxonomy. We can only infer human or animal rationality (an important category for Aristotelian innatism) by recourse to the individual effects of certain faculties "like the faculty of laughing (or 'risibility' as they say), or like the faculty of whinnying in a horse, and so forth."[99] And because "inner potentials are recognized only by outer acts,"[100] our discriminations among different objects are contingent and approximate. They predicate an entire vision of hypothetical and natural historical method, because over time and by "repetition" we might conceivably create increasingly approximate and predictable (though never isonomic) descriptions of what constitutes a human being, as opposed to a horse.[101] For example, because a horse, unlike a human being, does not laugh, in this scheme *what is not* is as important as *what is*—difference may adumbrate, but emphatically cannot prescribe, identity. Moreover, though knowledge is now constructed as a system of differences, Gassendi makes it clear that human beings cannot completely survey and thus regulate that system.[102]

Baxter primarily attacks Gassendi in his critique of the new somatists, but he also attacks Marin Cureau de la Chambre, whose works enjoyed a considerable vogue in mid-seventeenth-century England.[103] La Chambre's arguments against Pierre Chanet's Cartesian essentialism within the debate about animal rationality help to elaborate one consequence of Gassendi's views of the sign.[104] In his *Discourse of the Knowledge of Beasts* (1647; trans. 1657), la Chambre insists on the primacy of the represented image for the discursive reason (constituting true knowledge) and for the capacity of will or choice (as the basis of ethical action).[105] Just as the intrusion of the image into a conceptualist version of cognition modifies an intuitionist or essentialist epistemology, la

Chambre resists the bald assertion that animals have no souls by a sceptical strategy that argues that we can only know the soul by its actions and
that beasts evince sufficient tokens of rational choice based on sensational
responses to mental images.[106] Even if animals lack the human faculty of
abstraction,[107] they nevertheless appear to be endowed by some distinctive form of reason.[108] La Chambre's defense of an orderly universe
assumes the ontological proportions among its various parts,[109] such
that to determine that human beings are *uniquely* possessed of reason is
to divorce them from their relation to other creatures, as well as arrogantly to claim a knowledge of human, as opposed to animal, essences.
We cannot know more about the human than the animal mind, because
our knowledge of both is merely inferential. Thus la Chambre is capable
of defending the probability of animal rationality on the conjectural and
contingent grounds that Gassendi inherited from Epicurus.

Writing and Assent

How does Gassendi's peculiar conceptualism translate into a vision for
literary representation? In his *Vie de Pierre Gassendi,* Pierre Bougerel
suggests a comparison between the two greatest mid-seventeenth-
century French philosophers, writing that "l'exemple de ces deux grands
hommes devroit réconcilier leurs disciples avec la poësie," reminding his
readers that most ancient philosophers were also poets.[110] Modern as-
sessments would probably put Descartes's claims as a stylist well above
Gassendi's; but these claims partially conflict with Descartes's own views
about the usefulness or necessity of literary expression. Descartes's
strange hesitancies between his convictions of certain, intuitive, essential, simple knowledge on the one hand, and his usually grudging admission of contingent and probable forms of knowledge and behavior on the
other,[111] register an eloquent and lifelong ambivalence toward the accommodation of writing and rhetorical figuration.[112] Because for him
certain knowledge is demonstrative, it denotes a direct, unmediated apprehension of simple natures, and language, symbolized variously by
images, fables, and riddles, denotes a radical and analogical displacement
of knowledge from its true focus.[113] Descartes struggles with the necessarily rhetorical function of accommodating expression to the lower
imaginative faculties of the mind, as well as (by extension) to lower and
less gifted individuals: for Descartes, the power of fables degenerates all
too easily into the frustrating obscurity of riddles.[114] In its purest search
for true knowledge, the mind must slough off its incarnated state and free

itself from ordinary vision, the body, writing, and the contingencies of persuasion.[115]

Gassendi is never as ambivalent as Descartes about linguistic mediation. Gassendi may occasionally appear to denigrate figurative expression, especially hyperbole, suspicious of its tendency to overwhelm or distort the decorum of human cognition.[116] But in viewing cognition as already a matter of representation or approximation, Gassendi insists on the necessity of rhetoric as such. Like Epicurus, whose prescriptions he echoes, he desires a rhetoric that enacts the economy of mental representation.[117] In the early pages of the *Exercitationes,* he announces that "I am neither Ciceronian, nor the least bit scholastic. I favor an unaffected prose style which flows spontaneously, for I am no more painstaking with words than with other things," a view that adumbrates less a simple 'plain style' than an ideal of "extemporaneous" expression.[118]

Gassendi is already hinting at his operationalist view of language, which links "words" and "things" in an encompassing theory of represented behavior. That is—to remember la Chambre's argument—language is to the human being what neighing is to the horse. In this view, the significance of a linguistic utterance is rhetorical (rather than, to use a false distinction, straightforwardly referential), because it is a linguistic action that does something specifically different from a similar utterance in a different circumstance, or a different utterance in the same circumstance. An utterance is an externally constituted sign within an externally constituted universe: we have no more access to linguistic intention (and thus ideal reference) than we do to the inward essences of bodies. Thus, though Gassendi appears to dismiss the elaborations of Ciceronian style, it is precisely Cicero's scepticism, as expressed in the *Orator,* that informs Gassendi's entire critique of the Aristotelians.

The *Orator* supplies one means by which Gassendi's critical reading of the history of philosophy can implode the pretensions of Aristotelian hegemony. For Cicero's reading of Aristotle's *Rhetoric* is the vehicle for Gassendi's own deployment of the rhetorical device of *in utramque partem.* Gassendi reminds us that, according to Cicero, "Aristotle trained his young students in their school exercises not to discuss subtly in the manner of philosophers, but with the richness of the rhetoricians, both for and against, so that they could speak more elegantly and more richly."[119] Thus, the paradoxical device of arguing on both sides of the question denotes a scepticism embedded in Aristotelian rhetoric, which questions the certainties of Aristotelian scholasticism. Sponsored by

Cicero, the scepticism embedded in a rhetorical view is the point at which Aristotelianism paradoxically defeats itself. The necessity of reading alone deflates certain epistemological claims. So like Cicero, and unlike Descartes, Gassendi wants to expose and celebrate language in order to serve his philosophical motives.

Gassendi almost obsessively reiterates that all human knowledge is nonessential in character. What knowledge we obtain arrives by sufficient though arbitrarily selected signs for the apparent differences among species: access to Nature is nominal, not real. Because they provide only a part to suggest a whole, or make comparisons between unlike figures, synecdoche and analogy more properly reflect this empirical view of representation than the fiction of radical metaphor, which aspires to unite signifier and signified. Especially in his attack on Cartesian ontology, Gassendi anticipates the poststructuralist critique of the Romantic metaphysic of metaphor or symbol: an analysis of its logic reveals an inevitable and fatal reliance on metonymic or analogical modes of apprehension, which invariably displace the mind from what it would apprehend or control.

For Gassendi, then, all signs can be treated as *ostensive*. With Gorgias "specifically in mind," he writes that language must inevitably substitute for the yearning after a sustained and unmediated *haecceitas*. Words merely indicate objects by performing "the same function for our ears that fingers perform for the eyes when we point at those things for the same purpose."[120] Ostension is a means of typifying Gassendi's consistently operationalist view of language.[121] That is, the externalized instrument of the teaching gesture (ostension) suggests that knowledge is not a matter of apprehending essences, but, like the operations in the laboratory or the organization of cultural symbols, a matter of learning to negotiate and interpret external forms or operations. If, as we have seen, action is the image of a thing's nature, language constitutes an activity (such as laughing) that distinguishes a human being from a horse. An individual utterance operates in equivalent fashion to other modes of contingent and significative behavior, a point made very early by Gassendi in the *Exercitationes*[122] and elaborated both in his later writings and by la Chambre, who in his *Discourse of the Knowledge of Beasts* writes "that Knowledge ought to be an Action." Even la Chambre's rival, Chanet, admits this point, "but he consents not with me, that this Action is a representation; otherwise he would be forced to confess, that there is no other means of knowing, but by forming the images of objects, because no representation can be made but by making the picture of the thing which is represented."[123]

It may, of course, be philosophically imprecise to yoke the idea of the image to the idea of an action in this way. But the conflation is habitual to neoclassical assumptions about language. To Gassendi, the two are intricately allied under the same epistemological rubric. Language is both known *by* action (the ostensive gesture that teaches us the use of language) and known *as* action. In both cases, knowledge is communicated by an external, contingent, somatic sign. Like the ostensive gesture that links a given word to a given object or event, an utterance can itself create an indicative moment, a kind of atom of linguistic action within an accumulated understanding of language-as-use. By an admittedly loose kind of logic, this analysis of language proceeds from interpreting words as *referring* to interpreting words as *acting*. Significantly, language is thereby displaced from its position as a privileged instrument of knowledge into an arena in which it must compete on equal terms with all other modes of expressing and signifying social behavior, and must partake of the same phenomenal and contingent status.

As we saw in section one above, Gassendi expounds his view of language by describing it and by converting his own philosophical text into a canvas to exemplify it. By making the reader the center of this textual, behavioral scene, Gassendi not only recommends and exemplifies his operationalism but also succeeds in showing where and how he believes linguistic authority should be delegated. Already in the *Exercitationes,* Gassendi flatly denies that specialized and technical tools for language acquisition either describe or assist the way language is actually learned or used within a social context. Rather, as Augustine points out, language acquisition and use occur within the context of already-constituted rules of conduct symbolized by the nurse, geometer, orator, monarch, musician, politician, and craftsman, who, "bringing [their] own natural judgment to bear," employ "a method of simple prudence."[124]

Further, in response to Descartes's fugitive and cloistered definitions, Gassendi offers the *loquens vulgaris* as a criterion of what we mean by what we say, and converts his own philosophical delivery into an instance of such socially circumscribed use. In a brilliant move, he demonstrates how, within "the practice of everyday speech," we use "the expressions 'to have an opinion' and 'to know' interchangeably." Here, like Wittgenstein, Gassendi shows that all assertions of knowledge, once examined within their social context, can never escape a merely probable

and strategic condition.[125] To believe in the externalism of social behavior, the defining context for language, is to see culture through a
sceptical lens, which automatically prevents *assertions* of certainty being
anything but contingent *in practice*. Thus in the *Syntagma*, Gassendi
implies that the soul of language, like the human soul, is to be found in
qualities manifested by a repertoire of explicit forms of behavior, not in
some essential being: "The qualities of the human soul are of this kind, by
which we understand that it is such that in the same man it not only gives
life, feels, and moves, but also understands, reasons, wonders, probes
abstruse questions, speaks, laughs, makes laws, discovers skills, and so
forth. The nature of the soul is located in these qualities."[126] Gassendi
finally subordinates the potentialities or powers of reason to social actions, to the rules of cultural symbolism. And because all utterances
partake in the fabric of symbolic action, Gassendi thus cleverly collapses
theoretical arguments about knowledge into a question of ethics.

Given this argument, language now represents and reinforces wider
forms of social behavior. The question then becomes, How are we to
regulate its behavior in such a way as to make it exemplary for a desired
social or political effect? Because—like Epicurus's and Gassendi's view of
the cognitive image—words are objects of conscious cognitive apprehension, Gassendi's view of language necessitates the activity of assent or dissent. And as in Epicurus, the analogy between the atomic
constitution of the physical world and the mind once again shows its
importance. Gassendi retains the postulate of the void, as well as the
indivisibility of physical minima, in order to preserve a dual notion of
physical and ethical integrity. The reader will remember that the void
always sustains the view that physical bodies have some freedom of
movement: the void represents a space across which atoms must move in
order to combine. And though Gassendi rejected the Epicurean *klinamen,* or swerve, it also underscores the way the physical metaphor of
movement in space translates into a means to preserve the fiction of free
will—the mental equivalent of free movement in space.

Although the physical metaphor can thus support a certain kind of
voluntarism, what is distinctive about Gassendi's position is not that
Gassendi propounds a voluntarist physics, such that God by the exercise
of his will can intervene at any moment in the laws of nature.[127] Rather it
is Gassendi's cognitive and ethical voluntarism that is distinctive, and
that he uses to attack the essentialist epistemologies of (variously) the
Aristotelians, Stoics, and Cartesians. The hypothesis of the physical void

serves as a metaphor for this ethical motive. We have seen that the void interposes a differential between the elementary and internally coherent constituents of matter, allowing for the free physical movement of atoms. Similarly, the discrete cognitive image serves a view of the mind as atomically constituted; the construction of the fabric of knowledge operates like the construction of the physical cosmos, as a binding and elaboration of originary particles. Gassendi's conceptualist metaphor assumes the activity of individual acts of judgment, which willingly select and bind the atoms of cognition into some larger construct. Hence the perceiver's assent to the cognitive image is inherently voluntary, a determinate act of bridging the cognitive differential between the originary particles of cognition and the perceiver.

Because the cognitive image is imagined in Gassendi's conceptualist model as inevitably mediated to the mind, as a form of representation, the voluntarism preserved by Gassendi's atomic model applies to all forms of representation, including words, pictures, or moments of symbolic action, which, like the cognitive image partake of a purely contingent, mediated status. Thus to Gassendi as much as to Epicurus, a plenist physics inhibits the possibility of momentarily drawing back from presentations of knowledge and, accordingly, of judging, discriminating, and finally assenting to what is proposed. As in an essentialist taxonomy, plenist physics seizes us in its grasp, and we are whirled involuntarily in a vortex of action, whose corollary is an involuntary assent to the propositions of knowledge, and potentially the construction of an absolutist state.[128]

The Self as Example: Gassendi versus Descartes

Both Descartes and Gassendi use the architectural metaphor for knowledge, but, by emphasizing its value for a plastic and mediated description of knowledge, Gassendi reveals his determination to make philosophy real as and by example.[129] The way philosophy is conducted should itself exemplify the contingent, mediated status of all knowledge and must therefore convert itself into an arena for the kinds of symbolic action we have just discussed, not least in the reader's engagement with a text. To know a philosophical proposition is to assent to or dissent from it in the way in which we assent to any other socially constituted text, of which, of course, history is the most obvious corollary. Gassendi uses Aristotle's career to make this point: he draws an early distinction between Aristotle's theorizing and his concrete scientific practices, in order to show how the Scholastic rage for certainty merely produced millennia of empty speculation. By contrast, Aristotle's zoological research, by exemplifying productive experimental practice, not only shows his true genius but also neatly exposes the hollowness of his theorizing.[130] If Aristotle had translated the methods embedded in his practical experiments to his theories of knowledge, he would have provided a worthwhile general description of experimental method. Similarly, what seemingly most disturbs Gassendi about the drift of Descartes's *Meditations* is that, having negotiated its complicated and abstruse logic, we emerge with no new equipment for handling the practical concerns of everyday life.[131] "Solid physics," Chapelain asserts in a letter to Gassendi, is intimately united with "palpable example,"[132] as if to say that our experimental and social lives should be mutually reinforcing. Thus Lynn Joy argues that Gassendi refused to conceive of philosophical practice outside the genres of biography and history. It is biography in particular that iterates the primarily exemplary and ethical role of such a practice. Accordingly, Gassendi's theory of exemplification is, as we have seen, habitually enacted by the exemplary rhetoric of his own philosophical arguments.

It could be objected that Descartes frequently recommends and uses example. Bernard Williams points out the exemplary rhetoric of the *Meditations,*[133] and Descartes explicitly presents the *Discourse* as just such an example of his own personal enquiries into truth.[134] But ultimately, within the wider perspective of the Cartesian project, the function of example is merely proleptic, a contingent fable, which, if adequate to the merely probable realm of knowledge, cannot represent those certainties upon which true knowledge must proceed. Descartes finally displays an impatience with such contingent modes of representation, such that for him the act of writing is a tool for concentrating the attention, a shorthand for the true and unmediated activities of mental deliberation.[135] And his letters operate as frequently as a means to dictate or announce Cartesian Truth as a discursive space in which writer and audience can cooperate in the construction of a mutual form of social knowledge. For Descartes, the exemplary becomes a *tool* to be used up or disposed of in the expectation of an unmediated certainty; for Gassendi, the exemplary denotes an encompassing historical *mode,* which informs the primary and inescapable means of human and social apprehension. That is, these different attitudes to the exemplary are simply another dimension of Descartes's and Gassendi's respective attitudes to the linguistic constitution of all knowledge.

This difference manifests itself finally in a tonal (and, by implication, ethical) difference between Descartes's and Gassendi's modes of representing themselves and their projects. Descartes's letters of dedication tend to move between embarrassing self-abasements to authority and arrogant assertions that only he and his addressee are worthy members of his new society of knowledge.[136] These gestures represent two sides of the same coin—namely, an obsession with obtaining access to centralized and absolute fonts of authority.

The tenor of Gassendi's *libertinisme érudit,* by contrast, demands a continuous and more modest series of negotiations between writer and dedicatee or reader, such as to emphasize the inevitably dispersed, textualized nature of cultural exchange and to encourage *our* participation in its ethical and epistemological process. Gassendi appropriately launches his philosophical career with two texts that make his commitment clear—his biography of Peiresc on the one hand,[137] and the *Exercitationes* on the other. The latter opens with a scene of laughter, an imaginative participation between Gaultier and Gassendi, whom Gassendi imagines reenacting the moment when Democritus first saw Hippocrates.[138] Gassendi's modesty places him in an equivalent position to Hippocrates, at whom Gaultier (like Democritus) may laugh if he pleases. But the laughter itself plays a Hippocratic or thaumaturgic role, because the exorcism of Aristotelian tyranny achieved by the *Exercitationes* heralds a new philosophical and social liberty, of which the permissive freedom of laughter is the perfect figure. At the end of his career, Gassendi still typifies the philosophical enterprise as heuristic and forensic—as a posture of inquiry and instructive ignorance—with the image of Theseus pursuing Ariadne's clue, just as Gassendi's career has begun by unearthing the "traces of the ancients," themselves of course nothing but a series of dispersed and tantalizing texts.[139]

Descartes's and Gassendi's respective projects differ, then, because they propound different political ideals for knowledge. Gassendi's exemplary and historical mode of cognition is predicated on a mental atomism, which resists centralization and consequently requires an ethic of cooperation toward the construction of viable (if not certain) models of knowledge. In the final moments of the *Institutio Logica,* Gassendi anticipates the ethical cast of Charleton's and Boyle's appropriation of atomism: the resoluto-compositive method here presupposes the integrity of discrete atoms of knowledge, as well as their subsequent organization within a cooperative framework, so "distribution will be effective if all the members are orchestrated to form a single harmonious unit."[140] Descartes's *Discourse*, by contrast, ultimately propagates an autocratic vision of knowledge: for all its gestures toward a rhetoric of moderation, it moves seemingly inexorably toward visions of an individual and absolute mastery of knowledge and Nature,[141] sweeping aside all the possibilities of majority agreement and contingent method,[142] like the military commanders of the absolute French monarchy to which Descartes explicitly refers.[143] This autocracy applies definitively to Descartes's prescriptions for scientific organization: whereas by implication Gassendi's experimental ideal necessitates mutual cooperation, Descartes will not admit true co-workers into his experimental polity. Like the military commander, the experimenter dominates his sphere of activity, limiting his recruits to mercenaries. The individual observer cannot "usefully employ other hands than his own, except those of artisans, or such persons as he could pay, who would be led by the hope of gain (a most effective motive) to do precisely what he ordered them to do."[144] If for Gassendi (and even Hobbes) contract is an occasion for exchange and assent, for Descartes it is the grounds for a dictatorial control.

Epicurus's Example: The Quest for Epicurus's Image

As Diderot reminds us, Epicureanism is deeply attached to the figure of Epicurus the benign philosophical master. Epicurus's personal authority is transmitted to subsequent generations by his icon and *suggrammata,* a textualized and fragmented version of his ethos, for which his theory of knowledge and representation prepares us. The image of Epicurus discoursing in the confines of his garden, surrounded by the trees he planted, itself becomes a discrete emblem of true Epicurean knowledge. Because he or she must reassemble that textualized or mediated knowledge from its fragments into some general proposition, however contingent, the modern reader comes to fulfill Epicurean method at an individual level, actualizing in the process an ethical ideal of voluntary assent. I have argued a similar relationship between knowledge, method, the cognitive image, and the textualized version of the self in Gassendi's philosophy. That conception is bound up with an ideal of an exemplary culture, which, in mobilizing a scepticism about our access to the essential properties of bodies, other minds, or God, transfers its energies into a rhetorical notion of knowledge, whether physical, textual, or social. Gassendi also imitates Epicurus's philosophical and cultural posture and thus also transforms himself into an exemplary image of conduct for later generations. As he seeks to do so, he engages in a forensic and historical inquiry into Epicurus's icon, itself a successful and evocative token of cultural transmission from ancient to modern times.

We shall see in chapter five that the mid-seventeenth century did indeed develop something of a cult of Gassendi's personality, but it is also evident that Gassendi represented for his generation the detailed, concrete practices of experimental science.[145] His essentially ethical reputation may explain the scholarly conundrum by which both Alexandre Koyré and Richard Westfall treat Gassendi's purely 'scientific' contributions as insignificant or unoriginal,[146] though Koyré can still admit that Gassendi's cultural reputation far transcended Descartes's in the second half of the seventeenth century.[147] Thus Gassendi (rather than Descartes or Hobbes) seems to have represented a model for contemporary experimental physics.[148] In this light, that Gassendi was the first European to publish the law of inertia is probably more important than is commonly admitted.[149] For this publication appears as one instance within a wide range of experimental activities. It is not Gassendi's 'scientific' or philosophical formulations merely, but, precisely, his *influence,* his *example,* that should draw our attention. What is important for Gassendi is not the mere propositions of knowledge, but, because he sees language as part of an encompassing notion of symbolic action, how they act and thus recommend action to the reader or hearer.

Gassendi not only made significant physical and astronomical experiments at sea but also sought to extend that experimental view of knowledge by acting out the part of the chief mid-seventeenth-century French savant.[150] For example, its practical and social energy divides Gassendi's *libertinage érudit* from the more cynical libertinism earlier advocated by Théophile de Viaux.[151] The intimate débauches with Gabriel Naudé and others provide the arena not for indulgence, but for a distinctively neo-Epicurean libertarianism, defined by the virtues of friendship, freedom of discussion, and moderation: on account of his digestion, Gassendi, like Epicurus, reportedly preferred water to wine.[152] And in rare glimpses of Gassendi's social manner and affect, we capture a sense of moderation and harmony, which appears especially to distinguish him from Descartes.[153] Certainly Hobbes seems to have found in Gassendi an exceptional friend.[154] This ethic is most clearly realized in Gassendi's attitude to his correspondents and disciples:[155] the reverence he seems to have created converted his originally private correspondence into a widely disseminated semipublic literature.[156] And his concern about ensuring

Juſt as I was now concluding this Diſ-
courſe, I received the following *Epitaph*
from a worthy and learned *Friend* out
of *France:* It is the *Inſcription* upon the
Monument of the admirable *Gaſſendus,* who
for being ſo great an Aſſertor of *Epicurus's
Inſtitution,* the *Doctrine* delivered by our
Carus, and a perſon of ſuch excellent
erudition, deſerves highly to be remem-
bred by Poſterity.

The *Epigraph* is as follows:

HIC

HIC JACET

Non unus è ſeptem Sapientibus,

Verum

Tota Sapientum Familia

Philoſophi omnes,Politici, Philologi,Mathematici,Theologi,
Eodem Tumulo teguntur!
Academiæ veteris & novæ, Lycæi, Stoæ, Hortorum
Rudera, Veſtigia,

E Quibus

Jam jam reparanda, et multò Splendidius reſtauranda
Edita doctrinâ Sapientum Templa Serena.

Ubi

Veluti totidem Oracula,
Siſtendi erant Redivivi & Audiendi
Thales, Anaxagoras,Pythagoras, Hippocrates,Democritus,
Socrates, Plato, Ariſtoteles, Zeno,
Epicurus, Lucretius, *Cicero,*
Seneca,Plutarchus,
Sextus.

Et quotquot huiuſcemodi Heroum
Ad noſtra uſque tempora exſtitere.

HIC JACENT
Cum Muſis, Pallade, & Apolline,
Pudor, & Juſtitiæ Soror Incorrupta Fides,
Nudaque Veritas.

Quæ Univerſa
Magnum Petri Gassendi Nomen
Complectitur.

Tu Viator Erudite,
Luge Sortem Generis Humani,
Cui Mors invida eripuit
Fidiſſimum, Diligentiſſimum Naturæ Interpretem,
Virtutis, Solidæ Pietatis, Bonæ mentis
Cultorem, Vindicem, Propagatorem
Integerrimum, Acerrimum, Feliciſſimum.

Vixit
Sine querela, ſorte uſa contentus,
Interioris notæ Amicis Jucundiſſimus,
Viris imperio,auctoritate,doctrinâ,ſapientiæpreſtantiſſimis
Acceptiſſimus, Chariſſimus,
Non apud Exteros ſolùm,
Sed & in Patriâ ſua,
Amorem, Venerationem
Meritus,conſequutus,
Annos LXIII. Mens. IX. Dies XIII.
Æternum ſui deſiderium relinquens
Lutetiæ Pariſiorum
A. d. IX. KAL. Nov. clɔ lɔc. lv.
A P. T.M. S. S. F.B.
Amico Veteri, Præceptori bene merito,
Grati animi Monumentum
M. M.   P. P.

Gassendi's epitaph (reprinted in Evelyn's *Essay on Lucretius* [1656]
and Bougerel's *Vie de Gassendi* [1737])

control over the published *Opera Omnia*—Gassendi's equivalent to Epicurus's *suggrammata*—is communicated by Sorbière's dedicated supervision of that posthumous work, to which Sorbière attached a preface.[157]

If it is historically inevitable that our knowledge of 'Gassendi' must finally be a knowledge of his literary and textual self-construction, this is a kind of knowledge that Gassendi himself anticipated. For only by a recourse to literary interpretation can we move from impressionistic and scattered statements about Gassendi's ethos toward a proper understanding of Gassendi's rhetorical self-presentation. The example of his correspondence already suggests the ethical purposes of Gassendi's wider historiographical mode, just as it obeys Epicurus's advice to make oneself known in one's writings (a habit Christianized by Paul). We might say that his letters, like his other writings, make real or exemplary by textualizing a whole method of cognition and behavior. Here again, as Joy argues, Gassendi's early biography of Peiresc anticipates Gassendi's philosophico-literary career,[158] just as the *De Vita et Moribus Epicuri* (1647) acts as a preface to Gassendi's specifically neo-Epicurean projects, the *Animadversiones* (1649) and *Syntagma Philosophicum* (1658).[159] Biography perfectly epitomizes that delicate balance between a fragmentary, textualized past, and the postulate of some stable knowledge to be transmitted to the future.

It seems appropriate therefore to close with Gassendi's biography. In its organization and range of documentary (particularly epistolary) material, Bougerel's *Vie de Pierre Gassendi* (1737) displays a rare sensitivity to the internal logic of Gassendi's career. Partly by quoting freely from numerous letters written throughout Gassendi's life, Bougerel presents a thinker intent on making himself known (like Epicurus in his garden) as an actor performing at once in a textual and social space. Gassendi's biographer registers a consciousness that biography is the ideal correlative to Gassendi's sceptical historiography, with its concern with the problems of historical, especially textual, evidence.[160] The manuscripts of Diogenes Laertius were an important occasion for Gassendi to formulate his critical method;[161] Bougerel also understands how Gassendi's imaginative revision of Epicureanism might occur by means of a vehicle that itself dramatizes the use of probabilist and hypothetical modes of representation and interpretation.[162] The Gassendi we see here is an already-textualized persona, a character who, because he is historically known, is accordingly masked. Bougerel therefore emphasizes the effect of Gassendi's epistolary rhetoric, both (in the "Avertissement" to the

Vie) as a pervasive irenist ethic[163] and, in regard to Gassendi's 'scientific' colleagues, as that cooperative purpose assists the spread of experimental knowledge.[164] In homage to his catalytic role, Bougerel writes that "Gassendi n'étoit pas seulement un homme d'une grande érudition, mais encore un homme d'une politesse & d'une douceur infinie: ses lettres ne respirent que la paix & l'union; il ne pouvoit supporter que les sçavans se brouillassent entre-eux, encore moins qu'on parlât mal des grands hommes."[165]

Bougerel finally wishes to transform his biography into an image of an ethical agent who exemplifies a defined yet permissive mode of conducting social and intellectual exchange. He is accordingly careful to cast Descartes into a decidedly autocratic role. Much as he recognizes that the very genre of biography propagates the quality of Gassendi's epistemology and hermeneutic, Bougerel displays an interest in Gassendi's own fascination with the iconic, even totemic powers accorded the ancient philosophers' posthumous images. These images served to symbolize the master's philosophical powers to his disciples. At one point Godefroy Wendelin writes to Gassendi about "l'exemple de Platon qui ne voulut pas priver ses amis de sa statue."[166] Much earlier in the biography, Bougerel has already seized on Gassendi's peculiar focus on the image of Epicurus, which historically assumed considerable powers in the organization and maintenance of the Epicurean community.[167] In part, Bougerel paraphrases some of the Latin correspondence reprinted in volume six of the *Opera Omnia,* and he cites a letter of 1632 from Gassendi to Gabriel Naudé that requests a picture of Epicurus's statue at Rome. Although Bougerel seems only to refer to one letter of that year, the *Opera Omnia* reprints two letters from 1632, in both of which Gassendi displays some concern about the minute disposition and posture of Epicurus's statue.[168] However, Bougerel makes the same point by citing some seemingly different and later correspondence with François Lullier. In 1634 Gassendi is inquiring again about Epicurus's disposition in his represented image, as well as about whether Epicurus should be grasping a scroll, a question he has already put to Naudé two years before.[169] It is also a question that he raises in a letter to Lullier in 1633; though Bernard Rochot notes that Gassendi is seeking a picture for an engraved frontispiece, Gassendi nevertheless lavishes an astonishing energy on the details of the planned engraving.[170] In 1633 Gassendi insists to Lullier that Epicurus must hold a roll of parchment in one hand, not a book.[171]

Gassendi's motives are scrupulously historical: the book is a modern object, thus an anachronism.[172] Like his mentor, Peiresc, strenuously examining the traces of the ancients, Gassendi wants exactly to apprehend the figure of Epicurus itself, which signals the strain and artifice of historical recuperation. This inferential stance toward the scattered atoms of human knowledge simply underscores the contingent and mediated terms by which we are, as knowing subjects, forced to function. The precise protocols, then, under which a reader becomes acquainted with Epicurus's image stand for the discriminations by which we may recuperate history, or focus, sort, and combine the discrete components of our mental economy—themselves the products of our private histories. The image of Epicurus represents a great moralist; Gassendi's purpose is evidently to combine it with other prolegomena to a modern realization of his peaceful, modest philosophy of the garden. The image is here only a fragment, a momentary means of organizing and signaling our responsibility to what we see. In this it is no more or no less effective than the final moments of Bougerel's *Vie de Gassendi*, which marmorealize Gassendi in his epitaph, the textualized trace for which Gassendi's neo-Epicurean ethic is a vast prolegomenon.[173]

5. "Living and Speaking Statues": Domesticating Epicurus

If Galilaeus with his new found glass,
Former Invention doth so far surpass,
By bringing distant bodies to our sight,
And make it judge their shape by neerer light,
How much have you oblig'd us? In whose mind
Y'have coucht that Cataract wch made us blind,
And given our soul and optick can descrie
Not things alone, but where their causes lie?
Lucretius *Englished, Natures great* Code
And Digest *too, where her deep Laws so show'd,*
That what we thought mysteriously perplext
Translated thus, both Comment *is and* Text

Sir Richard Browne, "On My Son *Evelyns* Translation of the First
Book of Lucretius" (1656)

Cartesius reckoned to see before he died the sentiments of all philosophers, like
so many lesser stars in his romantic system, wrapped and drawn within his
own vortex.

Jonathan Swift, *The Tale of a Tub* (1710)

Translating and Domesticating Epicurus

In 1656 John Evelyn published the first English translation of Lucretius.[1]
His "Animadversions upon the First Book of T. Lucretius Carus De
Rerum Natura" (appended to that pioneering translation) refers Evelyn's
reader by a marginal gloss to Gassendi's life of Epicurus (*De Vita et
Moribus Epicuri* [1647]). Paraphrasing Diogenes Laertius, Evelyn writes
that Epicurus "was a person of super-excellent candor and integrity, as
testified by his Countrey in general; the costly *Statues,* and glorious
Inscriptions erected to his memory; his many Friends and Disciples; and
lastly, that *promiscua erga omnis benevolentia;* nay, and (what the Reader
little expected) even his *Religion* and *Charity.*"[2]

Evelyn reminds us that Epicureanism sustained itself after the death of its master by referring to the memorial inscriptions dedicated to Epicurus. And Gassendi's and Bougerel's textualization of the self continues that tradition. Similarly, Evelyn could well be commenting on his own text, which serves as a kind of epitaph for Gassendi. Indeed— anticipating Bougerel—Evelyn concludes his translation with a printed facsimile of Gassendi's epitaph (p. 136). Evelyn's famous translation of Lucretius appeared less than a year after Gassendi's death in 1655: even the title of the "Animadversions" fortuitously echoes the title of one of Gassendi's two most important neo-Epicurean works.[3] The gesture toward Gassendi's *Animadversiones in Decimum Librum Diogenes Laertii* (originally published in 1649 and only fragmentarily reproduced in the 1658 *Opera Omnia*) seeks to remind us not only of Gassendi's revision of Epicurus but also of his more comprehensive schemes to construct his own *Syntagma*.[4] Thus by translating book one of *De Rerum Natura* with its speculative physics, Evelyn not only propagates Lucretius's sublime understanding of "the Principles of things"[5] but also reminds his compatriots of Gassendi's neo-Epicurean cosmology.

In 1657, only a year after Evelyn's translation of Lucretius, William Rand translated Gassendi's important *Viri Illustris Nicolai Claudii Fabricii de Peiresc,* his life of Peiresc issued in English as *The Mirrour of True Nobility and Gentility.* Rand's dedication celebrates Evelyn, whom Rand associates with Gassendi's neo-Epicurean ethos. And just as Gassendi saw in Peiresc an anticipation of the ideal Epicurean gentleman and scholar, so Rand depicts Evelyn as an English version of the same *"Peireskian Vertues."*[6] Rand concludes his dedication to Evelyn by celebrating Mary Evelyn. In the hope that the Evelyns' offspring will generate a newly reformed English gentry, Rand beseeches "Almighty God to make you the happy and joyful Parents of many faire, wise, and well-bred Children, that may tread in their Parents steps, and as living and speaking Statues, effectually present your names and vertues to succeeding Generations."[7]

Evelyn and Rand evidently conceive of the transmission of culture (here spoken of as "vertue") as a process by which an image becomes over time a kind of archaeological counter or coin, which it is the purpose of texts—such as Peiresc's antiquarian endeavors—to secure against dissolution. This view applies equally to Epicurean inscriptions, Peiresc's biography, Gassendi's epitaph, or Evelyn's children, whom Rand imagines as "speaking Statues" conveying Evelyn's virtues to later generations. Accordingly, Rand carefully links Gassendi's deliberations on history to Peiresc's fascination with its concrete (as opposed to merely verbal) remnants: whereas "Philosophy instructs men indeed with words, . . . History inflames them with examples."[8] And the exemplary force of historical knowledge is only fully realized by an essential supplement to textual evidences, what Peiresc saw as the "incorrupted witnesses of antiquity"—namely, "Charters, Letters, Seales, Coates of Arms, Inscriptions, Coins and other such like things."[9] The attitude is perfectly captured in the specular image of Peiresc "looking through certain spectacles of Augmenting glasse upon Papers and Coins, whose letters were exceedingly small, and half eaten away."[10] Just as this biography is intended, for the similarly attentive reader, as a "Mirrour of True Nobility & Gentility," so "by Statues and Coins" (Peiresc would retort to his detractors) "we may know what was the Countenance and habit of renowned men and illustrious women, whose actions we delight to hear related."[11] Antiquarian ideals such as Peiresc's predicate Rand's striking invocation of a statuary trope to prophesy Evelyn's propagation of knowledge and virtue.

Evelyn's and Rand's two translations indicate the extent to which Gassendi played a catalytic role in the development of a specifically English neo-Epicureanism. This role has been misunderstood, because, as I have already argued, Gassendi has usually been treated *either* as a contributor to mid-seventeenth-century European atomism (taken as the most marketable product of the neo-Epicurean revival) *or* as a figure in the development of European libertinism and free thought. By restricting its field of focus, either genealogy unnecessarily distorts the historical picture. If we separate Gassendi's physics from his larger cultural program, we fragment the coherence of his writings and in so doing allow more powerful claims to 'scientific' influence on British natural philosophy to dominate the discussion. Descartes's enormous modern reputation, for one, is always in danger of blocking our vision.[12]

More importantly perhaps, neoclassical thinkers often sought to absorb and domesticate their intellectual debts silently. Consequently, to measure the effect of a given cultural figure, we must examine methodological rather than purely thematic issues. For example, without explicitly referring to him, Dryden's epistle to Charleton uses Epicurus to exorcize Aristotle from its new discursive polity: Epicurus authorizes the contingent modes of apprehension the poem enacts, which themselves connote an epistemology that resists Aristotle's.

An equally frequent and misleading habit is the tendency of seventeenth-century writers to refer to figures of intellectual authority for purely polemical purposes. For example, if we examine the figure of Descartes in the *Vanity of Dogmatizing* for the epistemological and methodological role he plays in Glanvill's text, we discover that he acts out a part that in its details is closer to the 'actual' Gassendi than the 'actual' Descartes. By invoking Descartes, Glanvill evidently lends a certain philosophical grandeur to his text, and he neatly avoids the difficulties of consorting too openly with Epicureanism, which others might associate with the abominable Hobbes. I have been arguing so far that a particular method betokens an ideology, an entire approach to personal and public knowledge, which encompasses natural philosophy, theology, criticism, and literature. Consequently, we now discover philosophical debts not primarily by hunting out explicit allusions, but by calibrating the ways in which epistemology and method are understood, used, and represented.

Thus I argue that Gassendi's peculiar methodical appropriation and domestication of Epicurus set the stage for an entirely critical and uniquely English reappropriation of Gassendi and Epicurus. Speaking of himself as the "interpreter" of Lucretius,[13] and conscious of the "latitude" his interpretive method permits,[14] Evelyn gauges his own cultural distance both from Lucretius the ancient and Gassendi the modern, while still offering an entirely exemplary vehicle—his translation of Lucretius—to make both authors available to his reader. Rand similarly encourages a series of contingent negotiations among the figures of Peiresc, Gassendi, and Evelyn. Like the "living and speaking statues" by which he describes Evelyn's children, Rand's *Mirrour of True Nobility and Gentility* recognizes both the continuities and the disruptions involved in the transmission of culture, because it occurs like a series of translations on translations, mediated texts succeeding mediated texts. (And by reminding us of Evelyn's earlier translation of Lucretius, Rand simply amplifies this recognition.)

Gassendi is not a figure without whom the English neo-Epicurean revival is inconceivable. But it is clear that his presence on the European intellectual scene helped to organize and catalyze it: in short, his neo-Epicureanism establishes a precedent for the whole neoclassical move. Both French and English culture possessed the same classical texts, and Boyle's early and seminal manuscripts on atomism contain no explicit references to Gassendi.[15] But the onset of translations of Lucretius from the mid–1650s on testifies strikingly to a new sense of the applicability of the Epicurean model to this particular crisis in English history.[16] Here was a crisis that required a critical reflection on the founding premises of culture, and such criticism was in part enabled by Gassendi.

The determination to nationalize and domesticate English cultural resources, which fluctuates between desire and resistance, has also made it difficult to measure the influence of earlier sources on the Restoration. For example, the precise impact of Bacon or Descartes on Restoration culture is still inadequately understood.[17] Bacon's hugely exaggerated reputation as the founder of English science derives in large part from the Restoration anxiety to preserve the native quality of its intellectual debts. Bacon frequently appears in Restoration texts, but his role—like his presence in the title page of Thomas Sprat's *The History of the Royal Society*—is more polemical than methodological.[18] The appeal to Bacon serves a double purpose. On the one hand, it Anglicizes the institution and practice of natural philosophy. Thus Bacon's atomistic theories were republished at midcentury in order to provide an English claim to a movement whose sources were primarily Continental.[19] On the other hand, Bacon provides an intellectual authority from some antique past divorced from associations with the late civil upheaval.[20] A large number of scholars agree that, apart from a generic emphasis on experimentation, Bacon provided no adequate methodological tool or model for the practice of Restoration natural philosophy.[21] It is therefore misleading to revitalize R. F. Jones's highly positivistic appreciation of Bacon first to argue some founding distinction between the "mechanical" (or "corpuscular") philosophy and the "experimental," and second to apply the ideal of "experiment, observation and natural histories" to Locke's philosophical practice, as if Locke had more in common with Baconian experimentalism than with atomism.[22] Locke's understanding of method (and thus of history, however defined) could not operate further from Baconian inductivism: Locke believes that without hypothetical modeling (very like that described by Gassendi), particulars will never form themselves into universal propositions.[23] In his discussion of philosophical style, which has profoundly methodological implications, even Sprat evidently views Bacon as stylistically archaic: it is Hobbes, as Sprat describes him, who echoes the prescription for philosophical prose laid down in *The History of the Royal Society*.[24]

The English pretense to fabricate a cultural norm without the assistance of Continental philosophy is demonstrated in a notorious debate between Sprat and Sorbière. In 1664, Sorbière, long Gassendi's disciple and an individual highly qualified to comment on the European intellectual scene, published his *Relation d'un Voyage en Angleterre*.[25] To this tendentious but nonetheless detailed and informative report, Sprat issued a shrill and frequently *ad hominem* reply, his *Observations on Monsieur de Sorbier's Voyage into England* (1665), dedicated to Christopher Wren. Like his belief that the English are innately xenophobic, some of Sorbière's observations are indeed impressionistic and offensive, and they belie his general acuity. But many of the judgments to which Sprat most objects are highly suggestive, such as Sorbière's view that there is widespread resistance to Anglican hegemony.[26] Sorbière's attitudes provide an occasion for Sprat to demonstrate a meanness of temper, a mediocrity of mind, and a deeply suppressed fear that Sorbière's views might have foundation. If Sorbière indulges Catholic prejudice, Sprat vents a strident anti-Catholicism, and he equally stridently declaims that nothing is rotten in the state of England. The Anglican Church and the Stuart State, he writes, receive the full support of the people.[27]

Interestingly, Sorbière records a visit to the Royal Society, in which he is first and foremost struck by the prevailing ideals of intellectual moderation and cooperation, to which he refers at least twice.[28] He emphasizes that such a moderate intellectual climate prohibits any uniform adherence to a single intellectual source of authority; but he nevertheless notices a distinction between the "simple Mathematiciens" and "les literateurs," the former group inclined toward Descartes, the latter toward Gassendi.[29]

Whatever Sorbière meant by his distinction between simple mathematicians and "literateurs," it is possible to imagine a working methodological difference between the mathematical and experimental traditions within the Royal Society, which was later epitomized in the difference between Newton's *Principia* and *Optics*. Sorbière presents two native groups of figures to represent this difference: he describes meeting John Wallis (he also mentions Wallis's mathematical dispute with Hobbes) and also "les immortels ouvrages" of Boyle, Willis, Glissonius, and Charleton, referring especially to Boyle's air pump, on which he has performed "une infinite d'experiences."[30] It is entirely likely that (even if they allowed the distinction) neither group would have admitted an allegiance either to Descartes or Gassendi. Sorbière notes precisely this resistance to factionalism, which Sprat's outrage fully confirms, but he nevertheless arguably intuits something about the different styles of philosophic practice available to the Royal Society.

Sprat, however, displays nothing but impatience with Sorbière, whose qualified judgments he caricatures as absolutes, which in turn predicate his own absolute (and absurd) declaration that "neither of these two men [Descartes and Gassendi] bear any sway amongst them [the Royal Society]: they are never nam'd there as Dictators over men's Reasons; nor is there any extraordinary reference to their judgments."[31]

Sprat's double polemic against foreign intellectual 'dictatorship' and the memories of domestic strife discloses two motives for the English determination to translate and domesticate its sources, for which Bacon is the perfect instrument. Bacon swells the native strain and lends an image of primitive purity that releases the Restoration from obligations to more recent and painful events.

The appeal to an ancient past can also help avoid those charges of atheism or heterodoxy to which the age was highly attuned, and thus Bacon and similar figures could stand in for more immediately valuable but problematic sources, such as Epicurus. To recognize this strategy of camouflage is not only to recognize that the appeal to certain older figures of authority was frequently more strategic than truly methodological, but also that it reveals the extent to which the Restoration desired to appropriate the methodical power of texts, such as Epicurus's, that could be seen as subversive. Nevertheless, it is important to recognize that modern interpreters have sometimes exaggerated the degree to which such texts were, or were taken to be, subversive. Hence, contrary to a comfortable historiographical myth for which Thomas F. Mayo is primarily responsible, Epicurus was not the object of attack by all outside the decadent "Restoration world of fashion,"[32] though there were grounds for concern. At one level, the neo-Epicurean movement merely revitalized a familiar Renaissance problem of how an officially Christian culture could adopt or accommodate pagan authors. And at another level, Epicurus's distinctive theology did indeed raise particular difficulties: Epicurus is sometimes associated with Hobbes's putative materialism and atheism.

The calculus of responses to Epicurus in the early Restoration (and immediately before) will remain elusive unless we permit a kind of circular device, which earlier chapters have urged. That is, neo-Epicureanism was already understood as a highly sophisticated cultural organism. By 1660, it had long been the object of careful modifications in the direction of Christian orthodoxy. Epicurean theology creates the greatest difficulties, but these had been variously pruned by Erasmus, Valla, Gassendi,

Charleton, and others. Thus to many during the Restoration, neo-Epicureanism denoted not only an extraordinarily powerful physical hypothesis but also a probabilist epistemology, imparting a specific cognitive principle, an hypothetical method, and an irenist and apparently latitudinarian ethic.

Baxter's hostile but still comprehensive grasp of the new "somatism" reflects the extent to which by the mid–1660s Gassendi was known even to his detractors. Moreover, English publications represent a very significant percentage of European editions of Gassendi from the 1650s on, beginning with the *Institutio Astronomica,* published at least as early as 1653, and frequently reprinted into the early eighteenth century.[33] Descartes was published no more frequently in England after 1640,[34] but the number of Gassendi's books (unimpressive even by late-seventeenth-century standards) is less significant than the overall intellectual profile of Gassendi it presents. English readers would encountered a sceptic attacking hermetic forms of knowledge, a practicing astronomer, a biographer, a historian of ancient philosophy, and a powerful theorist of method, which provides the rationale for all other intellectual practices. Indeed, in the 1660s, in an apparently unusual departure from Continental modes of publishing Gassendi's works, there were two editions of the relatively youthful *Philosophiae Epicuri Syntagma,* issued in tandem with that fruit of Gassendi's most mature deliberations, the *Institutio Logica.* In consequence, access to Gassendi's recuperation of Epicurus entailed its most syntagmatic and revolutionary distillation: Gassendi's meditations on knowledge and method. Perhaps significantly, the first of these editions appeared in 1660.

If Epicurus and Epicureanism were attacked, C. T. Harrison, in a judicious essay published the same year as Mayo's book, demonstrates the range of responses manifested by seventeenth-century English writers.[35] Harrison describes some unambiguous attacks on Epicureanism after midcentury by such figures as Samuel Parker and Henry Stubbe. But for the most part, resistance to Epicurus is limited to isolated implications of his philosophy and (as with John Pearson) heavily qualified by a solid knowledge of Epicurean texts and respect for Gassendi's work.[36] Taking the picture as a whole, Harrison's painstaking account creates the impression that, even for many of its critics, the Epicurean myth had already deeply permeated some English cultural assumptions. Although Kargon credits Charleton with the acceptance of atomism after midcentury, Harrison mentions a host of reputable and influential thinkers, for whom Epicureanism represents an established if involved fact, among them John Pearson, Edward Stillingfleet, John Tillotson, Henry More, Ralph Cudworth, John Wilkins, Thomas Sprat, Robert Hooke, John Ray, Gilbert Burnet, Aphra Behn, Jeremy Taylor, William Temple, and Isaac Newton.[37]

With many of these figures, the use of an etiological myth proved useful. First, Democritus could serve as a figure for a version of the *prisca theologia* in which the more ancient and primitive philosopher acts as proxy for Epicurus, whose more elaborate formulations invited more detailed charges of paganism.[38] (This is not to say that Democritus entirely escaped charges of materialism.) A second and even more neutral device was sometimes to refer to Epicurean physics as the "corpuscular philosophy," which was also a way to refer loosely to all atomic theories of matter. Nevertheless, in Boyle's case "corpuscularianism" also denotes an entire probabilist method bolstering a calculated irenist ethic. There is no question that Boyle must have learned both from Gassendi's and Descartes's physics, but what is often interpreted as Boyle's refusal to swear allegiance to Epicureanism as a system (and hence as a proof he was no Epicurean)[39] constitutes part of a distinctive view of hypothetical knowledge that Epicureanism propounds.[40] M. A. Stewart thus quite properly chides Richard Westfall and R. H. Kargon for their assumptions that the young Boyle wished to escape the embarrassments of Epicureanism.[41] (Ironically, the Boyle manuscripts that Westfall publishes in company with his contention constitute an extended series of deliberations on method that a neo-Epicurean would instantly recognize.[42]) What Sorbière noticed on his visit to the Royal Society was exactly that irenist, moderate, exemplary, and hypothetical ethic of intellectual conduct which reminds him of Gassendi, and which paradoxically encourages Sprat to conflate his Francophobia with a resistance to intellectual tyranny, a resistance that Gassendi himself actually symbolizes. If his very successful *Plague of Athens* (1659) is any indication, Sprat was not averse to associations with Epicureanism as such; his translation not only celebrates the famous closing passage of *De Rerum Natura* in its choice of subject but also adopts its resonances more than those of Thucydides, to whom Sprat also genuflects.

The third device by which Epicurus could be adapted to orthodox Christianity was to construct a Christian, rather than a pagan, etiology for the atomic hypothesis. It is well known that Cudworth's *True Intellectual System of the Universe* (1678) wishes to save atomism as "unquestionably true"[43] and does so by ascribing its invention to Moses, and its gradual corruption and increasingly materialist emphasis to Pythagoras, Empedocles, and Anaxagoras, then Democritus, Leucippus, and, finally, Epicurus.[44] Apparently, Cudworth had conceived his project by May 1671, when it received Samuel Parker's imprimatur,[45] in which case Cudworth is registering the substantial success of the neo-Epicurean scheme by that date, the same year in which Locke completed Drafts A and B of his *Essay*.

An earlier work by a younger man, Theophilus Gale, Boyle's and Temple's close contemporary, commenced publication in 1669. All four parts of *The Court of the Gentiles* remained incomplete until 1677, but part one, which was reissued in 1672, provides another view of the effect of the neo-Epicurean revival by the end of the 1660s. Like Cudworth (who clearly aided Gale in his project[46]), Gale seeks to Christianize the substance of ancient cosmology by claiming priority for an Hebraic, if not expressly Mosaic, dispensation. Insofar as their respective aims coincide, Cudworth and Gale may at first appear to share an affiliation with a vestigial Renaissance hermeticism, detecting in ancient wisdom the traces of divine footsteps outside the circle of revealed religion;[47] but unlike Cudworth, Gale reveals how much Restoration historiographic method secretly owes to a neo-Epicureanism that it is his purpose in part to confine.

Cudworth lies on the far side of an epistemological watershed from Gale: though willing to entertain atomism as a model strictly for physics, Cudworth steadfastly refuses uniformly to apply the phenomenalism it entails.[48] He is dismayed by the notion that questions of faith may have to subject themselves to the same criteria of evidence as secular history,[49] and the final pages of the *True Intellectual System* elaborate a rejection of all notions of artificial justice and thus of contractual societies. Both positions depend on momentary but crucial suspensions of sceptical judgment, betokening on the one hand a belief in the accessibility of certain noumenal essences, and on the other an argument increasingly at odds with the age—namely, the view that because political obligation enjoys its own actual, ontic being, "private judgment of good and evil . . . is absolutely inconsistent with civil sovereignty."[50] Appropriately, Cudworth manifests more patience with the Stoics than the Epicureans.[51]

By contrast, Gale rigorously grounds his massive project on precisely those inferential and analogical foundations that neo-Epicurean methodology had sought to advertise. If his intentions appear to us strange and remote, his method is recognizably less so. By examining and presenting only those (phenomenal) records available to us, Gale seeks to show that it is "very probable"[52] that pagan mythologies embed "*traces* and *footsteps* . . . of *Jewish,* and *sacred Dogmes.*"[53] Thus he writes (citing Chillingworth):

> From so great a *Concurrence* and *Combination* of *Evidences,* both *Artificial* and *Inartificial,* we take it for granted, that the main con-clusion will appear more than conjectural, to any judicious Reader. Or suppose we arrive only to some *moral certaintie* or strong *proba-bilitie,* touching the *veritie* of the *Assertion;* yet this may not be neglected: for the least *Apex* of truth, in *matters* of great moment, is not a little to be valued. Besides, we may expect no greater certaintie touching any subject, than its *Ground* or *Foundation* will afford.[54]

Even as early as the late 1660s, Gale's case shows us how far in some instances an anti-Epicurean (or antimaterialist) polemic could marshal expository devices that it owes in part to the neo-Epicurean contribution to method. Admittedly, Gale's references to Chillingworth and other "*Modern Criticks,*" such as "*Ludovicus Vives, Stenchus Eugobinus, Julius* and *Joseph Scaliger, Serranus, Heinsius, Selden, Preston, Parker, Jackson, Hammond, Cudworth, Stillingfleet, Usher, Bochart, Vossius* and *Grotius,*" testify that certain approaches to criticism had long been possible.[55] But Gale's appropriations of comparative and contingent method are typical of the later seventeenth century. The same point could be made of Glan-vill's approach to witchcraft.[56]

Richard Bentley dutifully attacked Epicurean and Hobbesian mate-rialism in the first Boyle lectures of 1692.[57] But these demonstrate how, by the end of the century, the role of Epicurean atomism in Boyle's cosmol-ogy was widely understood. Bentley therefore selects for criticism only those distinctly pagan and unorthodox features of Epicurean thought which contradict the truths of the Christian faith. By contrast, Bentley reminds his audience that "the Mechanical or Corpuscular Philosopy, though peradventure the oldest as well as the best in the world, had lain buried for many Ages in contempt and oblivion; till now it was happily restor'd and cultivated anew by some excellent Wits of the present Age. But it principally owes its re-establishment and lustre, to Mr. *Boyle.*"[58] Bentley asserts that select doses of Epicureanism may serve as an antidote to more dangerous forms of atheism, because they contribute to a proper understanding of the true nature of matter, which cannot think. Such a cosmology, he writes, "being part of the *Epicurean* and *Democritean* Philosophy is providentially one of the best Antidotes against other impious Opinions: as the oil of Scorpions is said to be against the poison of their stings."[59] Epicureanism as such was ceasing to become quite the loaded subject it once had been. Mayo interprets the apparent decline in Epicurean texts published in the first quarter of the eighteenth century as a decline of interest in Epicureanism,[60] but it is possible to take the same phenomenon to indicate a less intense anxiety about its implications. Thus, when Thomas Creech published the first complete English translation of Lucretius in 1682, he had to deflect potential attacks by elaborate and defensive annotations. But in the 1715 edition of Creech's translation, the annotator (who is not the translator) clearly no longer feels impelled so vigorously to vilify Lucretius's pagan attitudes, though he carefully signals his own orthodoxy, especially in his preface.[61]

In view, then, of what seems a predominantly silent absorption of neo-Epicurean method and hermeneutic (going well beyond atomistic physics), Gassendi's specific contribution to English culture has understandably remained somewhat of a mystery. On the one hand, critics have tended to rely on broad analogies between Gassendi's formulations and a defined version of English 'empiricism.'[62] On the other hand, finding such correspondences insufficiently compelling, and unable to forge more concrete connections between Gassendi and the English, Lynn Joy fails to admit any valuable link.[63] I have already disputed Joy's contention that Gassendi's historiography decisively separates him from the late seventeenth century; but she also contends that we possess no adequate textual evidence for Gassendi's influence on the Restoration.

I believe, however, that there is more evidence than most earlier scholars (except perhaps Kargon) have generally recognized.[64] First, we have presumptive evidence both in the contemporary English publications of Gassendi's works, and even more so in Charleton's imaginative, compelling, and stylish naturalization of Gassendism in a body of work initiated by *The Darkness of Atheism Dispelled by the Light of Nature* (1652) and continuing with his *Physiologia Epicuro-Gassendo-Charletoniana* (1654), *Epicurus's Morals* (1656), and *The Immortality of the Human Soul, Demonstrated by the Light of Nature* (1657). The immense range of Charleton's interests can be seen as integral to his "physio-theologicall" habilitation of Epicureanism in general and Gassendi in particular. Charleton's authorial career had begun in 1650 with two translations of

Jean Baptiste van Helmont's works, representing an earlier tradition of natural philosophy.[65] Nor, I would argue, are Charleton's adaptations of Gassendi anything short of original, a claim that even Kargon has resisted.[66]

Second, Thomas Stanley's influential *The History of Philosophy* (1655–60), in its section devoted to Epicurus, incorporates translated portions of Gassendi's *De Vita et Moribus Epicuri,* some passages from book ten of Diogenes Laertius, and the complete text of Gassendi's *Philosophiae Epicuri Syntagma.*[67] Stanley, a charter member of the Royal Society, was reckoned—along with Richard Crashaw—one of the two finest translators of mid-seventeenth-century England, and he proved an exceedingly successful poet. Stanley's edition and translation of Aeschylus (1664), with which John Pearson may have assisted, gained him lasting fame,[68] and his *The History of Philosophy* proved to be something of a publishing wonder. First issued serially between 1655 and 1662, it was reissued complete either seven or eight times before 1743, both in England and on the Continent. Sections of Stanley's *The History of Philosophy* also appeared in four separate books before 1701 in the guise of *The History of Chaldaic Philosophy* and *The Life of Socrates.*[69] Jean Le Clerc included Stanley in his *Opera Philosophica* of 1704. *The History of Philosophy* appears in the listings for Evelyn's, Locke's, and Newton's libraries.[70] Cope shows how heavily Glanvill also drew upon this source.[71] The section of *The History of Philosophy* devoted in part to Epicurus (originally in volume three) was issued in 1660, but the title page of the "Fifth Part" of Stanley's work claims that it was printed for Humphrey Moseley and Thomas Dring in 1659; that is, only a year after the appearance of Gassendi's Lyons edition of the *Opera Omnia.*

Furthermore, not only does Stanley indicate a primary debt to Gassendi's historiographical approach in his dedication to John Marsham, his uncle,[72] but the work constantly reminds us of the special values of embedding all philosophical knowledge in biography and history. Stanley's preface applies the lessons of history to painting, because both vindicate the cognitive priority of the particular, such that "he who rests satisfied with the general Relation of Affairs, (not fixing upon some eminent Actor in that Story) loseth its greatest benefit; because what is most particular, by its nearer affinity with us, hath greatest influence upon us."[73] The epigraphs to volume three, taken respectively from Bacon's *Advancement of Learning* and Montaigne's *Essais,* not only amplify the theme but also do so just as the reader approaches the Hellenistic

PETRI GASSENDI

ANIMADVERSIONES
IN DECIMVM LIBRVM
DIOGENIS LAERTII,
QVI EST

De Vita, Moribus, Placitifque
E P I C V R I.

Continent autem Placita, quas ille treis ſtatuit Philoſophiæ parteis;

I. CANONICAM *nempe, habitam* DIALECTICÆ *loco:*

II. PHYSICAM, *ac imprimis nobilem illius partem* METEOROLOGIAM:

III. ETHICAM, *cuius gratiâ ille excoluit cæteras.*

EPICVRI EFFIGIES,
Ex Cimel.Cl.Viri Eriel Puteani.

L V G D V N I,
Apud GVILLELMVM BARBIER, Typogr. Reg.

M. DC. XLIX.

CVM PRIVILEGIO REGIS.

Portrait of Epicurus on the title page of Gassendi's *Animadversiones* (1649)
(also reproduced in *De Vita et Moribus Epicuri* [1647])

EPICVRI EFFIGIES.
Ex Cimel. Cl. Vivi Eriel Puteanj.

Portrait of Epicurus from Charleton's *Epicurus's Morals* (1656)

philosophers, culminating—as in book ten of Diogenes Laertius—in the lengthy section devoted to Epicurus.

Joy rightly objects that Stanley's *The History of Philosophy* provides no final proof of a true English appreciation of Gassendi, because she argues that the *Animadversiones* and the large *Syntagma* represent the core of Gassendi's real contribution to mid-seventeenth-century natural philosophy. But the objection ignores several important facts: the small *Philosophiae Epicuri Syntagma,* translated in 1659 by Stanley, was not only supplemented by other English publications of Gassendi's *oeuvre* but also by three reprintings (1660, 1668, and 1718), the last two offered first as a presentation of the *Institutio Logica* and only subsequently of the small *Syntagma.*[74]

Moreover, Evelyn, whom Margaret C. Jacob treats as "a veritable weather vane of latitudinarian sentiment on political matters,"[75] and who was a close friend of Taylor and later of Boyle, whose executor he became,[76] assumes that the English readership of his Lucretius is fully and intimately conversant with Gassendi's work, including explicitly the *Animadversiones.* Again, it is arguable that Stanley assumed some similar fund of associations or knowledge on his readers' part, because the Latin Leipzig edition of his *The History of Philosophy* (1711) supplies marginalia to the now more pointedly renamed *Philosophiae Epicuri,* which not only more carefully elaborate the classical sources than Stanley's original translation but also supply almost seventy running references to both volumes of Gassendi's 1649 *Animadversiones.*[77]

Despite the imputation of atheism, which neo-Epicureanism never entirely managed to elude, it is remarkable what kinds of texts register Gassendi's impact. On the Continent, Leibniz's *Nouveau Essais* pays homage to Gassendi as a significant feature of the intellectual landscape. Vico's *Autobiography* also testifies to the pervasiveness of Gassendism in late-seventeenth-century Europe. Vico records the moment at which he is forced, by its success, to encounter Gassendi's neo-Epicureanism. Only after reading Lucretius does Vico feel authorized to criticize the grounds of Gassendi's metaphysic, a process that anticipates his investigation and subsequent rejection of Cartesianism.[78] Closer to home and much earlier in the Restoration, Glanvill's *Vanity of Dogmatizing* (1661) and *Plus Ultra* (1668) both display a knowledge and approval of Gassendism, as does Boyle's *Works,* whose index devotes only slightly less attention to Gassendi than Descartes. For example, Boyle recommends Gassendi's *Institutio*

Astronomica as the best single exposition of "the *Copernican Hypothesis*."[79] Boyle's *Examen of Mr. T. Hobbes His Dialogus Physicus de Natura Aeris* (1662) explicitly commends Gassendi's atomism but attacks Hobbes's unfortunate materialism.[80] Here Gassendi stands as the foremost among "many other Atomists (besides other Naturalists) ancient and modern [who] expressly teach the sun-beams to consist of fiery corpuscles, trajected through the air, and capable of passing through glass," a view Boyle first associates with "the Epicurean hypothesis."[81]

Finally, as if to register and seal the orthodoxy of these earlier Restoration figures, Edward Phillips (a contemporary of Dryden and Locke) introduces Stanley and Gassendi into his *Life of Milton* (1694), still the most reliable early biography of his famous uncle. Gassendi appears as the last of a distinguished line of biographers stretching from Plutarch through Diogenes Laertius, Cornelius Nepos, Machiavelli, Fulke Greville, Thomas Stanley, and Isaac Walton. The "great Gassendus" occupies his position as "the worthy celebrator" of "the noble philosopher Epicurus" and Peiresc, in order to empower Phillips's own celebration of the greatest Christian poet in English.

The English in Paris: Gassendi versus Descartes

In the 1640s and 1650s there were some very different and much more personal contacts between Gassendi and important representatives of English society. Kargon admirably describes the émigré group in Paris circulating around Sir Charles Cavendish and Lady Margaret Cavendish, and known as the Newcastle circle. The group, which included Digby, Hobbes, and Pell, regularly communicated with the greatest representatives of French intellectual life—Marin Mersenne, Gassendi, and Descartes—as well as figures such as Pierre de Fermat, Gilles Personne de Roberval, and Sorbière. Kargon treats the Newcastle circle as a decisive vehicle for importing the new mechanical philosophy directly into England, a judgment with which Robert G. Frank concurs.[82] But because he is chiefly interested in the history of atomism, Kargon focuses equally on the physical theories of Descartes and Gassendi, a strategy that appears to lend them equivalent authority in the midcentury development of English atomism.

For his picture of this Paris circle, Kargon draws on the well-known correspondence between Sir Charles Cavendish and Dr. John Pell, partly published in an influential article by Helen Hervey.[83] Hervey's purpose is to illuminate the contacts between Hobbes and Descartes. But the

value of the correspondence is that it provides an almost phenomenological report from the scene and, taken as a whole, more accu-
rately reports on English attitudes toward Gassendi and Descartes, with
somewhat less focus on Hobbes. Although Hobbes is an assumed member of the group, we can witness in this correspondence, which chiefly
covers the years from 1644 to 1646, the formation of a series of personal
and intellectual prejudices, which finds Gassendi more persuasive than
Descartes as a mentor for English cultural motives. By examining another epistolary exchange, we shall also see how these attitudes are
shared both by the royalist émigrés and the Dury and Hartlib circle at
home, of whom the young Boyle was an impressionable member.[84]

The Paris group evidently fosters frequent and intimate contact
among its members: in November 1645 William Petty thanks Pell for the
ease with which his letters of introduction to Hobbes have also introduced him to Sir Charles Cavendish, Sir William Cavendish, and Mersenne.[85] Furthermore, Hobbes has happily provided Petty with access to
the latest French mathematics. Consequently, in part owing to his decidedly generous intellectual disposition, Sir Charles evinces a concern to
heal the obvious friction between Hobbes and Descartes. He feels indebted to Descartes for unnamed favors and finds Cartesianism "most
ingenious."[86] But Sir Charles's concern seems, from the evidence, the
response to a more widespread irritation with Descartes. Pell reports that
Descartes is difficult to handle on intellectual matters ("I perceive he
demonstrates not willingly").[87] Overall, we receive the impression that
Descartes is exacting, prickly, and dogmatic.

By contrast with Descartes, Gassendi is a welcome and intimate
member of the social and intellectual scene. It is true that Gassendi and
Hobbes were allied in rebutting Descartes's *Meditations;* but again, the
sense of the preference for Gassendi seems to stem from his general
ethical and intellectual *modus operandi.* Thus, in September 1644, Pell
doubts that Hobbes and Gassendi can reconcile with Descartes.[88] Despite his "esteem" for Descartes's "last newe booke of philosophie," Sir
Charles Cavendish admits that "I am of your opinion that Gassendus and
De Cartes are of different dispositions," adding that "Mr. Hobbes joins
with Gassendes in his dislike of De Cartes his writings."[89] He volunteers
in the same passage that Hobbes "is joined in a greate friendship with
Gassendes."[90] In the letters written between August 1644 and October
1646, Gassendi circulates almost as frequently and certainly more fluently
than either Hobbes or Descartes, to such an extent that, after a noticeable

absence, he reappears in a telling aside. Sir Charles Cavendish has been tempted by Athanasius Kircher's "book . . . of light and shadow," but because "Monsieur Gassendes doth not much commend it . . . I have no encouragement to buy or to read it."[91] Gassendi's authority is perhaps subtle, but it is real.

It is possible to cull from these exchanges solely the whims of personal prejudice, an early but familiar version of academic politics. But the grouping of alliances seems as consistently intellectual as social: Pell carefully selects the word "genius" to describe the difference between Gassendi's (thus Hobbes's) and Descartes's ethic.[92] Sir Charles Cavendish knows that the degree of difficulty between Hobbes and Descartes is in direct proportion to their philosophical differences. Like Gassendi's, Hobbes's physical theories are much more Democritean than Descartes's—one cause for the failure of their meeting.[93]

The intellectual content of such enmities and alliances is vividly illustrated by two features of the correspondence. The first concerns the theme of Descartes's intellectual envy, which Pell introduces in a letter dated August 1644, and which informs my epigraph from Swift. Descartes has attacked "Monsieur Hardy" for buying an expensive "Arabicke manuscript of Apollonius."[94] Searching to explain this behavior, Hardy interprets it "as a signe of envy in Des Cartes, as being unwilling that we should esteeme the ancients, or admire any man but himself for the doctrine of lignes courbes."[95] Not only does Descartes later refuse fully to cooperate in conversation with Pell by offering mathematical demonstrations, but his attitude informs a singular approach to the ancients, of whom "he magnifies none but Archimedes," though he "hath a high opinion of Euclid and Apollonius for writing so largely y^t which he conceives may be put into so little roome."[96] In sum, Descartes refuses to credit the ancients with their own historical life apart from his most immediate intellectual desires, because he resents the philosophical space that historical baggage occupies. History mediates and frustrates the search for absolute philosophical categories. Predictably, "he suspects Diophantus might be excellent in the books w^{c}h are lost," because that permanently muted knowledge suits his own intellectual supremacy.[97] Of course, the moderns fare no better: Pell would be embarrassed to repeat what Descartes has said about Vieta, Fermat, Roberval, and Golius, and he has been too wise even to mention Hobbes.[98] The same month (March 1646), Sir Charles Cavendish (ultimately in vain) encourages Pell to publish his own works, despite Descartes's persuasions to the contrary.[99]

The second feature of the correspondence that lends an intellectual weight to its social preferences is the writers' fascination with the latest philosophical publications. Many of Sir Charles Cavendish's letters to Pell begin with either requests or thanks for some new tract or book. Cavendish's letters of 1644 engage, for example, with the publication and reception of Descartes's *Principles of Philosophy*. Although Cavendish discovers he likes the work, Pell reports that Gassendi remains unconvinced (August 1644), whereas Cavendish predicts that Hobbes will not like it either, a suspicion that proves correct (October 1644). The letter of October 1644 reveals that Hobbes, who had already read and dismissed the manuscript of Descartes's *Principles of Philosophy*, has received support for his intellectual judgment from a friend who also has seen it. It is possible that this friend is Gassendi, who immediately provides the next topic: Hobbes has seen an impressive manuscript of Gassendi's, and he judges it to be "as big as Aristotle's philosophie, but much truer and excellent Latin," which Kargon concludes to be a draft of the *Animadversiones*. Cavendish requests Gassendi's *Disquisitio Metaphysica*, his rebuttals of Descartes, about which he has been inquiring for a month. In December, Cavendish gratefully records its arrival.

Now writing in 1648, Sir Charles Cavendish again indulges his interest in Gassendi. Cavendish believes that *De Vita et Moribus Epicuri* (1647) and the *Animadversiones* compose an integral project, because he reports that "Gassendus . . . proceeds with his Epicurean phylosophie, the halfe of which; I doubte is not yet printed" (August 1648). In early 1649, Descartes's *The Passions of the Soul* has appeared, but Cavendish is anxious by March to obtain a copy of Gassendi's *Animadversiones* ("Mr: Gassendes his Epicurean philosophie"). In May Pell announces its long-awaited publication, describing its cost and size. He has, he says, met Sorbière, who supervised the publication of Gassendi's *Disquisitio Metaphysica* and translated Hobbes's *De Cive* into French. Sorbière also mentions that the *Animadversiones* have sold so well that a second printing is contemplated. A year later (June 1650), Cavendish has finally received his own copy of the *Animadversiones*. Significantly, especially in light of their mathematical biases, Cavendish and Pell think of Gassendi's work not even primarily as a treatise on physics, but as the exposition of an organic and refined philosophical scheme. It is therefore no accident that Cavendish retails Hobbes's remark that the *Animadversiones* will effectively displace Aristotle in scope, penetration, and style.

Hartlib, Gassendi, the Air Pump, and Boyle

The Newcastle circle also anticipates the neo-Epicurean strain in Restoration culture because it was indirectly linked with a significant group of individuals in England, which did not share its party political affiliations. Through Petty, both Hartlib and Boyle seem to have learned of Gassendi's *Animadversiones* at a point in Boyle's career that has remained somewhat of a mystery. Steven Shapin and Simon Schaffer have argued that Boyle's belief in the vacuum (defended by experiments with his air pump) served an ideological debate with Hobbes, on the grounds that his plenism was the physical equivalent to his political absolutism. But these were the actions of a mature Boyle, and Shapin and Schaffer's book does not connect this ethical use of a physical hypothesis with Epicureanism as a cultural organism, which specifically encourages a cohesive link between method, the void, and an ethical voluntarism. The void, in short, represents the possibility of movement and negotiation among the constituents of matter or society, and thus it encourages the notion that, on the one hand, the discrete particles in this economy must retain their integrity and, on the other, that we must discover a literary technology that promotes the dual possibility of integrity and assent. I have also argued that the integrity of the atomic particle encourages a view of the example that resists reduction and that therefore encourages the movements of assent or dissent. Like Evelyn, Boyle seems to seek an idea of the exemplary suited to new ethical and cognitive requirements, and to intuit very early on that the rhetoric of the dialogue and the epistle seems to offer the desired effect.

By attending to the rather fragmentary correspondence between Hartlib and Boyle, I want first to suggest that, before he could explore Gassendi in full, the young Boyle already associates a certain literate method with a distinct ethic, that he knew of the *Animadversiones* before they were published, and that his early interest in atomism must therefore have occurred in an atmosphere which treats that physical hypothesis as part of an entire methodological and ethical program.

In a letter to Hartlib dated 8 May 1647, Boyle indicates that "*Gassendus* [is] a great favourite of mine."[100] But at this point relatively little of Gassendi's important work had been published. Boyle's full appreciation of Gassendi almost certainly had to wait a year or more, because the

Animadversiones was published in 1649. It is Hartlib's contact with Petty in particular that first connects Boyle to the Newcastle circle. Hartlib introduces Petty to Boyle in a letter dated 16 November 1647: Petty, it transpires, is "a perfect *Frenchman,* and a good linguist in other vulgar languages besides *Latin* and *Greek,* a most rare and exact anatomist, and excelling in all mathematical and mechanical learning, of a sweet natural disposition and moral comportment."[101]

In May 1648, in a pivotal letter Hartlib writes again to the youthful Boyle (he is only twenty-one). Here Hartlib acts as purveyor of intellectual goods: his main purpose is to enclose an extract of a letter from Sir Charles Cavendish to Petty, which Hartlib has received through Benjamin Worsley (the surveyor general under whom Petty was to work in Ireland after 1652). Clearly, Hartlib's general motive for copying the extract is his detailed interest in intellectual affairs on the Continent. But the more specific motive is captured by the letter's suggestive conjunction between Gassendi and the air pump, which was to play such an iconic role in Boyle's career. Gassendi "hath now" his *"Philosophy of Epicurus"* in "the press at *Lyons"*; the existence of the *Animadversiones* (to which Cavendish refers) thus seems already to have been introduced to English intellectual circles by mid-1648.

Gassendi's text seems to fit with Hartlib's and Boyle's correspondence in several ways. Because Gassendi seeks, like Epicurus, to fuse all intellectual issues with ethical ones, the reference to his *Animadversiones* could mirror Hartlib's evident concern to treat Petty's intellectual credentials and certain social and moral values as one. Petty meets Hartlib's criteria for reforming and harmonizing philosophical enquiry and political conduct, a project that deeply influenced Boyle, even before he could articulate it by reference to the embryonic neo-Epicurean revival.

Before Boyle could have known of Gassendi's *Animadversiones,* Boyle's series of letters to Hartlib and Dury of 1647 discuss Dury's and Hartlib's utopian projects, themselves of course responses to the unsettled times. But, more interestingly, Boyle's letters seem to anticipate the neo-Epicurean texts we have examined, because they are highly self-conscious dramatizations of a mode of intellectual and ethical behavior that display a moderate and irenist ethic. The point here is that Boyle seems to seek a rhetoric that in its method will itself enact the contingent epistemology that—as a response to the civil war—would make forms of social negotiation necessary and desirable. Indeed, the first letter (19 March 1647), which mentions two of Hartlib's utopian tracts, as well as suggestions for a universal character, begins with an invocation to the epistolary muse. "I need a great deal of rhetoric to express to you, how great a satisfaction I received in the favor of your letter," Boyle writes, "both for the sake of the theme, and more for that of the author."[102] Boyle believes that rhetoric is the contingent instrument for lending ideas phenomenal weight within the social and intellectual arena. In the final letter in the series, he determines not to neglect "improving my rhetoric to the uttermost," in order to assist Dury's logical schemes (themselves integral to the social program) "by exemplifying his rules, to clothe with flesh and skin his excellent skeleton of the Art of Reasoning."[103] Here Boyle clearly speaks in terms of incarnating knowledge, of rendering it somatic in order to propagate it.

Other very closely related metaphors for incarnating and textualizing knowledge in order to render it socially negotiable also appear in these letters from Boyle. The first occurs in the title of Hartlib's now lost *Imago Societatis*. Like Hartlib's description of Macaria (1641), this tract seeks to propose a society that exemplifies a Christian reformation of education and politics. The subtitle to Hartlib's *Macaria* conceives of its polity as "an example to other nations," which mirrors the theology of 1 Pet. 1:9: "But ye are a chosen generation, a royal priesthood, an holy nation, a peculiar people; that ye should show forth the praises of him who hath called you out of darkness into his marvellous light." However, the imaging or "showing forth" of the new nation exploits the device of the dialogue ("between a scholar and a traveller"), which enjoys more classical than biblical antecedents and, like rhetoric in general, presumes the merely contingent negotiations of knowledge. That is, "showing forth" can be seen as an incarnation of knowledge, which is made possible by the enactments of dialogue. And, curiously, as Boyle reports his response to having read "your *Imago Societatis* with a great deal of delight," he himself has "lately traced a little dialogue in my thoughts."[104] A few lines later, he expresses his hope for Mr. Hall's "Divine Emblems," which itself distills Boyle's interest in the ideal exemplary image, whose power he describes as "probable."[105]

The letter of May 1647 in which Boyle mentions his special regard for Gassendi is devoted to a discussion of the *"Invisible College,"* and it is explicitly in this relation that Gassendi appears.[106] The letter is also deeply concerned with the question of exemplarity. Having introduced the topic of Hartlib's invisible college, Boyle pauses to thank Hartlib for his letters and reaches for a doubly numismatic and plastic metaphor:

"And truly, Sir, for my particular, had you been to coin and shape news, not so much to inform, as to delight me, you should scarce have made choice of any, that were more welcome."[107] Although ostensibly serving private communication, the epistolary manner, Boyle tells us, achieves a kind of public value and a capacity for circulation and exchange, like a coin or statue; it then gathers the power to instruct and delight. Like the epistolary mode, the invisible college will become a discrete concrete example to the nation. And, like his role in the Newcastle circle, it is possible that Gassendi could already represent to Boyle the advancement of knowledge in association with an ideal of essentially private, cooperative, and even redemptive social behavior, which as we have seen, is dear both to Sir Charles Cavendish and Hartlib.[108]

The degree to which Gassendi's neo-Epicureanism could specifically provide a vocabulary for that ideology was a mere potential in 1647: Boyle's letter of May was written three months before Gassendi's *De Vita et Moribus Epicuri* received royal approval,[109] and two years before the *Animadversiones* appeared. But by 1648, things have changed. Petty arrives on the scene, importing his knowledge of Continental affairs, and Hartlib, in two letters to Boyle, can now convey more details of Gassendi's neo-Epicurean project.

The letter that Hartlib copies for Boyle in May 1648, and that I introduced above, fortuitously realizes some of the terms of Gassendi's neo-Epicureanism, now a matter of public record. For just as Petty represents to Hartlib an ideal combination of philosopher and moral agent, so Gassendi embodies a strikingly similar complex of values, and thus he serves to link Sir Charles Cavendish and Petty, the society they create, and Hartlib's friendship with Boyle. Cavendish refers to Gassendi as "your worthy friend and mine,"[110] thereby uniting an ideal of intellectual inquiry with the exemplum of friendship, a virtue appropriately textualized in the intimacies of the private letter. For all his personal feelings for Descartes, Cavendish never accords him the particular value that Gassendi not only assumes here but also had himself described in his *De Vita et Moribus Epicuri*.

We also saw that Cavendish—in the same letter that Hartlib copies for Boyle—discusses Gassendi's *Animadversiones* and enumerates the details of the air pump. The conjunction is significant, because the air pump represents "an experiment how to show . . . that there is or may be a vacuum."[111] In contrast to Cartesian or Hobbesian plenism, the existence of a vacuum establishes one of the premises of neo-Epicurean physics, of which the *Animadversiones* is a revolutionary vehicle. And by virtue of the characteristically isonomic Epicurean device, the vacuum (like the atomic swerve that Gassendi revised out of the physics) represents not only the physical space in and through which atoms can move but also its ethical corollary, the desideratum of social and intellectual accommodation and choice. If Shapin and Schaffer are correct, it is precisely this corollary that Boyle was later to implement, with devastating effect, against Hobbes's physics.

If Hartlib's letters of 1647 and 1648 represent any development in Boyle's early and express enthusiasm for Gassendi, then we might ask how Gassendi's neo-Epicureanism was to achieve through Boyle a revolutionary effect on English culture—that is, how closely can we link Boyle's enormously influential adoption of corpuscularian physics to a knowledge of Gassendi at midcentury? Richard Westfall believes that Boyle's earliest extant manuscripts concerning "Ye Atomicall Philosophy" were written by 1653. Westfall argues that they postdate 1649, when, he tells us, Gassendi published his *Philosophiae Epicuri Syntagma*. By implying that the Epicurean *Syntagma* alone was published in 1649, Westfall conveniently supports his assumption that Boyle was embarrassed by his own putatively illicit interest in Epicureanism, because the small *Syntagma* does not present Gassendi's revisions of Epicureanism. However, M. A. Stewart's challenge to Westfall is supported by the fact that the *Philosophiae Epicuri Syntagma* originally appeared in 1649 as a condensed appendix to volume two of the much more comprehensive *Animadversiones,* and Boyle's access to the Epicurean *Syntagma* could only occur by his knowing of the entire *Animadversiones.* The implications for our view of the early Boyle are at least twofold. First, if—as is highly probable, and in practice Westfall and Kargon must assume— Boyle had read the *Animadversiones* in 1649, Boyle's understanding of Gassendi would then extend well beyond the biography and redaction of Epicurus. Second, because Gassendi's adaptation and modification of Epicureanism sought to transpose pagan requirements into Christian ones; because both the ancient and the modern forms of Epicureanism provide perfect equivalents to Boyle's early union of method, physics, and ethics; and because the figure of Gassendi evidently circulated as easily in the Hartlib as the Newcastle circle, there seems little reason to see in Boyle an urgency to reject associations with Epicureanism. Thus, writing about Boyle's physics to Spinoza in 1663, Henry Oldenburg is wonderfully unembarrassed by the current status of "Epicurean" physics.

He reports that Boyle wishes to adopt it in order to displace "the chemists and the schoolmen" and then to reform it on experimental grounds, themselves reflecting—as Boyle himself at one point writes—neo-Epicurean method: "Our Boyle is one of those who are distrustful enough of their reasoning to wish that phenomena should agree with it."[112]

John Evelyn: The Neo-Epicurean Naturalized

John Evelyn's career epitomizes the matrix of cultural and philosophical attitudes that neo-Epicureanism came to symbolize in the Restoration. Evelyn served as an important vehicle for translating French cultural attitudes into English ones during the Interregnum; he was closely in touch with the developing interest in natural philosophy, both in the royalist and Cromwellian camps; and he developed a vocabulary of cultural knowledge, which owes something to the Epicurean *Suggrammata* and to Gassendi's ideal of biographical and historical modes of reading. The probable occasion of Evelyn's contact with Gassendism, if not Gassendi—his trip to Europe in the 1640s—itself manifests the distinctive combination of royalist, Anglican, and irenist commitments, which was to form Evelyn's entire reputation. E. S. de Beer records that Evelyn left England in 1643, unwilling to swear allegiance to Parliament. In 1646 he established contact with the group of émigrés in Paris, which worshipped at the chapel of Sir Richard Browne, the king's emissary to the French court. Browne had instituted his chapel—significantly—as a visible reminder of his devotion to a uniquely Anglican polity, which increasingly dissociated itself from the courtly and predominantly Catholic circle gathered around Queen Henrietta Maria.[113] Evelyn married Browne's daughter, Mary, who was to design the frontispiece to the *Essay on the First Book of T. Lucretius Carus De Rerum Natura; Interpreted and Made English Verse* and whose virtues Rand celebrates in his translation of Gassendi's life of Peiresc. Additionally, in 1656, Browne cemented a public and literary relationship with his son-in-law by dedicating a poem to Evelyn's Lucretius.

Evelyn's return to England in 1652 marks the point at which Evelyn began systematically to cultivate himself as a palpable example of that confluence of private and public virtue for which he became famous, and which Taylor distills in a reference to Tusculanum.[114] Cicero's *Tusculanian Disputations* enacts a search for, and the methods appropriate to, a probabilist epistemology by dramatizing a series of dialogues conducted in Cicero's seaside villa at Tusculanum, itself symbolizing a studied perspective on the turbulence of public life in Rome.[115] Evelyn's posture of moderation and virtue permitted him to reconcile a fervent Anglican and royalist temperament with an astonishingly wide range of acquaintance.[116] Evelyn articulated his cultural and personal projects by several means. First, especially in the form of letters, he developed a marked and novel ideal of intimate friendship.[117] Second, with an almost mystical enthusiasm, he appropriated and elaborated the image of hortulan retirement in a number of concrete forms: his renowned garden at Sayes Court (Evelyn's aforementioned Tusculanum and, in Taylor's words, his "Terrestrial Paradise"); his extensive writings about horticulture; and his equally extensive collection of books on the subject. Third, Evelyn patiently explored and articulated the nature of the exemplary phenomenal image, a fascination that unites his concern over the minutiae of printing with his antiquarian and numismatic interests.

The correspondence of Taylor and Evelyn breathes the atmosphere of a cultivated, intense, and intimate friendship of the kind Taylor describes in his *Discourse of the Nature, Offices and Measures of Friendship* (1657).[118] Not unlike Boyle, Taylor and Evelyn stretch the capacities of their epistolary styles to manufacture an original and urgent language of friendship. A deeply moving exchange between them occurs at the loss of Evelyn's young son in February 1657/58; but we also catch something of the artificiality of the pose, an emblem of the discourse under construction, as it were, in a letter from Taylor to Evelyn dated May 1657, written during the composition of Taylor's *Discourse*: "I only can love you, and honour you, and pray for you; and in all this I can not say but that I am behind hand with you, for I have found so great effluxes of all your worthinesses and charities, that I am a debtor for your prayers, for the comfort of your letters, for the charity of your hand, and the affections of your heart."[119] The spatial trope, by placing the author temporarily *behind,* implicitly at a competitive disadvantage to his addressee, predicates the quality of the prose, which seeks by a flurry of activity, accumulating clauses, to close the distance. What is artificial, however, is no less felt. On completing his *Discourse* (June 1657), Taylor proclaims Evelyn the concrete realization of the ideas it describes. "Sir, your kind letter hath so abundantly rewarded and crowned my innocent endeavors in my description of Friendship," Taylor begins,

> that I perceive there is a friendship beyond what I have fancied, and a real, material worthiness beyond the heights of the most perfect

ideas: and I know now where to make my book perfect, and by an appendix to outdo the first essay: for when anything shall be observed to be wanting in my character, I can tell them where to see the substance, much more beauteous than the picture, and by sending the readers of my book to be spectators of your life and worthiness, they shall see what I would fain have taught them, by what you really are.[120]

In Taylor's allegory, true perfection resides not in the implicitly Neoplatonic perfection of ideas, abstracted ("beyond the heights") from the mundane, or so much in the *particular,* as in the "material," substantial, or "real." And Evelyn consciously strove to articulate this incarnated perfection in his Kentish garden, and, by extension, in his numerous schemes for improving the forestry, ecology, horticulture, and habitable spaces of England.[121] Evelyn strives comprehensively to embody and enact the conditions for a new variety of citizen, for which private friendship is a prolegomenon. Sayes Court, as an image of that desired culture, attracted precisely such spectators of Evelyn's art as Taylor imagines, in the form of Cromwellian and Stuart grandees.[122] Executing Taylor's prescriptions for friendship in his *Discourse,* Evelyn subtly revises his polity away from the Ciceronian and Plutarchan models of social intercourse to embrace female company. Addressing the question of "how friendships are to be conducted,"[123] the *Discourse,* an epistle addressed to Mrs. Katherine Philips, inveighs against "the morosity of those cynics, who would not admit your sex into the communities of a noble friendship."[124] Like the Epicurean community, which in this respect was unique within classical culture, both Evelyn and Mrs. Philips conscript their spouses into a mythology of friendship, which seeks at once to reform the conventional terms of marriage and to embrace other individuals. They share Taylor, the "Palaemon" to Mrs. Philips's "Orinda."

Mary Evelyn is a silent partner in this discussion of friendship, but her engagement within the hortulan virtues of Sayes Court has a striking parallel in a different textual space of her own making, namely the frontispiece to John Evelyn's *Essay upon Lucretius* (p. 168). (Rand was later to refer to John and Mary Evelyn as "true yoak-fellowes."[125]) It should first be noted that Mary Evelyn inherited the main features of her design from Michel de Marolles's translation of Lucretius (1650), the first full translation into French. Marolles's frontispiece in turn owes something to Jan Jansson's Amsterdam edition of 1620, which Cosmo Alexander Gordon believes to be "the earliest printed illustration" of *De Rerum Natura.*[126]

Frontispiece to Evelyn's *An Essay on the First Book of T. Lucretius Carus De Rerum Natura* (1656), designed by Mary Evelyn

Mary Evelyn's appropriation of Marolles's frontispiece should be read in at least two directions: it comments on the general project, shared by Marolles and John Evelyn, of translating Lucretius into vernacular languages; it also comments on the specifically English desire to import and so domesticate French cultural artifacts at this historical juncture. The one commentary occurs in Marolles's original, in which the conventional iconology of the four elements is subtly altered; the other occurs in Mary Evelyn's equally delicate adjustments to that original. The four main figures represent earth, water, fire, and air.[127] But by a series of intricate iconological adjustments, the design subtly revises the political connotations of its emblems by Christianizing, feminizing, and particularizing their cultural associations. The most obvious and important fact is that it is Evelyn's wife who supervises the reader's entrance upon her husband's translation, a fact engraved on the lip of Neptune's urn. Mary's name thus publicly cooperates in a cameo of cultural reinterpretation with her husband ("J.E.") and Wenceslaus Hollar, the period's most distinguished engraver and illustrator. Second, the design balances the presence of three male figures (Neptune, Vulcan, and John Evelyn) with three female figures by adding the presiding allegorical figure of *begnignita*, or *sostanza:* Cesare Ripa's *Iconologia* allegorizes both virtues with a woman whose breasts, like Ceres' fruit, represent abundance. At the same time, Mary Evelyn has also differentiated the sexes by substituting Vulcan for the more habitual female representation of fire. The Vulcanic hammer can now economically allude to Lucretius's mechanistic universe.

The frame accordingly achieves a temporary balance between its representations of gender; however, on closer examination, the rhetorical weight shifts from the masculine left to the feminine right. The conventional grammar of reading pictures favors the move, but, as if to assist it, the rather bland allegorical figures of Neptune and Vulcan stolidly clutching trident and hammer, respectively, lose something by comparison to the more fertile, lavish, and polyvalent female figures. (The action is articulated by the sweeping gesture of the gown on the top of the frontispiece, which directs the eye in a circular movement toward the right.) The seated Ceres, for example, concentrates several associated iconological possibilities. Her coronet is borrowed from Cybele, founder of civilizations, while Ceres herself inherits from medieval iconology the image of the nourishing church, apparently the central edifice on the coronet. Ceres shares with Minerva the serpent, representing, in this connection, prudence and logic. Hence Ceres not only plays a part in the generic allegory of the four elements by symbolizing earthly plenitude but also infuses a Christian tonality into the Lucretian fascination with the founding elements of human civilization, as well as the cosmos.

The act of feminizing and Christianizing is, however, by no means unambiguous. Just as the Christianized possibilities of the frontispiece exploit a pagan mythology, such that the pagan image only hazily predicates a submerged Christian icon, so the cultural resonance of translating Lucretius in the mid-seventeenth century is at least double-edged. By presenting the lion peeping from beneath Ceres/Cybele's gown, it is almost as if the frontispiece dramatizes this peculiarly destabilized hermeneutic: the classical iconology surrounding Cybele usually requires two lions, the transfigured forms of Atalanta and Hippomenes,[128] but the single lion here, though admitting that pagan tradition, invokes the Christian iconology by which a lion could represent either Christ or Satan. The lion rises as a warning to the Christian about to engage Lucretius's pagan masterpiece.

The figures in the frontispiece do not behave in a uniformly allegorical manner. The tension within the frame questions the nature and role of allegorical interpretation itself and, in so doing, revises the epistemological and political terms under which representation operates. John Evelyn's portrait directly faces a figure ambiguously representing air, and only by default: apart from occupying the conventional space given to the fourth element, she has been denuded of Juno's emblems—the peacock, or an anvil on each foot signifying her punishment for disobeying Jupiter.[129] The political premises of the frontispiece preclude such images of female subservience. The absence of such iconological cues, as well as this most realistic and Christianized allegorical figure of all, invites the consideration that the image setting itself against Junoesque vanity and submission may stand for Mary Evelyn herself. The postulate encourages the historical and concrete to emerge from and even escape general and abstract knowledge. It inscribes a moment of translation. The figure of Mary Evelyn can be felt to resist the weight of inherited, reflex modes of interpretation constituted by male, classical, and pagan influences, yet she also approaches and greets her husband.

Where the top and right frames of the frontispiece succor the feminine, its bottom frame curiously mingles male and female. Technically, the snake is Ceres' possession; the urn, Neptune's. But here their juxtaposition confuses such identities. First, Mary Evelyn's name marks the gushing urn: the rim identifies her genius within the frame, and the action of the water mirrors the fruit spilling onto Ceres' gown and the milk of abundance raining down from the officiating figure of sustenance. The snake and the urn, moreover, move away from their proper points of origin, causing them to mingle, so the womblike urn is about to swallow the snake. The water gushing from the urn's mouth further mixes male and female polarities, because it seems to drench both Ceres' and Neptune's feet. The feminized terms of the emblem absorb rather than exclude the masculine.

Hence by juggling the tropes of an emblem that, like *De Rerum Natura* itself, raises the most elemental questions about civilization and the cosmos, Mary Evelyn's frontispiece effectually contributes to the wider debate to which neo-Epicureanism was also tributary. In short, the frontispiece constitutes its own discursive space, which, by alluding to and revising the presumptions of iconological reading, establishes its own delicate critique of interpretive authority and behavior. The polity of the Epicurean garden, made real in Sayes Court and in John Evelyn's conduct of friendship, can foster Mary Evelyn's subtle but ambitious claims for the role of women and for cooperation between the sexes within her own design for a new social order.[130]

The ambiguous emblem of the lion curiously focuses something of Evelyn's own ambivalence about his *Essay on Lucretius*. He expresses his hesitation about his project in terms of his frustrations with a sloppily printed edition—something that later irritated him about the printing of his *Numismata*.[131] But in response to Taylor's much more uncomplicated admiration for the translation, Evelyn also rather vaguely fears that he might indeed have loosed a lion on an unsuspecting public. A penciled gloss appended to a letter from Taylor in 1656 reads: "I would be none of yᶜIngeniosi malo publico."[132] Years later, in his guardedness about popular misconceptions of Epicureanism, Evelyn tells William Wotton that his recently dead friend Boyle "was a *Corpuscularian* without Epicurus."[133]

Curiously, however, it is in the context of the elaborately constructed letters of friendship between Evelyn and Taylor that we detect not only the fascination Lucretius could exercise for Taylor's immaculate orthodoxy but also the terms in which Lucretius's pagan theology was debated and revised. Like John Wilkins, Taylor is deeply impressed by Evelyn's translation, and he urges Evelyn more than once to finish the final four books of *De Rerum Natura*. Taylor's initial enthusiasm is somewhat tempered by his advice that Evelyn should strategically distance himself from Lucretius's theological views;[134] subsequently, the friends discuss the immortality of the soul,[135] only some time after Evelyn has written that "my animadversiones . . . will I hope provide against all . . . ill consequences, and totally acquit me either of glory or impiety."[136] None of these gestures even hints at rejecting neo-Epicureanism *tout court*.

Evelyn might attempt to preserve Boyle from Epicurean heterodoxy. But if we step back from the minutiae of Evelyn's response to *De Rerum Natura,* and particularly if we register his *obiter dicta,* we see how profoundly he associates neo-Epicureanism with the new philosophy, especially the community it signifies. Returning to his diary entry for 12 May 1656, which records the initial publication of the *Essay on Lucretius,* Evelyn retrospectively comments that "little of the Epicurean Philosophy was known then amongst us." The temporal logic here is critical. For if Evelyn's correspondence—treated as a coherent allegory of English culture between 1647 and 1704—describes a triumph of knowledge, it occurs in the form not of atheism or materialism, but of "the new philosophy," which, he declares in 1703, "has since obtained."[137] At this point, Wotton is researching the life of Boyle, a project to which Evelyn attaches absolute significance; it is uniquely biography which can preserve that fragile relation between natural philosophy and culture, for which neo-Epicureanism is a perfect figure. For Evelyn, Gassendi's life of Peiresc has achieved the task definitively by transmitting the memory of "that illustrious and incomparable virtuoso."[138] Whereas Peiresc exemplifies a mode of knowledge for which Gassendi has invented the perfect literary vehicle, Wotton's biography can now make of Boyle an ideal example for future generations. By the end of Evelyn's life, Boyle's name evokes in him such powerful resonances for a peculiar set of philosophical and cultural values that Evelyn finally indulges in a fanciful and elaborate myth that will permanently link the Boyles with the Evelyn family name.[139]

The impulse behind Evelyn's mythologizing of Boyle derives from his earliest dealings with him. Like his visit to the Oxford philosophical group in July 1654, prompted by "my excellent & deare Friend *Dr. Wilkins,*"[140] Evelyn's relationship with Boyle extends the ideals of intimate friendship to more public models of social exchange. Evelyn lends his own diary and correspondence the weight of a developing but coherent narrative in a series of retrospective comments, which by hindsight realigns the allegory of events as they were originally recorded. The result is a vision of the gradual expansion of his private ideals into the cultural and political landscape. Evelyn editorializes his visit to Oxford in

1654 by later inserting the comment that Wilkins is "now Bishop of *Chester*," an institutional turn taken by other members of the Oxford group, and that Evelyn describes in a letter of 1703.[141] Evelyn himself accentuates the activity of a historical narrative in which an ever-widening circle of friends seems to have begun—like Evelyn tending his garden—at some intellectual and geographical fixed point. The general concern with the transmission and propagation of cultural knowledge also discovers a convenient metaphor in the figure of the expansion of knowledge by an ever-widening series of concentric circles.

Of this activity, Boyle is a persistent feature. In 1659 Evelyn writes to Boyle about "our common and good friend Mr. Hartlib"[142] and alludes to a work "concerning the ornaments of gardens, which I have requested him to communicate to you."[143] Evelyn's assumption of an *imago societatis* later finds unpremeditated reinforcement in 1665, when Evelyn rejoices in the prospect of Wilkins, Petty, and Hooke living together at "my Lord Geo. Barclay's at Durdans near my brother" and discussing all kinds of schemes, which excite in Evelyn the reflection that "I know not of such another happy conversation of Virtuosi in England."[144] Evelyn's enthusiasm is to be expected not only on account of his hortulan and familial *imaginatio* but also because such a conversational and harmonious society is the subject of an elaborate proposal he presents to Boyle in 1659, less than a month after he hopes Hartlib will have conveyed Evelyn's work on gardens. The letter lays bare the motives that combine the interests of friendship, hortulan virtue, and social exemplification united under a single rubric—the determination to resist cultural and political instability ("that fond morigeration to the mistaken customs of the age").[145] Prevented by his family ("an aggregate person") from offering himself as the founder of his proposed community, Evelyn finds in Boyle the embodiment and seminal figure of his design.[146] A plot of "thirty or forty acres of land, in some healthy place, not above twenty-five miles from London"[147] will provide space for the cultivation of true religion and "experimental knowledge,"[148] while a kind of sabbatical system will infuse into the larger body politic those virtues cultivated in Tusculan retirement. Evelyn's precise spatial descriptions emphasize how this society may fill the gap or interruption in culture that he characterizes as "this sad *Catalysis*." Evelyn describes his general aim:

> In order to this, I propound, that because we are not to hope for a
> mathematical college, much less, a Solomon's house, hardly a friend

in this sad *Catalysis,* and *inter hos armorum strepitus,* a period so uncharitable and perverse; why might not some gentlemen, whose geniuses are greatly suitable, and who desire nothing more than to give a good example, preserve science, and cultivate themselves, join together in society, and resolve upon some orders and oeconomy, to be mutually observed, such as shall best become the end of their union, if, I cannot say, without a kind of singularity, because the thing is new: yet such, at least, as shall be free from pedantry, and all affectation?[149]

The spatializing of knowledge that actuates a coherent cultural image implies specular activity at two levels. Each participant, cultivating an individual garden within the boundaries of the smaller world, sees in each cohabitant a reflection of the ideals that the community desires. Similarly, the community serves as a complete example to official culture, signaled by the relative proximity of London—a Rome to Horace's Sabine farm. Knowledge of the example is enacted in terms primarily of *circulation*—the circulation of virtuous examples within the community's confines, as well as the recycling of continuously refurbished images to and from the wider society. It should not surprise us, then, that Evelyn's antiquarianism should lead him to a fascination with numismatics—material images confronting us from the past—or that Gassendi's biography of Peiresc should represent both sets of values to Evelyn.

A number of letters from the 1680s and 1690s develop Evelyn's elaborate conception of the use and function of medals as cultural artifacts. Medals assume a peculiar value, which they share with pictures, title pages, and illustrations, but to which they literally lend unusual weight and compression. Evelyn's discussion of these images from the past occurs within a heightened consciousness of their historical and epistemological status. Such images "transmit anything valuable to posterity"[150] only by a lucky chance, a happy union of fragmentary evidences. But Evelyn wants to regularize conditions of misfortune, malice, and accident by prescribing methods for collecting and maintaining books, pictures, and medals. His most extended deliberations on the topic occur in a letter to Samuel Pepys, dated 12 August 1689, in which he repeatedly indicts the "sad dispersions" of great repositories of culture—such as King Charles I's, Prince Henry's, and the Earl of Clarendon's collections—in the recent past and especially during "the late fanatic war."[151] Clarendon provides the most public and magnificent ideal of the collector, to whom (in Evelyn's epistolary drama) Pepys plays the most appropriate, if more modest and private, late Restoration equivalent. Moreover, whereas Clarendon's art collection is dispersed, his palace demolished,[152] and his political career wrecked,[153] Evelyn places hope in Pepys's library as a more secure and long-lasting repository of cultural images. Evelyn conveys his determination to repair the damage done to the great art collections and libraries during the civil wars in a generational metaphor of the kind that opens Dryden's "Astrea Redux." A younger generation must assume the responsibility for reassembling and re-animating a culture that has suffered a series of lacunae not only by war and fire[154] but also by the negligence and greed of prodigal children, even though Clarendon provides an exception.[155]

The responsibility of a younger generation to an older one is reflected in a parallel responsibility of the English to themselves. Again, Clarendon provides the perfect vehicle for Evelyn's argument, because his criticisms of "the open and avowed luxury and profaneness which succeeded, [in the Stuart court] *à la mode de France*"[156] motivated his disgrace and exile to that country. Like the frequent sale of great English collections on the Continent, it is all too easy for a culture intent on dismembering itself to export or otherwise to dispose of those "effigies" (to adopt Evelyn's term) that it finds inconvenient. Evelyn wants to control and regulate the wholesale exportation of cultural artifacts to France, as well as indict the indiscriminate taste for foreign, especially Italian, painting, in order to reinvent and propagate a native virtue and integrity. Thus he unequivocally defends his panegyric to Clarendon (an encapsulation of Clarendon's historic value) in the dedication to his translation of Gabriel Naudé's *Advis pour Dresser une Bibliothèque* (1627; trans. 1661).[157]

The determination to compete with the institutions of French culture (in particular) is both domesticated and cleansed of any associations with pomp and grandeur by a dual metaphor of circulation juxtaposed with a highly specialized conception of space. The circulatory and spatial assumptions driving Evelyn's argument meet in an image of the Thames flowing by Lambeth Palace: like the commerce the Thames allows, the formerly plundered palace can become one of several new loci of cultural wealth, realized most profoundly in terms of books, pictures, and medals. Like Harvey's circulation of the blood, an English discovery that Evelyn remembers here, the circulation of artifacts will restrengthen the sinews of the body politic.[158] And like the library of Lambeth Palace, the

Medals from Evelyn's *Numismata* (1697), showing how Evelyn interprets narrative
history from these compressed items of evidence

new spaces Evelyn imagines as repositories of knowledge (from the virtuoso's cabinet to the Wren library at Cambridge[159]) both copy and revise French models, especially the Académie Française. However, whereas Cardinal Mazarin's library and the Académie connote an almost stifling grandeur and a vision of the state control of culture, Evelyn desires a public effect to be achieved by more local and domestic means. The linguistic functions of the Académie are, in Evelyn's imagination, transferred to a group—such as the "three or four meetings . . . begun at Gray's Inn, by Mr. Cowley, Dr. Sprat, Mr. Waller, the Duke of Buckingham, Matt. Clifford, Mr. Dryden, and some other promoters" of wit[160]—which is "brought together into conversation" in "one competent room in [a] gentleman's house."[161]

Evelyn is profoundly concerned with the ontic and epistemological status of the artifacts that will compose the counters or currency of his new cultural economy. Evelyn's hostility to art collectors' undiscriminating preference for Italian mythological paintings denotes a wider resistance to the speechless and "dusky lumber" of history.[162] Part of Evelyn's argument is that such representations are not historical enough in nature; because the "real image"[163] or "instructive types"[164] only achieve power by marking their space in some larger cultural grammar, they must be framed in some way by the contexts and aims of history. This is the purpose of Evelyn's confessedly "promiscuous" but equally prescriptive catalogue of famous individuals, who represent, singly or together, for good or for ill, examples for the kind of society he postulates. As we might expect from the striking mutuality of John and Mary Evelyn's personal and intellectual relationship—Mary evidently accompanied John as an intellectual peer on that famous visit to Oxford in 1654—John Evelyn calculatedly includes women in his ideal society.[165] Indeed, the most vivid individual heading his vast list of historical figures is Helen Cornaro, who, as a member of "one of the most illustrious families of Venice," refused all offers of marriage and preferred to cultivate a "universal knowledge and erudition," and died a celebrated public figure.[166] Evelyn, of course, mentions Katherine Philips and Princess Elizabeth of Bohemia.[167]

Evelyn believes that the meaning and eloquence of such portraits derive exclusively from an implicit or explicit context—manufactured from received knowledge or embedded in the image—which explicates their moral and cultural significance. That is, the portrait's significance lies less in its status as a fragment, a piece of isolated historical lumber cast up on the shores of the modern consciousness, than as a synecdoche, a concreted and objectified sign of a history whose movements and motives remain largely unreified and whose true process remains largely inaccessible. Moreover, because writing and inscriptions compose another, larger body of the actual history we inherit, no single historical image more perfectly encapsulates, embodies, and condenses historical significance than the medal, whose emblematic constitution fuses the pictorial and linguistic. Writing under the shadow of Ezekiel Spanheim's revolutionary contributions to numismatics, Evelyn treats the medal as a plastic example of the wider hermeneutical problems attendant on history, for which the Cotton manuscripts also serve as a figure.[168] But medals, though distinct, are also obviously associated with coins—they share a common origin at the mint—and in 1696 Evelyn links their peculiar weight as cultural currency (with its attendant metaphors of circulation and potential inflation) to the current debate on the coinage.[169] By implication, Evelyn's activity of "gathering up all. . . . Medals as I could anywhere find had been struck before and since the Conquest . . . relating to any part of good history"[170] seeks at a cultural level to resist the decline of value in "this mercantile nation" by "clipping, debasing, and all other unrighteous ways of perverting the species."[171]

Medals, then, bear a special cultural burden, because "we are not only informed whose real image and superscription they bear, but have discovered to us, in their reverses, what heroical exploits they performed; their famous temples, basilicae, thermae, amphitheatres, aquaducts, circuses, naumachias, bridges, triumphal arches, columns, historical and other pompous structures and erections."[172] Like the Epicurean icon, the medal provides a peculiar arena for the play of instructive images and discourses, which resists the entropy of history.

Evelyn's own strategy of resistance and gathering is captured in his last major publication, the *Numismata* (1697). Like the museum, the library, and the cabinet, the book now establishes a space for the selection, concentration, and ordering of cultural artifacts (p. 176). And curiously, like the medals that the facticity of the book imitates, the book is itself—as Evelyn is painfully conscious—subject to a process of clipping and debasing. What created in Evelyn the most intense anxiety during the publication of his *Essay on Lucretius* and equally his *Numismata* (almost exactly forty years later) are the errors created for posterity by his printer's negligence. Sir Geoffrey Keynes writes that the publication of *Numismata* "brought no satisfaction to its author, for he was deeply mortified to find that, in spite of the trouble he had taken, it was full of errors and misprints."[173] By the intervention of Richard Bentley and Benjamin Tooke, Evelyn was dissuaded from inveighing against these errors in his preface, and he compiled instead "an immense list of *Emendata*."[174]

Evelyn's response is less explicable as an obsession with tidiness or accuracy as such than as a response to his own aesthetic of cultural imagery. So, again in that historic letter to Pepys, he advises Pepys that because oil paintings are expensive, clumsy, and sporadic vehicles of historical knowledge, a cheaper and more useful device would be to convert his library into a kind of cultural gallery, where, like medals, books enclose the pictorial and verbal. Evelyn advises Pepys "to add to your title-pages, in a distinct volume, the heads and effigies of such [historical figures] as I have enumerated, and of as many others as either this or any other age have been famous for arms and arts, in *taille douce*, and with very tolerable expense to be procured amongst the print-sellers."[175] As William Rand recognizes in his translation of Gassendi's life of Peiresc, it is finally in the book itself that the life, the image of the life, can be textualized and—like Epicurus's *suggrammata*, Gassendi's biography of Nicolas-Claude Fabride Peiresc, Bougerel's biography of Gassendi, and Evelyn's own children—can become a kind of statue "living and speaking" to posterity. Similarly, just as Sir William Temple imagines the inhabitants of his ideal Epicurean garden contemplating, within its space, the statues that punctuate it, so Evelyn imagines Pepys standing within the virtuoso's cabinet, turning to his books to contemplate "the effigies of those who have made such a noise and bustle in the world, either by their madness and folly, or a more conspicuous figure by their wit and learning."[176]

If we began the story of neo-Epicureanism by meditating on the relationship between Epicurus's physics, cognitive mechanism, and his own contingent and mediated view of the propagation of the self in the *suggrammata*, Evelyn now imagines an entire culture, which those series of imaginative relations define. Like the woman in Le Clerc's *Ars Critica*, Pepys is finally handed to us as an image of the neoclassical reader contemplating the necessarily phenomenal, though atomized, remains of a history he must strenuously and methodically reassemble.

PART 3

Activating the Word: Linguistics, Theology, and Literary Criticism

6. "Somaticall Science": Neoclassical Linguistics, Action, and Writing

Is it credible that the polite and learned orators and historians of Greece and Rome should, out of choice, use a method [FIGURATIVE EXPRESSION] to perfect their eloquence, which the first rude and barbarous nation employed out of necessity, and which rude and barbarous nations shall employ, for want of intellectual ideas, and more abstract terms?

William Warburton, *The Divine Legation of Moses Demonstrated* (1738–41)

Let us imagine a picture story in schematic pictures, and thus more like the narrative in a language than a series of realistic pictures. Using such a picture-language we might in particular e.g. keep our hold on the course of battles. (Language game.) And a sentence of our word-language approximates to a picture in this picture language much more closely than we think.

Ludwig Wittgenstein, *Zettel* #241

Introduction

The last chapter closed with the image of Pepys surrounded by his books, which, like the coins and medals of Evelyn's *Numismata,* serve as the inscribed, exemplary tokens for a new cultural economy, just as Rand designs Evelyn's children as "statues" to posterity. I have hitherto been arguing that, within the neo-Epicurean scheme, the monumental power of books and medals perpetuates an influential reading of human cognition, in which all knowledge is cognitively mediated. And at the same time, the discrete, atomic value of such icons also serves a model of cultural circulation, in which the flow of continuously reminted artifacts promotes an ideal of exchange, to nurture and strengthen the body politic.

We now turn from Evelyn's specifically neo-Epicurean vision of cultural transmission and expansion to a series of texts published between the 1640s and 1730s, which we may loosely describe as 'linguistic.' I shall not rehearse the period's engagement in language schemes and language reform, because what interests me about, for example, Wilkins's famous *Essay toward a Real Character, and a Philosophical Language* (1668) is less its impossible claim to create a new language *ex nihilo* than the degree to which it echoes a wider nexus of attitudes composing a distinct philosophy of mind, language, and society.[1] Inasmuch as neoclassical linguistics is prescriptive, it attempts (like neo-Epicureanism) to force home the institutional and ethical consequences of a behavioral theory of language in which theories of action, of words, and of writing are mutually reinforcing.

I do not believe that we witness a sudden Foucaultian shift in linguistic attitudes in the 1670s or at the turn of the eighteenth century.[2] Rather, I would argue that the changes having the greatest importance for literary representation had already occurred between 1640 and 1660, and, however strange we may find Wilkins's *Essay,* it is by no means as secure about its ideal of linguistic reference as Jonathan Swift thought or as Wilkins's modern critics have often assumed. Nor am I persuaded by the view that we have a seventeenth-century tradition of Aristotelian taxonomic essentialism, which is only revised late in the century by a nominalism represented best by Locke.[3] For the Joseph Webster–Seth Ward debate of 1654, when Hartlib also published *The True and Readie Way to Learne the Latine Tongue,* already reflects an epistemological shift, which conscripts print culture as an instrument of a sceptical, empirical view of knowledge, in which the natures of things are at best only indirectly available to the human mind.

Similarly, I fail to detect any clear distinction between a view of grammar that, during the Restoration, focuses on the semantic, nominal elements of language, and only later in the eighteenth century emphasizes its syntactic nature.[4] Because the Lucretian analogy between physical atoms and linguistic letters is so pervasive, we see no simple shift from signs to propositions, for to imagine the elements of language as letters motivates a corresponding need to underscore its linear (if logically and temporally subsequent) form: we must consider letters, then syllables, then words, and, by extension, phrases and entire utterances.[5] Language is not composed of nouns alone, but of a system of links, which qualifies and articulates them. And language is thus encouraged to assume—even in the 1650s—its own narrative integrity, which provides one reason why the appeal to Aesopic fable occurs frequently in discussions of the child's grasp of language-as-we-have-it.[6] The neoclassical interest in bodily gesture and the pictorial hieroglyph unites an interest in the particulate and particular grounds of knowledge with the search for a means to describe language's entire form. Thus, however revolutionary Lockean linguistics may appear, they distill attitudes that were already in formation well before 1671, the date of the earliest draft of Locke's *Essay*. For example, Locke's journals and notebooks are full of references to George Dalgarno's linguistic treatises. From John Bulwer's deliberations on the deaf and dumb in the 1640s, to Warburton's massive study of Egyptian hieroglyphs in *The Divine Legation of Moses Demonstrated* (1738–41), we discover an enduring fascination with the grounds of human cognition, hence of language, and a growing belief that those grounds must be imagined in terms of spatial or somatic metaphors, whose visualism seeks to reinforce the primacy of written or printed over aural media.

Part of the ambiguous effect of Wilkins's *Essay* occurs because, though the work attempts to resist the mediations of ordinary language in favor of some referential transparency, its intricate mechanism can only be revealed in the pages of an elaborate, printed document, which effectively celebrates its graphic status by detailed systems of tables, diagrams, and at least three large fold-out pages. Half a century later, Daniel Defoe displays a certain anxiety about a great mercantile people such as the Phoenicians ("a kind of universal Merchants"), who "knew nothing of Letters." And, he adds, "their Money"—unlike Evelyn's coins and medals—"had no Inscription upon it, but consisted chiefly of Rings of Copper, and Brass, and Iron, with only a Stamp of an old Tower or Castle."[7] The Phoenicians' lumpish form of coinage signifies a sterility at the heart of their cultural as well as their mercantile economy, and thus it acts as a parable of Defoe's chief thesis that healthy civilizations require the services of alphabetic writing.

Hans Aarsleff, for one, has repeatedly insisted that we treat the neoclassical fascination with the origins of language not as some naïve historical view of how languages actually developed, but as a device by which to disclose the underlying rules of ordinary language.[8] The imaginative scenes in which language is either thought to originate or to realize its most 'natural' form reveal a subtle marriage of apparently distinct theories of physical action and reading and writing. The link is made possible by a double assumption—first, that all human knowledge is mediated and somatic, conveyed by bodily gestures or some process metaphorically akin to them. It follows that there are at least two concepts of a universal language—one, like Descartes's famous proposal to

Mersenne, a universal language, which corresponds to the arrangement of the elements of thought;[9] and another, in which our animal, physical nature might provide the context for a physiognomic science.[10]

The second assumption is that the sceptical terms that encourage this view of knowledge as embodied or mediated also require its perpetuation by a literate—as opposed to an oral—culture.[11] Precisely because an oral culture might also easily encourage tyrants or sectarians to mystify knowledge for their own purposes, it could allow absolute claims that are subject to no public, visible scrutiny. This is also to realize that the neoclassical scepticism about eloquence does not constitute an outright rejection of rhetoric, because that very scepticism commands a more rigorous commitment to the partial, inferential, and analogical terms that define human knowledge. "Words" cannot simply submit to "things," because language must enact our 'natural' forms of cognition: in abandoning 'metaphor,' we cannot escape the conditions of representation, but we must rather cultivate a synecdochic and metonymic form of figuration, because it is precisely by associative and analogical means that we apprehend the world. The entire argument eventually translates into a highly sophisticated defense of the rhetorical or symbolic nature of human culture as a whole, in which the body—like the hieroglyph—stands at one and the same time for an entirely natural and an entirely cultural sign. As Kenneth Burke says, human beings are "bodies that learn language."

The discussions about hieroglyphs (e.g., were they invented by the Egyptian priesthood in order to preserve knowledge for an élite?), the grand concern with the cultural transmission of knowledge, and the more domestic concern with language teaching, all demonstrate how persistently language theory returns to the question of who controls cultural and textual spaces. Attempts to prove that Moses, not Cadmus, originated Western literacy are really means to link the possession of literate culture to Christian—usually Anglican—institutions. The point is made brilliantly by Augustine, whom many of these language theorists lavishly cite, because his fiction about his childhood acquisition of language by ostension presupposes the instituted authority of the family: it is the power of the adult's gesture that for the child decisively attaches the name to the thing.[12] And a related, operationalist view of knowledge—external, visible operations occurring within clearly defined institutional spaces—informs, for example, Hartlib's, Hooke's, and Petty's ideas of how to teach languages or to propagate philosophical knowledge.[13]

The Visible in Wilkins and Creech

John Wilkins and the "Power of the Vowel"

The Baconian and millennial impulse in Wilkins's *Essay* is finally muddied by its own scepticism. Although Wilkins declares that he wishes to repair the ruins of Babel—that is, to rectify the confusion of languages,[14] it soon becomes obvious that if he can manufacture a lingua franca, it cannot have much to do with the language spoken by Adam. Yet Wilkins, in more or less opening his monumental work by citing the two chief Restoration myths about the origin of language, must elect the biblical account. Nevertheless, it is significant for the subsequent conduct of his argument that he gives more space to the pagan, Lucretian myth, than to its biblical, Adamic counterpart. Wilkins recounts that the ancients believed that

> either *Men* and *Languages* were *eternal;* or, that if there were any particular time when men did spring out of the Earth; and after inhabit alone and dispersedly in Woods and Caves, they had first no Articulate voice, but only such rude sounds as Beasts have; till afterwards particular Families increasing, or several Families joyning together for mutual safety and defence, under Government and Societies, they began by degrees and long practice to consent in certain Articulate sounds, whereby to communicate their thoughts, which in several Countries made several Languages.[15]

By contrast, "to us, who have the revelation of Scripture . . . 'tis evident enough that the first Language was *con-created* with our first Parents, they immediately understanding the voice of God speaking to them in the Garden." Within two pages, the vision of returning to such a pristine form of communication has dissolved, not only because Babel (signaling the Fall) intervenes, but also because Wilkins demonstrates the impossibility of recovering the traces of *"Mother-tongues"* from the present welter of languages and dialects. He also punctures the hope that we can still detect "the agreement of . . . remote Nations in some radical words." Imperial conquest further exaggerates the historical, cultural, and geographical dispersions of languages, utterly erasing all traces of Adam.[16]

Wilkins's answer to the problem is, curiously, to reinstate something of the conceptualist and contractual view in the Lucretian account of language, which he has apparently rejected. Using a terminology also indebted to Aristotle's *De Interpretatione*,[17] Wilkins insists that his new language will refer not transparently to "things," but *things and notions,*[18] showing how he assumes a tripartite structure of any language's relation to the world—namely, "Things, Notions, *and* Words."[19] Wilkins's failure of scepticism lies not in the view that words and things can be seamlessly fused, but that notions more or less act as an exact template for our perceptions of things. Notions naturally substitute for things; words, arbitrarily for notions. A "natural Method" therefore would require "the Enumeration of things and notions, as that they may be full and *adaequate,* without any *Redundancy* or *Deficiency,*" a project Wilkins effectively admits is doomed at the very moment he embarks upon it, because he writes rather lamely that it constitutes his "chief Difficulty and Labour."[20] His "natural Method" thus creates something of an internal tension for Wilkins's project, because it directly conflicts with the probabilistic, comparative, and historical terms on which his argument is predicated, a view of knowledge he was to explicate at length in *Of the Principles and Duties of Natural Religion* (1678), to which John Tillotson added a preface.

Nevertheless, Wilkins clearly remains committed to the view that words can methodically designate discrete elements in the ordinary workings of the human mind.[21] Although at times he seems to treat writing as subordinate to speech ("Writing being the Picture or Image of Speech"[22]), he also converts that subordination into a temporal rather than a structural matter, because he sees that, whether spoken or written, a sign plays the same signifying role in relation to its signified.[23] His attack on linguistic mutability and ambiguity has primarily a political motive, because he distrusts those "great swelling words, whereby some men set up for reputation."[24] What he seeks in their place is not a transparent set of counters (any more than he can dispose of the mediation of "Notions"), but a language that is readily apprehensible. And to be apprehensible, words must be, Wilkins says, *"effable":*[25] the mediations of speaking and writing achieve an equivalent figural status, because they are equally public and thus "legible to men of all Nations and Languages."[26] If words refer, they still do so by symbolic substitution.[27]

Wilkins, of course, insists that his real character must function by arbitrary signs that are distinct, discrete, and methodically arranged.[28] This commitment to the symbolic, representational character of human language is played out specifically in relationship to the sounds that to Wilkins represent the atoms of ordinary language. Although he makes an apparent distinction between language "which is *Customary* and figura-

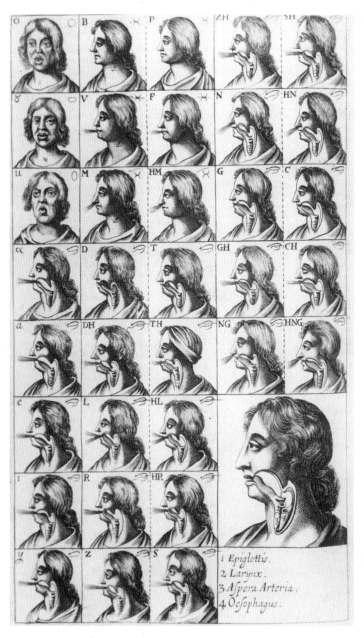

Table from Wilkins's *Essay towards a Real Character* (1668),
showing the physical productions of words by the mouth and head

	1	2	3	4	5	6	7	8	9	10	11	12	13	14	15
1		α	a	e	o	u	y			α	a	e	o	u	y
2															
3	h								H						
4	w								W						
5	y								Y						
6	b								B						
7	p								P						
8	v								V						
9	f								F						
10	d								D						
11	t								T						
12	dh								Đ						
13	th								Th						
14	g								G						
15	c								C						
16	gh								Gh						
17	ch								Ch						
18	z								Z						
19	s								S						
20	zh								Zh						
21	sh								Sh						
22	l								L						
23	hl								hL						
24	r								R						
25	hr								hR						
26	m								M						
27	hm								hM						
28	n								N						
29	hn								hN						
30	ng								Ng						
31	hng								hNg						

Table from Wilkins's *Essay towards a Real Character*,
showing an alphabet corresponding to the somatic production of words

tive" and "that which is *Natural* and regular,"[29] the argument here assumes that the better we account for the natural bases of language, the more carefully we must attend to the inevitable fact of representation. Indeed, what precisely disqualifies Chinese as a philosophical language is an argument repeated well into the eighteenth century: that the tonal nature of the language defies the apparent stability of its graphic signs; what should be effable is instead ineffable.[30]

Wilkins's project, by contrast, is to determine in part what sounds within developed languages represent the palpable cries of passion and desire within the (implicitly) Lucretian scene of origin and then to fix them onto a negotiable, visible, *legible* grid of knowledge by referring them to their somatic, physical origins in the human body, specifically the mouth.[31] Wilkins wants "to give a rational account of all the simple sounds that are, or can be framed by the mouths of men,"[32] by describing "all the kinds of Actions and Configurations which the organs are capable of, in order to Speech."[33] Wilkins is in effect arguing that vocal sounds are ineluctably somatic and thus already legible within the human, embodied economy, and that a graphic system should attempt to represent the configuration of that somatic ground of language. Having decided, therefore, that vowels naturally precede consonants within animal utterance, we should attempt to adapt writing to "the material circumstances" of speech (pp. 189–90):[34] writing should correspond to the "shape" of sound, that "shape," or "power," being understood as equivalent to its physiological means of production within and by the organs of speech. Words are what the mouth molds, not what the mind conceives. So whether in his project for a real character or his ruminations on natural grammar, in Wilkins's system the visible synecdochically reproduces the visible, not some luminous source of knowledge beyond or outside what must, for epistemological and political motives, be rendered legible and negotiable, laid open to common agreement.

The Frontispiece of Thomas Creech's Lucretius

The so-called second edition of Creech's famous translation of *De Rerum Natura,* which was first published in 1682, appeared a year later. The book includes a frontispiece (p. 192), which combines the most celebrated arguments of books one and five, concerning the physical constitution of the world by atoms, and the gestural, somatic origins of language, which in turn explain the origins of human civilization. The frontispiece effectively serves to propound the analogy between atoms and letters, because

Frontispiece to the second edition of Creech's translation
of *De Rerum Natura* (1683)

(as we have seen) arguments about the way we know or represent the foundations of matter dovetail with Lucretius's arguments about the visible origins of speech. Significantly, the figure of the poet dominates the page, gesturing with one hand toward the flood of atoms raining down on him, and clutching in the other hand a book, which stands at once for Lucretius's original poem and Creech's translation, upon which the reader is about to embark. The poet's gesture sets in motion a complicated but circular set of relations, which matches the analogical and inferential structure of the atomic hypothesis to the similar structure of literate experience.

The organization of the frontispiece encourages us to notice immediately what comes first in the order of Lucretius's poem—his explanation for the nature of matter. But the visual means by which the argument is pursued seems to suggest both its substance—the fact of atoms as the elementary particles of matter—and the methodological device by which we must argue for their existence and nature—the hypothetical means by which we infer causes from effects. The point comes across partly because of a pun on *casus* (fate, chance) and *causa* (cause): the odd displacement of the sphere in the top right corner of the frame from the attentive poet indicates the way that all causal explanations (even those proposing 'fate' as an explanatory mechanism) are only derived from what we observe—by implication, the *eidōla* created by atoms striking the poet's eye. The strangely flattened quality of the band of atoms raining diagonally from the sphere contrasts curiously with the clumsy though patently more realistic figures mapped onto a three-dimensional landscape, and this quality succeeds in almost setting it apart from, or behind, the rest of the frontispiece. This itself amplifies a visual corollary to the pun on *causa/casus,* because all causal explanations—the postulate of unknowable submicroscopic particles—are only made possible as a condition of our knowledge of gross bodies, as if the abstractions of metaphysics are spatially displaced from our common apprehensions of things.

That our negotiations with gross bodies is the central epistemological issue is suggested by the curious feature at the back of the populated landscape: a human figure in the process of emerging from the earth. Here the natural and artificial finally collapse, because the material terms by which the idea of the human body comes to bear any significance at all within the frame of the frontispiece are precisely determined by the habits of reading both the frontispiece and poem must assume, not to mention our knowledge of what it means to have a visual artifact introducing a literary one and emblematically condensing its arguments. The most visible kinds of representation are the most rhetorical, a corollary implied by the unicorn—not an actual animal, but a fabulous device composed of a juxtaposition of the features of known animal bodies. As Locke shows about our ideas of species even in the real world, we classify differences according to a nominal—hence figural—system using external, contingent observations based on an atomic hypothesis.[35] In Locke's words, "the Boundaries of the *Species* of Things" are synecdochic at best, and thus they are linguistically constituted.[36]

Locke's argument is anticipated by Lucretius's account of language, which the various bodies emerging from the ground in Creech's frontispiece are supposed to recall. Lucretius argues for an entirely physiological account of the origins of language, symbolized both by the human body arising from the earth and the visual imperatives of the frontispiece. Human beings share with the animals the physical capacity to signal desire and fear, such that "As *Infants* now, for want of *words,* devise / *Expressive* signs, [and] speak with Hands and Eyes; / Their *speaking* hand the want of Words supplies."[37] Creech's happy choice of "*Expressive* signs" should again recall the intimate alliance between *exprimere* and *imprimere*—which share a common root that the frontispiece is keen to preserve—because it invokes the terms by which Lucretius's myth of the material origins of language (by an act of embodiment) is itself made material (by the act of printing). To the right flank of the poet, who is clutching his final product, the book, lie the implements of writing. The fiction of expressive origins, only made possible by the poet, are in Creech's translation literally impressed onto the frontispiece and made real by the visual mechanics of publication. As Evelyn is well aware, the frontispiece thus becomes a discrete emblem minted within a literate economy upon which it depends and which it helps to stimulate. We come full circle, because the inferential and analogical mechanisms that yield the hypothesis of atoms and void also determine the contingent activities of the neoclassical reader confronting the title page, a mediated, visual sign, which reenacts Lucretius's own myth of the origins of language.

Webster and Ward: *Vindiciae Rhetoricae*

The most prominent feature of Creech's frontispiece is the figure of the poet, who fills a good third of the frame. His ostensive gesture is an

"*Expressive* sign," which helps to set the semiotic logic of the frontispiece in motion. It also disturbs us by exposing the extent to which the frontispiece's publicly negotiable ideal of representation may seem to liberate the reader by requiring a series of merely probable manipulations, but it nevertheless cannot escape the need for some center of interpretive authority. This is a major issue in the much-discussed Webster-Ward debate of 1654, whose epistemological and pedagogical implications are fully explicated in Hartlib's educational anthology, *The True and Readie Way to Learne the Latine Tongue,* also published in that year.

Only if we attend to the arguments about method (hence language) in Webster's *Academiarum Examen* and Ward's riposte, *Vindiciae Academiarum* (with which Wilkins also helped), can we see that classical interpretations of the debate have tended to reduce it to one of two thematic—as opposed to epistemological—dramas.[38] On the one hand, a progressivist view, epitomized by R. F. Jones, treats Ward's attack on Webster as a triumph of a modern over an archaic attitude toward "science."[39] On the other hand, Charles Webster and Allen Debus have criticized Jones's allegory, arguing that we should understand Webster's enthusiastic gnosticism, indebted to Paracelsus, Boehme, and Fludd, as allied to a pervasive midcentury millenarian motive for the advancement of learning, which bore fruit in Comenius's, Dury's, and Hartlib's educational reforms and led indirectly to the establishment of the Royal Society.[40] Thus Hugh Trevor-Roper talks about the shift from an earlier, more millenarian Baconianism to a later, more utilitarian "vulgar Baconianism," which forgot its millenarian roots and vocabulary.[41]

I would argue, however, that, corrective though these responses to Jones have been, they have obscured the central issues at stake precisely by focussing on a thematic rather than methodological criterion over which Webster and Ward disagree. Ward *does* finally herald a set of attitudes that the Royal Society was centrally to endorse: he displaces the imagination represented by Webster, not (like Jones) by merely mocking Webster's millenarian impulses (though he does do that), but by adopting a series of arguments, which vindicate a rhetorical ideal of human knowledge against Webster's transcendental, mystical form of hieroglyphic knowledge, by which the mind can penetrate, by a gnostic device, into the essences of things. Thus Webster celebrates the true "*Metaphysical,* or supernatural," against the "corporeal or materiate."[42] The argument becomes explicitly political because all parties agree that philosophical and institutional "tyranny" must retreat before some new edu-

cational ideal. Here the disagreement is also conducted squarely on epistemological grounds, because, if Ward and Hartlib only amplify Webster's libertarian rhetoric, they show a common anxiety to ensure that the
kinds of educational freedom they desire occur within visible institutional boundaries. Unlike Webster, neither Ward, Hartlib, nor their suc-
cessors in the Royal Society wish to escape the contingencies of instituted authority. Ward defends Aristotle and the universities primarily
to this end,[43] because Webster's more anarchic desire for a general clearing of intellectual underbrush fails to recognize the need for any educational program to make itself known through the encumbrances of educational institutions. Thus, against "the gang of vulgar Levellers"[44]
represented by an "angry fanatick man,"[45] Ward's commitment to the
universities accompanies a contingent, formal view of knowledge, which
itself suggests the necessity of mediating such knowledge through visible
institutions, which must also include and depend upon the institutions of
printing and foreign correspondence.[46] Like Lucretius's indicative gesture in Creech's frontispiece, Ward's argument seeks to translate the
somatic properties of "pointing & indication" into an educational method, which will make both knowledge and language "effable."[47]

Webster's text is particularly germane to my larger thesis, because it
almost revels in the notion that the ideal of *"English Liberty,"*[48] sought by
all disputants, can only emerge from direct competition among different
epistemological or philosophical postulates. Thus, as in Dryden's epistle
to Charleton, Aristotle stands for the tyranny of "one methode,"[49] which
must be displaced by the profusion of alternatives suggested by *"Pytha-*
goras, Thales, Democritus, Zeno, Plato, Phyrrho, Epicurus, and others."[50]
But Ward brilliantly exposes the methodological contradiction in Webster's polemic by arguing that to invite a comparative reading of cultural
alternatives must necessitate a contingent, probable view of history,
which entirely subverts what he rightly interprets as Webster's epistemological nostalgia for "infallible demonstration."[51] More provokingly,
Webster anoints Descartes[52] and Bacon as joint apostles of this epistemic
gospel, in which "a certain way and infallible rules be found out for the
adeaquation of notions and things, and fitting of genuine *Denominations*
to notions,"[53] against which the syllogistic method is "no infallible Science . . . but . . . probable and conjectural, not . . . firm and certain."[54]
Although Webster uses a vocabulary that appears to anticipate Wilkins's
conceptualism in the *Essay,* and though he recommends a series of research and teaching programs that Ward happily embraces as at least

partly adopted by the universities, his "things" and "notions" do not legislate a series of cognitive mediations (however well calibrated). They are collapsed instead into the self-proclaiming force of God's "Caelestial signatures,"[55] indelibly imprinted on the cosmos[56] and effortlessly revealed by Paracelsus's "Magick, and Cabalistick science."[57]

Against Webster's enthusiasms for Cartesian and Baconian infallibility, Ward explicitly summons Gassendi for a number of related reasons. For all Webster's interest in language schemes and language acquisition, Ward's invocation to Gassendi crystallizes, for our purposes, the central issue in the debate—namely, the relationship between a literate culture and human institutions. Thus, Ward most obviously argues that Webster cannot with any theoretical consistency rely on the comforts of Cartesian certainties while depending on Gassendi's *Exercitationes* to attack Aristotle, or consistently unite Fludd's cabalism with Baconian induction.[58]

Ward makes the devastating point by raising the issue of citation and by literally transposing it onto the visible negotiations of the printed page (p. 199). By accusing Webster of inadequately citing his dependence on Gassendi and by graphically revealing his legerdemain, Ward satirizes Webster's central desire to escape the entanglements of institutional authority and deflates the hollow, aural pretensions of Webster's Pythagorean transcendentalism in favor of the inescapably rhetorical force of the printed page. By affording a visual comparison between Gassendi's original text and Webster's derived one, Ward permits the fiction of readerly discretion without pretending to escape his own authoritative action. The implication for Webster's position is clear: it is false, because in its urgency to escape obligations to the past it silently imperializes the past upon which it depends. Like the émigrés in Paris, Ward sees the political and epistemological debate centrally in terms of how the various parties use texts. Again, the comparative, hypothetical method, which Ward sees as central to true science, and which he explicitly associates with Gassendi, serves to embarrass the false jocularity of the Cartesian literary monolith by exposing its urge to absorb other texts. Ward converts his own text into an example of the purely contingent ways to knowledge that a literate culture necessitates, not only by graphically comparing Gassendi's original polemic with Webster's later one but also by engaging in an act of furious parody by which Ward signals the dependence of his own dissenting argument on Webster's attack.[59] Because acts of parody, in Sir Thomas Browne's phrase, are "no

new inventions, but old Fancies reviv'd,"[60] Ward uses a literary device to
reduce Webster's identities to mere equivalences.

Gassendi also assists Ward in exposing another contradiction in
Webster's argument—namely, the attempt to combine the sensory benefits of "ocular experiments" and language teaching by "use and exercise,"[61] with his drive for complete certainty, whose linguistic aim is to
unite "words and matter, names and things."[62] For Ward is irritated that
Webster can exploit Gassendi's authority against Aristotle, yet casually
dispose of Gassendi's epistemological and cognitive attitudes. Although
at one point Webster says that reason follows the senses,[63] at a more
significant juncture of his argument he takes issue with the empirical
view of knowledge, clearly alluding to Gassendi as its prime exponent by
assaulting as "barren and fruitless" the view "that there is nothing in the
Intellect that hath not first some way or other been in the Senses."[64]
Webster rightly recognizes that this view of human cognition is "a weak
means to produce *Scientifical* certitude,"[65] an attitude that Locke was to
transform into a positive cornerstone of his *Essay*.

Like Richard Baxter, then, Webster wants to preserve a special re-
gion of knowledge against the somatists. But, paradoxically, it is precisely
what Webster derides as "corporeal or materiate" that distinguishes him
from Johan Amos Comenius, to whom he appeals,[66] because Comenius's *Orbis Sensualium Pictus* opens (in the 1659 translation by Charles
Hoole) with the announcement that *"there is nothing in the understanding
which was not before in the sense,"*[67] a sentiment that Antoine Arnauld only
three years later (according to James Dickoff and Patricia James) associated with Gassendi's form of empiricism.[68] Ward realizes that when
Webster seeks to preserve the special knowledge offered by the Scriptures
from "the carnal instruments of mans wit and reason,"[69] he believes that
he can in some ingenious way bypass the linguistic medium through
which the Scriptures have historically been communicated. Webster's
version of Baconian millenarianism finally holds that we can dismiss mere
philological approaches to the Scriptures and spiritually commune with
them.[70] Because languages change, we must suppress them in order to
penetrate into a translinguistic sanctum of stable truths.[71]

Ward's defense of the universities amounts to nothing less ambitious
than a critique of the rhetorical, formal, and linguistic terms by which
human culture operates. His attitudes are all of a piece, enunciating a
consistent phenomenalism, which drives home our inescapably inferential and probable dealings with Nature and Language. Hence the pur-

Gaffendis Exercitations *adverfus Ariftoteleos*, befide a little out of *Helmont*, to fpare words I have annexed this Table.

Webfter. Page	*Gaffend.* Page	Here come in the *Defiderata,* Afterwards	
53	53,54,55		
54	56		
55	58,59,60		
56	60	*Webfter.* Page	*Gaffend.* Page
57	62,63	78	141
58	64	79	146,167
59	78	80	167
60	79	81	170, 171,172
61	81,83	82	186
62	84	83	189,195
63	90,92		
64	93		
Webfter. 65 66 67	*Helm.* 46 *& deinceps.*		

You may think Sir I love the man, otherwife *I* fhould not take this paines with him; this concernes his Learning, that which difcovers his ingenuity is,that in the tranfcription of all thefe 18 whole Pages out of *Gaffendus,* he never quotes him . only for a line or two by the by,*pag.* 66. he names him.

Q. But you will wonder why this chafme fhould be betwixt *pag* 67.and *p.*78.and why he could not have given *Ariftotle* his lurry altogether?

Anf. I anfwer becaufe his Tranflator failed him, who fhould have brought it to him altogether.

M*r Webfter* being above,or without all skill in Languages,and deftitute of revelation, was forced to get another to tranflate (he onely attempting at one fmall parcell *pag.*64. *Accedebat ad hæc ingenium viri (Ariftotelis) tectum & callidum &c.* which he conftrues, *there happened to thefe things the clofe wit of the man &c.*though his tranflator ftayes,yet (fenfible in how great need the world ftood of his la-

E 2   bour

Table comparing Gassendi's *Exercitationes* to Webster's unacknowledged uses of it in *Academiarum Examen*. Printed in Ward, *Vindiciae Academiarum* (1654)

pose of educational institutions is to inculcate a respect for contingency; Ward defends the philological approach to the Scriptures against "the mysteries of the *Gnosticks*" and *"Cabalists";* he insists that the universities do encourage cryptography and universal languages; and he vindicates the necessarily hypothetical, speculative grounds of natural philosophy, writing that we are "all employed to salve Mechanically, and statically the Phenomena of nature."[72]

According to the mechanical philosophy that Webster and Ward jointly wish to promote, we must save the phenomena, because, according to its sceptical and inferential premises, second causes are all we have. Again, Ward reveals that Webster resists the consequences of this position for perception and language: Ward propounds a conceptualism based on a strictly methodical analysis and a compounding of "simple notions,"[73] and he mocks Webster's presumption that we can conduct disputes outside the boundaries implied by such *"Notions."*[74] By emphasizing the merely probable terms by which Aristotle's rhetoric and syllogistic operate, Ward can argue that it is Aristotle who symbolizes the hypothetical approach to physics[75] and the "Methodicall" "fitting" of contingent modes of knowledge and expression to the contingencies of "Institutions" rather than the search for "truth or infallibility."[76] Thus Ward prefers Aristotle's "Historicall parts of nature" and "his Rhetorick" to his physics, which "time and observation have manifested to be untrue."[77]

It is this emphasis on the manifest that finally brings Ward closer to the neoclassical reading of perception and language which we have been examining. Ward seems to see that Webster himself provides instances of how human knowledge must function by manifest, formal vehicles— Webster suggests the language of the deaf and dumb as an example of a universal or natural language.[78] But Webster collapses that kind of natural knowledge into a Rosicrucian "language of nature,"[79] which is entirely occult. Ward thus accuses Webster of believing in transubstantiation[80] and dismisses his "Language of Nature" as nothing more than "a Canting Language,"[81] to make the point that Webster can provide no philosophical grounds for preferring his hieroglyphs to what he treats as "dead paper idolls" and "mute statues," which deaden by rendering visible the powers of a Pythagorean, aural, Adamic perception, which communes with the "secret and internal vertues and qualities" of things.[82] For Ward—as for Rand—inscriptions on paper are the occasion of knowledge rather than the death of it, not mere idols or "mute statues," but inescapably formal and phenomenal icons, which act as the contingent instruments by which we negotiate the world.

"Our Virgin Philosophy of Gesture": Somatic Action and Language Theory from Wilkins to Dalgarno

Hartlib's *A True and Ready Way to Learne the Latine Tongue* is largely composed of a series of educational tracts, the longest of which is written by Eilhardus Lubinus, who may have had some influence on Comenius's educational theories. Lubinus argues that the child best learns the rudiments of language by perceiving them in animal forms, because then they appear to the mind almost literally as bodies. The child subsequently learns to understand the linearities of linguistic, and thus historical, experience by being immersed in Aesopic fables. Therefore Lubinus articulates a vision, later reiterated by Petty and Hooke, of the culturally symbolic and constitutive nature of human activities. This Aesopic prejudice is shared by a strange and distinctive series of arguments about bodily language, which takes shape during the 1640s and culminates in the vast tradition of eighteenth-century physiognomy.[83] Contrary to a common assumption, fueled by its author's characteristic failure of modesty, Descartes's *The Passions of the Soul* (1649) is relatively unimportant for the distinctively English tradition of discussing the relationship between the passions and the body, and the possibilities of finding a means to teach the deaf and dumb how to communicate.

Descartes can achieve a certain clarity in his famous discourse partly because he is less willing than English writers to admit his debts to ancient rhetoric.[84] The English texts (many published before 1649) seem to elude modern categories of analysis, because they often want methodically to elaborate the rhetorical notion of *actio* in terms drawn from an emerging physiology and because, at the same time, they wish to preserve Cicero's and Quintilian's scepticism about human behavior and language, which precludes knowledge of mental acts and must consequently parse language in terms of a pathology of bodily action.[85] Earlier texts, such as Bulwer's, also display some epistemological hesitancy when they reflect the oblique movement of Galen's influential *On the Natural Faculties* between an inductive and deductive approach to pathology. If Bulwer, in his somewhat untypical *Anthropomorphosis* (1653) (pp. 202 and 204), seems to propose (through Galen, among others) that the form of the human body expresses the divine order,[86] his sceptical and inferential attitude to bodily signs contrasts markedly with Charles

Frontispiece to Bulwer's *Anthropometamorphosis* (1653)

Le Brun's *Conférence de M. Le Brun sur l'Expression Générale et Particulière* (1698) (p. 204), which not only treats "PHYSIOGNOMY" as a tally of "certain and permanent Signs, which indicate the Passions of the Soul,"[87] but also proposes that we can exactly read human character from a rather mystical analogy with certain animal features, themselves reducible to purely geometrical properties. Le Brun's *Conférence* had some success in the earlier eighteenth century, but it is significant that it seems to have been reborn in the nineteenth century, owing to that century's romantic interest in occult relations between the head and human character.[88]

The title of Bulwer's dual treatise, *Chirologia: Or the Naturall Language of the Hand Composed of the Speaking Motions, and Discovering Gestures thereaf. Whereunto is added Chironomia: Or, the Art of Manuall Rhetoricke* (1644), precisely locates the balance of interest that English writers manifested on gesture from the early 1640s on. Rather than tabulating a set of isonomic relations between a given shape of head or body and a given moral character (as Le Brun did), the primary concerns are, first, to describe the mechanical processes by which the affections of the mind register themselves as bodily motions, and, second, to propose a gestural rhetoric that might introduce the deaf and dumb to social intercourse. Both arguments are also, of course, ways of reimagining the behavior and rules of ordinary language. Thus, though there is talk of the "universall and naturall Language" of gesture, this does not imply that what appears as a natural motion allows more than a hypothetical view of what has caused it, or that individual acts created by momentary impulses can of themselves, without recourse to an artificial and contractual method, construct what we can properly describe as language.

William Holder's *Elements of Speech* (1669) puts the point particularly well.[89] Although writing appears briefly in some secondary, derived relation to speech ("*Language* in *Counterfeit*"[90]), it soon becomes clear that all language, whether spoken or written, is an artificial, contractual fabric of "*Materiall*" signs. Like the elements of speech in Wilkins's *Essay*,[91] spoken letters have some origin in the physiology of the mouth, but this is not the same as language as we know it. Nature yields to Culture: "Now these Letters considered, as to their *Genesis, i.e.* as they are made and fram'd by several *Motions* of the parts of the *Mouth*, are the natural Elements of Speech, but the use of them is *Artificial, viz.* when they are composed, and designed by several Signs of Respective Notions: and hence Languages arise, when by institution and agreement, such a

never ceaſeth nor reſteth, as in many French Men
Silly Phiſiog. and Spaniards, and the like in certaine Germans,
hath been obſerved and noted. For when the forme
of the Head is through rounds then is the middle
Ventricle large, and the Spirits working in the ſame
ſo large, untill theſe finde a large place, which in the
meane time are not ſufficiently united: and in ſuch
wiſe is the vertue Eſtimative weakened, by that the
Spirits are carried round about the bounds of the
ſame; inſomuch that ſuch Men having the like formed Heads are ill reported of for their proper qua-
Albertus   lities and conditions in Phyſiognomie. Albertus
magn.de ſecret Magnus (indeed) commends a round-Head, and
Mulier.   would have Boyes loved that have round Heads, be-
cauſe that is the moſt Noble Figure: Therefore, Nur-
ſes ſaith he are wont to compreſſe and endeavour to
make Boyes Heads round, which hence ſeems to have
Spigel de   been accuſtomed either in Padua or Ratisbone.
Hum.Corp.
Fabr.lib.1.   The Muſcovites,
who are for the
moſt part of a
ſquare proportion,
broad, ſhort and
thick, have broad
Heads, which is in
Faſhion with them
at this Day. And
when they are
young Infants,and in
their tender Age apt
to be drawn and
bent to any ſhape,
their Faces are explained and flatted by Art, and
ſo

ſo directed to grow into this Gentilitian forme.
The Apichiquis Pichunſli, Sara, People of Purchas Pilgr.
the Indies, affect the ſame mad Gallantry of a 4.lib 7.
broad Head and platter Face; to bring their
Children to which Affected deformity, they
lay one board on the Forehead and another on
the Neck, ſo keeping them in preſs from Day to
Day untill they be foure or five Yeares old.

     The Women of
Cumana affect a ve-
ry long Head and
Face, as accoun-
ting it the moſt
comely and Beau-
tifull Figure of the
Head.A long Face
and thin Cheekes
being their chiefe
Beauty. To attain
unto which deſi-
red Deformity,
they gently com-
preſſe the Heads of their Infants between two little Pillowes to extend them. Such contradictions there is in the Phantaſies and opinions of
Men and claſhings in point of Elegancy in the
Figure of the Head, that we may well cry out
with Pliny, that there is no thing ſo vaine and ſo Plin.Nat.Hiſt.
Proud as Man.

                         In

Page from Bulwer's *Anthropometamorphosis*, comparing different
cultural uses of the body

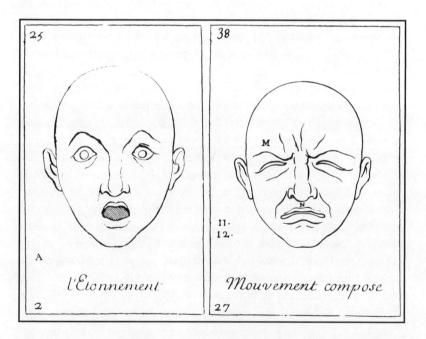

Plates from Le Brun's *Conférence . . . sur l'Expression Générale et Particulière* (1698),
showing how signs of complex emotions derive from simple ones

composure of Letters, *i.e.* such a Word is intended to signifie such a certain thing."92

Because the mechanism must presume a series of displacements from a merely hypothetical point of origin, it does not encourage a naïve theory of reference: language is made from what we inherit. The oral habitually loses precedence to the written, printed, the manufactured, because the gestural myth inevitably favors the materiality of the visual over the immateriality of the aural. Thus (possibly echoing Wilkins again) Holder devotes the bulk of his essay to describing the *"variety of Motions* and *Figures,* made by the Organs, which serve for Articulation,"93 partly in order to transfer the possession of language to "Persons Deaf and Dumb."94

Although perhaps to say so is to invite a false teleology, it is striking how the argument gains in clarity and coherence between Wilkins's *Mercury* (1641) and Dalgarno's *Didascalocophus* (1680). Whether spoken or written, language exists "as a thing very materiall in commerce,"95 a collection of numismatic counters circulating within a larger cultural space, "Expressions being currant for conceits," as Wilkins puts it, "as money is for valuations."96 The individual and privately motivated 'natural' actions of the body only discover their significance within a wider context of socially constituted activities.

Wilkins's Mercury: *The Assault on Secrecy*

> . . . *your diviner hieroglyphics tell,*
> *How we may landskips read, and pictures spell.*
> *You teach how clouds inform, how smokes advise;*
> *Thus saints with incense talk to deities,*
> *Then by dumb creatures we instructed are,*
> *As the wise men were tutor'd by a star.*

Richard West, "To His Honoured Friend J. W. On His Learned Tract. The Secret and, Swift Messenger"

Although it announces itself as a discourse on secret communication, Wilkins's *Mercury* (p. 206) explodes rather than preserves the boundaries of secret knowledge. Its activity begins with the mythological gesture of translating Hermes into Mercury, which domesticates by Latinizing and implicitly displacing the more oriental and mystical associations of Hermeticism.97 Because the Romans, more explicitly than the Greeks, attached Mercury to matters of commerce, Wilkins also subtly encourages a public notion of linguistic trade: we have seen how *Mercury*

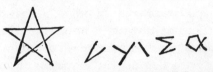

This marke was esteemed so sacred amongst the Ancients, that *Antiochus Soter*, a perpetuall conquerour, did always instamp it upon his Coine, and inscribe it on his Ensignes; unto which he did pretend to be admonished in a dream, by an apparition of *Alexander* the great. And there are many superstitious women in these times, who beleeve [this to bee so lucky a character, that they alwayes worke it upon the swadling clothes of their young children, thinking thereby to make them more healthful and prosperous in their lives. Unto this kind also, some referre the characters that are used in Magick which are mayntained to have, not only a secret signification, but likewise a naturall efficacie.

This short-hand writing, is now so ordinary in practice (it being usuall for any common Mechanick both to write and

Page from Wilkins's *Mercury* (1641), which graphically explodes the mysterious pentagram

indulges the metaphor of coinage.[98] Entirely conscious of his own mythological move, Wilkins recalls that Mercury was both a deceiver[99] and an inventor of alphabetic writing,[100] in order to show that, as communicative creatures, we can escape neither language nor its capacity for deceit and violence.[101] As the figure of Mercury in the frontispiece of Le Clerc's *Ars Critica* shows, nor can we escape our hermeneutical situation, for there he stands as the figure for interpreting a bookish culture, and one also engaged with interpreting the past. Only angels have unmediated knowledge,[102] but human beings, because they have "Organicall bodys . . . have need of some corporeall instruments, both for the *receiving* and *conveying* of knowledge."[103] The plastic quality of Wilkins's numerous charts and diagrams, as well as the graphic versions of a primitive Morse code and so on that fill the pages of *Mercury,* simply underscores our corporeality and its implications within a specifically literate culture. 'Secrecy' becomes a matter of how the instruments of a material and literate culture are used, rather than an intrinsic quality.

Wilkins is not, however, sentimental about this epistemological necessity. Admittedly, he does briefly speak of writing as a 'confinement' of "those different sounds of voyce . . . within the bounds of those few letters in the Alphabet,"[104] and he recalls the "troubles and contention . . . the art of writing" has caused (adding that "the Inventor of it, is fabled to have sowne Serpents teeth"),[105] but it is clear that such fictions create no nostalgia for him. To interrupt the texture of literacy is tantamount to a vicious act of self-mutilation, an outbreak of barbarism: "And yet is was but a barbarous act of *Thamus,* the Egyptian King, therefore to forbid the learning of letters. We may as well cut out our tongues, because that member is a world of wickedness."[106]

Wilkins also unhesitatingly confronts the kinds of power and violence that circulate within a literate economy—implicitly, within any human civilization. He thus provides a specific example to illustrate how the preliterate Native Americans "could scarce make themselves beleeve that a paper should speake."[107] An "Indian slave" who is twice sent on a journey with a basket of figs and a letter by his master on both occasions eats some figs en route and, being brought to account, in the first instance curses the paper "as being a false and lying witnesse," and in the second hides the letter under a stone, "assuring himselfe, that if it did not see him eate the figges, it could never tell of him."[108] This structure of power relations in any collision between literate and nonliterate societies is also suggested by Wilkins's description not only of food[109] and birds[110] as the *"materials"*[111] of conveyance but also, in one case, of "Hystiaeus [, who] took occasion to imprint his secret intentions on his servants head."[112]

Wilkins also vindicates the necessities of writing, because his own tract constitutes an attack on superstition and magic—realms of behavior that draw "suspition."[113] Certain kinds of power are prescriptively necessary to preserve the integrity of ordinary language (understood descriptively and as coterminus with writing): Wilkins links the attempt to subvert that integrity to the aural maneuvers represented by "Melancholicke Chymicks," "the *Canting* of beggars," or "the *charms* of Witches, and language of Magitians."[114] These represent false modes of secrecy.[115] Because the aural so subtly confuses our capacity for discrimination, "'Tis probable, [the devil] did invent such horrid and barbarous sounds, that by them, he might more easily delude the weake imaginations of his credulous disciples."[116]

The ontogenetic myth of the origins of language, then, serves Wilkins's motives in at least two related ways. By treating the body as the site of our most primitive articulations, Wilkins can vindicate and exploit the tactile possibilities of a print culture in which language assumes visual, corporal, material form. Its powers are best captured in the twin metaphors of *embodiment* and *inscription* or engraving, such that the visible potential of gestures finds its equivalent in the idea of the emblem, which Wilkins demystifies as a vehicle of knowledge by comparing it to "the stamps of many ancient medalls, the Impresses of Arms, the frontispices of books, &c." and by reducing the noun etymologically: "Emblems, from the Greeke word *[emballesthai]*, interserere, injicere."[117]

Applied to an analysis of the elements of language—individual words or signs—Wilkins's view amounts to a vindication of the inevitably metaphorical (more properly, metonymic) nature of language. And applied to the composite fabric of language, it amounts to a theory of allegory, in which all knowledge assumes exemplary and symbolic force. Thus gestures can signify primal motions of animal expression[118] and can serve to teach children their first words[119] but, when articulated into an entire vocabulary, can also serve to express the symbolic nature of religious and political life—constituting what Wilkins calls "actions of forme."[120]

Individual actions are articulated into complete statements by a process of digital atomism; that is, like letters (the atoms of written language), "the particular wayes of discoursing by gestures, are not to be numbered, as being almost of infinite variety, according as the severall fancies of men shall impose significations, upon all such signes or actions, as are capable of sufficient difference."[121] Notice here, as elsewhere in the discussions of gesture, that the originary, putatively 'natural' elements of motion can only achieve symbolic significance by submitting to an entirely contractual device: we select and combine signs entirely by mutual agreement.[122] Given this artificial, culturally local consequence of his view, Wilkins also wants to ensure the principle of similarity and difference: "sufficient difference" requires individual signs to be distinct, yet comparable. Furthermore, in his analysis of individual signs, such as hieroglyphics, if signs refer 'naturally,' they do so entirely metonymically: "the *Egyptians* were wont to expresse their minds, by the pictures of such creatures, as did beare in them some naturall resemblance to the thing intended. By the shape of a Bee, they represented a king, intimating, that hee should be endowed with Industry, Honey, and a Sting."[123]

The principle of *"Combinatio"*[124]—casting linguistic atoms into sets of relations—informs all of Wilkins's proposals for sending coded messages, and it also highlights the artificiality of universal languages.[125] Applied both to writing and the body as mutually reflective metaphors, this principle introduces a defense of all parabolic, poetic, and rhetorical knowledge. Like the body, knowledge is best realized in graphic, spatial, and pictorial terms,[126] whose closest narrative equivalent is the parable or fable. Like the metaphor or hieroglyph, the parable can create and preserve secrets ("mysterious Fables, underwhich the ancients did veile the secrets of their *Religion* and *Philosophy*"[127]). The parable can sustain knowledge for the few—the Egyptian priests, Christ's disciples—by obscuring it from "common understandings."[128] But, significantly, Wilkins does not seek to dissolve those obscurities in favor of some simpler ideal of linguistic plainness, because he introduces a second notion of secrecy. This time, secrecy is the inevitably rhetorical effect of any linguistic utterance whose constitution, relative to some transparent referentiality, is obscure and to that extent most fully realizes the phenomenal grounds of human cognition. Thus Wilkins concludes this section of his argument by transforming a hesitant into a more prescriptive approach to the obscurities of fables:

> By this Art, many men are able in their ordinary discourses, so secretly to convey their counsels, or reproofes, that none shall understand them, but those whom they concerne. And this way of teaching hath a great advantage above any other, by reason it hath

Frontispiece to La Chambre, *The Art How to Know Men* (1659; trans. 1665), exemplifying a Continental fascination with physiognomy in the middle of the seventeenth century

much more power in exciting the fancy and affections. Plaine arguments, and morall precepts barely proposed, are more flat in their operation, not so lively and perswasive, as when they steale into a mans assent, under the covert of a parable.

To be expert in this particular is not in every mans power; like Poetrie, it requires such a naturall facultie as cannot be taught. But so farre as it falls under the rules and directions of Art, it belongs to the precepts of *Oratory*.[129]

John Bulwer: Vox Corporis

When Bulwer writes that "the Spirit is Corporeall,"[130] he is not expounding a wholesale materialism, but rather a précis of Wilkins's view that the body is a metaphor for the metaphorical nature of language.[131] In a series of books, *Chirologia . . . [and] Chironomia* (1644) (pp. 212–14), *Philocophus: or, The Deafe and Dumbe Mans Friend* (1648),[132] and *Pathomyotomia, or a Dissection of the Significative Muscles of the Affections of the Minde* (1649), Bulwer, like Charleton a physician, seeks not to tabulate (unlike Le Brun's *Conférence*) the characterological significance of gesture, but a merely inferential "Corporeall Philosophy"[133] or pathology of muscular motion.[134] An entirely contingent method assumes that bodily movements compose an act of accommodation,[135] at best "a kind of semblance and representative proportion, to the *motions* of the mind."[136] The dedicatory poems to *Chirologia* reveal a Baconian hope that Bulwer's revitalization of the art of gesture can repair the ruins of Babel.[137] But even in 1644, Bulwer's vision of such a "universall and naturall Language,"[138] as he calls it later, is fundamentally colored by his epistemological scepticism. His "Praeludium" to *Chironomia* spins a myth in which the Greeks, inhabiting a rarefied climate, "had naturally both motions of the Mind and Body to explaine and unfold their cogitations and recondite senses with an incredible facilitie."[139] But, like Adam's vision of Eve's "words and actions" in *Paradise Lost,* a different world has intervened, as if real historical time is not experienced as such linguistic unselfconsciousness. The artifice of Roman oratory, with its "books of Institutions,"[140] serves to displace Aristotelian epistemology, because, whereas the "learned Ancients . . . prove . . . Cosmetique gestures of the *Hand* to be things of great moment, & the very Palme and Crown of Eloquence,"[141] Aristotle mistakenly held that "these Chironomicall Notions [were] things of no great matter."[142] Knowledge now operates in some ironic, rhetorical relation to its putatively

Frontispiece to Bulwer, *Chirologia* (1644)

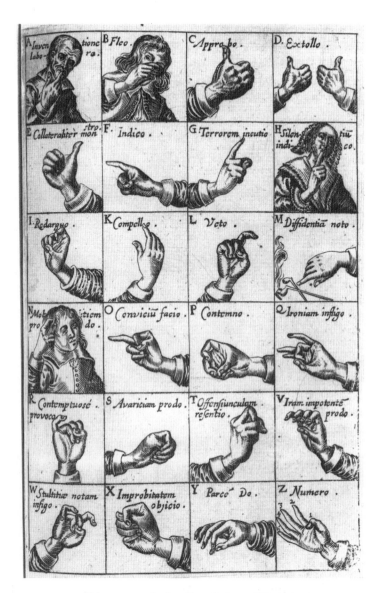

Chirogrammatic plate from Bulwer, *Chirologia*

Frontispiece to Bulwer, *Chironomia* (1644)

'natural' ground: for us, "the actions of the *Hand* are not perfect by Nature."[143]

Bulwer's pathology thus serves to expound what he calls the "mediation of the *Muscles*."[144] Careful to dispel imputations of radical scepticism,[145] his work in the 1640s vindicates the "concrete,"[146] "evident,"[147] "manifest"[148] properties of bodily signs, whose powers, known entirely inferentially, must depend solely on the eye. To some extent, Bulwer's modified scepticism still views the structure of inference as relatively stable. Although he supplies the expected clock metaphor to illustrate it,[149] he treats Sextus Empiricus's classic example of indicative signs with perhaps unwarranted confidence: "smoke which in darke vapours expires from incensed fuell is a certaine signe of fire."[150] Nevertheless, Bulwer still assumes the necessity of evidentiary, essentially probable arguments: it is only by analogy with other minds that we can infer the significance of others' gestures ("by experience judging and approving in themselves those affections that outwardly appeare to worke upon others");[151] greater evidentiary certainty arises when two senses rather than one seek to judge signs.[152] Hence for Bulwer the persuasions of gesture flow from "raising Allegoricall inferences"[153] by providing "ocular assurance."[154]

Bulwer's visualist and evidentiary posture explains how language is both natural and yet rhetorical. Local involuntary gestures supply the most natural signs of occult mental processes; but Bulwer is fully aware that in themselves they cannot approximate ordinary language. Because all knowledge is physically mediated by appearances, even the most primal, instinctual knowledge requires a critique of representation. Language as a recognizable human medium is produced by the voluntary manipulation of "arbitrary motion"[155]—naturally derived signs—and, like Wilkins's digital atomism, which Bulwer echoes in *Chirologia*,[156] their equally voluntary sophistication from simple into compound structures (what Bulwer also calls a "Conjugation of Letters"). Bulwer can accordingly suggest seven pairs of actions that produce "the *generall* discourses of the *Head*."[157]

The rhetorical nature of all human communication is authorized by the ancient rhetorical tradition of *actio*, which Bulwer expands into a peculiar physiognomic interpretation of language. He celebrates the primacy of somatic knowledge with two kinds of arguments. First, a kind of private language argument, which serves again to displace "some zealous Patriots of the *Aristotelian* Philosophy,"[158] holds that because mental actions and intentions must remain entirely impotent without bodily activity,[159] only the human body distinguishes communication as human: "For were the abilities that proceed from *motion* and its instruments, separated from the Body, without doubt man would almost cease to be man, and would degenerate into a Plant or Stock."[160] Because motion is our necessary means to knowledge, fictions of pure being, of essence, must yield to forms of action.

Second, because knowledge and language are inevitably formal, the imagery of gesture more fully satisfies the tastes of the mental palate than mere sound. Bulwer proposes that if the rhetorician were deprived of all but a single means of expression, he should invariably choose *actio*. Words are not pure sound, but rather the issue of the *"Appulsive Motions"* of "the bodies of the Tongue, Lips, and Teeth";[161] and in consequence "all Histories abound with the exploits of the *Hand* which hath performed and brought to passe more things by a significant silence, then the Tongue hath ever done by an audible demonstration."[162] "Hence, the ingenious are forced to confesse that all things are more expressive in the *Hand,* as that which doth garnish the sense of words, and gives the shape, figure, and winning glory unto eloquence."[163]

The frontispiece of *Philocophus* (p. 217) clearly implies that the nature of motion requires a visual rather than an aural epistemology, which the very existence of the frontispiece emphasizes. The metamorphosis of sound (the viola da gamba at the front left) into sight (the miniature on the table at the front right) occurs under the rubric *"ad motum labiorum."* The corporeality of all language, whether spoken or written, is conveyed by a double effect. First, the physical nature of music—vibrations made by a combination of horsehair, strings, and wood—allows the central, kneeling figure to apprehend its effects by applying his mouth directly to the instrument—significantly, the carved ear at the top of the neck. Body communicates only to body. Parodying an aural fiction for language, the mouth here receives knowledge from the ear, not vice versa. The figure in the middle effectively executes the prerogatives of translation that are reinforced by his mediating gestures: he mediates between one vocabulary and another, so the language of the musician can be read into the more universal language of vision, represented by the seated figure at the right. Second, the visual conventions of reading, which presuppose print technology, require the simple movement from left to right—scanning both the emblem and its verbal tag—to make real the transformation from sound to sight.[164] Of course, the very direction of Western habits of reading (from left to right) also shows how the priority of the aural is a

Frontispiece to Bulwer, *Philocophus* (1648)

kind of hypothesis imaginable only within a scene constituted by visual presuppositions.

Bulwer evidently intends his linguistic discussions as a commentary on the turbulent times in which he writes. Broadly, he anticipates the irenist tone of neoclassical arguments for contingency, both by stressing the voluntarist potential of his cognitive theories and by treating the theoretical primacy of somatic knowledge as a means to displace the urgencies of rebellion and tyranny. Because items of knowledge are formal, visual, and contingent, and because the mind uniquely possesses inferential mechanisms, the manipulations of knowledge must follow *"the Command of* [the] *Will."*[165] This is a consistent theme of *Pathomyotomia* in particular. The mechanisms of *"intelective cognition,"* which are distinguished from the unreflexive processes of animal cognition, free the mind from the dictates of pure impulse, the prompting of every exterior force that affects it.

Bulwer's voluntarist rhetoric does not support a simple libertarian position, because he assumes the necessity of rule: the head must rule the bodily "Oeconomy [, which is] as 'twere a City govern'd by good Laws."[166] An ideal balance between liberty and rule emerges in *Chironomia,* in which a series of tableaux shows that if we take its universal somatic grounds to signal the essential constitution of language as such, language will always elude the attempt to monopolize it, whether for the purposes of sedition or tyranny. The "secret property"[167] of gesture appeals so widely and deeply that Bulwer writes that it could quell popular rebellion, though Bulwer is more interested in its power to resist. Indeed, the origin of pantomime or the art of the *chironomons* is symptomatic and anticipates another moment, in which "the malice of *Antonie* forced teares and lamentations into the eyes of the Romans, when they saw *Cicero*'s Right Hand, the instrument of his divine Eloquence . . . nail'd fast unto his head, and set upon the *Rostrum*."[168] We learn that

> the scene of this Art (as is thought) lay first in Syracusa, and [it is further thought] that these *Chironomicall* expressions sprang from the immane cruelty of Hieron, the Tyrant of that City, who among other his barbarous edicts, prohibited the Syracusians all commerce of speech, and the vocall liberty of communication, commanding them to call for their necessaries by nods and significant motions of their *Hands,* eye, and feete, which [prohibition] soone necessitated them to fall into these dancing conferences and declarations of their mindes.[169]

Senault, Charleton, and the Scene of Passions

Bulwer frequently draws on a theatrical metaphor to show how knowledge is embodied and dynamic. The theatrical trope emphasizes the externalism of all cultural symbology: for example, Bulwer remembers the elder Cato's question "whether *Cicero* could write better then Roscius could speake and act; or Roscius speake and act better then Cicero write." This is not an attack on writing as such, but rather a vindication of the phenomenalism of all language: thus the "Pantomimicall *Roscius . . .* could vary a thing more by gestures then either *Tully* could by phrase."[170] Bulwer translates this external vocabulary into his view of the cognitive process, of which the gestural terms of public knowledge are a representational corollary. He discovers "two Amphitheaters . . . in the Body, whereon most . . . patheticall subtilties are exhibited by Nature, in way of *discovery* or *impression . . .* or the voluntary motions of the Minde."[171]

Whether or not Charleton read Bulwer (whose *Chirologia* is quite rare), the theatrical metaphor of the mind serves similarly to expound the inevitably figural, dynamic, and bipartite nature of the cognitive process, in which the passions themselves become peculiarly reified actors within the individual mind. As with Locke, an essentially private process is paradoxically reimagined as if it occurs in public. Charleton—writing twenty-five years after Descartes's *The Passions of the Soul* (1649)—draws deliberately on Jean-François Senault's *De L'Usage des Passions* (1641), which Henry, Earl of Monmouth, had just translated in 1671 as *The Use of Passions* (p. 220).[172] Senault's reputation as a model of Christian humility and as one of France's great preachers and rhetoricians[173] provides Charleton with a precedent to displace Descartes's account of the passions and to embark on a neo-Epicurean expansion of Senault's safely orthodox cognitive theories.

Senault's aim is to vindicate the corporeal condition of human experience, into which the passions are finely woven. Launching an attack on the pride of the Stoics, who deny the body,[174] Senault fervently embraces the divine sanction on our incarnation. Both Adam[175] and Christ[176] experienced passions, and to minimize Christ's sensory and passionate experience is utterly to vitiate the power of his vicarious suffering:[177] "If it be permitted to suffer the tears of the Son of God to pass for illusions, one may make his sorrow pass for Imposturism, and under the pretence of reverency a man may overthrow the ground-work of our souls welfare."[178]

Because Adam's and Jesus' virtue arose not from the denial of the

The VSE of PASSIONS
Written in French by
J. F. Senault.
And
put into English
by
Henry Earle of
Monmouth.
1671.

Divine Grace
Reason
Joy
Feare
Despaire
Sorrow
Choller
Hope
Boldnesse
Love
Eschewing
Hatred
Desire

Passions araing'd by Reason here you see,
As shee's Advis'd therein by Grace Divine:
But this, (yow'll say)'s but in Effigie!
Peruse this Booke, and you in ev'ry line
Thereof will finde this truth so prov'd, that yow
Must Reason contradict, or grant it True.

M.sculp:

Frontispiece to Henry, Earl of Monmouth's translation of Senault's
The Use of Passions (1671)

body, but from regulating and directing the passions,[179] Senault lays down a corporal theory of cognition, which can display the proper balance between raw animal sensation and the mind's capacities to combine, abstract, and direct what it receives. Senault's central principle maintains that God authorizes even his fallen creation, because "he [is] shed abroad in all the parts thereof; there is no *intermedium* which he fills not up."[180] The soul is similarly "disposed in the body,"[181] such that our knowledge, however partial, is both sensory and purposive: Senault can then write that "*Sin* is the *Theatre* of [Christ's] *Power*."[182] Senault's scepticism about the truth value of sensations necessitates a fideistic view of "the truths which Religion proposeth unto us [, which] are of so high a nature as our understanding cannot comprehend them."[183] But apart from that point at which we must accept in faith what is revealed, we are implicated in a world of sensation: "To part the Soul from the Body, so to exempt it from [passionate] agitations, were to overthrow the Fabrick of man."[184] We inhabit a realm of imagination and desire, which the Christian somatist must direct by an exercise of judgment and will. Senault effectively contrasts an ontological to a hermeneutical approach to the mind's activities, assigning three functions to "the Soul, whose power is limited, [and] cannot operate without dependance upon the Organs."[185] Senault treats the first function cursorily, because it involves the consciousness of pure being, in which the soul approaches "near the Dignity of Angels."[186] The second and third functions adumbrate the Lockean distinction between sensation and reflection, define the sensory and dynamic nature of our temporal existence, and amount to a defense of the representational character of cognition. In her second "estate," the soul "becomes sensible, and begins to have inclinations and notions, she uses Objects by the Sense which their reports make unto the Imagination, this trusts them or commits them to memory, which obligeth her self carefully to keep them, and faithfully to represent them."[187]

Passions are "differing motions" drawn by the mind's desire of, or aversion to, the images of sensation; in this, human beings are like "the Beasts, which discover Objects by Sense, which receive the sorts thereof in their Imagination, and preserve them in their Memory."[188] The soul's third estate describes that condition in which she becomes self-conscious and, in obedience to her divine origin, begins to examine, judge, and abstract from the raw objects of sense—a conjectural process that confirms our historical and contingent state.[189] That the "Understanding" presides over the "Imagination" encourages Senault to extend the forensic possibilities of his nakedly spatial metaphor. The imagination and the passions compose a citizenry, which enjoys a certain "Liberty" before the understanding, which acts as a "Judge [rather] than their Soveraign."[190] The forensic purpose of the understanding presumes that, like the figures in the frontispiece to *The Use of Passions,* and like the imagination to which they are bound, they retain a certain atomic and objectified weight. Within the courtroom drama of the mind, the understanding must discriminate among the passions, here not entirely successfully: "These Passions arising from the Senses side alwaies with them; whenever Imagination presents them to the Understanding, he pleads on their behalf, by means of so good an Advocate they corrupt their Master, and win all their Causes. The Understanding listens unto them, weigheth their Reasons, considereth their Inclinations, and lest he may grieve them, oft-times gives Sentence to their Advantage."[191] Whether Senault intends the effect or not, the palpable motions of personified affections within his own language curiously enact his own argument for the palpable motions of passion within the theater of the mind. As so often during this period, the reader's experience graphically confirms a distinctive matrix of cognitive attitudes.

Charleton is even more comfortable than Senault with the moral consequences of his theory of the passions. Charleton's *Natural History of the Passions* is markedly less devotional than its predecessor, more grounded in the pure mechanisms of cognition.[192] It is also more clearly advertised as a hypothetical exercise in the operations of the soul— ignorant of its "mysterious Essence," we only infer its mechanisms by its *"Operations."*[193] Charleton's main motive is to unify his hypotheticalism as regards physical knowledge with an account of cognition, which equally guarantees the necessity of mediation.[194] Possibly taking a cue from Senault's anti-Stoic polemic, Charleton finds Descartes's relation between spiritual and corporal knowledge insufficient because he treats body and soul as two single, indivisible properties, whose being is utterly unlike,[195] while he hypothesizes that they cooperate in the pineal gland.[196] Charleton emphasizes his debts to a number of thinkers, including Descartes,[197] but he accuses Descartes in particular both of bad anatomy[198] and of an unsatisfactory theory of translation or mediation: "*Des Cartes* left it still unconceivable, how an Immaterial Agent, not infinite, comes to move by impuls a solid body, without the mediation of a third thing that is less disparil or disproportionate to both."[199]

It is perhaps true to say that perhaps Charleton's main purpose is to supply what he finds missing in Descartes. Charleton thus needs to account for two features of our mental life. Recalling the Pauline experience of *"[psuchomachia]*, or *civil war,"*[200] Charleton divides the soul into two principles, which roughly correspond to Senault's second and third estates. "What then," Charleton asks, "can remain to cause this dire war daily observed within us, betwixt the allurements of our *Sense*, on one side, and the grave dictates of our *Mind*, on the other; but two distinct Agents, the *Rational* Soul and the *Sensitive*, coexistent within us, and hotly contending about the conduct of our Will?"[201]

This principle of two souls provides a two-edged weapon. It maintains that the act of unifying the soul as a single, indivisible entity (whether in Aristotle[202] or Descartes) may appear philosophically or aesthetically attractive, but it flies in the face of universal experience. But, more significantly, the principle allows Charleton to elaborate a theory by which the spiritual can be accommodated to the material and can account simultaneously for human sensation and our capacity to create abstractions and universals. Clearly, "the *immortal Gassendus*"[203] and "our *Oracle, Epicurus*"[204] preside over Charleton's suggestion that we should imagine the "Corporeal Soul" as "composed of particles extremely small, subtil, and active,"[205] like fire.[206] Like the figure mediating between sound and sight in Bulwer's frontispiece to *Philocophus*, Charleton's corporal or sensitive soul translates knowledge between our material, animal experience and our rational and spiritual capacities.[207] This soul is plastic and divisible, and thus it is responsible to the multiplicity of sensations; it is a fine medium and thus can translate the activity of raw sensation to the rational soul and vice versa.[208] The rational soul is "a substance purely spiritual,"[209] and to have commerce with the body appeals to "the *Sensitive* Soul, conjoyned with her, to be a convenient *Medium* betwixt herself and the gross body, according to her will and pleasure: that it is, that she should *immediately* move and actuate the body, to receive her immediate influence, and actuate the body, betwixt whose nature and her own there is great disparity."[210]

The mediations of the sensitive soul sustain Charleton's anxiety to ensure the primacy of empirical experience, a "Harmony of *Reason, Sense,* and *Motion*."[211] That the sensitive soul is "closely intertexed with all parts of [the body]; as the warp and woof are interwoven in cloth" depicts the "mutual cohesion" of bodily and sensate life, known primarily as a form of action: like a flame, "the Existence of this Corporeal Soul depends intirely upon the *Act*, or *Life*," of the body.[212] The corporeal soul is marked by its own behavioral symptomology,[213] but it nonetheless disperses the moment the body dies.

Governed by a pleasure-pain principle, "the various *Gestures* of the Soul" compose a series of responses to "*sensible* objects,"[214] which can variously stimulate or react to gross bodily motions and can differ in degrees of violence or energy. One detects some confusion in Charleton's separate analysis of passion and the imagination. But it seems that in themselves, the sensitive soul's "postures" in response to what it desires or fears (with their varying visible effects on the body) compose those elements of passion that Charleton catalogues.[215] Apparently, the same mechanical and corpuscular view of motion also underwrites Charleton's general view of empirical knowledge, which, in modifying motion into a familiar visual and spatial theory of cognition, smacks indelibly of Charleton's neo-Epicureanism. The body's spatial and tactile undulations become the conditions of a knowledge based on images. First, "th'impression made by an external object upon the instrument of sense, doth by impelling the Animal Spirits inwards, and by disposing them into a certain peculiar figure, or mode (as the *Cartesians* speak) cause the act of *Sensation,* or simple *Perception;* and . . . then the same spirits rebounding, as it were by a reflex undulation, outward from the brain into the nerves and muscles, produce *local motions.*"[216] The transactions between this unreflexive experience and the rational soul are made possible by the visual knowledge that the sensitive soul conveys to the rational soul in the form of images, so introducing a distinctly human self-consciousness into an otherwise reductively "*material*" account.[217] Thus, "the *Rational* Soul, as president of all th'inferior faculties, and constantly speculating the impressions, or images represented to her by the Sensitive, as by a mirrour; doth first form to herself conceptions and notions correspondent to their nature, and then proceed to acts of *reason, judgement,* and *will.*"[218] When the rational soul comes to "*know, speculate* and judge of all Phantasms or images,"[219] we transcend the instinctual, "*Innate*" behavior of animals:[220] simple apprehension is animal; intellection is human.[221]

To the possible objection that Charleton's cognitive theory does not belong to a chapter on neoclassical linguistics, the reader should notice that, like other somatists, Charleton almost casually collapses his cognitive theory—perpetrated by various metaphors of space, vision, printing, the speculum—into a linguistic theory. Hence the combinatorial and abstractive powers of the rational soul produce "*Propositions,* by compounding or dividing the simple notions of sensible things," a resoluto-compositive activity anticipated by the sensitive soul, which "when an image of some new object newly admitted, meets with one or more images either formerly stored up in the Memory, or at that instant suggested by natural instinct; and is found associable, or repugnant to them."[222]

The recurring specular metaphor used to depict the self-reflexivity of the rational soul also serves to emphasize how its products—in the form of abstractions and universals—are voluntary and to that extent artificial, though "it is from the *Imagination* alone that she takes all the representation of things, and the fundamental *ideas,* upon which she afterward builds all her Science, all her wisdom."[223] Charleton's hypothesis of the double nature of the soul almost immediately shows itself to be about language in at least two senses: the 'natural' grounds of language are themselves "representations sensible," and language-as-we-have-it is an artificial fabric woven from what our bodies have supplied. It is not surprising, therefore, that Charleton should compose his treatise in re-tirement and discover his materials equally in *"Reading"* and *"Medita-tion,"* because negotiating the printed page is cognitively equivalent to observing "the theatre of my own breast."[224] And Charleton encourages his reader to repeat this exercise in analogy, moving at the end of his *History* "to a more profitable conversation with your own thoughts."[225]

George Dalgarno's "Dumb Eloquence"

Dalgarno's *Didascalocophus: Or, the Deaf and Dumb Mans Tutor* (1680) rehearses the neoclassical effort to conceptualize language as gesture, though with a forcible clarity. His central principle is that "all signs, both vocal, and written, are equally arbitrary, and *ex instituto.*"[226] Conse-quently, Dalgarno may briefly entertain the priority of speech over writ-ing,[227] but speech only serves to confirm the phenomenal circumstances of human knowledge, language, and society.[228] The physicality of sign language and writing (what Dalgarno introduces in his diagram of inter-pretive arts as "Dactylology" and "Grammatology," respectively) thus assumes a central place in Dalgarno's scheme, and not only because he wishes to reassure the deaf and dumb that they also can acquire language.

In his most complicated chapter, *"A Deaf man capable of as Early Instruction in a language as a Blind,"*[229] Dalgarno presents us with scenes of deaf children learning the meanings of words by ostension.[230] This alone should show how he takes it "for granted, That Deaf people are equal, in the faculties of apprehension and memory, not only to the Blind; but even to those that have all their senses."[231] The deaf simply experience, in a specialized state, the visual and corporal conditions of common apprehension. Dalgarno begins his tract by declaring his conceptualist and visualist prejudices: "Tho the Soul of man come into the world, *Tabula Rasa,* yet it is withal, *Tabula Cerata;* capable, thro study and discipline, of having many fair, and goodly images, stampt upon it."[232]

The blind depend for their knowledge of words on their hearing alone, and for their knowledge of bodies on touch. This gives them two distinctive advantages. They can hear the onomatopoeic residue in some words,[233] and they know that "Words" must substitute artificially for "Words," not "for Things,"[234] because they apply entirely disjunctive faculties to the separate realms of language and the world. However, because the deaf and dumb employ their chief faculty of sight uniformly to gross bodies and to language, they may mistakenly assume some natural connection between "words" and "things." But it is in turn precisely that commonality which interests Dalgarno and persuades him that though language is an unequivocally artificial medium, it can, by its bodily and visible manifestations, grow by analogy to symbolize our most fundamental cognitive habits.

Dalgarno interprets cognition as already mediated, persistently as a visual experience conveyed best by the metaphor of printing, and occurring perhaps originally as a series of isolated, atomic encounters with objects, which when accumulated obey the continuities of space and time. For Dalgarno, seeing represents a more stable form of perception than hearing: retaining "the Images of things, by the conveiance of Figures, thro the Eye," the deaf person evinces "a more distinct and perfect perception, of external Objects" than the blind one.[235] This visual stability stimulates a self-reflexive attitude to the accumulated tokens of our knowledge, which, because distinct, allow for studied review and comparison, giving rise to memory and a sense of history. With the blind, the comparative indistinctness and confusion of sounds in speech—no sound standing alone but prone to run into the next— Dalgarno depicts as a solipsistic, circular apprehension incapable of self-reflexivity,[236] or as "the scriblings and blottings on the Table of the Blind mans memory . . . [which] breed confusion."[237] In the clearer atmosphere of the visual world, by contrast, the deaf person's mind is "like clean paper, and therefore takes the impression the more easily, fair and

distinct,"[238] a graphic metaphor, which must treat mental representations as "a constant progressive motion."[239]

Language proves an artificial version of cognitive behavior, which
itself can only be represented as a series of such graphic metaphors. Thus
Dalgarno embraces the "permanency of the Characters"[240] in writing
and printing, because they best approximate the discrete imagistic mechanisms of perception. Whereas the mind manufactures memory and
history from accumulated images, language is likewise (though entirely
artificially) constituted of letters, syllables, words, sentences, whose linear development is best realized in scriptural narrative, "Aesops Fables,
and some playes where there is much of action."[241] Dalgarno can thus
describe his own text as "the following Scene of action."[242] (More particularly, Dalgarno recommends guiding the deaf through this cumulative
process by ostension, pointing out first nouns, then adjectives, then
"verbs of bodily action,"[243] and finally entire narratives, which the
coherence of the teaching gesture already predicts.) Because both cognition and writing (and especially printing) share a visual and corporal
context, the deaf experience certain linguistic and social advantages over
the blind: they can enjoy a true "intercourse of letters,"[244] because
"words laid up in the deaf Boyes memory, are like Characters engraven in
Steel or Marble: the blind boyes words are but chalked out, or, *nigro
carbone Notata,* and therefore easily defaced."[245]

Every dimension of existence ("1. *Supernatural,* 2. *Natural,* 3. *Artificial*") presents a realm of "Interpretation . . . in its largest sense," whether
God communicates by "visions, apparitions, &c."; whether in "Physiology . . . when the internal passions, are expressed by . . . external signs";
or whether human beings invent their own tool, "Sematology; that is, an
Art of impressing the conceits of the mind upon sensible and material
Objects, which have not the least shadow of affinity to the images of the
things they carry imprest upon them."[246]

Dalgarno subdivides sematology into "Pneumatology, Schematology, and Haptology," corresponding to the respective "three senses of
Hearing, Seeing, and Touching."[247] But because "the Soul of Man . . .
[depends] in its operations upon the bodily Organs,"[248] it is already clear
that, as a rhetorical art, pneumatology yields in cognitive importance
to schematology (comprehending "Typology or Grammatology, and
Cheirology or Dactylology") and to haptology, because these latter represent the graphic and somatic vehicles of cognition.

In a distinctive elaboration of the somatic tradition of linguistics,

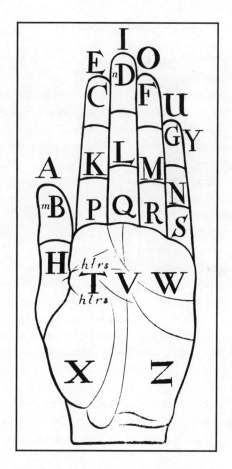

Plate from Dalgarno, *Didascalocophus* (1680),
illustrating the principle of digital atomism

which we have been following, then, Dalgarno moves comfortably from
discussing the art of teaching the deaf to write, and thus introducing
them to narrative consciousness, to a scheme for *"an Alphabet upon the
Fingers"* (see above).[249] Although an entirely artificial linkage between
individual letters of the alphabet and specific points on the hand, there is
a sense in which Dalgarno does 'naturalize' his rhetoric by transcribing it
onto the body, as if to recall the principle that "the Soul of Man . . .
[depends] . . . upon the bodily Organs,"[250] which presumes the instru-
mentality of visual and spatial knowledge.[251] Graphically reproduced in
Dalgarno's text, and mapped onto the hand, Dalgarno's dactylology
makes visible the articulations of language from its simplest, founding
elements into entire utterances.

A grotesque and strange fable of Dalgarno's invention presses the implied argument a step further, to suggest that, stripped of all but essentials, language can, without losing its features as language, be reduced to dactylology—body-to-body contact. By combining Homer and Aesop as its protagonists, the fable brilliantly conflates two discussions which (at least *in potentia*) belong to the somatic tradition from *Mercury* on. The contact between Homer (epic writer) and Aesop (inventor of the fable) asks us first to reimagine the relationships between metaphor as a linguistic base and the exigencies of genre as a sophisticated linguistic construct—in short, between figuration and allegory. The mechanics of Dalgarno's tale then reveal that the answer to the first problem hinges on the relationship between literacy and violence. Dalgarno seems to ask us to move from a narrow consideration of language as a metaphorical artifact, to examining its activities within generic conventions, of which epic is the most rarefied. In the process, we then discover that the sophistications and abstractions of genre as a form of civic conduct, which signal the imposition of ideology, must violently control and shape their materials.

Dalgarno introduces his fable as a four-act drama, each act representing a reduction of linguistic possibility in the direction of a purely somatic language. At first, "Blind *Homer*" purchases the deaf Aesop, blessed with the advantages of sight and "trained up in . . . Sematology," as a slave "to write out his *Ilias* fair, from his own blotted Copy."[252] Any difficulty Aesop encounters in reading Homer's manuscript, Homer can correct "upon his fingers."[253] In the second movement, Homer then mistakes Aesop's stuttering as an attempt to deceive him, and, "in a sudden passion, he cuts out his Tongue."[254] Ordered, however, to wait upon a dinner party, Aesop presents his own tongue as the sole delicacy, upbraiding Homer by communicating on a pipe ("Glossology"). Dalgarno suggests the fragility of aural communication at this point, because Homer angrily throws Aesop's pipe on the fire, and he is only placated, as well as converted to "fear, and admiration," when Aesop takes his hand and communicates by gestures ("Haptology").[255]

Homer arranges another dinner party for the following night, requiring Aesop to provide "the oldest, and leanest carrion, he could find," which inevitably proves once again Aesop's own tongue. Furious at the repeated trick, Homer signals to his friends ("by Dactylology") to pluck out Aesop's eyes.

Homer finally suffers an illness that deprives him of hearing. This "reconciled him again to *Aesop;* for he judged him the fittest companion he could find, with whom to bemoan his folly, and misery. After this," we hear, "they lived good friends, passing the time in telling old stories; some times upon their fingers ends, and sometimes with hand in hand, traversing the Alphabetical *Ilias*."[256]

The tale drives Homer and Aesop to maneuver around each other as personified postulates about the constituents of various kinds of narrative, themselves proposing different forms of knowing and representing the world. Homer declines to Aesop's state, and they meet over "old stories" conveyed by gestures. The visual and tactile necessities to which both figures are reduced are already embodied in Aesop (not Homer) from the start, as if from the very idea of Aesopic fable emanates some universal property of narrative, thus of language. Homer's violence upon Aesop implies that Homeric epic—a sophisticated code of narrative convention abstracted from these elementary properties of language and narrative—must control, enslave, and violate the integrities of the materials upon which it depends. And the inescapable imbalance of constituted political structures (master-slave) is revealed by the mechanics of power that attempts to sustain them. This is, of course, one version of the ideology of contingency (as I have called it), inasmuch as it holds that, in revealing the origins or grounds of knowledge and language (an experimental means to describe ordinary language), we can expose the epistemological forgeries of tyrants and rebels and thus embarrass their forms of ideological mystification. Dalgarno ends his fable not with two inarticulate, lumpish bodies deprived of language—this would argue the possibility of recapturing some impossibly prelinguistic, natural scene of knowledge—but with Homer and Aesop, now reconciled, reconstructing a society with a fully conventional language of the hand. Even the devices of tyranny are artifices (such as "alphabetical lines"), themselves ideological prescriptions, which cannot cancel their debts to what they supersede. We may escape the impositions of a given allegory, but we cannot escape metaphor.

"The Voice of the Sign": Hieroglyphic Knowledge and the Material Universe of Signs

Hieroglyphs: The Pictorial Grounds of Ordinary Language

Exactly paralleling the emergence of the somatic tradition, a new interest in Chinese pictograms arose in the mid-seventeenth century and flourished in the Restoration. As one commentator puts it, the rich Renaissance theories about hieroglyphs "had been illusions based on Neo-Platonic speculations and an entirely erroneous conception of the script," and now the direction of interest was decidedly philological. It is a mistake, however, to see this development as "inspiring nothing but learned quarrels generally unedifying and barren in themselves," though useful as a harbinger of true (i.e., modern) linguistic science.[257] If as technical linguistic treatises they remain inadequate, discussions of hieroglyphs and pictograms—like the somatic texts—provide a rich source of meditations about the nature and grounds of ordinary language. The flood of publications issuing from the pen of Athanasius Kircher (1602–1680), beginning in the 1640s and continuing unabated for almost half a century, catalyzed an interest in hieroglyphs and pictograms precisely because they appeared as strangely reified linguistic tokens.[258] Like the somatic tradition, these scripts seemed to offer more evidence that language is indeed transculturally constituted as phenomenal, atomic, sequential; moreover, as a happy coincidence, they offered a confirmation that the conditions of the scribal and printing culture inhabited by neoclassical theorists was a late manifestation of graphic tendencies embedded in the very fabric of language.

Writers frequently hint that hieroglyphs and pictograms (usually treated as distinct categories) confirm the possibility of realizing a universal language.[259] Somewhat less frequently, they also propose the pictorialism of Chinese or Egyptian signs as evidences of some 'natural' language, but they apparently never confuse the postulate of universality or naturalness with some uninhibited referential engagement with the world. None of the writers I discuss imagines (as somatic writers are more tempted to do) that we can elude the conditions of representation. For example, Gabriel de Magalhães writes that "it is the nature of Hieroglyphicks not to be the natural figures of the things which they signifie, but only to represent them either naturally, or by the Institution of Men."[260]

Magalhães's crucial distinction between natural representation and "the Institution of men" illuminates the bifocal character of the argument conducted on the evidence of Chinese and Egyptian writing. That Magalhães so easily moves in one sentence from one to the other also supposes certain analytical continuities between them. We have seen how, for the somatic tradition, the brute fact of the body becomes the occasion for a critique jointly of the corporeal origins of the founding particles of language and of a behavioral description of ordinary language. Similarly, the hieroglyphic tradition exploits the material and visual implications of Chinese and Egyptian writing in order to examine not only the putative grounds of language but also how language works as a sophisticated cultural organism.

All the writers I mention—from Pierre Gautruche, to Magalhães, Jan Nieuhof, Defoe, and, eventually, Warburton—seem to assume a conceptualism that Stillingfleet, writing in *Origines Sacrae* (1662) perhaps most vigorously expresses: "It is most agreeable to Reason, that Names should carry in them a suitableness to the things they express; for Words being for no other end but to express our Conceptions of things, and our Conceptions being but . . . *The Resemblances and Representations of the things,* it must need follow, that where there was a true knowledg, the Conceptions must agree with the Things; and Words being to express our Conceptions, none are so fit to do it, as those which are expressive of the several Natures of the things they are used to represent."[261]

It is possible to hold that what amounts to a radically referential theory must defeat an account of the contractual, arbitrary nature of language viewed as a human artifact. But Stillingfleet sees that though the graphic, pictorial status of pictograms and hieroglyphs is a useful metaphor for this side of his conceptualism, the results gained do not describe language as a system of tokens carrying a contractual, culturally specific, weight. That is, all the writers above are drawn to one vision of hieroglyphic representation and are disturbed by another: because we think by images, the argument goes, the pictorialism of the hieroglyph might provide a laboratory in which to examine the figural status of human signs as atomically represented to the human mind. Yet viewed almost anthropologically, though that same pictorialism serves as a metaphor for material culture, which language helps to organize, alphabetic writing realizes an elegance and efficiency that the attempt to trade pictorial symbols never could. Thus Stillingfleet is one of the first writers to express disappointment at the clumsiness and ambiguity of what he calls "representative Symbols" as a vehicle of cultural transmission and, also discarding the "vocal Cabala" of "Speech," prefers the flexible exactitude of "Letters."[262] The loss of the alphabetic letter's strict accountability to a mimetic or pictorial model of representation releases it into a different signifying economy, in which patently nonmimetic marks submit to purely contractual regulation.

Gautruche can characterize the hieroglyph as an "Emblem" or "Ænigm,"[263] because it shows its advantages over the body for the politico-linguistic discussion by remaining stubbornly visual: it cannot be imagined as a site or symptom of speech. And it is precisely the precisions associated with vision that for Nieuhof (in John Ogilby's translation) reveal the superiority of the pictogram over spoken Chinese, which he depicts as a form of interpretive chaos: "Now though all the Subjects of that Empire use several Characters in their Language, yet in speaking there seems to be little or no difference in them, all their words sounding alike, notwithstanding the difference of form and signification in Writing."[264]

Warburton merely summarizes a long tradition, then, when he notes that "WRITING and LANGUAGE, throughout all their various modes, ran exactly the same fortune."[265] If not chronologically, which is something we cannot judge, writing is *epistemologically* prior to speech, because it plays to the visual requirements of the human mind. Gautruche argues that hieroglyphs are a response to a universal apprehension of the *"shapes of things,"*[266] or what Nieuhof similarly describes as "the Characters of the Antients, which presented the shape of things."[267] In the progress of the argument, the Chinese pictogram—like the body—is subsequently selected as a space from which the commentators read a curiously frozen, condensed history of writing. The pictogram is therefore to be distinguished from the hieroglyph proper, because the latter represents only an early phase in humankind's graphic development. Magalhães and Nieuhof believe that the pictogram can itself be anatomized as a palimpsest, in which the traces of a cruder picture writing remain; Warburton juxtaposes Aztec, Egyptian, and Chinese scripts, from which we read essentially the same story.

Magalhães anticipates the steps of the argument by insisting first that in "their first Original . . . without doubt [Chinese pictograms] are Hieroglyphicks," which is to say "the Images and Figures, tho' imperfect, of the things visible which they signifi'd." "For example," he adds, "the Ancient Letter, which signifi'd the Sun was this, ⊙ *ge,* and that which is now in use is made thus 且 *ge.*"[268] And Nieuhof pursues a similar line of criticism by writing that

> at first the *Chineses* Characterized their meaning in a kind of Hiero-
> glyphic shape, as of four-footed Beasts, Birds, Creeping Creatures,
> Fishes, Herbs, Boughs of Trees, Ropes, &c. which were variously
> made and contrived, as the fancy of the User thought meet: But
> after-ages by a long series of time, and a constant practical use

thereof, finding a great confusion in such a vast number of differing Creatures and Herbs, imitating the form of some of the Ancients in their Characters, made or added some little Points and Lines about them, to distinguish them one from another.[269]

At this juncture, Nieuhof prints a table (see p. 235), which graphically displays the two principles about language at work in the pictogrammatic discussion. The first reiterates the purely artificial, representational character even of picture signs by remarking that language is always an instrument of social use and that even the primitive "User" of hieroglyphs manufactured signs that are in essence synecdochic, "contrived, as the fancy . . . thought meet" from arbitrarily selected visible appearances of objects. Warburton makes the point particularly clearly. The "MEXICANS [Aztecs] painted their conceptions" by "tracing out the images of things." This is no simple copy-theory of language, however, for though "things that have a bodily shape were represented by their proper figures; . . . those which have none, [were represented] by other significative characters." The hieroglyphic refines this clumsy method of "simple painting" by creating a "more ingenious . . . pictured character,"[270] whose two methods of representation are synecdochic and metonymic: "The first way was, *to make the principal circumstance in the subject stand for the whole*" (synecdoche), and "the second, and more artful method of contraction, was by putting the instrument of the thing, whether real or metaphorical, for the thing itself. Thus an *eye,* eminently placed, was designed to represent God's omniscience" (metonymy).[271]

Nieuhof's second principle—also more fully expounded by Warburton—takes its direction from the first: simple strokes of the pen are evidently a more economical means of achieving the same effect as hieroglyphs (which clearly signify primarily by agreement, though they are conceived from a representational model), and this is partly because they more effectively execute the combinatory method entailed in hieroglyphs. The patently particular quality of alphabetic marks condenses and lubricates the potential in hieroglyphs by assuming their symbolic role in a smaller space, as well as by more clearly admitting of potentially endless recombinations. Thus Magalhães comments that

the *Chinese* Letters are either Simple or Compounded. The Simple Letters are made of Lines, Points and Folds, as 忘 *sin,* 本 *mô,* 吐 *tú,* 玉 *chú.* The Compounded Letters are formed of several Simple Letters put together, as 恕 *xú,* 柱 *chú.* The Letter *xú* signifies

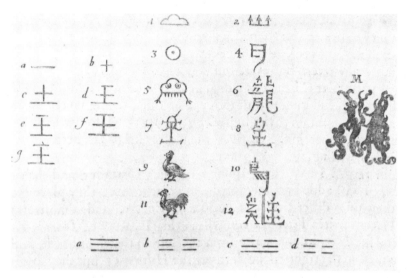

Plate from Ogilby's translation of Nieuhof's *An Embassy to the Grand Tartar Chan* (1669), showing the development of alphabetic writing from pictures

sincere, sincerity, and is compos'd of the Letter 𝔛 𝔇 *iu,* which signifies, *as*; and the Letter 𝔛 *sin,* which signifies a *Heart;* for that the Countenance and Words of a sincere Man are like his Heart.[272]

Defoe vividly describes the recombinative method as "Coupling."[273] And Warburton explains that the reason the Egyptian priests "called their hieroglyphic and symbolic marks *[stocheia],* was that, in this way of writing, they employed all kinds of natural entities, to denote their mental conceptions; the proper signification of *[stocheia]* being the first elements and principles of things, out of which all beings arise, and, of which, they are compounded."[274]

However distantly, alphabetic letters remain cousins to the hieroglyphs or (in Warburton's comparative anthropology), Aztec picture writing. We have seen that, as a crucible in which pictures transform to letters, the Chinese ideogram serves as a concentrated emblem of the history of writing, an exposition equally of phylo- and onto-genesis. But neoclassical pictogrammarians also anxiously cherish the discrete integrity of pictorial signs, because they take them to guarantee the visual and graphic force of individual letters and consonants of the alphabet. Their motives are largely that all representative signs must be accountable to mental habits, the need—in short—to focus the mind's attention, and thus create a relaxed cognitive atmosphere in which to erect the constructs of true memory (hence history).

This principle is one obvious implication of Descartes's announcement that "a plurality of things cannot be of assistance to the intellect in distinctly intuiting individual things. Rather, in order to deduce a single thing from a collection of things—a frequent task—we must discard from the ideas of the things whatever does not demand our present attention, so that the remaining features can be retained more readily in the memory."[275] Additionally, the signs that so help to focus mental attention are derived synecdochically from the world: "It is not the things themselves which should be displayed to the external senses, but rather certain abbreviated representations of them; and the more compact these are, the handier they are, provided they act as adequate safeguards against lapses of memory."[276]

Unsurprisingly, then, Dalgarno can append to his *Didascalocophus, A Discourse of the Nature and Number of Double Consonants,* because the view of corporal knowledge predicating his version of digital atomism presupposes the atomic constitution of ordinary languages, such as Hebrew, in which "all their Radical words consist generally of a single consonant, and a single vowel, succeeding one another alternatly."[277] Magalhães had already enunciated the atomic principle twenty-two years earlier, this time emphasizing its advantages in securing distinction and discrimination within and among the components of language—a version of what modern linguistics has characterized as difference:

> In regard the *Chinese* Letters are not simply Lines or Characters, but figures appointed to represent or signifie something, it follows of consequence that they are not simple Letters like ours, but Hieroglyphicks. Where we are to take notice that these Hieroglyphick Letters which extreamly help the Memory to remember them, and contribute much to know and distinguish what they signifie, in regard that every Genus and every Species has a distinct Letter which is to be found in all those that signifie the things contain'd in the same Species.[278]

The symbiosis between the atomic and somatic features of language, which the hieroglyph apparently confirms, is perhaps most fully explicated by an important passage in Warburton's *Divine Legation of*

Moses.[279] Only because the mind works by "the uniform voice of nature"[280] can we convert different modes of writing into stages in the
growth of civilization. Prior to the invention of letters, "all the barbarous
nations upon earth . . . made use of hieroglyphics, or signs for things, to
record their meaning: the more gross, by *representation;* the more subtle
and civilized, by *analogy* and *institution*." Therefore, "the general history
of writing [developed] by a gradual and easy descent, from a PICTURE to
a LETTER." Warburton offers "Chinese marks" as that liminal point or
"border" in which the transition from "Egyptian hieroglyphs on the one
hand" to "alphabetic letters on the other" can be detected.[281] The derivation of many alphabetic systems ("being only a compendium of that large
volume of arbitrary marks") from hieroglyphic representation is expressed in many ancient "names which express letters and literary writing": " Thus the Greek words *[SEMEIA]* and *[CHĒMATA]* signify as well
the images of natural things as artificial marks or characters; and
[GRAPHŌ] is both to paint and to write."[282] Failure to attend to the
artificial and incremental progress of graphic signs as human artifacts
misled Plato and Cicero to ascribe to language a divine origin.[283]

It is also Warburton's purpose to show how this artifice is naturally
derived, as if the human mind tends, when engaged naturally with the
world, to fabricate and refine systems of increasingly flexible symbolic
forms. Speech cannot therefore logically or historically *precede* writing or
its origins, because, by implication, the mind's contacts with the world
must mobilize all the instruments the body provides. Thus, "as St. Austin
elegantly expresses it, *Signa sint* VERBA VISIBILIA; *verba,* SIGNA AUDI-
BILIA."[284]

Historical evidence suggests that language was "at first extremely
rude, narrow, and equivocal," the use of analogy to express general ideas
being a later development. "Accordingly," Warburton writes in a crucial
passage,

> in the first ages of the world, mutual converse was upheld by a
> mixed discourse of words and ACTIONS; hence came the eastern
> phrase of *the voice of the sign;* and use and custom, as in most other
> affairs of life, improving what had arisen out of necessity, into
> ornament, this practice subsisted long after the necessity was over;
> especially amongst the eastern people, whose natural temperament
> inclined them to a mode of conversation, which so well exercised
> their vivacity, by motion; and so much gratified it, by a perpetual
> representation of material images.[285]

Warburton shows all indications of knowing exactly where he is going. The "significative actions" of the prophets of the Old Testament (an instance of divine accommodation) anticipate the figural terms of the New. And the economical reduction of picture to letter in the progress of writing finds its somatic parallel in "the birth of the FABLE,"[286] which similarly declines over time from the apologue, to the proverb, then to the simile, "in which men consulted closeness as well as brevity,"[287] the argument being that the simile services the mind singularly neatly, because the two terms of comparison are closely juxtaposed in a single observation. The inevitable fourth step is already implied by the foregoing. Language, we learn, is metaphorical at root, and the dialectical relationship between language and history is also the dialectical relationship between metaphor and allegory: "As from [Chinese] *marks* proceeded the abbreviated method of *alphabetic letters,* so from the simile, to make language still more expedite and elegant, came the METAPHOR; which is indeed but a simile in little; for men so conversant in *matter* still wanted sensible images to convey abstract ideas."[288]

After again offering Old Testament prophecy as an example, Warburton continues: "Quintilian considering this matter in an inverted order, yet makes an observation, where he speaks of *metaphors,* much to our purpose—Continuus [usus] vero in allegoriam et aenigmata exit. That is, as the allegory may, by degrees, be contracted into a metaphor, so the metaphor, by beating long upon it, may be drawn back again into an allegory." Like the simile, of which it is a contraction, metaphor never pretends to anything but its own artifice. That deceit is the province of what Warburton calls the "EPITHET, which soon discharged all the colouring of the figure." Epithet tricks us into forgetting that language serves the appetite of human cognition, which requires it to sustain its figural, plastic, and material power: "The common foundation of all these various modes of WRITING and SPEAKING, was a PICTURE or IMAGE, presented to the *imagination* through the eyes and ears; which [is] the simplest and most universal of all kinds of information."[289]

7. Text and Action in Biblical Criticism

And as our Sensations carry the notions of Material things to our Under-standings which before were unacquainted with them; so there is some Ana-logical way whereby the knowledge of Divine Truth may also be revealed to us. For so we may call as well that Historical Truth of Corporeal and Material things, which we are informed by our Senses, Truth of Revelation, *as that Divine Truth which we now speak of: and therefore we may have as certain and infallible a way of being acquainted with the one, as the other.*

John Smith, "Of Prophesie" (1660)

But Jesus stooped down, and with his finger wrote on the ground, as though he heard them not.

John 8:6

The New Climate of Knowledge

Christian theology must begin with the Word. For that reason alone, religious apologetics in the culture I describe could provide a major forum for linguistic debate. The Genesis account habitually provided the furniture for imagining the origins of language, even when the motive was to replace the familiar Adamic theory of naming with a conventionalist view of language. And important 'linguistic' explorations such as Defoe's *An Essay upon Literature* and Warburton's *Divine Legation of Moses* extend their arguments from biblical history, just as Brian Walton's prolegomenon to his *Biblia Polyglotta* deliberates on the nature and origin of language.

In an influential book, Hans Frei describes a hermeneutical revolution taking place by the late-eighteenth century.[1] Whereas the reformers interpreted all human history by recourse to a spiritual master plot educed from the Bible, which they treated as factually precise, the eighteenth century began to judge biblical events by criteria drawn primarily from nonbiblical or more empirically verifiable patterns of history.[2]

Some may interpret this change as an expression of a new secularizing impulse, but I shall argue that, even if it added to that movement, it is possible to see the changes Frei discusses as occurring earlier, and as motivated by arguments about the nature of Christian knowledge itself.

Thus, as Frei himself suggests, Hugo Grotius's and Richard Simon's forms of biblical criticism had already adumbrated new approaches to biblical knowledge; I therefore propose that it is roughly during the middle of the seventeenth century that new epistemological pressures foment a new set of attitudes to recuperating biblical texts and interpreting both ancient and modern languages. Defoe centers his defense of the supremacy of writing as a vehicle for all forms of cultural expression and transmission on the image of Moses taking dictation from God. Warburton's equally encompassing prejudice for the phenomenality of language, and hence of all cultural symbology, takes the form of appropriating the familiar theory of accommodation to his hieroglyphic interests, such that "the prophetic style seems to be a SPEAKING HIEROGLYPHIC."[3] Similarly, both John Owen and Richard Simon—approaching textual criticism from diametrically opposed viewpoints—recognize that debates about recuperating biblical evidences must assume general theories about the nature of language. Owen's integralist defense of the antiquity of Hebrew vowel points briefly receives support from his friendship with Wilkins.[4] And Simon explicitly mobilizes the Lucretian account of language to talk about the relation between instinctual utterance, which is a divinely given rational faculty, and the artifices of human intercourse, which arose in the natural course of time.[5]

Although my generalizations apply throughout to more than Anglicans alone, Gerard Reedy's book about Anglican theological method in the Restoration perfectly articulates one premise of this chapter. Celebrating "the smoothly psychological unity"[6] of Anglican apologetic, he shows how it plays out the epistemological and evidentiary issues that form part of our larger topic. Henry R. McAdoo's magisterial study, *The Spirit of Anglicanism,* unearths a three-pronged criterion of reason, Scripture, and tradition, which lies at the heart of Anglican hermeneutics; but Reedy's focus on evidentiary arguments shows how this criterion supplies a distinguishable method of interpretation. I am not entirely convinced, however, that the theoretical consequences of textual criticism—most radically expressed by Hobbes, Spinoza, and Simon— eluded the Anglican tradition.[7] Inasmuch as to recognize the fragmentation of ancient sources helped to dissipate monopolies of knowledge associated with certain nonconforming and Catholic epistemologies, Anglicans gladly invited textual criticism into their theological practices. Part of the purpose of this chapter is to show that, by focusing on relatively few Anglicans, the textual-critical position did emerge with greater clarity as the Restoration wore on, and that, because the epistemic and linguistic ramifications went well beyond the Anglican camp, we cannot comfortably divorce Anglican method from related Protestant attitudes. Yet Reedy is still right to imply that the Anglicans' probabilist arguments for reconstituting texts took place in a fairly comfortable atmosphere, in which the methods educed to reconstitute texts were treated as effectively identical to the ways in which—within these texts— miracles were readily validated by the quality and number of witnesses confronting the reported event.

We observe here a vital dynamic between the critic using empirical criteria to judge the relative value of sources, and the actors, participating within the biblical accounts, forced to make inferences from prophetic utterances, parables, or miracles.[8] The inferential and analogical structure in both cases is the same, and it serves the point neoclassical linguists want to establish—namely, that our negotiations with language are purely positional. Theological writers often go one crucial step further by expressly establishing the reader as the enactment and embodiment, the present realization, of this forensic principle. The necessity of choice is then promulgated by treating texts and words as material objects to be negotiated, and it thus finds an apt theological ally in Arminianism, which vindicates the will as that faculty with which human beings must encounter the contingencies of a purely mediated experience. The talk about the "plain" places of Scripture does not amount to a belief in linguistic transparency; rather, it describes those points at which textual evidences are 'sufficient' to provide minimal agreement about the sense of a passage, though those minimal points happen to coincide with the rudiments of the *kerugma*. The cooperation between philosophical method and theology is not in this sense 'scientific.' Moreover, because (as Reedy has again shown) reason in this context must imply a capacity of the mind to judge on limited, probable grounds the evidence that it faces, it follows that this kind of rational theology is hardly rationalist in tenor. As in 'linguistic' texts, the logic of the argument drives together a theory of action with a theory of language, because, if we picture our manipulations of language as a contingent negotiation of textual elements into some sufficient model of spiritual apprehension, we treat language as a matrix of formal, not essential, properties, much as we may at best infer causes or generalities from the specifics of observed action.

This peculiar form of scripturalism (as I call it) thus marries text to action. An entirely circular logic first holds that, given the equal corruption of words and documents, multiple, if only teasing, references to a series of activities must indicate the temporal priority of such events. But conversely, what might imply a certain positivism—a perfectly accessible event securing *post hoc* the text's minimal reliability—is precluded by the sceptical recognition that inevitably an event is a feature of the text it is summoned to stabilize. The phenomenal terms that empower an event also determine a reading of the text that transmits it: text and action simultaneously emerge as visible symptoms of each other. The linearity of ordinary language (reinforced by print) and the sequentiality of narrative (history, event, parable) cooperate to assert the comparably palpable quality of language and action. The act of reading now becomes finely accountable to its empirical grounds, which interjects a moral imperative into the cognitive argument, because the judgments that the scriptural narratives evoke from the reader entail inescapable theological consequences.

Even in the work of Simon, who is writing ostensibly as a Catholic, the argument cuts equally against Catholic and inspirationalist views, because it balks at the inevidency of certain abstract theological propositions that serve to control others. Against all evidence of sense, the doctrine of transubstantiation claims impossibly to preside over the occult transmutation of bread and wine;[9] the inspirationalist equally improbably assumes the capacity to chart the mysterious movements of the Spirit in the believer's inmost self. I know of no modern commentary that sees how this resistance to abstraction from the phenomena of text and world encourages a distinct theory of close reading: on this view, any generality must evidence itself as the demonstrable product of inferences drawn from commonly observed particulars.[10] Both Hobbes and Locke argue that selective or spasmodic reading must disturb the intrinsic integrity of the text:[11] Locke even castigates the "crumbling" of Scripture into printed chapters and verses, because the false elements of knowledge so proposed reify and obscure the self-regulating movements of the text.[12] Although the phenomenalist argument thus parades as a political attack on one dimension of false reading—creating a resistance to cognitive tyranny—it simply substitutes, as Hobbes and Locke are well aware, another politics of reading.

That this genuinely permissive theory of religious and textual apprehension is nonetheless enmeshed in institutional commitments is already clear in William Chillingworth's *The Religion of Protestants the Safe Way to Salvation* (1638). In this work, which is conducted as a debate with his Catholic opponent, Father Edward Knott, over a vast textual canvas, this spectacularly reconverted Anglican pursues Catholic infallibility armed with a distinct and massively influential theological probabilism.[13] Like Lucius Cary, Viscount Falkland, to whose distinguished circle he belonged[14] (and like William Laud, his godfather),[15] Chillingworth effectively demolishes Catholic fideism and infallibilism by uniting faith and knowledge as dimensions of a single epistemological critique,[16] which insists on the essentially mediated, prudential character of human cognition and human institutions.[17] The formal properties of language, texts, cultural symbols embedded in the liturgy, all inform Chillingworth's famous outburst: "The Bible, I say, the Bible only, is the religion of protestants!"[18] Like our knowledge of history,[19] which provides one of Chillingworth's motifs, our knowledge of textual evidences is contingent. And it is precisely on that basis—employing a contingent and prudential criterion—that by implication Chillingworth exhorts us to select an institution by which visibly to exercise our faith,[20] yet no institution that oversteps the divinely ordained limits on human understanding to abrogate the natural flexibility of individual judgment. That these formal conditions of knowledge can be brought against radical inspirationalism as much as Catholic fideism explains how Chillingworth's epistemological moderation can be associated with Laud's immoderate defense of Anglicanism for essentially prudential motives.[21]

The Anglican position revealed a theoretical instability in Restoration theology, which spawned numerous skirmishes over the criteria distinguishing prudence from idolatry. Like the debates over transubstantiation, and like the attempt to rationalize God's unique act of speech in the Incarnation and by means of his Creation,[22] the question of language sits firmly at the center of the issue: Anglican prudentialism treats the formal properties of the church as an extrinsic means to cultural participation, as a purely *representational* medium, while it accuses Catholic polemic of veering between a false literalism and incantation (Cassirer's "word magic"), and hence as indistinguishable from nonconformist *"Fanaticism."*[23] We see in effect the emergence of a new kind of privacy, in which a representationalist view of language (symbolic in Kenneth Burke's sense) preserves the postulate of an inner life from

unwarranted inspection, while conserving civic and religious accountability for the public realm.[24] Anglican Erastianism here amounts to a
defense of "figurative expressions," in Stillingfleet's phrase.[25] Of course,
as Catholic polemicists were quick to notice, by their nonconformist
critics the Anglicans were ironically describing their own false position in
accusing the Catholics of idolatry; by what except arbitrary or mystic
authority could Anglicanism orchestrate even contingent forms of religious conformity?[26]

The epistemological thrust of Chillingworth's critique, frequently
elaborated during the Restoration, also attacks Catholicism for authorizing the arbitrary, nonnegotiable oral or nonwritten corpus. The main
aim was unequivocally to foreground written or printed texts as the
media on which to found religious knowledge.[27] Because Catholics
themselves remained confused about the distinction between 'oral' and
'non-written' evidences,[28] that confusion simply added fuel to the polemical fire.[29] Because, for all its faults, the written participates unequivocally in the public sphere of evidences, it was thought to resist the trade
in recondite knowledge, which exploits evidentiary lacunae created by
fictions of oral or nonwritten doctrines. That by the end of the Restoration the argument has become general is evidenced by Defoe's position
in *An Essay upon Literature:* true historical—that is, textual—knowledge
will expose the pretensions of tyrants for what they are. William Sherlock
epitomizes this textualism when he notes that "a Writing may be proved
Authentick, an obscure unwritten Tradition cannot."[30]

Owen, Walton, and Textual Criticism

It is also this textualism that ensures a harmony between epistemological
and textual-critical attitudes. Again, Chillingworth's Arminian emphasis
can vindicate the freedom of the will and resist Calvinist determinism by
suggesting the historical instability of biblical texts, which, though they
do not require papal arbitration, limit the kinds of claims any theology
can legitimately support. Perhaps the two presiding geniuses of textual
criticism in the early seventeenth century were Isaac Casaubon and
Grotius, both distinctively anti-Catholic and anti-Calvinist, and both
with close ties to England.[31] Mark Pattison's luminous biography of
Casaubon translates him into a Protestant hero and the originator of
modern textual criticism.[32] Although his reassessment moderates these
claims, Anthony Grafton reiterates the force and authority with which
Casaubon demolished Cesare Baronius's Catholic historiography, and

S.S.
BIBLIA
Polyglotta.
Complectentia Textus Originales
HEBRAICOS cum
Pentat. Samarit:
CHALDAICOS
GRÆCOS.
Versionumq. Antiquarum
SAMARIT. GRÆC. SEPT.
CHALDAIC. SYRIACÆ.
LAT. VULG. ARABICÆ.
ÆTHIOPIC. PERSICÆ.
Quicquid comparari poterat.
Brianus Waltonus
Anno M.DC.LVII.

Title page to the *Biblia Polyglotta*

TEXTUS HEBRAICUS,
Cum Versione interlineari Sanctis Pagnini, ad Hebraicam phrasin examinata per Ben. Ariam Montanum, & alios.

Vulgata LATINA
Versio, juxta exemplaria emendata Sixti V. & Clem. VIII.

VERSIO GRÆCA LXX. INTERP.
Juxta exemplar Vatican. Romæ impressa, subscriptis quæ aliter leguntur in vetustiss. MS. Angl. ex Alexandria allato, cum Versi. Lat. Edit. Rom.

Vulgata Latina

CAP. I.

IN Principio creavit Deus cœlum & terram. Terra autem erat inanis & vacua, & tenebræ erant super faciem abyssi: & Spiritus Dei ferebatur super aquas. Dixitque Deus: Fiat lux. Et facta est lux. Et vidit Deus lucem quod esset bona: & divisit lucem à tenebris. Appellavitque lucem Diem, & tenebras Noctem: factumque est vespere & mane, dies unus. Dixit quoque Deus: Fiat firmamentum in medio aquarum: & dividat aquas ab aquis. Et fecit Deus firmamentum, divisitque aquas quæ erant sub firmamento, ab his quæ erant super firmamentum. Et factum est ita. Vocavitque Deus firmamentum, Cœlum: & factum est vespere & mane, dies secundus. Dixit verò Deus: Congregentur aquæ, quæ sub cœlo sunt, in locum unum: & appareat arida. Et factum est ita. Et vocavit Deus aridam, Terram; congregationesque aquarum appellavit Maria. Et vidit Deus quòd esset bonum. Et ait: Germinet terra herbam virentem & facientem semen, & lignum pomiferum faciens fructum juxta genus suum, cujus semen in semetipso sit super terram. Et factum est ita. Et protulit terra herbam virentem, & facientem semen juxta genus suum, lignumque faciens fructum, & habens unumquodque sementem secundum speciem suam. Et vidit Deus quòd esset bonum. Et factum est vespere & mane, dies tertius. Dixit autem Deus: Fiant luminaria in firmamento cœli, & dividant diem ac noctem, & sint in signa, & tempora, & dies, & annos:

Versio SYRIACA cum Interpretatione LATINA.

In Nomine Domini Omnipotentis aggredimur impressionem libri legis Mosis Propheta. Ac primo librum Creationis.

CAP. I.

IN principio creavit Deus esse cœli & esse terræ. Terra autem erat deserta & inculta, tenebræque super faciem abyssi: & spiritus Dei incubabat superficiei aquarum. Dixitque Deus, Fiat lux: factaq; est lux. Viditque Deus lucem quòd bona esset. Et divisit Deus inter lucem & tenebras. Appellavitque Deus lucem, diem: & tenebras appellavit noctem: fuitque vespera, fuitque mane dies unus. Et dixit Deus, Sit firmamentum in medio aquaru: & fuit, divisitque inter aquas & aquas. Fecitque Deus firmamentum, & divisit aquas quæ sub firmamento, & aquas quæ super firmamentum: & fuit ita. Appellavitque Deus firmamentum cœlum: & fuit vespera, & fuit mane dies secundus. Et dixit Deus, Congregentur aquæ quæ sub cœlo sunt in locũ unum, & appareat arida: & fuit ita. Et appellavit Deus aridã, terram: congregationes vero aquaru appellavit maria: viditque Deus quòd bonum esset. Et dixit Deus, Producat terra germen, herbã quæ ferendo feratur juxta genus suum: & arborem fructus edentem fructũ juxta genus suũ, cujus plãta sit in semetipsa super terram, & fuit ita. Et produxit terra germen, herbã quæ ferendo seritur juxta genus suum & arbore proferentem fructum cujus planta est in semetipsã juxta genus suũ. Viditque Deus quòd esset bonum. Et fuit vespera, fuitq; mane diestertius. Dixitque Deus, Sint luminaria in firmamento cœli ad distinguendum inter diem & noctem: sintque in signa, & tempora, et in dies, & annos:

Page from the *Biblia Polyglotta*

with it slew the legitimacy of the *Corpus Hermeticum*,[33] which so dramatically concludes Frances Yates's classic account of Renaissance hermeticism.[34]

The central concern in the debate between Walton and Owen is the politic implications of textual criticism. During the Interregnum, as is well known, many Anglicans devoted themselves to scholarship—several, such as John Pearson, John Lightfoot, and Henry Hammond, with great distinction. The most visible fruit of this redirected energy was the monumental *Biblia Polyglotta* (pp. 245–46), which was edited by Walton, is reprinted to this day for scholarly use,[35] and was accompanied by Pearson's variorum commentary, *Critici Sacri* (1660). I have elsewhere described the *Biblia Polyglotta* as a watershed in English printing and publishing history;[36] if it failed to satisfy Simon's standards of criticism, it was the single major prior example of textual-critical method for which Simon had to account.[37] Whatever Reedy might imply by claiming that Anglican apologists remained largely undisturbed by textual-critical problems, the comparative textual method informing even the typography of the *Biblia Polyglotta* was both new[38] and entirely in accord with the comparative and probabilistic assumptions of Anglican (and much other) apologetic.

Because the *Biblia Polyglotta* atomized and by publishing rendered palpable the difference among biblical sources, it intentionally summoned the exercise of individual judgment: a unitary apprehension of the text could only emerge from an inferential and analogical method. Owen rightly saw these interpretive protocols as an assault on his most cherished views of Scripture, and *The Divine Original, Authority, Self-Evidencing Light, and Power of the Scriptures* (1659) and especially its weighty companion piece, *Of the Integrity and Purity of the Hebrew and Greek Text of Scripture,* reject the premises of Walton's *Prolegomena* and *Appendix* to the *Biblia Polyglotta*.[39] Owen's attack perfectly reveals how a common Protestant appeal to Scripture can camouflage utterly opposed readings of language, and thus of human society. Against Walton's strenuously historical, philological, and textual enterprise, Owen opposes an ideal of scriptural transparency and self-evidencing power, in which "Light manifests itself."[40] Owen's late scholasticism dramatically collides with an emerging neoclassical aesthetic: the believer's illumination by Scripture fully transcends instruments of persuasion or proof;[41] and the calm of epistemic transparency, self-evidency, and stability remains sublimely undisturbed by textual-critical niceties. God has orchestrated the virtually seamless transmission of ancient texts,[42] and he allows Owen to adjudicate a confident ratio between original texts and mere translations.[43] Owen believes that to display so many and various texts in such a public document sets a dangerous example.[44] Owen's luminist metaphor cherishes an ideal of transparent knowledge, whereas even Henry More's luminist metaphor already presupposes the exercise of the Spirit within an entirely mediated universe. And, like the contrast between Baxter's and Boyle's physics, the contrast between Owen's inspirationalism and Walton's empiricism unequivocally reveals how the construction of late-seventeenth-century empiricism required a particular defense of the rhetorical and contingent condition of human knowledge, even in biblical criticism, which was at the official heart of the culture. I depart at this point most decidedly from the implication Reedy entertains from a well-worn historiographical tradition, that the application of 'scientific' method to theological discourse by calling for a 'plain style' prompted a positivistic demand for referential transparency.[45] Indeed, I suspect that the successful defense of contingency as a condition of neoclassical theological method led Owen to modify his resistance to probable modes of inquiry, even within theology, in his *[Pneumatologia] or, A Discourse concerning the Holy Spirit* (1677),[46] to distinguish his method from enthusiasm, the *"immediate revelations"* of things not before revealed,[47] before reasserting that "the authority and veracity of God do infallibly manifest or evince themselves unto our faith, or our minds in the exercise of it, by the revelation itself in the Scripture, and no otherwise."[48]

Grotius's *De Veritate Christianae*

Owen's charismatic Protestantism erects an insuperable barrier between ordinary uses of evidence and our access to Truth, guaranteed by the Holy Spirit. Neoclassical theologians were correct to contrast their contentment with sufficiency with the inspirationalists' and Catholics' assertions of infallibility. As finally as any papal decree, the infallible witness of the Spirit in Scripture overcomes choice, the exercise of the will to engage the Scriptures, and Owen quite naturally attacked the Arminians in 1642 for building on "the sand of their own free-will and endeavours" and reducing the operations of the Spirit to matters of "moral suasion."[49] Characterized as the conjunction of a strictly philological approach to the text, and a rational posture that weakened its soteriological integrity (as Grotius recognized), to its opponents the Arminian admission of the efficacy of the will and the play of moral suasion invited the charge of

Socinianism, which carried roughly the same weight and precision as communism in American political rhetoric. Even Chillingworth had been attacked as a Socinian. Thus, almost inevitably, Owen came to indict Grotius (against his own and Hammond's asseverations) on precisely this charge.[50]

Like Casaubon—a friend of Lancelot Andrewes, Laud's mentor, and whose son Meric was an apologist for the Restoration settlement— Grotius was deeply implicated in the fate of neoclassical theological method.[51] His *De Veritate Religionis Christianae* (first published in Dutch in 1622, in Latin in 1627, and English in 1632) could almost, in its career in England, be said to trace the institutional fortunes of Anglicanism itself. More heavily published in England than anywhere else, it took off spectacularly after 1650, and even more dramatically after the Restoration; one of two 1660 editions was dedicated to Boyle; and it could receive no more official sanction than a translation by Simon Patrick in 1680, which was republished about seven times, but superseded from 1711 onward by John Clarke's translation of Jean Le Clerc's edition, which was reprinted almost twenty times in the course of the eighteenth century.

Grotius debates the major consequence of new movements in textual criticism that he and Casaubon represented. How can Scripture gain sufficient epistemic stability for the exercise of faith without, on the one hand, appealing, like Catholics, to church judgment, or, on the other, calling on comparative textual evidences, whose intrinsic stability is no greater than that of the Scripture they are asked to support? In response to the dilemma, Grotius becomes more radically scripturalist by making scriptural history itself the ultimate basis for the truths of the *kerugma*. Patrick's own contribution to his translation—book seven of *The Truth of the Christian Religion*—highlights the consequences of this turn. Patrick attacks Catholic reliance on church tradition as internally inconsistent, because it makes the infallibility of the church, which arbitrates even scriptural propositions, depend on a prior appeal to scriptural evidence. The church fathers do not help, because "they oft times propound divers interpretations alike probable. And sometimes plainly intimate their doubtfulness, and make imperfect conjectures." Patrick's permissive argument rehearses a familiar distinction between those truths no Christian can reasonably deny and those interpretations that may be "probable" but not essential to saving faith; thus "by following the Scriptures, we shall learn to bear with one another in our different opinions, about things which cannot thereby be determined."[52]

Grotius—accused in consequence of Socinianism[53]—balances rational method with an evidentiary construction of Scripture. Especially in book two, Grotius establishes Scripture as the ground of belief by treating it as authentic history without requiring it to support the burden of infallibility. Book one establishes some general propositions about God's existence and nature; and though Grotius relies variously on demonstrative arguments, arguments from consent and design, and specific historical evidence, because the first two kinds of arguments cannot establish a unique claim for Christianity, Grotius delegates to the third, to history, that task. By drawing on Phoenician, Egyptian, and Greek creation myths, Grotius evinces the comparative truth of the Genesis account, and an instance of the "many testimonies of such as were aliens from the *Jewish Religion,* which declare that the most ancient reports which passed for truth among all Nations, were agreeable to what *Moses* hath related in his Writings."[54]

Having introduced evidentiary criteria, Grotius now distinguishes narratives that resemble and thus support biblical history, while exposing the Koran as a skein of wildly improbable fictions. In book six, Grotius attacks the *"Many absurd things in the Books of the Mahumetans,"* claiming that "it would be *long* to relate how many things there are, contrary to the truth of *history;* and many things very *ridiculous* in the *writings* of the *Mahumetans.*" Without submitting biblical narrative to the test of nonbiblical history, yet without submitting nonbiblical narrative to obviously theological demands, Grotius effectively places all narratives into a comparative mode, which happens fortuitously to support biblical history as probable and persuasive. Grotius significantly offers a fable as a test case. In the Koran we get "that *fable* of a fair and beautiful *Woman,* that learned a solemn *charm* or Song of some Angels that were drunk, whereby she was wont to ascend into the Sky, and likewise descend again; and ascending once a great height into Heaven, she was caught of *God,* and there fixed, and made that Star which is called *Venus.*" Such absurdities also claim that "a *mouse* in *Noah's* Ark . . . was bred of an *Elephant's* Dung: and a *Cat* of the breath of a *Lion*"[55] Biblical miracles, however, occur in harmony with a reasonable and probable view of historical events, because they transcend, not conflict with, observable laws of experience. Precisely because as evidences they do not force belief, they focus Grotius's hermeneutical method.

Grotius anticipates a major thrust of Restoration apologetics by examining the terms by which we come to assent—on intrinsic grounds—to the actions recorded in the Bible. He focuses, for example, on the number and quality of witnesses congregated around a particular event, so that "those *miracles* and *prophecies* which are recorded in Histories . . . are testified by sufficient Witnesses living in the time when they came to pass."[56] Whether spoken of as prophecy, event, or miracle, all individual atomic constituents of narrative must submit to phenomenal inspection in a kind of experimental space. The criterion embarrasses Jewish unbelief, because it places the authority of Moses' and Jesus' actions on a par. Just as Moses' miracles are evidenced by "constant report" amongst the Jews, Christians "produce *twelve witnesses* of unblameable life to testifie that *Christ* ascended up into *Heaven*. And many more that saw him upon the Earth after his death."[57]

Grotius wants to preserve the fiction of individual, readerly assent and thus assists his reader in weighing various postulates, with an eye to what harmonizes with our common, contingent experience. The local political and ethical implications of the position in the atmosphere of the 1650s were, one imagines, inescapable; but it also retains its own epistemological force, because it can admit numerous inaccuracies and prevarications in the biblical texts without compromising a set of minimal propositions that arise from the texts' mutual, if often sporadic, cooperation. These are that "there was such a Person as *Jesus* of *Nazareth,* who lived heretofore in *Judea,* when *Tiberius* was Emperor of *Rome*";[58] that "the same *Jesus* was nailed to a Cross by *Pontius Pilate,* Governor of *Judea*";[59] that he wrought miracles that depended on superhuman power; and that historically he rose again, thus placing a seal on his doctrines.[60]

In one particularly striking act of imaginative extension, Grotius asks his reader to assume the perspective of the reasonable pagan before Christ. Like the child whom William Petty places in a *Theatrum Botanicum,* the seeker was confronted by a plethora of choices, all, however, empty because "grounded upon uncertainties; proving no more the happiness of a *Man* than of a *Beast*." Jesus' entrance onto the scene heralds a kind of methodological revolution, because now he unites a substantive theology, which can satisfy both body and soul, with a method adumbrated both by tradition and "probable conjecture."[61] In short, especially in his miracles, Jesus fulfills the desires of those who expect a sufficient, if not demonstratively certain, sign.

In a remarkably sophisticated defense of the rhetoric of history, Grotius subordinates Christian dogma to the minimal facticity of

Christ's life, miracles, death, and resurrection. If he can establish the conditions under which actions, events, and miracles appear real to us, then Grotius can leave the construction of dogma to an inferential process that confesses its derivation from such observed particulars. So the historicity of Christ is attested to not only by Jewish historians and chronicles but also pagan ones.[62] And the explicitly forensic opening of Luke shows how the Gospel writers *"writ the Truth, because they had certain knowledge of what they writ."* [63] Contrary perhaps to what we might expect, Grotius's minimalist reliance upon event leads him to celebrate rather than suppress the deviations and contradictions within the Gospel accounts. Like history itself, the Gospels convey facticity not by the smooth orchestration of details, which characterizes propaganda, but by their very roughness.[64] Although they must operate as a condition of the text, mistakes about facts tend happily to highlight the distinction between the phenomenon proper and the reporters' points of view.

At this logical juncture, Grotius turns from internal to textual matters, though he only hesitantly admits into theology those standards of criticism applied to classical texts. Nevertheless, Grotius develops a striking argument based on textual-critical considerations. Again, the dispersion and corruption of texts assists Grotius's minimalist argument, because they seem to force a distinction between those essential matters to which all texts attest, and inessential matters, the products of copier's mistakes or disagreements within the early church. To argue the complete insufficiency of Scripture, we would have to believe in the face of the evidence that "all the Copies were corrupted, and that in point of doctrine, or some remarkable piece of history." Although corrupted in part, the biblical sources never prove unreliable in exactly the same way or on the same subject, and therefore they sufficiently adumbrate the prior existence of the most crucial events and doctrines.[65] Thus, without admitting the Catholic call for an external interpretive arbiter, Grotius can suggest a distinctive Protestant hermeneutic protocol for reading, as well as for adjudicating historical evidences, which conveniently frustrates the kind of integralism Owen wishes to sustain, and which Grotius—and certainly Patrick—associates with cognitive tyranny.

Like others influenced by Arminian voluntarism (Hammond, Locke, Le Clerc), Grotius accords a privilege to discrete acts and events recorded by the text as a corollary to the reader realizing a liberty and discretion within it, and so executing a moderate cognitive politics, which implies a critique of epistemological absolutism. On the one hand, the phenomenal character of event, miracle, and action preserves its discreteness, its capacity to be seen *from without* and from several sometimes conflicting points of view; and, on the other, the reader's action relative to the text must view it (conceived either as material evidence, or as an organization of formal symbols) as similarly phenomenal. Theological doctrines exist in some difficult and abstracted relation to the immediacy of all such phenomenal events; it is precisely on these strictly textual grounds that Locke develops his non- if not anti-trinitarianism. For Locke, the trinity represents a highly strained extrapolation from what the concrete details of the text yield—it is insufficiently verifiable. Conversely, without observable actions that actualize their ethical requirements, mere assent to theological truths cannot secure salvation.[66] This sceptical criterion for salvific efficacy causes Locke, in a letter to Philippus van Limborch, to express his scepticism about a criminal who, on the scaffold, confesses his faith in the face of a life lived in transgression.

The position sketched in Patrick's supplement to *The Truth of the Christian Religion* typifies the kind of permissive rhetoric encouraged by this argument. The Scriptures serve to contain heresy, but they induce us to "embrace a Religion of admirable simplicity," free from Romish "Superstitions and Ceremonies." Catholicism violates the textual principle of simplicity because it demands absolute submission to a host of theological propositions, whereas the empirical commitments of Grotian textualism criticize elaborate and dogmatic abstractions: thus, "by following the Scriptures, we shall learn to bear with one another in our different opinions, about things which cannot thereby be determined."[67]

Henry Hammond and the Recovery of the Word

Like Grotius, whom he defended against Owen,[68] Hammond achieved posthumous fame after the Restoration.[69] Although known as King Charles I's former chaplain and as a Laudian, this ideological architect of the Restoration church achieved during the Interregnum a general reputation for learning and piety and was immortalized in a minor classic, John Fell's *The Life of the Most Learned, Revered and Pious Dr. H. Hammond* (1661), having died symbolically in 1660, on the eve of the new age.[70] In the decade after publishing his best-selling *A Practical Catechisme* (1645), Hammond established himself as one of the first English philologists, not only defending Grotius's criticism in the process but also producing his own *A Paraphrase and Annotations upon the Books of the Psalms* (1653) and *A Paraphrase and Annotations upon all the Books of the*

New Testament (1639) and eventually participating as one of the editors in the *Biblia Polyglotta*.

In "A Postscript concerning New Light, or Divine Illumination," which prefaces his *Paraphrase and Annotations upon all the Books of the New Testament* (1656), Hammond shows how far he diverges from Owen's hermeneutic.[71] The satisfactions of inspirationalism are too easily purchased by sacrificing textual difficulty, connoting the resistance of things to our often perverse desires, on the altar of self-evidence. Although couched as a respect for Scripture, claims to divine illumination often eliminate the text, simply feeding the self-reflexive desires of "uncharitable Gnostic heretics."[72] In a summary statement that also enacts his methodological presuppositions, Hammond expresses the substance of his objection. "And the pretension" of the enthusiasts "is this":

> That the understanding or interpreting the word of God, or the knowing his will, is not imputable to the use of ordinary means, (such are the assistance of God's Spirit joined with the use of learning, study, meditation, rational inference, collation of places, consulting of the original languages, and ancient copies and expositions of the fathers of the church, analogy of received doctrine, together with unbiassed affections, and sincere desire of finding out the truth, and constant prayer for God's special blessing on and cooperation with these and the like means), but either to the extraordinary gift of the spirit in prophesying, preaching, and expounding, or to illumination, not prophetical or simply extraordinary, but such as is thought to be promised to a new life, the work of the Spirit of God in the heart of every saint of his, which consequently supersedes the use of all external ordinances to such, even of the written word of God itself contained in the canon of the scripture.[73]

Here Hammond epitomizes what Werner Schwarz depicts as a contrast between a philological and an inspirationalist principle of analysis, which Schwarz believes distinguishes Erasmian from Lutheran method.[74] And almost more vividly than elsewhere, the reader will notice how the demand to attend to textual particulars serves the "external ordinances" of "rational inference" against a world of utterances, which for patently political motives, will not present themselves to rational—that is, visible—scrutiny. Hammond's own rhetoric, significantly, plays out the contrast between an inspirationalist "Divine economy" and his own rational one. By a series of absolute clauses, the dogmatic perspective seeks to close off the play of methods and proofs necessary to scriptural understanding, signaled by a juxtaposition of participial and nominal phrases. The one world is so palpably bracketed off from the other that again the reader must assume the individual responsibility for judging comparatively according to "rational inference," though the brilliance of Hammond's maneuver is such that merely to recognize the alternatives is already to subscribe to a cognitive economy that vindicates a certain theology, implying a certain politics. The fiction of epistemological transparency, encouraged by a focus on preaching as an unreflexive oral exercise, dissolves where the visible prerogatives of reading commit us to a merely probable, though consistently "sufficient," kind of knowledge, which harmonizes with the conduct of common life ("ordinary means"). The purpose of the entire "Postscript" is precisely to compare the difference between such "ordinary" and "extraordinary" methods.[75]

Hammond's knowledge of textual-critical matters is suggested by affectionate allusions to Grotius, Walton, and Casaubon.[76] As in Grotius, the bibliographical problem of establishing the relative reliability of texts shades off into the problem of how, in the light of manuscript variants, we agree on the "primary and literal sense" of ancient authors. The first task is obviously to assemble and compare sources, "which were probably designed by God for more honourable uses than only to be laid up in archives, as dead bodies in vaults and charnel-houses, to converse with dust, and worms, and rottenness." Hammond imagines the task of scholarship as life-giving, a resurrection brought about not by the mysterious movements of the spirit, but by spiritually informed, probable acts of comparative judgment. He offers himself as an embodiment of the new method, because "I have chosen to advise with" manuscript sources "and from them to offer sometimes a various reading; yet not permitting this to supplant or turn out that which hath vulgarly been received, but setting it in the inner margin, that those that have judgment may, as they see cause, make use of it."[77]

Whereas the "Gnostic" apprehension of Scripture must ignore its text as a manifestation of ordinary language used in a particular context, Hammond (like Davenant) defends 'vulgar' use as part of the institution of language we have inherited, part of that field of phenomena any rational human being must judge, just as all the elements printed on the page—even "in the inner margin"—offer themselves to the conscientious reader. Again, as in Grotius, this reader's activity parallels the activity of the scholar confronting choices posed by the dispersions of

historical evidences; that those choices have ethical implications Hammond admits by writing that their consequences are matters of "use."

Because the parallel between the first witnesses' judgment and the
reader's and scholar's judgment obtains, "that which was revealed to
[the] apostles is sufficiently communicated to us by ordinary means in the
writings of the scripture, so that there can be no necessity or use of
extraordinary."[78] The structure of neoclassical judgment resists lyric
force by demystifying its gestures: "we must appeal to foreign testimonies, and therein not so much to the diffused panegyrics which have
been largely bestowed on this holy book."[79] The comparative use of
multiple texts, of the different cultural habits, and of "some other means
which the reader will discern, (that especially of weighing the context,
and comparing one scripture with another)"[80] clarifies not by that act of
obvious control signalled by "diffused panegyrics," but by visibly dis-
tributing evidences and postulates in space, the most immediate and
potentially significant being the alternatives adumbrated for his reader by
Hammond's own rhetoric.

Hammond is quite explicit about this protocol. By his comparative
method, and by means of paraphrase, an admitted deviation from some
implied original, Hammond articulates what he understands as the "primary and literal" sense, while consciously steering between "all doctrinal
conclusions and deductions and definitions on one side, and . . . all
postillary observations and accommodations, moral or mystical ana-
gogies, on the other side." Such deviations and abstractions from a
primary sense—itself constructed by a contingent method—remain the
province of readerly discretion. Mystical readings can never encourage
consensus, because they reflect the vagaries of individual taste. But there
are matters, established by forensic devices, which should create consensus, while the individual remains free, within empirically verifiable
bounds, to develop a private sense of Scripture, most obviously in the
moral "application" of truths. Hammond only intervenes "when there
appeared some uncertainty and just reason for doubting betwixt two or
more senses, which should be preferred."[81]

Hammond must cope with the problem of "semantic" obscurity, as
in the linguistic texts we examined. We must make sense of difficult and
ancient languages and idioms, as well as problems of textual transmission. Hammond insists on treating Scripture as a special instance of
ordinary language, because interpreting the language of Scripture "is no
work of extraordinary illumination, but must be attained by the same

means, or the like, by which other writings of men are expounded," which pose a host of interpretive difficulties, such as "the conciseness or length of style, or sublimity of the matter of discourse, or intermixture of old forgotten customs, &c."[82] It is not only the figural nature of language or the inherent ambiguity of terms from alien and ancient cultures that destabilizes interpretation, but also hermeneutical conventions, such as typology ("for the most part the production of fancy"),[83] which tend to foreshorten or collapse distinctions between different languages, places, and times. The challenge is to discover a meaning as close to the original as possible, respecting the most ancient texts and manuscripts and also local historical and cultural nuances. Paraphrase comes to symbolize a resignation to such difference, as well as an attempt to approximate an utterance's original significance, while mediating among (for example) Chaldaic, Greek, and Syriac attempts to communicate the "primary and literal sense." Here, more words are better, because "the very design of a paraphrast [is] truly this, to render that fully in more words which an equal number could not sufficiently express."[84]

A scepticism about language leads paradoxically to a greater attention to its particulars. That scepticism, as expressed by Hammond, accompanies and serves a deep suspicion of enthusiasm as a claim to some hidden, essential illumination that abrogates the freedom of the will, and at the same time renders questions of spiritual truth unverifiable and submits the individual to a certain spiritual determinism. Hammond exploits a recognizably Arminian argument that the inspirationalist cannot finally claim access to hidden knowledge without appealing to a text or proving its validity by actions issuing from spiritual renewal, thus becoming caught in a contradiction. Precisely by paying attention to etymology—the external history of a word as a cultural phenomenon—Hammond shows that Greek notions of understanding conveyed by the New Testament argue for the necessary implication of the will in all matters of understanding: "Verbs of *knowing* or *understanding* (such as *learning* or *teaching*) do ordinarily include the will or affections also, so as *to know God* is to obey and serve him. 2dly, That verbs active . . . and passive . . . but especially adjectives participial, do frequently include a real passion, or an effect wrought in the subject of the passion."[85]

Knowing is no matter of static, absolute, and transparent apprehension, but a human activity made real by, for example, the pedagogical instruments by which we say we know things. Like other cultural symbols, words are the somatic and synecdochic symptoms that trace the

phenomena of human action and record their constitution in their etymology: the closer we go, the more they assert their palpability, like the
famous flea under Hooke's microscope. They represent the effects of
impenetrable human motives, and they act as counters to create subsequent effects. Hammond links this linguistic attitude to a theology of the
Incarnation. God has only communicated to us through a mediator, who
translates access to divine knowledge onto a lateral and phenomenal axis,
as opposed to a vertical and transcendent one. Because Jesus in himself
represents the agency of God's teaching, placing himself into dynamic,
spatial relations to his hearers, he requires not so much assent to a series
of propositions as a visible response to what he and his utterances create
at a particular moment. Hammond glosses "every one that hath learned
of the Father cometh unto me" "as the *coming unto me* is all one with the
coming unto me, that is, unto Christ, ver. 44, so they that had *heard* and
learned of the Father, being all one with the *taught of God,* must needs be
they on whom the effect of that hearing and divine doctrine was
wrought, that is, those who were obedient to God's grace."[86]

The mechanism of cause-effect relations acts as a corollary to the
Christian life enacted by obedience, and it opposes the inspirationalists'
penchant for collapsing cause and effect into a doctrine of representational immediacy:

> If the text be again observed, it would be a foul absurdity that
> would be consequent to that interpretation of it, that God the
> Father should be said thus immediately to *teach* them, who upon
> being so taught are said *to come to Christ;* for it is certain that Christ
> was set forth by God as the teacher of his will, and that was the end
> of God's *drawing* any man to Christ, that he might receive the full
> knowledge of his will from thence, which it were impertinent and
> even impossible for him to do, who were first taught by God in this
> sense.[87]

"Christ was set forth," that is, as a measurable, observable, yet contingent
sign of God's representations to humanity. And it is a short but obvious
step to the view that action or narrative—a linear articulation of such
signs, as opposed to doctrinal utterances—might serve to authorize
Scripture. Because perceptual acquaintance is a matter of contingency,
the contingencies of narrative might somehow, by giving words a context, embody them and control their tendency to become rarefied and
needlessly abstracted.

The life and actions of Christ assume, of course, the greatest burden,

and the Gospels are now to be judged as almost anthropological accounts. Thus the most convincing proof of the Psalms' status in the
scriptural canon is the authority conferred on them by their use within
the context of New Testament narrative. Hammond provides "two signal
instances" of the Psalms' significance: "the one at the institution of the
Eucharist, Matt. xxvi. 30, . . . *they sung a psalm*—closed the whole action
with a hymn—*and so went out.* . . . The other instance was that upon the
cross, being now at the pouring out of his peace-offering, Matt. xxvii.46,
About the ninth hour— . . . like a Levite's trumpet—*resounded with a loud
voice, Eli, Eli, Lamma Sabacthani,* the express words, in the Syriac reading, of the beginning of Ps. xxii."[88]

It is only in their use, by acting in a social context, that the Psalms
prove their "divinity," whereby Jesus, "by his own prescription, or practice . . . impressed a sacred character on each."[89] Hammond also discusses the word *testament.* Without forgetting the significance of *covenant,* Hammond argues for a notion of testimonial, "wherein the
Christian's inheritance is sealed to him as to a son and heir of God's, and
wherein the death of Christ, as of a *testator* (Heb. 9:16, 17), is set down at
large by way of story, and as it is applicable to our benefit."[90]

Story then proves the context and ground for the covenant between
God and humanity. Hammond elaborates the view at length in *Of the
Reasonableness of the Christian Religion* (1650), which follows Grotius's *De
Veritate* and obviously anticipates the main arguments of Locke's *The
Reasonableness of Christianity* (1696). Hammond writes that miracles are
sufficient and reasonable proofs of the faith and are validated by familiar
forensic criteria. Scriptural events participate within the fabric of history,
and God conveyed his truths to his creatures precisely by observing the
limits of his creation ("God's speaking to us in men, and upon earth"). If
God had chosen to communicate by some supernatural, unmediated
method, he would have obstructed the transmission of knowledge to
later ages, because—as Stillingfleet and Defoe vigorously argue—the
coinage of cultural transmission must appeal to the vehicles of human
understanding; namely, the visible, verifiable mediations of ordinary
language, for which writing becomes the best medium. Accordingly,
Hammond asks, "What ways would be expected to convince the ages to
come, who should not be present to hear it, of the truth of this, but the
constant affirmation of those who are now ear-witnesses of it, and by
their committing all this to writing now?"[91] Although Hammond exam-
ines aural events, Locke will examine visual ones. But in the Gospels,

both kinds of phenomena appear as public events obeying forensic criteria that are best conveyed by written documents: Hammond's use of aural events in the Gospels does not amount, in short, to some epistemological privileging of orality over writing.

Claims to immediate and supernatural evidences amount to a denial of the contingent terms of quotidien existence.[92] Thus the testimony that supports Christian truth (which, once proven, we might call "infallibly true"),[93] though it includes prophecies fulfilled in Christ,[94] almost exclusively consists of miraculous events occurring in public before numerous witnesses, some hostile, who nevertheless found no cause to question their experience. Like the Transfiguration, or Pentecost, or the Resurrection—the most central single such authorizing event, and a massive ostensive act confirming Christ's nature[95]—Saul's conversion "was not done privately, but every circumstance of the story was publicly known at that time." The fact that those with Saul on that fateful journey to Damascus did not hear the words addressed to him does not trouble Hammond, because that private knowledge became manifest by its palpable effects—ironically, Paul's blindness: "The obscurity of [such] words, and of the representation to which they belonged, was presently interpreted by the effect." Although Peter may apparently have experienced some gnostic communication at Cornelius's house, the Spirit "probably came down on them in some way of visible appearance," or in the speaking of tongues, which "was seen by the Jews, that were very far from being inclinable to believe such a thing of gentiles, and being convinced by the evidence were astonished at it, rapt with admiration at the strangeness, but no way doubting the truth of it."[96]

By placing the Jews outside the structure of belief that the evidences seem to confirm, Hammond tests the purely epistemic, cognitive value of events, which are thought to verify Christian doctrine, painting those events as discrete supernatural actions established by a plural perspective. The probable force of miracles establishes the essentials of faith; namely, the proposition that Jesus is the Christ. And Hammond simply elides its dogmatic ramifications, so part two of *The Reasonableness* recounts not theological niceties, but the benefits of a faith founded on the particulars of historical narrative.

Chronology, Narrative, and Myth in Jean Le Clerc

Like Grotius, Le Clerc represents an important connection between English and Dutch life in the period I describe.[97] A rival of Pierre Bayle and, like Limborch, a Remonstrant correspondent of Locke—whose *Essay*, in precis, he first published[98]—Le Clerc served the Dutch republic of letters as editor of three great periodicals, the *Bibliothèque Universelle et Historique*, then the *Bibliothèque Choisie*, and the *Bibliothèque Ancienne et Moderne*.[99] Like many others, he had read and was influenced by Simon's *Histoire Critique du Vieux Testament* (1678). But, on his own admission, Le Clerc belongs firmly to the tradition of Anglo-Dutch theology we are examining. He edited Erasmus and constantly cites Grotius, as well as Casaubon, Hammond, Wilkins, Ward, Vossius, Stillingfleet, and Burnet. Born in Geneva, Le Clerc epitomizes that Arminian criticism of high Calvinism which also distinguishes Casaubon, Grotius, and the English neoclassical line they influenced; thus, unsurprisingly, Le Clerc's works often appeared immediately in England after their publication in Holland.[100]

Coming after Simon and Bayle, Le Clerc has a theological scepticism that is more incisive than that of Grotius or Hammond, and Thomas Brown prefaces his translation of Le Clerc's *Twelve Dissertations [on] Genesis* with a defense of his author against charges of deism and atheism.[101] Le Clerc's aim is, however, like Grotius's and Hammond's, to rescue truth from the ruins of time. In the preface to *An Historical Vindication of the Naked Gospel* (1690), he writes:

> *The Design of this Work is of no less Importance than to discover the* Naked Truth, *as far as 'tis possible, after the Destruction of such infinite Numbers of Volumes by the Barbarity of former Ages: The little Fragments and Gleanings whereof, (that accidentally escap'd the Flames and Fury of those Times) tho' dispers'd up and down, yet do still afford some Light to a perspicacious* Enquirer; *and indeed give such a Landskip of things, as the Ruins now at* Athens, Carthage *and* Rome, *do of those Majestick Cities.*[102]

The philological researches of "Erasmus, Scaliger, Grotius, Capellus, *and* F. Simons *[sic]*" simply reveal how historical fact has been obscured by the institutional excesses of the church, pagan philosophy, and "Platonick Enthusiasm," exploited for their own ends by ecclesiastics.[103]

More clearly than for Simon, for Le Clerc an answer lies in the proper use of method. Method can serve both to cope with the problem of historical evidences and with that of linguistic ambiguity. Simon's energies go into the sheer amassing of detail, and less into disclosing his own agency within the text as a critical posture toward it, or promoting a form of participation in a critical community. Le Clerc, by contrast, describes his century, as well as his own engagement with earlier critics, as an emergence of critical method, which could become a means to intellectual toleration. Thus he describes "the general Bent of the last Age, rather towards Theological than Grammatical Learning, by reason of the new Controversies that then employ'd the whole Christian World; so that the Interpreters rather busied themselves to confute Errors, than give us a plain and critical Ennaration of the Words."[104]

The attitude is allied to a certain hypotheticalism, where, though Le Clerc seems to treat "hypothesis" as an order of judgment not founded on the "evident" or "manifest," he intends hypothesis to work as a mere postulate until verified by "positive testimony." Thus what Le Clerc denigrates as mere "conjecture" must give way, in the progress of method, to "opinion and probability."[105]

One aim of his first "Dissertation" on Genesis is to describe "The Method I follow'd in my Interpretation,"[106] because he believes it would be a "prodigious Advantage" to produce "a certain Method, made up of immutable Rules" of interpretation. The hope of the present age is that "we mightily exceed [the Massorites] in Method; for since we have most accurate Grammars, and follow fixt establish'd Rules, we no longer un-riddle the Construction of a Sentence by guessing, nor are we carried up and down by uncertain Conjectures, as we may observe the Ancients were."[107]

We must not confuse Le Clerc's optimism with a failure of epistemic scepticism, because it is precisely as an instrument for negotiating, and confirming, our contingent status that we should adopt method. Le Clerc's method is fundamentally comparative, seeking to discriminate on probable grounds the relative status of evidences; for example, when Le Clerc seeks to adjudicate the textual reliability of the Septuagint.[108] His prose itself conscripts the reader into the range of his interpretations, as here, where he both discusses and symbolizes his own critical strategies:

> But as we had often occasion to doubt, whether our Conjectures were right, and could not make out the meaning clear enough by the help of Grammar and Criticism alone, or else several meanings of equal Probability offered themselves: The Reader may observe, that both in our Paraphrase and Commentary, we use a doubtful and no Dogmatical Stile, and perhaps he will there discover fre-quenter Reasons for suspending his Opinion, than in most Writ-ings of this nature. But since every Man Believes and Doubts for

himself, I must inform those Learned Gentlemen that have a great insight into those Matters, that I writ for my self, and such as stand upon the same level, and may they hug themselves with the sweet Contemplation, that they know more than their Neighbours. Least [*sic*] we should betray any one into Mistakes, we made a scruple to assert some things positively, when neither by the assistance of others, nor by our own Endeavours, we are able to fix any certain Judgment: However it does not follow, that People do not invent, because they do not affirm.[109]

Against the dogmatic penetration of the "Learned Gentlemen," Le Clerc firmly, even with a touch of sarcasm, exposes the necessity of a kind of moderate activity of judgment, enforced in this translation at the level of typography, where the capitalized "Believes" and "Doubts" compete for attention. But Le Clerc almost rudely reminds us that if, in exercising that moderation he enacts, we withhold assent, we are still committed to an ideological position, though one we might prefer to the alternatives. This view obtains in the case of translation, where, like Dryden, Le Clerc argues for a "middle way . . . whereby the Translation shall neither be made so servile and close as to become obscure, and mis-lead those that are only skill'd in Latin, nor too lax or redundant, so as to shew the Interpreter rather than the Writer himself." The middle way cannot escape assuming the political weight implied here by Le Clerc's metaphors. The translator still imposes his will: "We find 'tis impossible to make a Translation of the Scripture, without a Man's interposing his own Sence against his Will."[110]

Translator and textual editor thus share the same position vis à vis historical texts. And Le Clerc tries to contain the degree of ideological imposition by pushing the historical, comparative method as far as he can. "The Grammatical and Critical way of Interpretation" must "borrow assistance from the neighboring Languages, . . . where the Sence and Circumstance of places will naturally lead an Interpreter" to understand the Hebrew.[111] The topological metaphor of place (as in "the comparing of places"), of neighborhood, and of "Circumstance," should suggest what is the case: that Le Clerc, like the neoclassical linguists discussed in chapter six, takes the sense of utterances to depend on their position within a culture, not as some stable semantic term. To paraphrase Gottlob Frege, *die Sprache immer nur bedeutet*. Thus "the ancient Interpreters," being closer in time to the culture they describe, have a better sense of "the use of the Languages then in being." Le Clerc argues for the final impossibility of translating one language into another without patiently and archaeologically situating the utterance in relation to the culture that produced it, a process so cumbersome as to become prohibitive.[112]

In practice, as in the case of Polyglot bibles, this leaves us with an analogical method, where the task of the editor, like Le Clerc, is "to referr to those [Interpretations] that seem'd to be the most probable of all, and lay down the Reasons that support them." Honesty must occasionally force us "prudently to suspend our Judgments"; but in leaving this final decision to the reader, the apex of the structure of inference within which he or she acts and so makes real, "if we do not discover the Truth, yet at least it is not excluded from the Mind."[113]

Etymology is yet another an interpretive aid. And again, though Le Clerc speaks of etymology as a search for "the Original of words," he means in alluding to their "trace" or "footsteps" not to uncover some originary scene but, by a kind of archaeological enterprise, their cultural history.[114] As in some of the linguistic texts we examined, the attitude is obscured by Brown's reference to the Royal Society motto, *Nullius in Verba,* and Le Clerc's own juxtapositions between "Rhetorical Figures, which only amuse and deceive ignorant People" and "the thing itself," or "Words and Stile" and "the things themselves."[115]

It is, significantly, Le Clerc's use of Cicero that shows how far he is from embracing some naïve referential or transparent ideal. Le Clerc's assault on "Words and Stile" comes within a clearly defined context, in which one target is not representation as such, but orality as a special site of language, one that, by obscuring the actual nature of ordinary language, based as it is on palpably figural operations, serves for political manipulation.[116] Thus at several points, he indicts etymology, conceived of as a fascination with the mere "chiming of words," or "empty Sounds."[117] His view of how language must nevertheless work figurally emerges in the course of his criticisms of Hebrew, which exploit criteria derived from Cicero. Precisely because Hebrew writers lacked "Grammar, Rhetorick, and the whole Circle of Philosophy," Hebrew literature is "unpolished and uncultivated," in comparison with the classical languages.[118] The Greeks and Romans have best prescribed, in the rhetorical tradition epitomized in Cicero, the terms by which all languages need "principally . . . three things, *viz* Plenty of Words and Phrases, Perspicuity of Speech, and Purity."[119] Unequipped with such rules, which merely describe the inherent behavior of language, Hebrew is indeed

crude by comparison with Greek. But by the same token, its very cru-
dities become a kind of experimental opportunity for Le Clerc to expose,
more dramatically than otherwise, the base necessities of language as
inevitably figural. By a philosophical approach to language, Le Clerc
means quite the opposite of what he could be taken to mean, for his
conceptualism assumes that the purpose of philosophy is to extend, not
limit and proscribe, the range of vocabulary, because the copiousness of
mental representation calls for a copious style. The limited nature of
Hebrew expression thus places a strain on linguistic resources in such a
way as to reveal how all language must be taken as metaphorical.

Where Le Clerc seems at first to desire one word for each notion, he
suggests a theory of reference; but where he—citing Cicero—admits
that no language can execute that ratio, he is resigned to the inevitability
of metaphor, or the intransigent slippage of words from some putatively
single sense to a borrowed one, in such a way as to make nonsense of any
clear distinction between the literal and figurative uses of words. This we
see in a crucial passage that seems to grasp at the literal, only to deny it
and to substitute in its place a clear reading of the culturally specific
position and use of words, so that one verbal token comes, in this case in
Hebrew, to bear a range of meanings. As in other instances we shall
examine, the passage assumes heuristic rather than prescriptive force:

> Want of words begot Ambiguity, for when we are destitute of
> proper Terms to explain our meanings by, we must wrest them into
> another Sence, or else express particular things in words common
> to several more. *For Metaphors,* as *Cicero* well observes, *l. 3. de Orat.*
> *c. 38. are all like borrowing, where what a Man has not of his own, he*
> *supplies himself with elsewhere.* Now if one and the same word sig-
> nifies several things, one in its proper Acceptation, the rest in a
> borrow'd or tralatitious Sence, 'tis no easie matter to distinguish its
> several Significations, and when Particulars are called by common
> Names, it often happens that we do not clearly understand, in what
> respect they differ from other things of the same Genus. For in-
> stance, *Erets* signifies among the Hebrews *Clay* that Vessels are
> made of, a *Tract of Ground* either more or less suitable to the present
> Occasion, the whole *Globe* of the Earth, and the *Men* that inhabit it;
> so that 'tis hard to say, which is its proper Signification, and which
> Figurative. When an universal Designation is fixed upon this word,
> which is express'd by *chol, All,* 'tis doubted whether the whole
> Kingdom, or a less compass of Ground, or the Globe of the Earth,

or whether all Men, or only some, are to be understood by it; so that nothing by the Context, or the Nature of the thing in debate, can assist our Conjectures.[120]

Cicero confirms that the activity of borrowing—the fact of language-as-metaphor—is equally a property of Hebrew, Greek, and Latin. We can only understand an utterance *("Erets," "chol"),* and that provisionally, by its cultural position ("Context"), or symbolic force, within linguistic exchange ("in debate"); and Le Clerc even recognizes that the proliferation of possibilities suggests more than a linguistic binarism. It is not the nature of the sign, but its cultural position, that makes it mean.

Moreover, Le Clerc also weds his conceptualism to this theory of symbolic action, again in a passage he uses heuristically. When we imagine language as a product of a certain local, provisional posture vis à vis the world, we can imagine—as Le Clerc does—that the original act of naming occurs precisely because words are attached to what strikes the observer as the sufficient token of an object or event. That is, linguistic signs arbitrarily denote mental signs—not fully, but only associatively, or by analogy representing the world. Thus in Le Clerc's reworking of the Adamic myth, words derive, apparently, from events, actions, features of the external world, which are empirically verifiable. *"Antedeluvian"* proper names did not depict an essential character bestowed at birth, but rather came to note typical features of individual experience observed over time: "They are to be looked upon as Sirnames, afterwards bestowed upon them for some particular Event or Accident that befell them."[121] That Adam had no need of language before the arrival of Eve indicates words have solely social significance.[122] And that words originally depicted by synecdoche only observable features of the world, not essences, is shown by Le Clerc's revision of Adamic naming. The animals did not "by a Miraculous and extraordinary Effect of the Divine Power" come trooping "to *Adam* to have names bestowed upon them"; rather, "words were invented by degrees, and . . . these Animals received their names as our first Parents happen'd to behold them, or to talk of them." In Hebrew, for example, names "are sometimes taken from something remarkably obvious in the Animals, which any one might have discovered at first sight."[123]

Le Clerc conceives of languages, then, in visual terms, derived from an empirical reading of how words were invented to respond to external stimuli. To work as intended, language-as-we-have-it must respect those habits of the mind that invented it. In a characteristic neoclassical slide, the way language is born (signs arbitrarily selected from the external world) expresses a demand for appropriate figures of speech—namely, analogy and metonymy—which are thought to rehearse that mechanism of invention. Thus the rhetoricians recommend that the analogical devices embedded in language be rendered perspicuous: this is the means to refining language, not some impossible search for linguistic transparency. Analogy assumes both similarity and dissimilarity, and the proper use of figures will calibrate and reveal the true proportions between each. On the one hand, we cannot have what Johnson was to abhor in the metaphysicals—namely, gross disproportion between the terms of a figure: *"All Disparity is to be avoided,"* the rhetoricians advise, "because every Metaphor is, or ought to be, grounded upon some likeness."[124] On the other hand, fictions of the literal forge absolute equations between such terms, which have clear political implications for Le Clerc. Like the doctrine of transubstantiation, what is invisible is politically subversive: the Catholics "defend their monstrous Opinion" by taking "the words of our Saviour, *This is my Body;* to infer a real Conversion of the Bread into the Body of Christ."[125] Thus, as regards his own theory of translation, Le Clerc wants to retain the difficulty of the original, because, like analogy, it preserves a cognitive resistance to the imperializing tendencies of the mind.[126]

God's use of Hebrew is a particularly strenuous proof of the necessity of figuration: Le Clerc simply retools the old device of accommodation. God communicates by and within the idiom of a given language; it is less that words are invariably mediated than that the utterances they compose are historically specific cultural actions. Part of the obscurity of ancient Hebrew results from the impossibility of recovering the idiom, which is now "above the reach of Human Understanding." God's grace toward humanity is expressed precisely by a divine communication embedded in the local accents of the language:

> But though God Almighty discover'd them to us by the Jews, yet he permitted them to use such a Stile as was most Familiar to themselves and their own Country-men: For the Spirit, by which they were influenced, by a wonderful Condescention, accommodated himself to the received Customs of their Language. Hence it comes to pass, that the Apostles deliver'd the Doctrine of Christ not in an Attick Stile, or with *Plato*'s Eloquence, but after their own way suitable to the People, for though they were Divinely inspir'd, yet

they were but indifferently skill'd in Humane Learning, as we were
told by St. *Paul*.[127]

Two major consequences follow from what I call an incarnationalist
position. God speaks in local, provisional terms, which emerges as a
commitment to narrative, as best representing the temporality of common experience. It also follows that complete translation between and
among cultures is impossible: as we have seen, Le Clerc expresses discomfort about the editorial exercise of textual criticism, and especially
translation, as entailing an unwarranted cultural and ideological imposition on its materials in the process of making them available to a wider
public.[128]

Even if the habits of the mind are universal properties, the structure
of lived experience differs according to climate and time. The mind may
manufacture words in a single way, but the cultural significance of languages varies: "Since Tongues are Images of the Sentiments of our Mind,
and are form'd and modell'd according to the Opinion of those People
that use them; it cannot otherwise happen, but that the common Speech
of any Country, must derive a great Tincture from the received Opinions
of the Inhabitants."[129] Thus the Babel story becomes for Le Clerc not so
much a literal as another heuristic device to describe the dispersion of
groups and the emergence of different dialects.

The double respect for the temporality of experience and its cultural
specificity, suggested by the verbal phrase "form'd or modell'd," leads to
an entire critique in Le Clerc of the habits and necessities of narrative—at
least its equivalents in a sequence of symbolic actions that carries peculiar
cognitive and cultural authority. Mosaic prophecy sanctions this mode as
a special method of exemplification: Moses "seems . . . to have design'd
to reform the Manners of the *Israelites* not only by direct and open
Precepts, but by a more oblique . . . way, of instructing them by Narrations."[130] Le Clerc here epitomizes his attitude to narrative, because
Moses conveys knowledge not perceptually, but in that more indirect,
somatic way best suited to human apprehension, and whose significance
carries force only in a specific cultural context.

Like the Protestant view of Jesus' utterance, "This is my body," it
follows that only by understanding the function of metaphor within a
specific society and language that the 'literal' significance of the narrations can unfold. Jesus did not mean his utterance to be taken 'literally,'
but (literally) meant it to be taken according to common usage; that is,

symbolically. Similarly, Moses' "Narrations" are utterances intended to be interpreted by their audience, the Israelites, and to understand them we need to recuperate their hermeneutic codes, to see them as provisional objects of interpretation. Thus it is by an appeal to probability, a consciousness of how we figure ordinary events in our own narratives, with their various motives embedded in what we intend or assume them to do, that we must reread both Mosaic and New Testamental narrative. Thus, at one level, Moses' narratives seem strangely improbable, but that is because the (probable) historical conditions of their construction caused them to be strangely truncated. Moses abridged his narratives, because he "writ for the Benefit and Instruction of a particular People called the *Jews*."[131] We cannot expect Mosaic narrative to act in ways we want our narratives to act.

Yet the mere fact of narrative still argues for a human response to some actual events, particularly if those events are adumbrated frequently enough in different accounts (a "concurrence" of "many Circumstances").[132] But at the same time, precisely because narrative is a metaphorical account of such events, Le Clerc wants to show the primacy of biblical events by treating subsequent interpretations, in Greek myths or rabbinic commentary, as displaying the results of wrong reading. These are less probable, highly abstracted impositions on more genuinely historical accounts, because they are unempirical, allegorical readings performed without regard to the local rhetorical and philological significance of a given historical utterance. By a kind of paradox, this false allegorizing springs from a too literal understanding of what critics think they see, just as Catholic theology has perversely taken Jesus' words of institution to denote the literal translation of bread into flesh. The rabbis "chose to commit Violence upon" Mosaic narrative,[133] raising "Romances and Legends" by their "Study of Allegories and Rites, but not of Philological Learning."[134] And the Greek fables—reworkings of genuine historical events already inscribed in Mosaic narrative[135]—irreparably damage those particulars by a similar allegorical turn. Allegory of this kind cannot respect the resistance of the rhetoric of history to the imperializing desires of the mind, just as the fiction of linguistic transparency (of the literal), in the larger fable of this book, indulges similar endogenous, narcissistic motives. The Greeks "had Vanity enough to adorn whatever they heard, with new fictions of their own Invention," with the result that "in the most ancient Histories of the *Greeks*, which are called *[muthoi]*, we find the innumerable Stories or Fables, not corrupted so much for the sake of Lying, but because the Narrations of the ancient Inhabitants were not understood well enough, and because their Metaphorical Expressions were erroniously interpreted in the proper or literal Sense."[136]

Because narrative enacts the temporal experience of the human mind, it is easier to translate than "the Books of the Prophets," which represent the mind's tendency to abstract and to ironize the atomic, sequential particulars of experience. Le Clerc links the sympathy that human thought extends to narrative with the criterion of "Connexion and Series," which not only asks probable narratives to obey "the Regularities of Time and Action" but also requires the grammatical sentence to follow an evident linear construction.[137] Like narrative, grammar and the printing culture Le Clerc summons to display it repeat and regulate the sequential and spatial quality of mental discourse. Accordingly, like Locke in *An Essay for the Understanding of St. Paul's Epistles* (1707), Le Clerc argues that the discontinuities in the reader's experience caused by typographical interruptions can obstruct the powers of syntax to articulate the processes of the mind. Le Clerc suggests how fragile the parallel between mental and typographical experience can be by observing that even the omission of one particle in a sentence can "render the Narration indirect and oblique," because "by this means an unskillful Reader will imagine, that some things are related *en passant,* while the Historian makes haste to go to others that are more material." He will therefore ensure that his typographical presentation of Genesis will respect the movements of the narrative, for though "we have distinguished the Verses by Numbers, . . . we have only had a regard to the Sence in the manner of our Pointing."[138] For Le Clerc, the palpability of cultural knowledge is executed by the tactile experience of the printed text.

Narrative Sequence and the Rise of the Harmony

It is in the "Harmony" that the perceptual power of linguistic, typographical, and narrative sequentiality is perhaps most clearly expressed. The emergence of method as I have described it seems to have coincided with the rise of the harmony, and evidently for similar reasons: Samuel Craddock claimed to have "Methodiz'd" the Evangelists' "Text," and to "Methodically set forth" the "Entire History of our Lord and Savior Jesus Christ."[139] The harmony was intended to "set forth," on the printed page, the true order of biblical action, even, in the more sophisticated versions, preserving the fragmentary texture of its sources. The first

MATTHEW.	MARK.	LUKE.	JOHN.
CHAP. XIV.	CHAP. VI.	CHAP. IX.	CHAP. VI.

MATTHEW.

21 And they that had eaten were about five thoufand men,

befides women and children.

☞

22 And ſtraight-way Jeſus conſtrained his diſciples to get into a ſhip, and to go before him unto the other ſide, while he ſent the multitudes away.
23 And when he had ſent the multi-tudes away,

☞

he went up into a mountain apart to pray :

MARK.

44 And they that did eat of the loaves, were about five thou-ſand men.

☜

☞

45 And ſtraight-way he conſtrain-ed his diſciples to get into the ſhip, and to go to the other ſide before unto Bethſai-da, while he ſent away the people.
46 And when he had ſent them away,

☞

he departed into a mountain to pray.

LUKE.

14 For they were about five thouſand men.

☜

☜

JOHN.

10 So the men ſat down, in number about five thouſand.

☜

☞ 14 Then thoſe men when they had ſeen the miracle that Jeſus did, ſaid, This is of a truth that prophet that ſhould come into the world.
☜

☞ 15 When Jeſus therefore perceived that they would come and take him by force, to make him a king,

he departed again into a mountain himſelf alone.

Women and Children, whom *Jeſus* thus entertain'd, and who perceiving this won-derful Miracle, concluded he was that extraordinary Prophet whom God had promis'd to ſend unto 'em, namely, the *Meſſiah.*

Jeſus immediately order'd his Diſciples (who obey'd him with ſome reluctancy at parting with him) to go on board, and ſail over before him to the other ſide of the Lake over againſt *Bethſaida,* where he then was, while he himſelf ſtaid to diſmiſs the Multitude. After which, underſtanding that ſeveral of thoſe whom he had thus miraculouſly treated were reſolv'd to take him by force, and proclaim him King over them, he withdrew into a Mountain alone to fruſtrate their deſign, and that he might be uninterrupted in his Devotion. The Apoſtles in the mean time,

G g   who

Page from Le Clerc, *Harmony of the Evangelists* (1701)

Frontispiece to Le Clerc, *Harmonia Evangelica* (1699)

notable series of harmonies was issued by the great linguist John Light-foot, a co-editor with Walton of the *Biblia Polyglotta,* and whom Gibbon, on account of his great learning in Hebrew, was to memorialize as "al-most a rabbi himself."[140] *The Harmony of the Foure Evangelists* (1644) was followed in 1647 by *The Harmony, Chronicle, and Order of the Old Testa-ment,* and in 1655 Lightfoot finally issued *The Harmony, Chronicle and Order of the New Testament.* To launch his project in 1644, Lightfoot wrote that "*The Harmony of the Evangelists* in our *English* tongue is rare to find, especially with that proofe of the order of the story, and that illustra-tion of the Text and Language, that a thing of that nature doth require, & that it hath found in other tongues."[141] Later he was to claim that the harmony succeeds in reducing scriptural texts "into their proper order," taking them "up in their proper places, in which the naturall Method and genuine *Series* of the *Chronology* requireth them to be taken in."[142] Like Hobbes's method of analysis and recombination, the harmony observes the "dislocations of Scripture" before "reducing them to their proper time and order."[143] It is not surprising to find Locke working on an elaborate harmony in his journal for 1676.[144]

After working on a Latin translation of Hammond's *Paraphrase and Annotations of the New Testament* (which he published in 1698), Le Clerc wrote to Locke that "j'ai travaillé, sans discontinuation, à une harmonie des Evangiles, que j'ai achevée en Grec, et en suite en Latin."[145] Pub-lished in 1699, Le Clerc's *Harmonia Evangelica* appeared in translation in London in 1701, as *The Harmony of the Evangelists. Being the whole Text of the Four Gospels dispos'd according to the Order of Time in which the Things related in them were done* (p. 271). The typography of this publication deserves especial attention, because, like Walton's *Biblia Polyglotta,* it sustains a perfect equilibrium between the atomic constituents of narra-tive on the one hand, and their articulation by typographical arrange-ment into some larger proposition on the other, while retaining the texture of history. The page divides vertically into four columns, one for each Gospel, with the bottom, horizontal margin devoted to the para-phrase that weaves the fragments into a virtually seamless sequence of events. The very arrangement of the page executes the Lucretian distinc-tion between the atoms of matter and words, as well as their articulation into the seemingly coherent fabric of the world, of knowledge, and of language. It also displays in the most graphic terms possible the entire architecture of analogical (comparative) and inferential (paraphrastic) relations that compose neoclassical method. In the frontispiece of the

Dutch first edition (p. 272), these methodical arrangements are realized in slightly different terms, with the four Evangelists cooperating to serve a picture of Christ, who stands above them as if to orchestrate their juxtaposition, mutually distributed as they are around the plinth on which he stands. And we know, of course, theologically that we only come to Christ *through* the Evangelists, just as the figure of Christ himself harmonizes their various accounts, signaled by the book each holds in his hand. Thus the Greek on the pedestal reads: "These things have been written that you may believe," and the final object of belief is indicated in the banner above the figure of Christ, which reads "this is my beloved son."

Commenting on his own book's performance, Le Clerc observes that "any man that has eyes may be convinc'd merely from dipping into this Book" that the "entire History" of Christ "has not been related by every particular Evangelist." The reader can see "one [writer] proceeding in a Relation, when all the rest are silent."[146] And because the method to which he is committed is cautiously reconstructive, Le Clerc can shamelessly embrace the Evangelists' "broken Narrative," because its fragments present a therapeutic challenge to the reader's inferential activity. Like all knowledge, the Gospel narrative arises from particular and apparently discrete events and utterances; Le Clerc's chronological pointing simply suggests how these atoms are not centrifugal, but centripetal, in impulse. Thus, "'tis plain [the Evangelists] have given us the same story in substance, tho differing in some Circumstances; which Variety arises from different Memories of the Historians, and their different purposes of writing in a short or more copious Stile."[147]

In the preface to his work, Le Clerc complains about the failure of previous harmonies to convey a sufficiently dynamic forward movement, which they obstruct by *"tedious Commentaries."* Le Clerc's own prescriptions crystallize his hermeneutical assumptions. The typographical arrangement of his harmony realizes the terms of Le Clerc's entirely neoclassical method. That cogent history arises from *"the connexion and dependance of one Story upon another"*[148] secures the necessary sense of continuity; but it also remembers that, unless it wants to abandon its moorings in empirical experience, narrative must inscribe the pressure of the particulars that it describes and that produced it, but that, paradoxically but no less inevitably, depend on its ministrations to remain real to other generations of readers.

8. Method, Image, and Action in Literary Criticism

The Academy Royal may pack up their Modes and Methods, & *penses
ingenieuses; the* Racines *and the* Corneilles *must now all dance to the
Tune of* Baptista. *Here is the* Opera; *here is* Machine *and* Baptista, *farewell*
Apollo *and the Muses.*

Thomas Rymer, *A Short View of Tragedy* (1693)

*It is one thing to think right, and another thing to know the right way to lay
our thoughts before others with advantage and clearness, be they right or
wrong. Well-chosen similies* [sic], *metaphors, and allegories, with method
and order, do this the best of any thing, because being taken from objects
already known, and familiar to the understanding, they are conceived as fast
as spoken; and the correspondence being concluded, the thing they are
brought to explain and elucidate is thought to be understood too.*

John Locke, *Of the Conduct of the Understanding* (1706)

The Rhetoric of Neoclassical Criticism

In earlier chapters, I have shown how neoclassical discourse—whatever
its apparent objects of knowledge—is remarkably conscious of its own
procedures. Far from attempting a watertight deductive or rationalistic
system, writers emphasized probable methods of apprehension both in
their explicit pronouncements and, equally significantly, in the manner
and form in which they cast their propositions. Locke's *Essay* remains
true to the method implied by its title inasmuch as it damages the fabric
of Locke's masterpiece to divorce its defense of contingency from its
contingent form and rhetoric. Its prior commitment to method explains
why it is impossible above all in neoclassical criticism to disentangle, and
so to reify, the various traditions to which it is indebted.[1] Thus Emerson
Marks can write that "we have to reject the view that in their serious
commitment to Aristotelian teaching Augustan men of letters were in
perverse reaction to the intellectual currents of the time" and adds that

"some hint of a sounder explanation is provided by their reiteration of that word *method*. . . . The method of any science was embodied in a set of rules, principles or axioms that were so many means to an end."[2] The inculcation of a methodical habit *in the reader* becomes this end: thus many neoclassical texts, while appearing prescriptive, also describe their aims by leaving their texts peculiarly open-ended.[3] Preparing to conclude his preface to *The Great Favourite*, Sir Robert Howard asks his reader to continue to extrapolate from the author's activity of judgment: "I would have all attempts of this nature be submitted to the fancy of others, and bear the name of Propositions, not of confident Lawes, or Rules made by Demonstrations."[4]

This is a particularly happy example, because it captures Howard's sceptical tone and reveals how his interest in method describes his own approach to the subject at hand, as well as his technique of inviting the reader into a common habit of discovery. In closing his preface to his translation of René Rapin's *Reflections on Aristotle's Treatise of Poesie* (1674), and after offering a final piece of evidence in support of his arguments, Thomas Rymer concludes that "the comparison might be much further improved to our advantage, and more observations made, which are left to the Reader's ingenuity."[5] Similarly, John Dennis's *The Impartial Critick* (1693), like Chillingworth's *Religion of Protestants* and Boyle's *The Sceptical Chymist*, employs the dialogue to realize a probable method of critical enquiry. One exchange between Beaumont and Free-man merges an explicit debate about probability in dramatic representation with the process of debating and a running commentary on the process.[6] The literary form of much neoclassical criticism—dialogue, informal addresses, prologues, and prefaces—naturally arises in part from its occasional milieu. But the mere fact of this contingency perfectly suits a wider ideal of contingency, which, like the letters exchanged between Taylor and Evelyn, seeks a rhetorical corollary to its epistemological, methodical, and ethical motives. Thus William Davenant's consistent allusions to his own poem within his preface to *Gondibert* infuse the argument with a kind of local and strategic value it would otherwise lack. At the end of the preface, Davenant turns to his friend and dedicatee, Hobbes, to bid him farewell and to remind him of the image of his creation, which has informed the discussion throughout: "And now, Sir, to end with the Allegory which I have so long continu'd, I shall (after all my busy vanitie in shewing and describing my new Building) with great quietnesse (being almost as weary as your selfe) bring you to the

Back dore, that you may make no review but in my absence; and steal hastely from you, as one who is asham'd of all the trouble you have receav'd."[7]

Davenant's cautiousness is echoed by Howard's in their common distrust of the absolute statement: Howard posits contingent, workable truths arrived at by inference ("Propositions") against what he dubs "confident Lawes, or Rules made by Demonstrations." Davenant is less straightforward: admittedly, he adopts a traditional stance of deference toward Hobbes, but he also plots to create a moment of indecision about the stability of literary judgment in order that the reader, like Hobbes, is cast onto his or her own judgment. The diffidence informing the tactic also determines the passage's mode of figuration. While reinvoking the architectural image, Davenant encourages us to see it as a barely suppressed simile ("Allegory") rather than a radical metaphor. So when he beckons Hobbes by the back door of his text, we must remember that analogy only obtains between terms that are unlike: we conserve the individual integrity and discreteness of 'building' and 'text.' The final placement of an explicit comparison ("and steale hastily . . . as one who is asham'd") secures the analogical mechanisms of the whole apostrophe. Clearly, literary figures of speech must observe the particular habits of the mind: Because we manufacture contingent truths by observing particular sensible signs in juxtaposition or combination, figures of speech can only convey understanding by playing, at a symbolic level, a similar role.

Davenant, Hobbes, and the Conceptualist Grounds of Criticism

The analogical habit observes the discreteness of signs in order to encourage a patient comparison between or among them. It cannot allow the arbitrary yoking of terms, but must ensure their organization into family resemblances according to some methodical prescription. For this reason it is at best anachronistic to state that Hobbes injected a new 'psychological' bias into English criticism in the course of his famous exchange with Davenant.[8] The emphasis is decidedly less affective than the allusion to psychology connotes.[9] Properly speaking, the assumptions are mentalist or conceptualist, because these focus on the mind's capacity to receive and arrange signs. And it must be in this primarily cognitive context that we should understand the neoclassical scepticism about language as it applies to the uses and abuses of figures of speech.

No critic contemplating neoclassical attitudes to style feels complete without alluding to Thomas Sprat's *History of the Royal Society*, of which both too much and too little has been made. I quote a purple passage at length:

> [We] should now keep up the Ornaments of speaking, in any request: since they are so much degenerated from their original usefulness. They were at first, no doubt, an admirable Instrument in the hands of *Wise Men:* when they were onely employ'd to describe *Goodness, Honesty, Obedience;* in larger, fairer, and more moving Images: to represent *Truth,* cloth'd with Bodies; and to bring *Knowledg* back again to our very senses, from whence it was at first deriv'd to our understandings. But now they are generally chang'd to worse uses: They make the *Fancy* disgust the best things, if they come not sound, and unadorn'd: they are in open defiance against *Reason,* professing, not to hold much correspondence with that; but with its Slaves, *the Passions:* they give the mind a motion too changeable, and bewitching, to consist with *right practice*. Who can behold, without indignation, how many mists and uncertainties, these specious *Tropes* and *Figures* have brought on our Knowledg?[10]

Read carefully, this is no less an appeal to the mental grammar by which we can know anything at all than a refutation of the figures of speech. Moreover, it assumes a grammar following almost exactly the Lucretian pattern: by impressing images on the mind, the senses set "Fancy" and "Reason" to work.[11] An etiology of representation is at least implied, because when words were used originally to convey truth, they organized images that approximated the effect of sense-impressions. Sprat calls us not away from language, but back to its founding properties. Curiously, especially in light of the Lucretian view of language and the somatic defense of figuration, Sprat conceives figures of speech as "Bodies," which can also import general concepts. That is, language operates metonymically, because the seen (the particular) entails the unseen (the general), a connection left to the reader's act of inference. What Sprat resists is not figuration as such, but its false application.

Davenant's fear of the abuses of language results in a similar revision of its rhetorical possibilities. To convey truth effectively, language must obey the rules that govern common observation. This is to convert the way the world is represented to the mind into a theory of literary representation. So, rejecting poetic rapture, he argues that the ancient poet-prophets "were long and painfull in watching the correspondence of Causes, ere they presum'd to foretell effects." Davenant has therefore submitted himself to an empirical poetic training, based not on "the names, but the proportion, and nature of things."[12] This neither naïvely displaces words in favor of things nor argues some ideal of referential transparency, but suggests rather that discourse can develop sets of internal relations, which somehow enact our apprehensions of the world. At this significant historical crossroads of English cultural history (Paris, 1650), these sets of relations effectively establish for the first time the central neoclassical criteria of wit.[13]

Davenant begins his revision of poetic habits partly by indicting the aural effects of language, removed as they are from "the vulgar Dialect," and only "fit for Sedition." Old men also mistake the nature of wit if they "think that it lyes in [agnominations, and in] a kind of alike tinkling of words." Only carefully selected visual images create the necessary effects, ones that Davenant even exemplifies in a description of his own verbal strategies as a search after "an unusuall dress."[14] It is precisely this power of working through image that allows poetry to assist the statesman to inculcate civic virtue. The poet differs from the divine, not because they do not equally seek to teach, but because the persuasions of the divine flow from his institutional position, depending ultimately on force, not assent. Unlike the sermon, which must exploit the fear of the afterlife and the church's status, "the persuasions of Poesy, in stead of menaces, are Harmonious and delightfull insinuations, and never any constraint; unlesse the ravishment of Reason may be call'd Force."[15] There is much here to remind us of Sidney, but the proportions between cognitive detail and ethical appeals by the critic have shifted: in his references to "Reason," Davenant is feeling his way toward a critique of the cognitive grounds of representation adumbrated in Sprat, but better explicated by Hobbes, the other party to this famous critical exchange.

In his "Answer" to Davenant's preface to *Gondibert*, Hobbes diagrams the course of poetic production: "Time and education begets experience; Experience begets memory; Memory begets Judgement, and Fancy: Judgment begets the strength and structure, and Fancy begets the ornaments of a Poeme." When Hobbes observes in passing that "the Ancients therefore fabled not absurdly in making memory the mother of the Muses,"[16] he adumbrates a conceptualist mechanism of representation, which he more fully explicates in *De Corpore* (1655). In the chapter "Of Method," he distinguishes between "METHOD" as "the science of causes, or . . . of the *[dioti]*" and "all other science, which is called the *[hoti]*, [which] is either perception by sense, or the imagination, or memory remaining after sense perception."[17] Like the geometric method of *Leviathan,* method is the formal organization of what has been derived from the world, which Hobbes describes as "the first beginnings . . . of knowledge." These are "the phantasms of sense and imagination; and that there be such phantasms we know well enough by nature; but to know why they be, or from what causes they proceed, is the work of ratiocination; which consists . . . in *composition,* and *division* or *resolution.*"[18] In outline, this exactly anticipates Locke's authoritative distinction between sensation and reflection, similarly founded on an atomic model of perception. Hobbes's conceptualist view of words follows: words are the arbitrary, voluntary signs of mental conceptions, not of things. "Seeing names ordered in speech (as is defined) are signs of our conceptions, it is manifest that they are not signs of things themselves; for that the sound of this word *stone* should be the sign of a stone, cannot be understood in any sense but this, that he that hears it collects that he that pronounces it thinks of a stone."[19] To argue for Hobbes's conceptualism is not necessarily to deny what critics such as J.W.N. Watkins see as a more radical nominalism also operating in Hobbes.[20] For an atomic account of perception can allow mental images, ideas, or conceptions to assume some symbolic life of their own, independent of their physiological origins, for, as I have argued at length, such a conceptualism presupposes a theory of representation. So whereas Epicurus talks of apparitions impressed on the mind by the external world as *[aisthēseis],* Hobbes similarly talks about *[to phainesthai].*[21] And the arrival of ordinary language certainly represents the emergence of a yet more arbitrary and voluntary principle.[22]

As is well known, Hobbes's conceptualism accompanies a deep suspicion of language, one shared with Dryden, Locke, and other major neoclassical writers. And like Montaigne, Hobbes associates the corruptions of speech with the times in which he lives. Unlike Montaigne, however, he offers the possibility of holding language responsible to human needs in two not entirely commensurable directions. Names serve in Hobbes's terms either for "marks" or for "signs." "Marks" are a means to fix the individual representations of the mind derived from the world (given "How unconstant and fading men's thoughts are"); "signs" denote the use of words as contractual, arbitrary social counters.[23] The latter, and more radical view, informs the entire strategy of *Leviathan:* if words are arbitrary impositions on our thoughts, then we can mutually contract for verbal significance in such a way as to construct a definitional and geometrical science. The former, which seems to inform Hobbes's theory of figuration, is more empirical, in that, if we attend to the habits of the mind, then we can regulate representation to reflect its activity. Both attitudes inform an outburst against the abuses of language in his "Answer" to Davenant:

> There be so many wordes in use at this day in the English tongue, that though of magnifique sound, yet (like the windy blisters of a troubled water) have no sense at all; and so many others that loose their meaning, by being ill coupled, that it is a hard matter to avoid them. . . .
>
> To this palpable darkness, I may also adde the ambitious obscurity of expressing more then is perfectly conceaved; or perfect conception in fewer words then it requires. Which Expressions, though they have had the honor to be called strong lines, are in deed no better then Riddles, and, not onely to the Reader, but also (after a little time) to the Writer himselfe darke and troublesome.[24]

Hobbes's rhetoric of clarity and light emphatically does not oppose some transparent ideal of representation to the darkness of linguistic (implicitly political) chaos. Although Hobbes never loses his faith in the prior fact of the world, giving rise through motion to sense-experience,[25] he knows that our experience is mediated by at least two systems of representation: the representations of the world to our mind occur as parts representing wholes, or as a sequence of causes and effects;[26] and our social interactions occur by a series of arbitrary signs. At one level, these operate as two different arguments, because a focus on signs as cognitive elements physiologically produced by motion does not amount to the analysis—for which Hobbes is famous—of language as a system of social symbology. But at another level they coincide in Hobbes's prescriptions for style, because on the one hand we allow partial representations of the world to stand for the whole, and, on the other, in order to communicate with others we must select sufficient, but only representative, signs to signify whole sets of ideas or universals.

Those prescriptions for style, that is, call for synecdoche and metonymy as the apt figures for expression. This is in part because they oppose a visual aesthetic to the flatulent chaos at present obtaining in the body politic. And it is also because, since they preserve us from the ambitions of those who seek to obfuscate the workings of signs, in order to retain linguistic clarity, they must be regulated to symbolize the partial habits of the human mind, which is limited by the methodical rules of inference and association or analogy. In an important passage analyzing the actual behavior of signs, what Hobbes calls *"natural"* and *"arbitrary"* signs partake of the same figure:

> Now, those things we call SIGNS are the *antecedents of their conse-*
> *quents, and the consequents of their antecedents, as often as we observe*
> *them to go before or follow after in the same manner.* For example, a
> thick cloud is a sign of rain to follow, and rain a sign that a cloud has
> gone before, for this reason only, that we seldom see clouds without
> the consequence of rain, nor rain at any time but when a cloud has
> gone before. And of signs, some are *natural,* whereof I have already
> given an example, others are *arbitrary,* namely, those we make
> choice of at our own pleasure, as a bush hung up, signifies that wine
> is to be sold there; a stone set in the ground signifies the bound of a
> field; and words so and so connected, signify the cogitations and
> motions of our mind.[27]

Metonymy and analogy signify a set of discriminations, a consciousness that signs are not identical to what they represent, which in Hobbes's political allegory happily dissipates the energies of those interests working to secure a cognitive monopoly by counterfeiting identifications between a sign and what it is said to signify. Thus Hobbes explodes the mystifications of Catholic idolatry in part four of *Leviathan* by the instrument of his extended analogy between the Catholic church and the Kingdom of Fairies. Neoclassical wit—whose criteria Davenant and Hobbes forge between them in the Paris of the 1650s—asks the poet to reflect the abundance and variety of empirical experience and visibly reproduce it in a calculated set of rhetorical strategies, one that, in Paul de Man's formulation of the opposition, perpetuates an allegorical over a symbolic reading of language.

Hobbes accordingly advises his friend that the empirical poet should come equipped with a wide range of experiences of Nature and of great men and actions, which encourages a clear and distinct series of mental images. The figural corollary to the variety of experience is no reductively 'plain style,' but "the admirable variety and novelty of Metaphors and Similitudes, which are not to be lighted on in the compass of a narrow knowledge." This poetics does not *refer* in any simple sense to experience, but it methodically reproduces the sensation of the mind's encounters with the world, a point Hobbes brilliantly makes by converting his prescription at this point into such a rhetorical parallelism: "As the sense we have of bodies, consisteth in change and variety of impression, so also does the sense of languadge in the variety and changeable use of words." This activity—and his own stylistic control palpably brings the *behavior* of his sentence home—Hobbes also figures as an act of "translation . . . in farre-fetch't (but withal apt, instructive, and comely) similitudes."[28] Knowledge, as Locke was later to say, is a series of juxtapositions, or verbal equivalences, on which human beings bestow symbolic and behavioral force.

Because we derive knowledge from the world first by receiving individual sense-impressions, and second by methodically organizing those impressions, we must apply the same criterion to poetry as guides our inferences from common experience or reading history; namely, probability. "For as truth is the bound of Historicall, so the Resemblance of truth is the utmost limit of Poeticall Liberty. . . . Beyond the actuall workes of nature a Poet may now go; but beyond the conceaved possibility of nature never."[29] The rules governing poetic behavior must operate not so much by referring to the world as by enacting the methods by which we engage with everyday life. Hobbes does not demand realism, only the symbolic performance of actual mental relations, which is to require poetry to observe, not obfuscate, the rules of ordinary language.

Like any neoclassical critic, Hobbes liberally avails himself of Horatian and Aristotelian vocabulary. But because his prescriptions for poetry are founded upon a particular methodical consequence of his conceptualism, his method, if not always his vocabulary, is modern rather than ancient. That is, Horatian and Aristotelian utterances provide neoclassical critics with ready-made verbal counters in a definitively nonclassical literary economy.[30]

Hobbes's revolutionary prescriptions for style inform a remarkable passage discussing the power of images. The passage is particularly evocative because it miniaturizes a device that typifies neoclassical criticism: it visibly exemplifies its assumptions about language in its methods of representation, not to mention its typography. To preface his translation of *The Odyssey* (1675), Hobbes discusses "the VERTUES of an HEROIQUE POEM." The "sixth Vertue," Hobbes writes,

> ancient writers of Eloquence called *Icones,* that is, *Images.* And an Image is always a part, or rather the ground, of a Poetical comparison. As, for example, when *Virgil* would set before our eyes the

fall of *Troy,* he describes perhaps the whole Labour of many men together in the felling of some great Tree, and with how much ado it fell. This is the Image. To which if you but add these words, So fell *Troy,* you have the Comparison entire; the grace whereof lieth in the lightsomness, and is but the description of all, even of the minutest, parts of the thing described; that not onely they that stand far off, but also they that stand near, and look upon it with the oldest spectacles of a Critique, may approve it. For the Poet is a Painter, and should paint Actions to the understanding with the most decent words, as Painters do Persons and Bodies with the choicest colours to the eye; which, if not done nicely, will not be worthy to be plac'd in a Cabinet.[31]

Hobbes's intense visualism scrutinizes objects with an optic glass and finally places those objects—including words, which act like "Persons and Bodies"—into a space for display. This space offers itself for the arrangement of what it contains and serves (like the page, to which Hobbes also gestures) as a three-dimensional correlative to neoclassical method. The piece concerns those images we apprehend in poetic experience, and the argument recommends finding apt analogies through image—comparative moments of knowledge that reenact mental relations, just as Hobbes supplies the phrase "So fell *Troy*" to balance the phrase "the felling of some great Tree." Nevertheless, Hobbes suggests how this therapeutic but fragile juxtaposition of figures, which stimulates the reader to infer the relations between unlike properties and thus to exercise his or her judgment, can too easily collapse under the weight of false convention, figured here by the potentially violent identification of terms in the Horatian metaphor "a Poet is a Painter."[32] That Hobbes perceives metaphorical yoking as an insidious politico-linguistic threat is expressed by his anti-Catholic polemic in the last half of *Leviathan,* and his related assault on the verb "to be," which offers as essential and total what is only contingent and comparative.[33] This momentary threat, therefore, passes with the return of simile; simile illuminates the final point ("as Painters do Persons and Bodies"), which the poet ideally, and this writer in fact, succeeds "nicely" in placing into his textual cabinet.

The General Argument of Restoration Criticism

Even in an age when *Leviathan* was widely vilified, most neoclassical critics shared with Hobbes his scepticism about words, his conceptualist assumptions about method, and his visualist approach to poetics, which they believe fulfills the inferential and comparative prejudices of cognition. This section attempts not a comprehensive survey of Restoration poetics, but, by reference to a range of critical utterances, an extension of the attitudes I have described. The reader will notice that a striking feature of Restoration criticism is that even in the midst of vigorous debates about content, the neoclassical critics' shared methodical presuppositions tend paradoxically to reinforce the antagonists' mutual hostility.

Writing against Dryden shortly after the Restoration, Howard, for example, expresses a conceptualist requirement for representation when he criticizes the use of verse in repartee because it fails to symbolize actual mental actions or images.[34] In the same year, 1665, Evelyn argues that we can remedy the abuses of language by compiling "a Gram'ar for the praecepts," by which he means to imply the regulation of rhetoric according to the *vernacula*, or idiomatic use.[35] Similarly, Sir William Temple defends Latin against the encroachments of modern languages, because (like Le Clerc's comparison between Hebrew and classical languages), he finds the poverty of the modern mind expressed by an impoverished language, "being patcht up out of the Conceptions as well as Sounds of such barbarous or enslaved People."[36] Although angrily opposed to Temple, William Wotton only repeats Temple's methodical assumptions by arguing that we apprehend modern literatures better than ancient ones because the conceptual structures that produced Lucretius and Vergil are lost, whereas we turn with pleasure to "*Milton, Cowley, Butler,* or *Dryden,* who wrote in their Mother-Tongue, and so were able to give that unconstrained Range and Turn to their Thoughts and Expressions that are truly necessary to make a compleat Poem."[37]

Although for Temple and Wotton the cultural value of classical learning is very much the point of debate, they share with Howard and Evelyn a premise that the effect of experience upon mental habits, and thus on the relations within language, is not. Indeed, even in this brief glimpse of a much wider-ranging argument, we can see that though the capacities of the mind may be imagined as universal and transcultural, Evelyn, Temple, and Wotton argue for an essentially culture-bound reading of the relative nature of languages. The latter adopt a more clearly Lockean vocabulary for their conceptualism than the two earlier thinkers; but George Granville, concluding the first stanza of his unashamedly bad poem *An Essay upon Unnatural Flights in Poetry,* reveals how Lockean the visualism of the Horatian *ut pictura poesis*[38] had become by the turn of the century:

> Poets are Limners of another kind,
> To copy out Idaeas in the Mind;
> Words are the paint by which their thoughts are shown,
> And Nature is their Object to be drawn;
> The written Picture we applaud or blame,
> But as the just proportions are the same.[39]

The neoclassical adoption of the Horatian trope serves to show that though words are thought to enact mental relations (figured in Granville's *"proportions"*), they are obscure inasmuch as, like the ideas they signify, they remain palpable, not transparent, vehicles of apprehension. If words are the dress of thought, that is because, like thoughts, words are embodiments and symbols of mental relations. In a very different sense, however, languages can be *made* obscure, and this because the actual function of language is misinterpreted or maliciously abused.

The most direct way of expressing this attitude acts, like the myth of Babel, as a myth of cultural entropy, one described as least as long ago as R. F. Jones's *Ancients and Moderns,* and elegiacally expressed in Dr. Johnson's wish that the instrument of language might be less apt to decay.[40] What has not been recognized, however, is that in different ways, the emergence of this trope in critical argumentation offers not so much the inevitability of linguistic decline as the notion that different cultural conditions place strains on language that cause us to forget its original purposes. It acts as a mnemonic to recall the mutual relations of knowledge and language, which Wotton associates with Ciceronian rhetoric, and which become the grounds less of a new than a renewed, methodical poetic.[41]

In the same letter to Sir Peter Wyche quoted above, Evelyn transforms the common trope of the decay from ancient to modern times into a different, more culturally specific narrative. For Evelyn, there is no greater logic to the decay of languages than the effects of social, political, and stylistic abuse, because languages bear the impress of "victories, plantations, frontieres, staples of com'erce, pedantry of schooles, affectation of travellers, translations, fancy and style of Court; vernility and mincing of citizens, pulpits, political remonstrances, theatres, shopps, &c."[42] However, Temple, in an evocative passage to which we shall return, invents another trope of decline, which argues that "*Poetry* was the first sort of Writing known and used in the several Nations of the World." Because this style is "regular" and "difficult," it reflects a tailoring of writing to the desires of the mind, even though modern prose may appear "easy and loose."[43] And Wotton repeats the argument in his own way by offering "the Writings of *Seneca* and the Younger *Pliny,* compared with *Tully*'s," as an example of the proposition that "there is such a Thing as a Decay of Eloquence in After-Ages."[44]

Part of the attempt to recall writing not so much to its original purity as to the ground rules of figuration itself is, of course, an attack on the perceptual confusions created by mere sound. Thus, though Temple celebrates the musical power of poetry, he also yokes it to the derangements described by Meric Casaubon's *Treatise concerning Enthusiasme* (1655), by calling for a natural history that can account for, and so legislate, its effects.[45] That Temple, clearly a neo-Epicurean in his own right, had been reading Walter Charleton's *Physiologia Epicuro-Gassendo-Charletoniana* is indicated both by its context and by a reference to the tarantula.[46] The tarantella has by a false etymology been long associated with the effects of the tarantula sting, and, in a rich and strange disquisition, Charleton depicts the autonomous powers of music in the world of the tarantula and its victims, who can only be cured by the music that drives them mad. This is a natural phenomenon that instantiates *"Occult Qualities made Manifest,"* but there are other capacities of sound, which, like false miracles, resist scrutiny and invite political manipulation. Charleton's book was published only five years after the king's execution, and the institutional significance of this picture—recaptured by Temple in his reference to Casaubon, and later by Swift in the "BELCHING" of the Aeolists in *A Tale of a Tub*—is unavoidable:

> That which deserves our highest Admiration, is this; that *this Venome of the Tarantula doth produce the same Effect in the body of man, which it doth in that of the Tarantula it self, wherein it is generated;* as if there were some secret Cognation and Similitude betwixt the Nature of that venemous Spider, and that of Mankinde. For, as the Poyson, being infused into any part of mans body, and set a work by Musick, doth, by a continual vellication or Titillation of the Muscles and Membranes thereof, incite the intoxicated person to dance: So likewise, while it remains in its own womb and proper Conservatory, the body of the Tarantula being once set a work by Musick, doth it incite the Tarantula to dance, and caper.[47]

What Charleton imagines here as strange, but nevertheless part of the order of Nature, can, when released into human control, become the matter of "Magical Practices, those Bombast Words, nonesense Spells, exotique Characters, and Fanatick Ceremonies, used by all Praestigitators and Enchanters [that] . . . import [nothing] more than the Circumvention of the Spectators judgement, and exaltation of his Imagination, upon whom they praetend to work the miracle."[48] In a less charged atmosphere, Howard attacks Dryden's justification of verse in drama by citing Seneca's command to close a door in the verse, *"Reserate Clusos Regii postes Laris,"* and comments sarcastically that "I suppose [Dryden] was himself highly affected with the sound of these words; but to have Compleated his Dictates together with his Arguments, he should have oblig'd us by charming our Eares with such an Art of placing words, as in an English Verse to express so loftily the shutting of a Door, that we might have been as much affected with the sound of his words."[49]

The Restoration revision of metaphor, as Brian Vickers has pointed out, occurs in a highly polemical atmosphere. But unlike Vickers, I am arguing that we should treat contemporary statements about language as conditioned not only by their polemical circumstances but also by contemporary theories of language. That is, such statements respond to genuine, alternative philosophies of language that imported, for all parties in the dispute, clear political implications. This is certainly true of Baxter, Owen, Webster, and their institutional opponents. Nevertheless, Vickers's most useful insight is that Sprat—as I have suggested—seeks not a critique of metaphor as such, but rather a critique of a false understanding of what metaphor is, and its potential for subversion.[50] Arguments about 'style' in the period are first debates about what metaphor in ordinary language *is,* as a prelude to prescriptions for a new poetic.

As an instance, we must therefore approach Granville's early-eighteenth-century attack on figures and ornaments with some caution. Dismissing "Fables and Metaphors that always lie, / And rash Hyperboles, that soar so high, / And every Ornament of Verse," like Sprat, he nevertheless does not propose a nonfigural discourse.[51] He describes instead the figural status of language "right apply'd" as a transparent veil, which perfectly summarizes the paradoxical argument for the necessary obscurity of language. Because the mind thinks figurally, it requires figures to apprehend knowledge: that is, representation viewed from one angle might appear to frustrate our desire for unmediated perception; viewed from another, it plainly serves the perceptual needs of the mind. Thus:

> As Veils transparent cover, but not hide,
> Such metaphors appear, when right apply'd;
> When, thro' the phrase, we plainly see the sense,
> Truth, when the meaning's obvious, will dispense.

> (ll. 14–17)

Even in this optimistic version of the poetics, as the embodiments of ideas that have no life apart from language, words are the sole, contingent terms by which we grasp the "sense." This view connotes a commitment to an inferential mechanism for approaching knowledge, which informs the prepositional "*thro*' the phrase." The same view is differently expressed in Granville's discussion of Homer's apt metaphors, in which he argues that metaphor misleads the mind unless it presents itself as metonymy or simile. The empirical method of inference and analogy requires that implied relations inhabiting a figure of speech (here "Achilles"/"lion") share a specific and local bond. This bond serves to prevent any arbitrary collapse of those implied relations: "When *Homer,* mentioning *Achilles,* terms him a Lyon, this is a metaphor, And the Meaning is obvious and true, tho' the litteral sense be false: The Poet intending thereby to give his Reader some Idaea of the strength and fortitude of his Heroe. Had he said, That Wolf, or that Bear, this had bin false, by presenting an Image not conformable to the Nature, Or Character of a Heroe, &c."[52]

In an earlier analysis of a couplet by Waller, Dennis presents a similar argument for the special status of metonymy. The couplet reads: "*Ships heretofore on Seas, like Fishes sped / The mightier still upon the smaller fed.*" And Dennis's debaters, Beaumont and Freeman, proceed to comment:

> *Freem.* That is to say, as a great Fish Breakfasts or Dines upon a small one, so a great Ship chops up a little one. I have known several, who, to their sorrows, have seen a Ship drink hard, but I never met with any who have seen one eat yet.
> *Beaum.* P'shaw, Pox, this is down-right Banter. This is to fall into the very same fault which you have condemned in others.
> *Freem.* I stand corrected, Sir; without rallery, then, this Metaphor *Feed* is too gross for a Ship, tho' I perfectly know what Mr. *Waller* means by it.[53]

Like Dryden's famous use of the dialogue in *Of Dramatic Poesy,* the dialogue itself becomes a device to play out, to externalize the kinds of strategies that must now inform poetic practice: metaphor is anatomized on the table of debate. And the epistemological assumptions that make the dialogue a significant pedagogical instrument (the reader being required to judge relative claims) are precisely what cause Freeman to object to "feed" as applied to a ship.[54] We cannot talk about a ship feeding because there is no obvious or ordinary circumstance which permits that comparison. We can, however, describe a ship drinking, for the obvious reason that a ship sails on water: far from criticizing figuration as such, Dennis is suggesting that no explicit metonymical relation allows a ship to feed as it might drink.

Although grudgingly, when Freeman allows "feed" to stand, he simply rehearses the mechanism. First, the gesture within the dialogue by which he submits to Beaumont argues that, within the behavioral context of ordinary language signaled by the dialogue, we still know roughly what sets of relations are intended by making a ship "feed." Like Gassendi, Dennis is showing how the conditions of conversation itself define the limits of verbal significance. Second, because the governing analogy of Waller's couplet compares ships to fish, the figural predicate "feed" can follow, for the whole statement is visibly controlled by that comparison. That is, though taken by itself, the second line seems to spring a hidden or private metaphor upon us, the explicit and public conditions of analogy secure Waller's figural activity against sudden and arbitrary conflations of terms. Thus, like Dennis's dialogue, Waller's couplet, in setting an analogical mechanism visibly to work—even as it occurs on the page—secures us against the insidious effects of radical metaphor that seeks to undermine the phenomenalism of language.

The atomic, discrete quality of cognition is what Dennis and Granville desire to protect, whether realized in the explicitness of analogy and metonymy, or in Granville's veiled sign. Neoclassical poetics execute the same methodical requirements that inform natural philosophy, in which probable knowledge is at once visible and contingent. And it is in this light that we should understand what Marks isolates as the two most important tropes of neoclassical poetics—"Nature" and "Probability." Marks denies that by referring to Nature, neoclassical critics rarely "subscribed to . . . naïve representationalism," or "art as mimicry"; but neither did they see themselves as acting by analogy to "God or nature."[55] By invoking "Nature," critics intended the elements of discourse (individual words, phrases, images, utterances) to behave according to the workings and principles of the physical world as made available to the perceiving mind, just as in natural philosophy all abstract concepts and laws had to derive from some union of demonstrable, representative, "materiall" particulars: where the architecture of the cosmos arose from the arrangement of atoms, an arrangement only hypothesized by inferring unseen from perceptible properties, so the architecture of literate experience depended on similar perceptible elements—namely, words—cast into probable relations. This is the inevitable implication of Boyle's obsession with the Lucretian parallel between atoms and words, and its consequences are clearly displayed in his own prose. Because metonymy or synecdoche suggests the activity of an inferential and analogical method applied to perceptible signs, they were felt to become not the transparent figures, but the apt ones, for such an empirical imagination.

Metonymy or synecdoche does not refer in any simple sense to what it denotes. Accordingly, the requirement of probability—as others, including Douglas Patey, have clearly demonstrated—does not entail a realist aesthetic. Probability becomes the formal, rhetorical presentation of the contingent relations by which the mind gets to know the world, or can imagine a future, or hypothetical, or fictional state. The key figure here is, of course, simile, in which (as also in allusion, the couplet, dialogue, the 'parallel,' the interlineary) the relations between terms of knowledge are presented for the reader to compare and judge; the reader's activity of judgment subsequently (often by 'habit') becomes a training in prudence, discrimination, or sagacity. Because it also implies the exercise of will or choice, such training itself becomes a figure for a certain mental and ethical liberty or "latitude": thus Neander in Dryden's *Of Dramatic Poesy* can brilliantly vindicate the liberty of English letters against the monopolies of the French state ("the servile imitation of the French") by claiming for English drama the right to "variety" and "copiousness" in its plots, which by placing on the spectator the onus of choice will thus resist the centralizing principles of strict neo-Aristotelianism.

As in John Ogilby's motto, appended to the title page of his *Fables,* "Examples are best Precepts," the assumptions of neoclassical literary judgment are primarily visualist.[56] This certainly seems the guiding principle of Davenant's preface to *Gondibert,* in that foundational exchange with Hobbes. Davenant responds remarkably sensitively to the peculiarly allusive mechanism of *The Faerie Queene,* which, however, he finds troubling because it enacts not the properties of waking cognition, but the condition of a fever or dream, and thus an "allegoricall Story" whose figural activity is "defective in the connexion." The power of example is disrupted, because, in Spenserian allegory, knowledge is represented by strangely illuminated episodic tableaux, which subvert the narrative grammar of experience. No sufficient parallel exists between Spenser's plot and the plot of our own lives for "use to humane application."[57] The aesthetic ideal of analogy or parallel that informs his criticism of Spenserian plot encourages Davenant to use an Horatian terminology to express his general revision of the exemplary power of narrative: in the course of his preface, he recommends comparing our lives with "actions on the Stage," Christian character in action, and instances of political virtue. He reminds us that the Spartans encouraged their children to eschew drunkenness by making slaves vomit before them.[58] And because the comparative function of imitation depends upon the precise calibration of the parallels between what we read or see, and the processes of cognition, it is clear that for Davenant the exemplary power of narrative is, precisely, visual. Thus he writes: "Since Nature hath made us prone to Imitation (by which wee equall the best or the worst) how much those Images of Action prevaile upon our mindes, which are delightfully drawne by Poets."[59]

Action and Fable in Restoration Criticism

Davenant evidently encourages the poet to refine the effect of narrative experience upon the reader, and not to anticipate it by an editorial moral or "Narratives." Because this effect requires a certain tact, the creation of a series of mnemonic cues that will invite, but cannot coerce, the reader into the appropriate posture, Davenant will edge his own critical pronouncements toward such an effect. He can do so precisely because the linearities of any discourse—such as his own—adumbrate the linearities both of narrative and of our cognitive experience:

> That which I have call'd my Argument, is only meant as an assistance to the Readers memory, by contayning breef hints, such, as if all the Arguments were successively read, would make him easily remember the mutuall dependancies of the generall designe; yet each rather mentions every person acting, then their actions: But he is very unskilful that by Narratives before an Historicall Poem, prevents expectation; for so he comes to have as little successe over the Reader (whom the Writer should surprize, and as it were, keep prisoner for a time) as he hath on his Enemy's.[60]

Hobbes repeats the distinction between philosophical abstraction and the narrative order of images. The special power of poetry lies in "her wonderfull celerity [, which] consisteth not so much in motion, as in copious Imagery discreetly ordered, and perfectly registred in the memory; which most men under the name of Philosophy have a glimpse of."[61] Just as the fabric of the physical world arises from a combination of individual particles, so the fabric of cognitive and poetic experience must arise from a similar articulation of discrete images. The spatial commitments of this poetic naturally lead to treating all literary narratives in terms of the drama. Thus Hobbes compares the "Fable" of *Gondibert* to "the Theater," which he then expands into a somatic metaphor, which exploits Harveian physiology and curiously anticipates the eponymous figure dominating the frontispiece of *Leviathan:*

> It hath the same resemblance also with a mans veines, which proceeding from different parts, after the like concourse, insert themselves at last into the two principall veynes of the Body. But when I considered that also the actions of men, which singly are inconsiderable, after many conjunctures, grow at last either into one great protecting power, or into two destroying factions, I could not but approve the structure of your Poeme, which ought to be no other then such as an imitation of humane life requireth.[62]

Howard repeats Hobbes's and Davenant's major premise about the primacy of specific images and actions when, glossing the *Ars Poetica,* he writes that "every thing makes more impression Presented than Related."[63] And by creating a heuristic distinction between "Substance" and "Form," Temple even goes so far as to suggest that any narrative construct, regardless of its "Form," can help preserve the "Substance" of narrative actions, such that "the variety of Events is seldom without Entertainment or Instruction, how indifferently soever the Tale is told."[64]

That morality derives from, and that abstractions depend on, the specific, concrete action of narrative is an implicit argument of the apparent ambiguity attaching to *fable* as a critical term, because it can denote the mere fact of plot, or its moral, or both at once.[65] This is certainly a happy ambiguity of Dennis's defense of English drama as conducive to morality. In effect agreeing with Beaumont that "the principal Actors being shaken by violent Passions, cannot be made sentencious," Freeman argues that the English stage can have a more genuine moral effect, because it moderates the passions represented on stage and "because it teaches some Moral Doctrine by the Fable, which must always be alle-

gorical and universal," by which notion of allegory he means the concrete, a posteriori uses of poetry, rather than the abstract, a priori ones.[66]

According to Davenant, plot, fable, or narrative has received its
highest authorization in Christ, because by the use of parables—concrete
fictions—he compelled the obedience so cherished by civil authorities.[67]
But Christ's use of parable is not original: it simply places the seal on the
sense in which the figural nature of poetry accommodates morality to
human apprehension, just as God accommodates himself to us by means
of his Creation.[68] Poetry and narrative equally come to represent the
figural status of human knowledge, as is demonstrated by classical uses of
parables to stir the citizens to political action, as when *"Demosthenes* sav'd
the *Athenians* by the Fable or Parable of the Doggs and Wolves, in answer
to King *Philip's* proposition."[69] By quoting the biblical phrase *"Without
a Parable spake he not to them,"* Davenant gestures toward that double
effect of biblical parable that also inhabits the neoclassical reading of
figuration, for, as Frank Kermode has shown, Christ speaks both to assist
and to obscure knowledge.[70] Parable obscures inasmuch as it seems to
obstruct some yearning for plain utterance, some direct access to knowledge through language; but the point of parable is that, just like language, it is an embodied form of knowledge that arises out of human
activity and serves as our sole means to apprehension. Although put this
way, the suspicion of narrative obscurity may be misplaced, in another
sense, one that Davenant articulates, it is not: for the sense of obscurity in
narrative, if it does not arise from a suspicion of figuration as such, may
arise from the recognition that a parable—like those Christ tells for his
disciples alone—can serve institutional, interested motives. For Davenant, the interests of power, which he directly represents, are not supplied by attacking figuration, but by ensuring that it is applied in certain
ways.

This is, of course, one argument that circulates within discussions of
the hieroglyph, because, as we have seen, the hieroglyph also can symbolize the metaphorical nature of language, as well as the use of secret
knowledge to maintain privilege. That it is in the interests of instituted
powers to have access to the most fundamental means of appealing to the
minds of the populace is also an insight offered by Temple. This he does
in two ways—one by showing the central function of "Story" in many
ancient cultures, and another by arguing that poetry represents the original form of representation, which is then appropriated in different ways
for different cultural purposes. Temple implies that in oriental and Mid-

dle Eastern cultures all knowledge depended upon the preservation and maintenance of narrative (whether history or myth). He twice connects "Knowledge" and "all Natural *Science* and *Philosophy*" to the health and perpetuation of "Story" and "the Registers of Times and Actions," showing that these cultures committed their preservation to "certain Officers of State" and "Priests." In Temple's analysis, the implication also emerges that because the progress of *"Astronomy, Astrology, Magick, Geometry,* Natural *Philosophy"* depends upon some means of storing, conserving, and propagating them, they are in some practical sense subsidiary to "Ancient *Story,*" or at least some mechanism like it.[71] It is this narrative and historical consciousness in ancient nations that shows its superiority to modern amnesia.

The conveyance of knowledge by story finds a different kind of support in Temple's essay "Of Poetry." Although he commends the aural powers of poetry, Temple treats these aural constituents as atoms within an essentially visual conception of language. The ancients evidently treated Apollo as the god of poetry because the heat of his heavenly body, the sun, not only generates the poetical impulse but also unearths, illuminates, and reveals as necessarily *embodied* the materials of poetic production: the poet "by the Light of that true Poetical Fire [discovers] a thousand little Bodies or Images in the World, and Similitudes among them, unseen to common Eyes, and which could not be discovered without the Rays of the Sun." Temple significantly deflects discussion away from developing critical precepts to a "History" of poetry, where we discover that poetry represents "the first sort of Writing . . . in several Nations to have preceded the very Invention or Usage of Letters."[72] Perhaps because it is not alphabetic in nature, it seems to signify—like the hieroglyph—the figural, imagistic nature of language as such. Like Dalgarno's fable of the relation between metaphor and allegory, Temple's essay also delineates the development of narrative conventions from the raw material of language.[73] So whereas poetry in the first ages preserved "Words and . . . Actions, which would otherwise have been lost and soon vanish away with the Transitory Passage of Human Breath and Life," the emergence of prose served a variety of purposes, not least "short Memorials of Persons, Actions, and of Times." And though poetry served a variety of purposes and genres in biblical and classical literature, the translation of poetry into prose betokens the definitive translation of metaphor into narrative or allegory: thus the first classical movement from poetry was "done first by *Aesop* in *Greek,*" and in biblical and

Eastern cultures, the same shift was "much in Vogue, as we may observe
in the many Parables used in the old Testament as well as in the New."[74]
Narrative also has suffered a sea change into "Romances," which Temple
obviously deplores. By arguing that the moderns are pale copies of the
ancients, Temple aims in part to call us back to the ground rules of
language itself: he feels no need to lay down specific critical rules, because
the poet need do no more than respect the founding conditions of
knowledge and language.

Temple's dislike of romances should suggest that, in recalling the
origins of language and narrative, he presumes the single criterion for
poetry and history also proclaimed by Hobbes. Unlike romance, which
subverts those originary terms, all forms of discourse must obey the laws
of probability. Davenant sets up a contrast between "austere Historians
[who] have enter'd into bond" with "Truth narrative, and past," which
they idolize, and poets, whose "Mistresse" is "truth operative, and by
effects continually alive."[75] But this defense of poetry only perpetrates a
distinction between events directly observed (historical facts) and the
portable, inductive principles established by observing such events (poetical fictions governed by probability). The hypothetical world can
create the illusion of possessing its own facts; but the laws governing
relations among them must arise from empirical, historical experience.
This focus on *relations* among fictional events, however grotesque or
fabulous each may appear, explains Davenant's comment that actions
"infer" character, because character is only one of many elements of a
literary text that, considered relative to one another, secure a probable
status for a fictional world. Thus, a satisfactory poem "ends with an easy
untying of those particular knots, which made a contexture of the whole;
leaving such satisfaction of probabilities with the Spectator, as may per-
swade him that neither Fortune in the Fate of the Persons, nor the Writer
in the Representment, have been unnatural or exorbitant."[76] And writing many years later in his "Discourse upon Comedy" (1702), George
Farquhar can defend the moral effect of English comedy on what Eric
Rothstein has called "radically empirical" grounds, but ones that Farquhar reveals by appealing to Aesop as the founder of the moral tale.[77]
Although couched in terms of animal character and action, and improbable in that sense, Aesopic fable—and similarly Christian parable
and English comedy—has a moral force that derives precisely from the
internal relations established by the mutual action of its atomic
constituents.[78]

Although Hobbes suggests some rules for representing character, plot assumes greater significance for neoclassical critics than character because we can assess the decorum of character only as a feature of plot acting in proportion to its entire "Design": only that proportion can parallel our cognitive expectations, and thus revise our moral ones.[79] To paraphrase Peter Brooks, neoclassical critics read for the plot.[80] This is certainly an implication of Hobbes's dictum that "as truth is the bound of Historicall, so Resemblance of truth is the utmost limit of Poeticall Liberty."[81] Similarly, in his preface to *Theatrum Poetarum*—dedicated, incidentally, to Thomas Stanley—Edward Phillips explains the significance of epic for this critical criterion. Like tragedy, epic concentrates in its procedures the very essence of narrative itself, so, however grandly, and however remote its materials, it also must obey the laws of probability. Because the laws, not the materials of narrative action, are the point at issue, this view of epic protocol also entails a reading of allegory:

> [Epic] must be [from] a brief, obscure or remote Tradition, but of some remarkable piece of story, in which the Poet hath an ample field to inlarge by feigning of probable circumstances, in which, and in proper Allegorie, Invention (the well management whereof is indeed no other than *decorum*) principally consisteth, and wherein there is a kind of truth even in the midst of Fiction; for what ever is pertinently said by way of *Allegorie* is Morally though not Historically true.[82]

Like the action of miracles in neoclassical theology, the action of epic and allegory can perhaps exceed common apprehension and belief, but they cannot positively contradict "the truth of History."[83] Romance infringes upon the dual requirement that a hypothetical world not only be reasonably self-contained, and consistently obey its own internal laws, but also run parallel to historical truth. If this is a referential theory of literature, it respects the processes and relations, rather than the mere details, of experience.

The power of narrative action as an empirical device is, finally, conveyed by Dennis's two debaters, Beaumont and Freeman, who argue the value of bringing a chorus on stage. Beaumont is not certain that the audience can retain the entire movement of the plot without what Dryden calls "narrations." Freeman reassures him by citing Aristotle, because "the Rules of *Aristotle* are nothing but Nature and Good Sence reduc'd to a Method."[84] Just as it is natural to seek to infer relations among perceptible elements of our experience, so the audience naturally makes connections between the elements of action on stage, thus creating its own sense of plot. Freeman argues that the division between the beginning, middle, and end of a plot supposes that any feature of a narrative, once contracted for, must act synecdochically for the entire plot: "This beginning and middle, are, according to *Aristotle,* Things that necessarily suppose something to follow."[85] Dennis perhaps allows for generic expectations within literary experience, but he certainly suggests that the parallel between literary and empirical experience extends to our common inferential habit of proleptically imagining as yet unrealized wholes from what we can see and know. It is, precisely, what is *left out* that makes literate experience interesting, and by the same token moralizes it, because the exercise of inference (as the reader is to discover in *Rasselas,* as Elizabeth is to discover of Darcy) becomes the vehicle of an isomorphism between cognitive and moral therapies. So Wotton advises that "it is a fault in Heroick Poetry to fetch Things from their first Originals: And to carry the Thread of the Narrative down to the last Event is altogether as dull. . . . Men should rise from Table with some Appetite remaining: And a Poem should leave some View of something to follow, and not quite shut the Scenes; especially if the remaining Part of the Story be not capable of much Ornament, nor affords a Variety."[86]

Postscript: A Short View of Rymer

Rymer has achieved a dubious fame by attacking *Othello* as an improbable fiction. But this is only one element of an entirely consistent set of empirical attitudes to literary study and performance, which finally shows how closely a prejudice in favor of decorous action follows a distinctly sensationalist, empirical criterion for literary response. In one sense, we can interpret Rymer's dramatic criteria as unhistorical in nature, committed to an imperial view of the permanent needs of the mind,[87] but it is precisely the empirical constitution of those needs that makes his critical approach both inductive and historical. He chooses Aristotle in part because his Aristotle is a descriptive analyst of drama.[88] His own historical description of the dramatic tradition shows how it has operated under different cultural imperatives, which Rymer even symbolizes by using different typefaces, as if to represent distinct historical forms of representation or consciousness. *A Short View of Tragedy* presents original documents, which show how, for example, King Francis I legislated the political function of drama in 1541.[89] And, following

Dryden's precedent, Rymer analyzes both *Othello* and *Julius Caesar* as examples of his general thesis. But of course this forensic attitude—as any critic of empiricism would point out—presupposes some permanent vision of how the mind assents to evidence. Rymer effectively admits this circular hermeneutic when he suggests that history—like the visual apprehensions of the mind—operates by a series of synecdochic compressions: like parables, pictures derive their force from their ability to editorialize and epitomize the general significances of historical experience. Descriptively, the mind needs exemplary tokens by which to grasp the flux of experience; prescriptively, this allows the Christian to restructure the morally amorphous quality of history into morally determined examples. The operation is, however, dynamic and dialectical, so if "the *last Judgment, of Mich. Angelo,* the *Massacre* of the *Innocents,* the *Baptist's* head, &c. . . .* yield any pleasure besides what proceeds from the art, and what rests in eye. 'Tis by the History, to which the picture serves only as an *Index.*"[90] Just as Evelyn takes Pepys's library as a collection of concreted moments of history, poetry and history here work together, such that poetry becomes a means of exemplifying while methodizing history's general epistemological and moral principles, thus making history *"more philosophical."*[91]

Like any general theory of history, then, Rymer's empiricism seeks within its historical materials correlatives to its own methods of appropriating knowledge and the morals it already wants to find. Because Rymer assumes that historical knowledge, represented by synecdoche, obeys a distinct forensic habit, he naturally objects to the improbability of placing the psychological—that is, evidentiary—onus of *Othello* on a handkerchief.[92] And he dislikes *Julius Caesar* because it contradicts the authority of historical facts.[93] The subversion of probability on forensic and historical grounds also saps the true moral function of literature, as is clear in the eccentric and grotesque manner in which *Othello* works. A uniform criterion of probability thus informs Rymer's historiography, his view of the relation between history and poetry, and his aesthetic demands on drama.

This peculiarly empirical version of probable knowledge also animates Rymer's attitude to decorum, though its criteria are also founded on Horatian principles. If perhaps we suspect the pressure of Horatian criteria within his discomfort at the perceived discrepancy between the actions of Shakespeare's plots and the "rumbling" of his verse, its language also deviating from the supposed status of the characters,[94] that charge perfectly reveals Rymer's general suspicion of the abstractions of words, which leads him to a visual prejudice in favor of plots, actions, and the parabolic foundations of literary representation. Rymer recognizes that action, left to its own devices, can become farcical and grotesque. But he believes that knowledge is a matter of similarly appealing palpably to the senses, so it is only in a constructive tension to action that language obtains its motive powers.[95] This criterion has two fascinating consequences or corollaries within Rymer's critical pronouncements: by returning to the origins and history of Western drama, Rymer can legislate what he understands as the invariable properties of all literary representation, of all language; and within that fiction, by expressing alternative linguistic postulates in national and political terms, he reveals that the philosophy of language cannot escape appropriation by competing institutions.

A local gesture of outrage at the beginning of *A Short View of Tragedy* perfectly encapsulates Rymer's jointly cognitive and political attitudes to drama, and hence language. We remember, he assumes, that Horace disliked "these empty *Shows* and Vanity" of fashionable Roman society; so we now see drama degenerate into the softening effects of French opera. Where "there is a Cup of Enchantment, there is Musick and Machine. . . . 'Tis a Debauch the most insinuating, and the most pernicious; none would think an *Opera* and Civil Reason, should be the growth of one and the same Climate."[96] If, like drama, opera requires sound and sight to coordinate its effects, it represents that dangerous— typically feminized, Frenchified—point at which musical bombast overcomes the vigor of true, that is, virtually tactile, dramatic representation. The Greeks, on the contrary, and fond of music as they were, permitted "no Metamorphosis to turn the *Drama* to an *Opera*. Nor did their Love come whining on the Stage to Effeminate the Majesty of their Tragedy."[97]

Like other aestheticians who return to the Greeks for some primal glimpse into art or language, Rymer does not want to celebrate every Greek. He constructs a precise chart of linguistic and political desiderata by reading the muscular virtues contracted in Homer against, on the one hand, the airy abstractions of Plato and, on the other, the seductive and perfumed romance of Eastern, especially Arabic, literature. Much like Derrida, but in precisely the opposite direction, Rymer allegorizes the same dichotomy between Platonic orality and some visual, figural, and allegorical ideal of apprehension. And to do so, he legitimizes Homeric fable as a classical version of biblical accommodation. To reach for the divine, Homer knew, condemns us to silence and forces a rejection of human contingency:

> Therefore [Homer] would not *banter* the World with hard words, and unintelligible gibberish, as *Plato* and others have since done; but did accommodate his Speech to our Human Senses, by Metaphors, Similitudes, Tropes, and Parables; after the manner of *Moses,* and the Old Prophets before him. He entertains and fills us to the utmost of our Organs and Capacity. Something he finds for all our Senses. He brings them to our Eyes, our Ears, our Touch: *Nectar* he provides for our Taste, and there always exhales an Ambrosial Odour in the Divine Presence. What *Plato,* or an Angel would say further, passes all understanding, would not enter our Organs; could have no relish or proportion to affect us, more than the Musick of the Spheres. Metaphor must be the Language, when we travel in a Countrey beyond our Senses.[98]

If metaphor is the raw material of apprehension, of accommodation, then its narrative articulations are *"Fables,"* which are "the most delightful means to convey Instruction, and leave the strongest Impression on our Mind." Thus Christ told parables, which, like fables, were literally untrue, but were moralized by allegory: "As for the *Fables* which in *Homer,* or on the Stage give offence: The Antients had a thing call'd an *Allegory,* which went a great way towards stopping the mouth of many a pert Observer."[99]

Although Rymer is careful to respect Homer's appeal to all the senses, it is nevertheless clear that the special sense is finally that of sight. The predominance of the eye causes Rymer to warn against the speed and subtlety with which Charles Hart, the famous stage actor, could dazzle his audience, and with which "this thing of *Action* finds the blindside of humane-kind an hundred ways," because "*Action* is speaking to the Eyes."[100] Rymer suggests the supremacy of action as a visual phenomenon not only by arguing that the plot is the soul of drama but also that if words fail in decorum, they simply cease to mean, whereas if actions fail in decorum, they captivate the attention all the more violently. So when asked for the secret of his oratorical powers "*Demosthenes* answered, *Pronunciation:* What then the next thing? *Pronunciation:* Pray then, What the Third? Still the answer was *Pronunciation.*"[101]

It is precisely the cognitive possibilities of action as a mode of exemplification that make the institutional control of drama an issue: Rymer describes King Francis I's legislation in 1541 to control the strolling players because of their subversive tendency to wander "up and down, acting Farce, or turning into Farce, whatever they acted."[102] I have already asserted that Restoration theorists knew very well that there was no necessary relation between the epistemological terms of an argument and its political implications. Here Rymer clearly invites central social institutions to appropriate a mode of representation that we can only treat as sceptical and contingent in its epistemological orientation, but no less the organ of ideological construction for all that. Lying behind Rymer's ambivalence toward the cognitive power of action is the fear that it might get away, a fear he readily admits, and that rehearses strikingly similar pronouncements in Davenant. For Rymer, "the Theatre is a Magazine, not to be trusted, but under the special eye and direction of a Virtuous Government";[103] Davenant, responding more directly to the pressures of the Civil War, exposes the same comparative terms by which exemplary—particularly dramatic—knowledge is thought to secure civil obedience:

> It may be objected that the education of the Peoples mindes (from whence Vertuous manners are deriv'd) by the severall kindes of Poesy (of which the *Dramatick* hath been in all Ages very successful) is opposite to the receav'd opinion, that the People ought to be continu'd in ignorance; a Maxime sounding like the little subtilty of one that is a Statesmen only by Birth or Beard, and merits not his place by much thinking: For Ignorance is rude, sensorious, jealous, obstinate, and proud; these being exactly the ingredients of which Disobedience is made; and Obedience proceeds from ample consideration, of which knowledge consists; and knowledge will soone put into one Scale the weight of oppression, and in the other, the heavy burden which Disobedience lays on us in the effects of civill Warr.[104]

We shall now see how the fragile balances between disobedience and oppression emerge in Dryden's great allegory of politics and language, *Absalom and Achitophel*.

PART 4

Reading Dryden/Dryden Reading

9. The Nod of God in *Absalom and Achitophel:* Dryden's Process of Speech

Nor are thy lips ungraceful, Sire of men,
Nor tongue ineloquent; for God on thee
Abundantly his gifts hath also pour'd
Inward and outward both, his image fair:
Speaking or mute all comeliness of grace
Attends thee, and each word, each motion forms.

John Milton, *Paradise Lost,* 8:218–23

Almost a century after the events that precipitated Dryden's poem, Dr. Johnson wrote of *Absalom and Achitophel* that "as an approach to historical truth was necessary, the action and catastrophe were not in the poet's power; there is therefore an unpleasing disproportion between the beginning and the end."[1] Johnson's literalizing and moralizing habit ascribes to the poem's "disproportion" a weight of historical responsibility that the relatively late appearance of the poem in the Exclusion Crisis could not have assumed.[2] As with most literary matters, however, it pays to respect Johnson, because he intuits a real problem that still remains largely undiscussed—namely, the relationship between the poem's beginning, middle, and end. Johnson's fear that, despite its greatness, *Absalom and Achitophel* was always constrained by its "political and controversial" origins[3] anticipates a second, related critical resistance: the unwillingness to accord the poem an independent mythic life. *Absalom and Achitophel* is a very great poem 'about,' among other things, Dryden's absorption and compression of *Paradise Lost* into its own poetic intentions, and, like that epic, it is also a poem engaged with the fall and decay of language, as well as the attempt to contain them by vindicating our actual linguistic condition for the contingent purposes of the poem's political subject. Only by admitting the force of the figurative drama of *Absalom and Achitophel* can we understand the nature and significance of its conclusion, in which divine agency restores not so much the order of things as the order of language.

Few of Dryden's modern critics have grasped the significance of *Absalom and Achitophel*'s ending. The anger of the poem is obviously directed against a moral and political threat and, less obviously but equally centrally, against an erosion of knowledge and language, which David's final speech in itself is powerless to correct.[4] This is not to oppose the immediate and concrete political motives of the poem to its allegory of language, because I have been arguing at length that these two motives were for Dryden's contemporaries intimately allied. A complex strategy informs Dryden's final appeal to the nod of God, the Divine Gesture, whose resonances achieve at least two things: first, like the miracles, those originary acts embedded in Scripture, this act authorizes the poem as a verbal, phenomenal artifact; second, it also crucially condemns the human lust for naked power by reinscribing the rule of Law, signifying the historical world we inhabit, itself symbolized by the linear constructs of ordinary language. The excitement of the poem derives from several dramas: the conflict between the plotters and the worthies; the erosion of speech in the body politic, most obviously in its great temptation scenes; and, not least, the struggle between the plotters' undisciplined discourse, associated primarily with the self-regarding, circular motives of orality, and another kind of language that is simultaneously the province of Scripture, human law, and poetry—namely, writing. Indeed writing, as we saw Defoe, Warburton, the Anglican polemicists, and Le Clerc arguing, is the very condition of history, which is at once Dryden's subject and the precedent for the exemplary and satirical method his poem exploits. Like Hobbes's, Dryden's aim is to contain unruly desires by an institutionally and divinely guaranteed discursive edifice.

Echoing Johnson, William Myers calls the poem's ending "unconvincing" and accuses Dryden of insufficient realism because he fails to treat the problem of power in "historically adequate terms."[5] But Dryden anticipates the objection by demanding that the reader apply to his poem the inferential methods of history itself. That is, we must attend carefully to the address "To the Reader," because it establishes, in explicit and methodical terms, the hermeneutical protocol for the entire poem. Here we might suspect Dryden, who makes no attempt to eschew his practical alliances with the royalists, with a certain political disingenuousness. He desires, he says, to please "the more Moderate sort" of readers with the "probability" that these will make "the best Judges," thus economically fusing the hermeneutics of literature, politics, and ethics. The poem's abundant gustatory activity identifies it with the

Menippean satire, the *satura* (mixed dish of foods), which allows Dryden to invoke at once historical, satirical, and epistemological motives.[6] The address "To the Reader" embodies Dryden's 'moderation' while recommending from the reader a similar attitude formed by the capacity to discriminate inferentially among the poem's particulars: for Dryden, true historical understanding follows "the guesses of secret causes, inducing to the actions," which are "drawn at least from the most probable circumstances, not perverted by the malignity of the Author to sinister interpretations . . . but candidly laid down, and left to the Judgement of the Reader."[7]

Thus Dryden is not merely disingenuous in claiming to be "only the Historian" in the poem. Wishing to avoid imputations of "malignity," the very motive informing the loose bandying of terms in the address "To the Reader," he anticipates a similar abuse of terms by interested and malign parties in the poem proper: "*Wit* and *Fool,* are Consequents of *Whig* and *Tory:* And every man is Knave or an Ass to the contrary side."[8] We already glimpse a world in which railing, like the cursing of the plotters, must be contained by the historical methods entailed in both poetry and Scripture and symbolized by the analogical relations among 2 Samuel, the Exclusion Crisis, and Dryden's poem, not to mention the alternations within Dryden's prose at this juncture. For Dryden, the laws of history, "truth of matter, method, and clearness of expression,"[9] inform *Absalom and Achitophel,* which, while respecting the particulars of biblical and Restoration events, achieves its own unique suggestiveness and life as a "fable."

As much as the desire tactfully to advise King Charles II, Dryden's notion of "method" explains his poem's procedure: indeed, one of his implicit criticisms of Charles is that he has forgotten the training in "Method" that makes him the hope of *Astrea Redux.*[10] That it is easy to forget or upset the delicate balance implied by Dryden's notion of moderation is an assumption in Davenant and Rymer. So, at the threshold of entering the poem, the reader is reminded of this analogical commitment one final time: "To conclude all," Dryden writes, "if the Body Politique have any Analogy to the Natural, in my weak judgment, an Act of *Oblivion* were as necessary in a Hot, Distemper'd State, as an *Opiate* woud be in a Raging Fever."[11] Dryden's own remedy is, of course, the moderating influence of the poem, which must be read, like this simile, with an eye to its comparative method: like Charles, the reader is asked to draw the appropriate inferences without forging absolute equations among the details of 2 Samuel, the Exclusion Crisis, and the poetic narrative. Because a "parallel" exists only as a juxtaposition of discrete narratives, it requires a given reader, in observing or applying the general principle to be inferred, nevertheless to preserve those mutual distinctions. And Dryden's gesture to us as we enter the poem reveals how far an analogical activity is at base a conditional and hypothetical, rather than an indicative, attitude to cognitive apprehension.

The rhetorical success of *Absalom and Achitophel,* then, derives largely from a twofold process: an openness to applications made directly from its descriptive particulars (i.e., Achitophel's body) to actual historical particulars (i.e., Shaftesbury's diseased body), and the generation of allusions that provoke more indirect inferences. Thus, once we admit the parallel between David's concubines and King Charles II's licentiousness, we might also recall Bathsheba, whom the poem mentions; her child, whom the Lord smites; and Nathan, who, by telling David a parable, pricks the king's conscience and saves the nation.

Because the poem is partly satirical and more centrally hortatory, it must establish its own epistemological vantage in order to secure apt moral judgments and find ("invent") the exact symbolic forms appropriate to such judgments. Thus Dryden's talk of "judgements" creates both verbal and political significance: without judgment, for example, how could we ever distinguish between Dryden's satirical energy and the babble of curses that seems to fill the poem? Dryden's conceptualism requires him to condemn Achitophel's "huddled Notions," for, as his and Sir William Soames's translation of Nicolas Boileau-Despréaux explains:

> As your Idea's clear, or else obscure,
> Th' Expression follows perfect, or impure:
> What we conceive, with ease we can express;
> Words to the Notions flow with readiness.[12]

And in his *Life of Plutarch,* Dryden warns that "if the method be confus'd: if the words or expressions of thought are in any way obscure, then the Idea's which we receive must be imperfect; and if such, we are not taught by them what to elect, or what to shun."[13]

By contrast to Dryden's address, in which the cues for reading are established, *Absalom and Achitophel* has arisen out of a national failure to discriminate on at least two levels. On the one hand, King Charles II has failed to act with sufficient vigor in response to events and, on the other, the casuistical devices of the Exclusion Bill and the Whigs' manipulation of evidence, courts, and juries betoken a potentially catastrophic abuse of forensics. The language of the poem and Dryden's attacks on Shaftesbury, Slingsby Bethel, and Titus Oates symptomize Dryden's pervasive assumptions about methods of presenting, using, and judging evidence. Like Dryden's attitudes to history as demonstrated in his lives of Lucian and Plutarch, and like Tillotson's attitudes to biblical texts, the articulation of the new empiricism in matters relating to law, whether in Hobbes, Locke, Boyle, Gassendi, or Charleton, accompanies a deep scepticism about language. Accordingly, the world that *Absalom and Achitophel* hypothesizes is, precisely, one in which words reverse their values, the distinctions among similitudes erode, the art of rhetoric decays, and poetry faces extinction. The poet's and reader's combined "judgment" becomes the cooperative site of preventing the looming disaster: a method of representation that can capture the discreteness of particulars must disperse, and thus render impotent, the urge to suppress political, spiritual, and mental categories of definition in favor of precipitate action.

Absalom and Achitophel is centrally an analysis of relations between language and power. Specifically, it proposes that natural instincts—particularly the lust for "solid Power" (l. 298)—chronically threaten to uproot, distort, and fragment language. The figures of instinct, lust, and ambition are, like Milton's, the way to symbolize the satanic subversion of the "procedure" of ordinary language. In the mouths of the plotters, abstractions such as "self-defence," "liberty," "public Good," and "just revenge" become arbitrary tokens to clothe their antinomian appeals to the law of Nature, and they threaten to debase the rhetoric of political expediency, which could justify David's response to the plot. The Jews' desire for Edenic liberty is nothing but an unruly impulse:

> These *Adam*-wits, too fortunately free,
> Began to dream they wanted libertie;
> And when no rule, no president was found
> Of men, by Laws less circumscrib'd and bound,
> They led their wild desires to Woods and Caves,
> And thought that all but Savages were Slaves.
>
> (ll. 51–56)

Achitophel's casuistical argument to Absalom that "Self-defence is Natures Eldest Law" (l. 458) betokens the power of instinct; but Dryden elsewhere, having posited a conflict between instinct and power, finds in

the notion of writing the potential for institutionalizing and thus historicizing it, an effect adumbrated by the Laws' capacity to constrain the
Jews' licentious desires. He implies that we can examine, and thus distance, the claim that instinct can instantly gratify us, and thus circumvent
the contingencies of representation, because we see how "once in twenty
Years, their Scribes Record, / By natural Instinct they change their Lord"
(ll. 218–19): Scribal records approximate Dryden's poem and the inscribed tablets contained in the Ark of the Covenant, which are associated with the "Form and Order" against which the Jews "employ" their
"Power" (l. 531). Against writing and inscription-as-Law, the Jews also
engage an instinctual—namely, an *oral*—speech, which symbolizes their
enthusiastic, self-gratifying effusions. Just as Anglican theologians deeply suspect the supposed Catholic infallibility of some transcendental,
oral, nonwritten Truth, just as Walton represents a threat to Owen's
attachment to unmediated access to God, and just as Defoe was to praise
the written records of antiquity as a means to deflate the exaggerated
pretensions of mythic heroes, so Dryden depicts the plotters' language in
the very process of erosion as it issues out of their mouths. Achitophel's
entire behavior is, of course, the most sustained example. For instance,
Achitophel claims that David has lost his popularity, but the terms in
which he does so ironically describe not only Achitophel's own character
but also speech: the apparent power of the "puff of Wind" that blows
away David's reputation actually describes the hollow fiction of Achitophel's Satanic speech act. It is a figure for empty figuration itself:
"Those heaps of People which one Sheaf did bind, / Blown off and
scatter'd by a puff of Wind" (ll. 277–78).

The very mouths of the plotters—as opposed to the pen of the
poet—are filled with cries, oaths, "Rayling and praising" (l. 555), and
curses empty of propositional force. The poet deliberately reminds us of
his own capacity to record the nature of his own "Verse" (l. 570), just as he
is about to introduce "Canting *Nadab*" (l. 575), as well as Jonas and
Shimei, who, though they draw up statutes and write, put those acts to
casuistical, circular ends and thus negate their potential (ll. 581–82; 614–
17).[14] That Shimei has "pact a Jury of dissenting *Jews*" to "free the suf-
fring Saint from Humane Laws" (ll. 607–9) signifies the bond between
his instinctual discourse and a wider abuse of law and an emasculation of
history and memory, those Lockean requirements for national and personal identity. Dryden characterizes the host of plotters as "the herd of
such, / Who think too little, and who talk too much," driven unwittingly

by "meer instinct" (ll. 533–35). And Corah/Titus Oates stands as a living monument to the perversion of memory and law. With a "Voyce . . . harsh and loud" (l. 646), Corah produces "wondrous Evidence" (l. 661); moreover, "His memory, miraculously great, / Could Plots, exceeding mans belief, repeat," which, precisely because they are improbable are credited, as if to illustrate Shimei/Slingsby Bethel's corruption of forensic processes (ll. 650–51).

The immediacy of the urge for power causes the plotters, like the devils in *Paradise Lost,* to inhabit a world composed of mere surfaces, of appearances, which they, like the mob, fail to penetrate, because the precipitousness of ambition provokes instant, self-mirroring judgment. Dryden has already described the idolatrous substitution of images for God himself in the Jebusites' love of their disgraced gods, which have been "burnt like common wood" (l. 97). And, generalizing about "Priests of all Religions," he writes:

> Of whatso'er descent their Godhead be,
> Stock, Stone, or other homely pedigree,
> In his defence his Servants are as bold
> As if he had been born of beaten gold.
>
> (ll. 100–103)

Further, on the one hand:

> The Sober part of *Israel,* free from stain,
> Well knew the value of a peacefull raign:
> And, looking backward with a wise afright,
> Saw Seames of wounds, dishonest to the sight;
> In contemplation of whose ugly Scars,
> They Curst the memory of Civil Wars.
>
> (ll. 69–74)

On the other hand, the *"Jewish Rabbins,"* ignoring the properly sceptical, retroactive "contemplation" of history and its "Scars," indulge rather in "believing nothing, or believing all" (l. 117), just as the other plotters and the crowd are quite satisfied with their own partial observations and dazzled by sheer spectacle. Achitophel has fallen from his eminence as a great judge with "discerning Eyes" (l. 189), and the "dazled" crowd "feed their eyes" unreflectively on Absalom's "goodly person" (ll. 686–87). Achitophel in particular makes Absalom conscious of how things appear, urging him to false and rushed conclusions: he speaks of the necessity to "watch and guide" the "Motions" of "Fate" and to seize the chance from "the first Impression" (ll. 253–57).[15] He also paints David "naked of Friends, and round beset with Foes" (l. 280), and, after having created a fiction by which Absalom is made to picture himself threatened by the Duke of York as a rapacious lion (ll. 441–54), he argues that when David "affects the Frown," he really wishes to be taken by force, or 'raped' (ll. 471–76).

Johnson was, of course, correct to comment that the first part of *Absalom and Achitophel* (to l. 810) overwhelms the remainder, in which Dryden places the worthies and David's speech. This is simply because the plotters talk too much, a garrulity that infects the narrator. The plotters fill their atmosphere with curses, oaths, and empty prayers. And Achitophel's satanic logic is marked by a predilection for a form of radical metaphor, in which the two logically discrete terms of the figure are forcefully conflated in defiance of the laws of probability, morality, and, significantly, linguistics.[16] Achitophel's ambition also claims an insight into the occult nature of things that he cannot have, such as the significance of David's 'mild' posture (l. 473). In addressing Absalom, Achitophel swamps his language by equating the young man with God, his prophets, Christ, and the deepest yearnings of the nation. Like Absalom, the reader cannot pause to judge the appropriateness of a given figure before another comes to sweep him or her on in a rush of images. The prince is his people's

> . . . cloudy Pillar, and their guardian Fire:
> Their second *Moses,* whose extended Wand
> Divides the Seas, and shews the promis'd Land:
> Whose dawning Day, in every distant age,
> Has exercis'd the Sacred Prophets rage:
> The Peoples Prayer, the glad Deviners Theam,
> The Young-mens Vision, and the Old mens Dream!
> Thee, *Saviour,* Thee, the Nations Vows confess;
> And, never satisfi'd with seeing, bless.
>
> (ll. 233–41)

Johnson's deep scepticism about the radical deployment of metaphor was to inform his attack on the violent 'yoking' of metaphysical conceits, much as Dryden fears Achitophel's 'forcing' of metaphor. And the language of "Vision" and "Dream" in this passage recalls Hobbes's similar doubts about religious certainty. Using the same distinction as

Edward Worsley between immediate and mediate forms of speech,[17] Hobbes seizes on the problems of authorizing claims to immediate converse with God: "How God speaketh to a man immediately may be understood by those well enough, to whom he hath so spoken; but how the same should be understood by another, is hard, if not impossible to know."[18]

More specifically, Hobbes indicts a hierarchy of four kinds of religious claims, whether issuing from "supernaturall Inspiration," "Holy Scripture," "Dream," or "Vision." Of the last two, he writes: "To say [God] hath spoken to [a man] in a Dream, is no more than to say he dreamed that God spake to him"; and further, "To say he hath seen a Vision, or heard a Voice, is to say, that he hath dreamed between sleeping and waking." Hobbes proposes in prophecy, as in all things, the "mediation of second causes."[19] But Achitophel's athletic disregard for an empirical control of the figures of speech explains in part his subordinating "even Heav'n" to "that Universal Call," the "publick Good" (ll. 421–22): Bleached of their moral and referential content, words become almost nominalistic counters, tossed about by the polymorphous perverse whims of a speaker driven by instinct and ambition, such that the cipher "publick Good" almost casually overwhelms "even Heav'n."

By osmosis, as it were, and like the narrator of Milton's epic, Dryden's narrator finds himself seduced by the plotters' verbal fluency. At least, there are junctures in the poem where the poet seems to adopt a false point of view. For one, we find the famous trope of "Guns, invented since full many a day," which, though distanced from "Our Authour," who "swears . . . not" that they will be used (ll. 131–32), invokes a radical anachronism, which signals the poem's wider corruptions of history. Further, he yields to the attractive ease of maxims, which, almost unwittingly, absorb this perverted perspective.[20] Concluding his general description of the problem of succession (ll. 1–84), he declares deceptively that "Plots, true or false, are necessary things, / To raise up Commonwealths, and ruin Kings" (ll. 83–84). Inasmuch as this axiom seems to confirm the necessity of unseating kings, this is a perverse judgment; though read another way, the poet here simply describes the mechanisms without which usurpation cannot succeed. Later, the poet writes, apparently agreeing with Shimei, that "Laws are only made to Punish those, / Who serve the King, and to protect his Foes" (ll. 610–11).

It is not clear whether the poet is merely describing or oddly conforming to a subversive attitude. We realize, as with the oxymoron describing David's "fatall mercy" (l. 146), that such judgments illuminate general and real problems within the political world of the poem. If they temporarily infect the narrator's point of view, that serves to underscore those problems, while distancing Dryden from them. We respond to an irony depending on an analogical perception of difference: we are asked to discriminate between alternative points of view potentially embedded in a single utterance, or between the local power of such an utterance, and the ironies generated by its relationship to some wider, controlling frame.

Accordingly, we witness a deflowering of the arts of poetry and rhetoric. The Ciceronian ideals of virtuous oratory are recast into Achitophel's self-regarding "successful Arts" (l. 289), his "Praise" (l. 303), his "Flattery" (l. 304), and his "blandishments" (l. 488), which Absalom, an eager pupil, retails to the mob. Poetry suffers the same fate, with Achitophel consoling Absalom for his meager portion from David:

> He to his Brother gives Supreme Command;
> To you a Legacy of Barren Land:
> Perhaps th' old Harp, on which he thrums his Layes:
> Or some dull *Hebrew* Ballad in your Praise.
>
> (ll. 437–40)

To Achitophel, words (his "Arts") can only be weighed on the scale of success, determined by the degree of power with which they endow the speaker; hence his damning contrast between the satisfactions of "Supreme Command" and the vacuousness of David's Psalms, to posterity the pinnacle of sublime poetry.

The problem is endemic from the beginning. Earl Miner writes that the temporal confusions of the poem's opening "refer to a time that never really existed except in the daydreams of masculine desires,"[21] and this depicts the degree to which those urges wreak havoc with the logical possibilities of discourse, because they aspire to operate outside the spatio-temporal constraints of writing or Scripture. The flush of temporal prepositions that overwhelm those lines ("In, e'r, Before, When, E'r, When, Then") enacts a perplexed world of discourse, which even puzzles the wise and symbolizes the narrator's own confusion: like David's lust, which has set the whole thing in motion, and like those lyric urgencies in Wordsworth that perplex the temporality of prepositions, the world of putatively masculine power and desire plays to itself. By recalling the Miltonic image of Eve caught up with her own image,

David's self-love, propagated in a series of indiscriminate self-coinages, ironically suggests a kind of failure of masculinity, which should be outwardly directed, and should preserve a syntactical distinction between subject and predicate.[22]

It is David, then, who predicates the poem's linguistic confusions. The beginning precisely determines not only what happens in the action of the poem (which is mainly talk) but also the structure of the end. By invoking the inevitable conflict between Nature and Law (or impulse and Scripture) (l. 5), Dryden forces us to see how, like the plotters, the mob, and the "well-hung *Balaam*" (l. 574), David has subordinated the necessity for rational discrimination to his lust. (For example, his court blurs the proper distinction between wives and concubines [l. 6]). The oxymoron "diviner Lust" (l. 19) signifies a more generic collapse of distinctions, as does the judgment implicit in the talk of promiscuity and scattering, which recalls how Onan, in spilling his seed, displeased the Lord.[23] Moreover, Dryden introduces his discussion of liberty and law by exploiting the moral confusion evident in David's taking several mothers like slaves into his bed. Paul argues in Galatians 4 that Hagar, the slave woman, represents "Jerusalem which now is, and is in bondage with her children," whereas Sarah represents the Jerusalem above, which is free.[24] We can only understand the trope properly in the context of the wider Pauline argument that sets not law and grace against each other, but faith and obedience to God's decrees (embodied in Scripture/writing) against the natural (and impulsive) law of disobedience. Paul insists that the law is holy[25] and that "the law was our schoolmaster to bring us unto Christ, that we might be justified by faith."[26] David's sexual license does not long escape the judgment on sin that "Priestcraft" entails (l. 1), even though the poet briefly intimates that David's promiscuity should not be "cursedly, confin'd" (l. 4).

To the problem of succession that David generates, Dryden adds two subtle and yet more precise failures of judgment, which he indicts as the seeds of the conspiracy itself. For David's "Lust" (l. 19), whose divinity is questionable, presupposes that mixture of impulse and superficiality which propels the plotters. Whether we know the circumstances of Absalom's origin or not, one thing is sure: none of David's "Numerous Progeny" is "So Beautifull, so brave as *Absolon*" (ll. 17–18). The perspectival qualifier "seem'd" alerts us to the implication that *David's* self-regard and indulgence are primarily pleased with Absalom's "motions" and "face" and transform them into an earthly image of *"Paradise"*:

> In Peace the thoughts of War he coud remove,
> And seem'd as he were only born for love.
> What e'r he did was done with so much ease,
> In him alone, 'twas Natural to please.
> His motions all accompanied with grace;
> And *Paradise* was open'd in his face.
> With secret Joy, indulgent *David* view'd
> His Youthfull Image in his Son renew'd.
>
> (ll. 25–32)

I have suggested that the putatively masculine activity of Davidic creation becomes in a peculiar way destabilized as effeminate, ineffective, and self-regarding. Both in this poem and later, Dryden extends the correlative between a failure of object-directed sexuality, which he associates with the discriminations of writing, and the circularities of a strangely deflected sexual drive, which he associates with a kind of instant, enthusiastic, pneumatic discourse. The "well-hung *Balaam*" and "canting *Nadab*" unite in MacFlecknoe's impotent "*Irish* pen," which finds expression in the collapsed verbal forms of anagrams, acrostics, and metaphysical conceits. A parallel failure in David is implied by the poem's soft description of Absalom, in whom David sees himself. Certainly, that Monmouth's beauty was associated with such values is suggested by a contemporary portrait of him as John the Baptist, which reminds one powerfully of Caravaggio's similarly strange and sexually ambiguous paintings.

The narcissistic subversion of judgment by the material world of surfaces propagates an act of casuistry fatal to the subsequent health of the body politic.[27] For David is both unable and unwilling to "see" Absalom's "faults" (ll. 35–36). Consequently,

> Some warm excesses, which the Law forbore,
> Were constru'd Youth that purg'd by boiling o'r:
> And *Amnon's* Murther, by a specious Name,
> Was call'd a Just Revenge for injur'd Fame.
>
> (ll. 37–40)

We experience here a crucial shift in voice: the active voice in the earlier lines places the failure of judgment clearly at David's feet; the shift now to the passive ("Were constru'd," "Was call'd") betokens an insidious decay, whereby an original and specific cause is dispersed into a general and impersonal process, which it has nevertheless precipitated. Significantly, this erosion occurs within the figures of medicine and law: in the former, hasty and expedient diagnosis replaces the careful analysis of symptoms (e.g., the worthies looking upon the "Scars" of the war); in the latter, the primal sin of murder is masked by a superficial and imperious casuistry, in which universals such as "Just Revenge" and "injur'd Fame" operate as counters in a perversely incestuous game. David has betrayed at once three of the central duties of kingship: he is a bad father, a weak judge, and an irresponsible speaker.[28]

David's identification with a refreshingly unconstrained "Nature" set against the constraints of "law" (l. 5) has subtly and catastrophically transmogrified into the poem's struggle between instinct and writing: the world of contingent, unconsidered naming that defends the boiling over of youth threatens to overturn the lawfulness of Scripture, which resists the easy conversion of "sin" (l. 2) into idolatrous self-justification, and which provides Dryden and the reader with the chief repository for the governing tropes of the poem, as well as the ultimate ground for its discriminations and advice. Dryden injects the figure of Scripture through the concept of law, which predicates David's final speech.

The very appeal to the common records of Christendom historicizes and contains the unruly impulses they describe and condemn, a power embodied in the fatal potentialities of the Ark of the Covenant. Achitophel scoffs at historical precedent, the "Successive Title, Long, and Dark, / Drawn from the Mouldy Rolls of *Noah*'s Ark" (l. 301–2), but he still recognizes the usefulness of Absalom's having his "doubtfull Title" inscribed in "Law" (l. 408). Like both arks, the Law represents the graphic spatialization of God's promises, fixing discourse in such a way that it can, like the houses of God and of State, encompass and compel the allegiance of humanity.[29]

Dryden quite casually conflates the Ark of the Covenant (which recalls Noah's Ark), the House of State, and the Temple of God in the lengthy passage on government (ll. 759–810). Here we witness the transformation of one world into another. The one is inhabited by Absalom's "Youth, Beauty, Graceful Action" (l. 723), the mob's "Common Interest" (l. 724), its adulation of the "Pomp" of "This moving Court" (ll. 739–40), and the distillation of "Religion, and Redress of Grievances" into "names, that always cheat and always please" (ll. 747–48). We inherit from the other a more sober determination, captured precisely in the poet's desire "here [to] fix the Mark" (l. 803). The moment of fixing or setting the limit, like that moment in *The Country Wife* in which

Horner's lie secures the continuance of social forms and completes the play, dictates by fiat the arbitrary, contractual point at which the conduct of politics, society, and discourse must circumscribe the free play of desire. That this is the condition of *graphē*, of writing or inscription, is confirmed in the identification of the fixed "Mark" with the Ark, which, in Moses' words of institution, establishes a permanent sign set against the Israelites' rebellion: "Take this book of the law, and put it in the side of the ark of the covenant of the Lord your God, that it may be there for a witness against thee. For I know thy rebellion, and thy stiff neck."[30] Dryden also invokes the power of that monument by recalling Uzzah, who kindled the wrath of God because he "put forth his hand to the ark of God."[31] The Ark stands as the repository of a spiritual and national stability, whose force depends on public inscription.

This process of 'fixing' stability not only informs the poet's own credo about the State but also introduces the society of worthies, in which the poet's "Naming" (l. 816) celebrates the Muse. Further, the reestablishment of law and the reconstitution of words ensure that poet, subjects, and king play their respective roles. The roll call of worthies introduces a polity in which the Muse recovers eloquence and arms and arts unite, all grounded on "experience" (l. 891). The "Recording Muse" (l. 828) subsumes the plotters' verbiage, and she mourns for Barzillai's noble son, who, illustrating the proper exercise of power within the body politic, operates in a "Narrow Circle" infused with "Pow'r Divine" (l. 838), in imitation of the ordinances of God and the poet's "Verse" (l. 858). Zadock epitomizes "sense," "fit words," "eloquence," and "Learning," acting as a pillar of the "Laws" (ll. 868–75). Adriel's gifts as a judge and Jotham's as a rhetor accompany those discriminations of "balance" (l.886), which Dryden, especially in this particular poetic moment, establishes in his verse. Talk of the "Circle" (l. 838), the "dome" (l. 868), "*Colleges*" (l. 872), "Pillars" (l. 874), and "Assemblies" (l. 884) expands into an architectural trope that union of spatial inscription and "Form and Order" (l. 531) with the Muse, or writing, ranged against the anarchic urges of naked power.

Not least in the Drydenian couplet, David's own speech reestablishes all those discriminations among figures that he has earlier suppressed. Restoring words to their negotiable denotative significance, he reverses the linguistic corrosion by which a "Patriots name, whose Modern sense / Is one that would by Law supplant his Prince" (ll. 965–66). As in the poet's description of Barzillai, David's speech freely employs strong caesuras, as if to stress the very activity of discriminating among words. Dryden has remarked earlier on the empirical constitution of synecdoche in the address "To the Reader," because we are to infer the complete action from what we see Dryden present.[32] And Zimri has come to symbolize the synecdochic function of representation as such, by standing as "all Mankinds Epitome" (l. 546). So David finally clarifies the synecdochic relationship between himself and his people: attacking the notion that "one was made for many" (l. 945), he declares:

> Votes shall no more Establish'd Pow'r controul,
> Such Votes as make a Part exceed the Whole:
> No groundless Clamours shall my Friends remove,
> Nor Crowds have power to Punish e're they Prove.
>
> (ll. 993–96)

Evidently, the restoration of this relationship accompanies the abolition of verbal pollution and the reinstitution of true legal procedure; the perjurers implicitly recant, and the plotters' devices fall upon their own heads.

However, all is not entirely well, because the return to regal authority cannot reside in David's speech alone. In describing the king's address, the poet admittedly paints a vision of political harmony, but the description is already compromised by its context. David's original abuse of words has radically destabilized a state that depends upon the judicious application of speech. How can the fiction of the king's authority solve a problem for which the king is responsible? And, further, how can the king's poet appear to speak truly, and achieve prophetic status, without arrogating to himself precisely the power that makes the plotters dangerous?[33]

Dryden presses home these problems in several ways, chiefly by emphasizing his process of speech, and also by remarking the nature of David's final pronouncement. As the poem progresses, the poet and his Muse increasingly intrude, until the poet must even restrain his Muse in midflight, caught up as it is in praise of Barzillai's son ("Here stop my Muse" [ll. 854–63]). Second, at the threshold of David's final speech, as the poet prepares to invoke the king, the curses of the plotters briefly erupt ("*Shimei* taught *Jerusalem* to Curse" [l. 932]), as if to remind us once more of the ominous alliance between orality and the unruly instincts of rebellion. Dryden thus invites us to treat David's speech as both an element of his own poem—and hence only text—and as an oral event of the kind, though not the intent, that has marked Achitophel. Whatever symbolic satisfaction we may draw from a corrective parallel between the corrosive effects of Achitophel's delivery and the thaumaturgic effects of David's, the very nature of both activities follows from David's original failure. The poet implicitly inhabits the world that the king has tainted, and he must therefore discover a source of linguistic authority that permits him to admonish David and buttress his poem, without becoming, like the plotters, an idolater, a "God-smith" or "*Adam*-wit" (ll. 50–51).

The psychological fulcrum of the poem anticipates its ending, by which Dryden can validate his text without making himself his own origin of epistemological and political authority. Dryden's scepticism prefers "deeds" over "words," as he puts it (l. 675), and, though Absalom is later to corrupt the Ciceronian art of *actio* by false and insinuating gestures (l. 690), we can mark by a gesture precisely the moment at which Absalom submits to Achitophel's wiles. Absalom first seems unscathed by Achitophel's temptation, but a series of unfelt monarchical axioms prefaces the discovery of his desire for power, which suddenly comes upon him:

> All but his Kingly Diadem he gives;
> And that: *But there he Paus'd; then Sighing,* said,
> Is Justly Destin'd for a Worthier Head.
>> (ll. 346–48; my emphasis)

God's eschatological power is signalled by a similar moment 'outside' or 'beyond' language, but that nevertheless partakes of 'writing,' just as in the Anglican hermeneutical tradition, miracles become the grounds for the contingent stability and "sufficient" authority of Scripture, in which they are inscribed. And just as the miracles are judged according to empirical criteria—the number and authority of witnesses—so Dryden presents himself as an independent witness of events. The voices of the plotters become a property of Dryden's text, which in turn the nod of God validates. For precisely the reasons that Anglicans dismissed Catholic claims to 'oral' and even 'nonwritten' church authority, Dryden will not invoke the *voice* of God: to do so would be to vitiate his and his poem's sceptical premises. Rather, the poet must find in poetic figure itself a symbolic equivalent to Scripture, a kind of writing that incorporates its own "foot-steps" of divine authority.[34] When Locke maintains that "the evidence of our Saviour's mission from heaven is so great, in the multitude of miracles he did before all sorts of people," he finds Scripture a satisfactory repository of proofs for the faith according to empirical criteria, especially owing to the public nature of Christ's miracles.[35] Similarly, the nations accede to David's "Godlike" nature because God testifies to it convincingly:

> He said. Th'Almighty, nodding, gave Consent:
> And Peals of Thunder shook the Firmament.
> Henceforth a Series of new time began,
> The mighty Years in long Procession ran:
> Once more the Godlike *David* was Restor'd,
> And willing Nations knew their Lawfull Lord.
>
> (ll. 1026–31)

The nod of God has its origins in an allusion to *The Iliad* (1:493ff.), in which Thetis begs Zeus to endow honor upon her son: Zeus nods, and Olympus shakes. R. B. Onians comments that in classical culture God was often represented by or as the head and that the nod came to represent a peculiarly binding form of promise.[36] But the nod is also a vital affirmation of the successive structure of historical time made real by the linear constructs of Dryden's poem, his parallel, and the very structure of the couplet. Even in this moment of confirmation, the sweeping hair of Zeus, like the dead strewn at the end of *De Rerum Natura,* recalls an activity of scattering as much as gathering. That scattering, as we have seen in the neo-Epicurean ethic, as well as in neoclassical linguistics, theology, and criticism, denotes an atomic view of knowledge, which asserts the phenomenality of language, as well as its inevitable articulation into the mutual mechanisms of narrative and syntax. The physiognomic sign from God reminds the reader, then, that cultural knowledge can only be enacted in those palpable terms, inscribed on Dryden's printed page, which must defy David's early desire to force language, against its nature, to his desires. The return to Law at the end of the poem is a return to the process of this poem, English syntax, and the comparative and temporal grammar of the couplet.

Postscript

In one sense, I have ended where I should like to have begun: with a critical reading of a neoclassical poem. In an ideal world, this book would act as a preface to a series of such readings. Its origins lie, precisely, in the question of what expectations we should bring to reading the literature of the Restoration and eighteenth century, because I believe that those expectations should respond to the culture's own attitudes to reading and representation. This concern explains my central interest in neoclassical linguistics.

I have also ended with an allusion to that most distinctive building block of Augustan poetry, the heroic couplet. For in the couplet is palpably embedded much of the argument it has taken many pages to develop. The couplet makes no attempt to hide its artifice: it makes no pretense to representational transparency, and Dryden's defense of dramatic rhyme against the objections of Sir Robert Howard only emphasize his recognition that plays do not aim at some realistic effect, even though Dryden accepts the criterion of probability. In its organization, the couplet perfectly enacts the conceptualist economy of the neoclassical mind. First, bound by its strong rhyme, the couplet serves most obviously as the foundational atom of poetic utterance, so an entire poem visibly displays the relations between individual *sententiae* or images and the entire fabric. Second, the internal organization of the couplet assumes a set of comparisons between the two lines, as well as between the elements of those lines, such that patterns can even be organized around strong medial caesuras to create a chiasmus. We might recall the athletic organization of Dryden's great opening to *MacFlecknoe*—"All humane things are subject to decay, / And, when Fate summons, Monarchs must obey"—or the suppressed zeugma in Pope's lines, describing Belinda in *The Rape of the Lock*—"On her white Breast a sparkling *Cross* she wore / Which *Jews* might kiss, and Infidels adore." Especially in Pope's hands, the couplet also becomes intensely organized at the level of the individual line, which itself emphasizes the printed materiality that directs attention to such minutiae of punctuation as commas. Here I can think of no better example than that memorable line, also from *The Rape of the Lock,* which simultaneously scans the material surface of the printed line and the objects arranged in sequence on Belinda's dressing table: "Puffs, Powders, Patches, Bibles, Billet-doux." In a poem that both celebrates and satirizes our obsessions with material goods, Pope must first exploit our apprehension of the printed page as an artifact before he can discomfort our very attempt at possession by placing the Bible into that purely physicalized cosmos. Pope can assume an aesthetic in which words are first endowed with discrete atomic weight before they become objects of authorial arrangement and readerly judgment.

Like Pope's line, the ending of *Absalom and Achitophel* can also assume that the normal processes of readerly apprehension are linear. In Pope, that linearity capitalizes on the Western action of reading, requiring the movement of the eye from left to right, which becomes a commentary on space and on how objects, placed within social spaces, become indices of our moral values. In Dryden, that linearity stands for the normal, sequential processes of history, which it is both immoral and impolitic to ignore or suppress. Both symbolic arguments substitute the normal behavior of language as such—its intrinsic atomism and linearity—for aesthetic and political theses. Dryden and Pope are each disturbed at the attempt by individuals to possess objects in the world (including human bodies), much as a reader may be said to appropriate the words of a poem into his or her cognitive universe. The therapy in both poets is to make the reader conscious of his or her activity, that is, to see the parallel between those various modes of appropriation and so to ironize the behavior that is nonetheless foundational to the very act of reading.

Something of what I have just described goes on in *Paradise Lost:* there, perhaps more fully than in later neoclassical literature, linguistic, cognitive, and spiritual behaviors serve as metaphors for one another. By becoming methodical, and conscious of their methods, those different forms of activity create a redemptive parallel between the movement of the reader in the text and the activity of the divine within the world. It is one of the persistent, though inexplicit, theses of my book that it is precisely in these terms that we should recuperate Milton's later poetry as belonging to the age in which it was published. Like *Leviathan,* which is much less a contested property of (loosely) Restoration culture, *Paradise*

Lost establishes a precedent for neoclassical aesthetics in treating method itself a focus of its symbolic argument, then attaching method to politics. This economy of method, readerly protocol, and ethics is what makes Jane Austen, writing some one hundred and fifty years after Milton, a neoclassical author. Following the precepts of a sceptical empiricism, neoclassical writers tend to treat good reading as a corollary to good character. (This is not to say that a similar commitment to method produces similar political attitudes.) Elizabeth Bennet finally knows that Darcy is a good man because he redeems Wickham and Lydia; but the reader may anticipate some such development of plot because Darcy is the only speaker whose verbal method matches Elizabeth's. And in her approach to Pemberley, Elizabeth can savor Darcy's good taste writ large upon the landscape, with all that that implies for his virtue. In its central readerly mechanisms, *Pride and Prejudice* is cousin to *The Country Wife* or *The Way of the World,* in which the parity of characters is established by a mutual ability to manipulate witty and apt comparisons in speech. I hope in this book to have provided a genealogy for the motives and protocols that determine those literate assumptions. The neo-Epicurean revival, as well as the parallel though often related developments in linguistics, theology, and literary criticism, provided the "materiall" conditions for a way of seeing and representing the world which survived a century and a half.

Notes

Introduction: Atoms, Bodies, and Words

1. Richard Foster Jones, *Ancients and Moderns: A Study in the Rise of the Scientific Movement in England* (Saint Louis: Washington Univ. Studies, 1936); and R. F. Jones et al., *The Seventeenth Century: Studies in the History of English Thought and Literature from Bacon to Pope* (Stanford: Stanford Univ. Press, 1951).

2. Robert K. Merton, "Science, Technology and Society in Seventeenth Century England," *Osiris* 4 (1938): 386; 390.

3. Timothy J. Reiss, *The Discourse of Modernism* (Ithaca: Cornell Univ. Press, 1982), 339.

4. For example, Peter de Bolla, discussing John Baillie's *An Essay on the Sublime* (1747), writes that neoclassical "writing, or more generally language is transparent, a neutral medium of representation"; Lennard J. Davis, discussing Defoe, retails the old view of the "plain style," writing that "the plain style claimed for itself a closer kinship with the Word of God than with the ornate words of man," a view Davis ascribes especially to the "Puritans"; and Antony Easthope, discussing Dryden, writes of the "presumed primacy of the real, the socially constructed real of British empiricism which denies its own construction." In various ways I challenge all these views, not least in their assumption that neoclassical culture did not see quite what was at stake in its adoption of certain linguistic postulates. See Peter de Bolla, *The Discourse of the Sublime: History, Aesthetics and the Subject* (Oxford: Blackwell, 1989) esp. 40–47; Lennard J. Davis, *Factual Fictions: The Origins of the English Novel* (New York: Columbia Univ. Press, 1983), 80; and Antony Easthope, *British Post-Structuralism since 1968* (London: Routledge, 1988), 205. Two essays that push in a different direction are Peter Dear, "*Totius in Verba*: Rhetoric and Authority in the Early Royal Society," *Isis* 76 (1985): 145–61; and Brian Vickers, "Analogy versus Identity: The Rejection of Occult Symbolism," in *Occult and Scientific Mentalities in the Renaissance,* ed. Vickers (Cambridge: Cambridge Univ. Press, 1984), 95–163.

5. For the importance of a rhetorical education based on Cicero, see, for example, the syllabus of Westminster School reproduced in James Anderson Winn, *John Dryden and His World* (New Haven: Yale Univ. Press, 1987), 521–24; and Daniel Defoe, *The Compleat English Gentleman*, cited in Carol Kay, *Political Constructions: Defoe, Richardson, and Sterne in Relation to Hobbes, Hume, and Burke* (Ithaca: Cornell Univ. Press, 1988), 55. Both Boyle and Locke recommend the study of Cicero. See Robert Boyle, *Some Considerations concerning Experimental Essays in General* (1661), in *The Works of the Honourable Robert Boyle,* ed. Thomas Birch, 2d ed., 6 vols. (London,

1772), 1:304–5; and John Locke, *The Works of John Locke*, 11th ed., 10 vols. (London: W. Otridge et al., 1812), 3:270–71. Locke's notebooks and journals are filled with references to Cicero.

6. Roy Porter, *English Society in the Eighteenth Century* (Harmondsworth, Eng.: Penguin, 1982), 18.

7. See J. H. Plumb, *The Growth of Political Stability in England, 1675–1725* (London: Macmillan, 1967).

8. Ronald Hutton, *The Restoration: A Political and Religious History of England and Wales, 1658–1667* (Oxford: Oxford Univ. Press, 1985), 1.

9. Thomas S. Kuhn, *The Structure of Scientific Revolutions*, 2d ed. (Chicago: Univ. of Chicago Press, 1970); and Imre Lakatos and Alan Musgrave, *Criticism and the Growth of Knowledge* (Cambridge: Cambridge Univ. Press, 1970).

10. See Kay, *Political Constructions*.

11. Steven Shapin and Simon Schaffer, *Leviathan and the Air Pump: Hobbes, Boyle, and the Experimental Life* (Princeton: Princeton Univ. Press, 1985).

12. Victoria Kahn, *Rhetoric, Prudence, and Skepticism in the Renaissance* (Ithaca: Cornell Univ. Press, 1985), chap. 6; Victoria A. Silver, "The Fiction of Self-Evidence in Hobbes's *Leviathan*," *ELH* 55 (1988): 351–79.

13. Thomas Taylor, ed. and intro., *The Works of Plato*, 5 vols. (1804; reprint, New York: Garland, 1984), 1:lxxxii.

14. James William Johnson, *The Formation of English Neoclassical Thought* (Princeton: Princeton Univ. Press, 1967); and Howard D. Weinbrot, *Augustus Caesar in "Augustan" England: The Decline of a Classical Norm* (Princeton: Princeton Univ. Press, 1978). See also Joseph M. Levine, "Ancients and Moderns Reconsidered," *Eighteenth-Century Studies* 14 (1981): 72–89; and *The Battle of the Books: History and Literature in Augustan England* (Ithaca: Cornell Univ. Press, 1991).

15. Bernard Frischer, *The Sculpted Word: Epicureanism and Philosophical Recruitment in Ancient Greece* (Berkeley: Univ. of California Press, 1982).

16. David Furley argues that though Epicurus dogmatically believed in atoms and the void, he did not—as Cyril Bailey and F. M. Cornford believe—hold to some unmediated means of knowing their existence. Epicurus's dogmatic beliefs depend on empirical and experiential criteria, very like those that occasion his probabilism. See "Knowledge of Atoms and Void in Epicureanism," in *Cosmic Problems: Essays on Greek and Roman Philosophy of Nature* (Cambridge: Cambridge University Press, 1989), 161–71.

17. John Bender, *Imagining the Penitentiary: Fiction and the Architecture of Mind in Eighteenth-Century England* (Chicago: Univ. of Chicago Press, 1987), 100.

18. See Robert H. Kargon, *Atomism in England from Hariot to Newton* (Oxford: Clarendon Press, 1966); and Thomas F. Mayo, *Epicurus in England, 1650–1725* (Dallas: Southwest Press, 1934).

19. N. H. Keeble, *The Literary Culture of Nonconformity in Later Seventeenth-Century England* (Athens: Univ. of Georgia Press, 1987), esp. 82–92.

20. James Clifford, *The Predicament of Culture: Twentieth-Century Ethnography, Literature, and Art* (Cambridge: Harvard Univ. Press, 1988), 22.

21. See BM Add MS 19.333. Lucy Hutchinson dedicated this manuscript to Lord Anglesey in 1675, but it is obvious from her dedicatory remarks that the translation of Lucretius occurred much before, perhaps as early as the 1640s, following her marriage to Colonel Hutchinson in 1638.

1. The Restoration as Cultural Moment

1. See *The Works of John Dryden,* ed. Edward Niles Hooker and H. T. Sweden-berg, Jr., 15 vols. to date (Berkeley: Univ. of California Press, 1956-), 1:43–44. Line numbers appear in my text.

2. Exactly this myth of generational and intellectual evolution occurs in Simon Patrick's famous pamphlet also published in 1662, *A Brief Account of the New Sect of Latitude-Men Together with Some Reflections on the New Philosophy* (London, 1662), esp. 18ff.

3. The 1725 edition of *Chorea Gigantum* appeared sandwiched between Inigo Jones's original and John Webb's defense of Jones, under the title *The Most Notable Antiquity of Great Britain, Vulgarly Called Stoneheng, on Salisbury Plain, Restored, by Inigo Jones. . . . To which are added, The Chorea Gigantum, or, Stone-Heng Restored to the Danes, By Doctor Charleton; and Mr. Webb's Vindication of Stone-Heng Restored, In Answer to Dr. Charleton's Reflections* (London, 1725).

4. See notes to the California edition of the poem for publication details of both Charleton's and Jones's works. (*Works of John Dryden,* 1:248–50).

5. Charleton attacks the Platonic and Stoic notions of the "universal," for pre-cisely these reasons. (*Epicurus's Morals* [London, 1656], Sigs. b2$^{r\&v}$).

6. Alexandre Koyré, *From the Closed World to the Infinite Universe* (1957; reprint, Baltimore: Johns Hopkins Univ. Press, 1968), 88.

7. Charleton dismisses Aristotle's dictatorship in his *Physiologia Epicuro-Gassendo-Charltoniana* (London, 1654), 90. He also discusses the dangers of philo-sophic secrecy in the same work (92).

8. Circularity is clearly an important figure. Harvey's notion of the circulation of the blood derives a cultural authority from other Renaissance notions of circulation, which endow the physiological metaphor with a preordained force. In breaking the logic of circularity, Dryden is not only taking issue with Aristotle but also declaring a new mode of perception and interpretation. See Walter Pagel, "William Harvey and the Purpose of Circulation," *Isis* 42 (1951): 22–38.

9. In an important article, Donald Greene argues that eighteenth-century litera-ture should be seen as "Augustinian" in its theology and "empiricist" in its epistemol-ogy ("Augustinianism and Empiricism: A Note on Eighteenth-Century Intellectual History," *Eighteenth-Century Studies* 1 [1967]: 33–68). Howard Weinbrot launched a sustained attack on the fallacy of seeing eighteenth-century literature as "Augustan" in *Augustus Caesar in "Augustan" England: The Decline of a Classical Norm* (Princeton: Princeton Univ. Press, 1978); and Howard Erskine-Hill has drafted a scrupulous qualification if not rebuttal in *The Augustan Idea in English Literature* (London: Arnold, 1983). If, as Erskine-Hill argues, the constellation of possibilities offered by the Augustan myth produced a "compound image in which compatibility was more evident than contradiction" (xii), this still does not amount to a methodical critique of culture, or a genuine mythology: it merely amounts to a source for a vocabulary—an imagery, precisely.

10. Christopher Hill, *The Century of Revolution, 1603–1714* (1961; reprint, New York: Norton, 1966); and see also Hill's *Some Intellectual Consequences of the English Revolution* (Madison: Univ. of Wisconsin Press, 1980).

11. J.G.A. Pocock, *Virtue, Commerce, and History: Essays on Political Thought and History, Chiefly in the Eighteenth Century* (Cambridge: Cambridge Univ. Press, 1985), 55.

12. For an account of the political events of 1709, and the Tories' attack on Marlborough as "Oliver" and "King John," see Edward Gregg, *Queen Anne* (1980; reprint, London: Ark, 1984), 286–87. In 1710, the riots accompanying the Sacheverell trial provoked in some fears of a new civil war (305–6).

13. The standard account of attacks on Hobbes is Samuel Mintz, *The Hunting of Leviathan: Seventeenth-Century Reactions to the Materialism and Moral Philosophy of Thomas Hobbes* (Cambridge: Cambridge Univ. Press, 1962). Steven Shapin and Simon Schaffer describe Boyle's determination to exclude Hobbes from the practices of the Royal Society in *Leviathan and the Air Pump: Hobbes, Boyle, and the Experimental Life* (Princeton: Princeton Univ. Press, 1985).

14. *The English Works of Thomas Hobbes of Malmesbury,* ed. Sir William Molesworth, 11 vols. (London: Bohn, 1839–45), 7:5. See also Edward Stillingfleet, *An Answer to a Late Dialogue between a New Catholic Convert and a Protestant* (London, 1687), 55–56, in which Stillingfleet attacks Catholic "Fanaticism," which clearly exploits the vocabulary made possible by fears generated by the Civil War.

15. See C. H. George, "Puritanism as History and Historiography," *Past and Present* 41 (1968): 77–104; Basil Hall, "Puritanism: The Definitional Problem," *Studies in Church History* 2 (1965): 283–96; and N. H. Keeble, in the introduction to his edition of *The Autobiography of Richard Baxter* (1974; reprint, London: Dent, 1985), xviff.

16. J.G.A. Pocock, "Clergy and Commerce: The Conservative Enlightenment in England," in *L'Eta dei Lumi: Studi Storici sul Settecento Europeo in Onore di France Venturi,* ed. R. Ajello et al., 2 vols. (Naples: Jovene Editori, 1985), 1:525–62. Christopher Hill writes that we should not "underestimate the effectiveness of the deliberate propaganda of the Anglican church, once it had been restored to its monopoly position" (*Some Intellectual Consequences,* 13). He also makes the absurd suggestion that the failure of the radical revolution irreparably blunted English literary sensibility, a naïve Romantic or inspirationalist myth that still lingers: "The immediate postrevolutionary hostility towards 'enthusiasm' had damaging effects on literature" (82).

17. Charles Webster, *The Great Instauration: Science, Medicine and Reform, 1626–1660* (London: Duckworth, 1975), esp. 19–31.

18. J. R. Jacob, *Robert Boyle and the English Revolution: A Study in Social and Intellectual Change* (New York: Burt Franklin, 1977), chap. 1.

19. Webster, *Great Instauration,* xiii; 43. Webster assumes the "dominance" of the "Puritans" in the mid-seventeenth century: "It has been decided to concentrate on the Puritans, the group which formed the dominant element in English society in the middle of the seventeenth century" (xiii). For a similar critique of *puritan* as a historiographical term, see T. K. Rabb, "Puritanism and the Rise of Experimental Science in England," *Journal of World History* 7 (1962): 46–67.

20. Webster provides an excellent account of the constitution of the groups anticipating the Royal Society (*Great Instauration,* 51ff.). Robert Frank provides even more detailed information in his equally fine *Harvey and the Oxford Physiologists* (Berkeley: Univ. of California Press, 1980), esp. 22–30. For an implicit critique of Webster, see John Henry, "Atomism and Eschatology: Catholicism and Natural Philosophy in the Interregnum," *British Journal for the History of Science* 15 (1982): 211–39.

21. Webster well describes some of the political constraints on the Royal Society (*Great Instauration,* 96–97).

22. Ibid., 497.

23. Ibid., 43. It may be fair to say that Webster has confused rather hazy intellectual or theological categories with forms of institutional affiliation. Many Presbyterians, including Matthew Poole, held a theology virtually identical to that of many Anglicans, though their views of Church government differed. Chillingworth, Milton, Browne, and Taylor shared very similar theological views, but their respective political fates varied widely. The two parties were frequently divided not by purely intellectual matters but by concrete political disagreements. R. S. Bosher's standard account of the achievement of Anglican hegemony at the Restoration is more precise and historically descriptive (*The Making of the Restoration Settlement: The Influence of the Laudians, 1649–1662* [London: Black, 1951]). I emphasize that a discursive ideology does not translate directly into the concrete possession of power, so Milton and Hobbes can be said to have contributed to a rhetoric that was employed by their enemies.

24. Raymond Williams analyzes the development of the modern, specialized senses of such words and concepts during the Industrial Revolution. What I have said here about "science," Williams says about "art." See *Culture and Society, 1780–1950* (1961; reprint, Harmondsworth, Eng.: Penguin, 1963), esp. chap. 2, "The Romantic Artist."

25. J.G.A. Pocock, *Politics, Language and Time: Essays on Political Thought and History* (New York: Atheneum, 1971), 18–21. I shall later discuss the multiple significance of terms such as *commerce* and *economy* in Locke's *Essay.* Similarly evocative and multivalent are the words *anxious* and *conscious.*

26. Boyle was described by contemporaries in the explicitly constitutional language of the "restorer of the mechanical philosophy," which appears to bind natural philosophy with political motives (see Marie Boas, "The Establishment of the Mechanical Philosophy," *Osiris* 10 [1952]: 414). Joseph Glanvill similarly describes Gassendi as "the *Restorer* of *Epicurus*" (*The Vanity of Dogmatizing: Or Confidence in Opinions Manifested in a Discourse of the Shortness and Uncertainty of Our Knowledge, and its Causes* [London, 1661], 176–77).

27. Keith Thomas's work suggests that though we cannot depict a moment when a set of attitudes changes, we can detect when institutions begin to speak differently about a certain phenomenon, which is not to say that things have automatically changed in the actual world. Nevertheless, a change in the patterns of verbal behavior constitutes a determinate historical event. Writing of the powers earlier accorded to charmers and sorcerers, Thomas claims that "the real change in attitude seems to have come with the Restoration of the Anglican Church after 1660" (*Religion and the Decline of Magic* [New York: Scribner's, 1971], 260).

28. Thomas H. Kuhn, *The Structure of Scientific Revolutions,* 2d ed. (Chicago: Univ. of Chicago Press, 1970).

29. See especially Sir Karl Popper's and Imre Lakatos's attacks on Kuhn in *Criticism and the Growth of Knowledge,* ed. Imre Lakatos and Alan Musgrove (Cambridge: Cambridge Univ. Press, 1970), 51–59; 91–197.

30. Wittgenstein's combination of epistemological scepticism and his vindication of the phenomenal nature of ordinary language serves increasingly as a model for commentators on neoclassical culture. See, for example, Michael G. Ketcham's excellent book on the *Spectator* as a means of ideological and representational dissemina-

tion, *Transparent Designs: Reading, Performance, and Form in the "Spectator" Papers* (Athens: Univ. of Georgia Press, 1985). See also Deborah C. Payne's judicious article "Reading the Signs in *The Country Wife*," *Studies in English Literature* 26 (1986): 403–19.

31. This characterization of Hobbes is not mine. Although these are indeed important features of Hobbes's philosophy, I also think that Hobbes is seminal to the creation of neoclassical discourse. The other side of the demonstrative absolutist is a propounder of a sceptical and contingent epistemology, involving an accompanying theory of reading and representation. Hobbes's founding strategy in *Leviathan* is to ask the reader to postulate a mere analogy between his or her experience and the anticipated experience of the text, a record of the author's private convictions. If we later assent to Hobbes's more absolutist and geometrical rhetoric, we do so only after acceding to this move. Thus to treat *Leviathan* as purely logical in its mode of argument is to ignore its own qualifications for our reading it.

32. Paul Feyerabend, *Against Method* (London: Verso, 1975), 145.

33. Ibid., 146.

34. Michel Foucault, *"The Archaeology of Knowledge" and "The Discourse on Language"* (New York: Pantheon, 1972), 74.

35. Ibid., 68.

36. Jonathan Brown, *Images and Ideas in Seventeenth-Century Spanish Painting* (Princeton: Princeton Univ. Press, 1978), 87–110.

37. Ibid., 106.

38. Ibid., 92.

39. Foucault, *The Archaeology of Knowledge,* 67.

40. Ibid., 225.

41. See variously, Nicolas Barker, *The Oxford University Press and the Spread of Learning: An Illustrated History, 1478–1978* (Oxford: Clarendon Press, 1978); Harry Carter, *A History of the Oxford University Press,* 1 vol. to date (Oxford: Clarendon Press, 1975); Colin Clair, *A Chronology of Printing* (Oxford: Cassell, 1969) and *A History of Printing in Britain* (London: Cassell, 1965); John Freehafer, "The Formation of the London Patent Companies in 1660," *Theatre Notebook* 20 (1965): 6–30; Katherine Eisaman Maus, "'Playhouse Flesh and Blood': Sexual Ideology and the Restoration Actress," *ELH* 46 (1979): 595–617; William Gaunt, *A Concise History of English Painting* (1964; reprint, London: Thames and Hudson, 1978), 40–56; and Antonia Fraser, *King Charles II* (London: Weidenfeld and Nicolson, 1979), 205.

42. Richard Ashcraft, *Revolutionary Politics and Locke's "Two Treatises of Government"* (Princeton: Princeton Univ. Press, 1986), esp. chap. 8.

43. Walter Charleton, *Epicurus's Morals,* 45–46.

44. John Evelyn also takes a similar line with Plato, accusing him of being a "Leveller" (*An Essay on the First Book of T. Lucretius Carus De Rerum Natura* [London, 1656], Sig. A7ᵛ). And in the light of my discussion, it is interesting that Baxter posits the Stoics as the classical corollaries to the Christians (*The Reasons of the Christian Religion,* in *The Practical Works of Richard Baxter,* 4 vols. [London: Virtue, 1845], 2:206). We shall later see how the new ideologists attack the Stoics as representing an epistemology too much like Baxter's, amongst others.

45. Glanvill, *The Vanity of Dogmatizing,* 150–51.

46. Ibid., 229. See also ibid., 104–5. There is a similar attack on the party politics implicit in maintaining opposed epistemologies in Boyle's *The Origin of Forms and Qualities According to the Corpuscular Philosophy* (1666). See M. A. Stewart, ed., *Selected Philosophical Papers of Robert Boyle* (Manchester: Manchester Univ. Press, 1979), 37.

47. *The Diary of Robert Hooke M.A., M.D., F.R.S., 1672–1680*, ed. Henry W. Robinson and Walter Adams (London: Taylor and Francis, 1935). Hooke's language against scholastic dogmatism also evokes his political orientation. In *The Present State of Natural Philosophy,* he attacks dogmatic practitioners of natural philosophy. See *The Posthumous Works of Robert Hooke* (London, 1705), 4.

48. For example, by Mintz, *Hunting of Leviathan,* 54.

49. It is important to note that Baxter has before him Gassendi's *Opera Omnia* (Lyons, 1658) and is consulting in particular Gassendi's posthumous masterpiece, the *Syntagma Philosophicum,* printed in volume 1. He quotes primarily from the section on physics.

50. On Baxter being offered a see, refer to Bosher, *Making of the Restoration Settlement,* 193–94; Michael R. Watts records Baxter's imprisonment in 1670 for leading a conventicle (*The Dissenters: From the Reformation to the French Revolution* [Oxford: Clarendon Press, 1978], 235). Baxter's own account of the Savoy Conference is indicative of the Presbyterian position very soon after the Restoration. See *Autobiography of Richard Baxter,* 166. See also Gilbert Burnet, *History of His Own Time,* 6 vols. (Oxford: Oxford Univ. Press, 1833), 1:327–30; 337.

51. For example, he calls Cicero a "moderate latitudinarian" (*Reasons of the Christian Religion,* 174).

52. Ibid., 181.

53. Baxter also displays his Aristotelian essentialism at ibid., 178: "When a moveable being is stopped from motion, it doth not thereby lose its mobile or active nature or disposition." He also argues that the postulate of an atomic *minimum* cannot explain the variety of beings: "To violate the harmony of God's works, and to deny all the steps of the ladder save the lowest, is but an unhappy solving of phenomena" (ibid., 176).

54. Ibid., 177. The principle Baxter states quite baldly: "We see that the natures of all things are suited to their several uses. *operari sequitur esse:* things are as they are. There is somewhat in the nature of a bird, or beast, or plant, which is their fitness to their various motions" (ibid., 183).

55. See also ibid., 193.

56. Ibid., 175 (my emphasis).

57. Johann Amos Comenius, *The Way of Light [Via Lucis],* trans. E. T. Campagnac (London: Hodder and Stoughton, 1938), 9. The 1668 edition was the first edition (though posthumous), whose publication was stimulated by the formation of the Royal Society. See Charles Webster, *Samuel Hartlib and the Advancement of Learning* (Cambridge: Cambridge Univ. Press, 1970), 36n.

58. Margaret C. Jacob, *The Newtonians and the English Revolution, 1689–1720* (Ithaca: Cornell Univ. Press, 1976), 25–26.

59. *The Leibniz-Clarke Correspondence* (originally, *A Collection of Papers which Passed between the Late Learned Mr. Leibnitz and Dr. Clarke* [London, 1717]), ed. H. G. Alexander [Manchester: Manchester Univ. Press, 1956], 6–7.

2. "Moments of Versimility": The Neoclassical Discourse of Contingency

1. Ian Hacking, *The Emergence of Probability: A Philosophical Study of Early Ideas about Probability, Induction, and Statistical Inference* (Cambridge: Cambridge Univ. Press, 1975), 18.

2. Douglas Lane Patey, *Probability and Literary Form: Philosophic Ideas and Literary Practice in the Augustan Age* (Cambridge: Cambridge Univ. Press, 1984); and Barbara Shapiro, *Probability and Certainty in the Seventeenth Century* (Princeton: Princeton Univ. Press, 1983).

3. For a study of the relations between scepticism and rhetoric in the Renaissance, see Victoria Kahn, *Rhetoric, Prudence, and Skepticism in the Renaissance* (Ithaca: Cornell Univ. Press, 1985); and for a close examination of the relation between the sceptical premises of ancient rhetoric and its arguments about rhetorical verisimilitude, see Victoria A. Silver, "'Sensible and Plausible Elocution': Rhetoric and the Shape of Knowledge in Bacon, Browne, and Hobbes," Ph.D. diss., Univ. of California, Los Angeles, 1984.

4. Hacking sees the new probability as taking two forms: "epistemological" and "statistical," the former involving methods of calculation based on common historical, physical, and legal evidences, the latter giving birth to more specialized arguments about mathematical probability theory (*Emergence of Probability*, 13–14). I am only concerned with the first kind. See also G.A.J. Rogers, "The Basis of Belief: Philosophy, Science and Religion in Seventeenth-Century England," *History of European Ideas* 6 (1985): 19–39.

5. Shapiro, *Probability and Certainty*, 13.

6. Simon Patrick, in his much-cited *A Brief Account of the New Sect of Latitude-Men Together with Some Reflections upon the New Philosophy* (London, 1662), assumes the perversity of those who will not conform to the Church of England. He regularly breaks with his own attempts at a moderate rhetoric. So the "Latitudinarians" "do highly approve that vertuous mediocrity which our Church observes between the meretricious gaudiness of the Church at *Rome,* and the squalid sluttery of Fanatick conventicles" (7).

7. Anthony Ashley Cooper, Third Earl of Shaftesbury, "A Letter concerning Enthusiasm," in *Works,* 3 vols. (London, 1744–45), 1:2.

8. Ibid., 1:11.

9. Ibid., 1:13.

10. Shaftesbury echoes Locke's argument about enthusiasm. The danger lies in subverting the concrete or weighted quality of primarily visual representation, or of aural evidences attested to by other signs, thus guaranteeing a public form of knowledge, as opposed to agnostic one. See *An Essay concerning Human Understanding,* ed. P. H. Niddich (Oxford: Clarendon Press, 1975), bk. 4, chap. 19, sec. 14–15.

11. Shaftesbury, *Works,* 1:13.

12. Ibid. (The contemporary edition reports Shaftesbury's statement as indebted to Harrington.)

13. I mention the historical economy because Shaftesbury significantly banishes, contains, or balances Pythagorean and Platonic philosophy by an appeal to the Epicureans and Academics (ibid., 1:14). Shaftesbury thus follows the neo-Epicurean mythology of philosophy I shall describe below.

14. Ibid., 1:17. Shaftesbury clearly does not want to abolish love, but the undertone of panic associated with the subversive powers of sound.

15. I am aware that the term *ideology* is analytically unstable. It should be clear, however, that I do not take it in its entirely pejorative sense. An excellent discussion of *ideology* appears in Raymond Geuss, *The Idea of a Critical Theory: Habermas and the Frankfurt School* (Cambridge: Cambridge Univ. Press, 1981), chap. 1.

16. Although it is a perplexed question, I think it unfruitful and unnecessary to debate whether we should conceive cultural and ideological articulations as primarily actuated by individuals or by larger and more impersonal and unconscious historical forces. Clearly, individual texts operating in individual contexts are part of what is evidently beyond the immediate control of individual authors. But I hope I can demonstrate that Restoration authors can be shown to have intended certain local strategies and effects as part of an ideological rhetoric. Unfortunately, perhaps, it is impossible to maintain a second-order discourse such as mine that does not on occasion appear to impute intention, will, desire, action, and so forth to texts if not to authors.

17. See, for example, Catherine Belsey, who adopts Benveniste's categories to construct a distinction between "declarative" and "interrogative" texts, which for her import different political possibilities (*Critical Practice* [London: Methuen, 1980], esp. 90–91). And Michael Ryan, who cannot credit Hobbes with knowing that his own language is already metaphorical. Ryan thus argues that Hobbes's authoritarian position finds its corollary in a naïve attempt to bypass metaphor. See "Introduction," in *Marxism and Deconstruction: A Critical Articulation* (Baltimore: Johns Hopkins Univ. Press, 1982).

18. As I have suggested already in chapter one, I thus disagree with John Yolton, who allegorizes Locke's anti-innatist argument as an intrinsically and historically progressive maneuver—innatists are backward and conservative; Locke's epistemology is a progressive critique. See *John Locke and the Way of Ideas* (Oxford: Oxford Univ. Press, 1956).

19. On neoclassical reading, see, especially, John M. Wallace, "Dryden and History: A Problem in Allegorical Reading," *ELH* 36 (1969): 265–90; and "'Examples are Best Precepts': Readers and Meanings in Seventeenth-Century Poetry," *Critical Inquiry* 1 (1974): 273–90.

20. This is the implication of Hobbes's assault on the verb *to be*, because the copulative can appear to forge identifications between terms of a proposition, and thus to promote the fantasy of knowing essences. See *The English Works of Thomas Hobbes,* ed. Sir William Molesworth, 11 vols. (London: Bohn, 1845), 7:81.

21. Thomas Hobbes, *Leviathan,* ed. C. B. Macpherson (Harmondsworth, Eng.: Penguin, 1968), 83.

22. Shaftesbury, "Letter," in *Works,* 1:6. Glanvill writes that "we love nothing but what hath some resemblance within our selves; and whatever we applaud as good or excellent, is but *self* in a *transcript,* and *e contra*" (*The Vanity of Dogmatizing: Or Confidence in Opinions Manifested in a Discourse of the Shortness and Uncertainty of Our Knowledge, and Its Causes* [London, 1661], 120). Locke similarly recommends to his reader to "make use of thy own Thoughts in reading" and believes that "if thou judgest for thyself, I know thou wilt judge candidly" ("Epistle to the Reader," in *Essay,* 7; italics reversed).

23. A similar mechanism describes the "methods" by which Charleton came to write his *Natural History of the Passions* (London, 1671), employing both "reading and meditation" which are equivalent activities (Sig. A4ᵛ).

24. This is of course true for great landscape gardens such as Stowe, where the walker's (thus reader's) experience is constructed as a corollary to the Temples' Whig politics, made real as a cognitive experience in the formal "freedom" of the landscape garden. Walter Charleton carefully aligns his notion of cognition with an idea of landscape. See his *Physiologia Epicuro-Gassendo-Charletoniana* (London, 1654), 163–64.

25. Boyle applies the notion of contingency to prognostication. We cannot know the future for sure, and we cannot grasp it by the mere exercise of human will. Only God has foreknowledge, but we are nevertheless expected to exercise our limited faculty of free will within those constraints. See *A Discourse of Things above Reason* (1681), in *Selected Philosophical Papers of Robert Boyle,* ed. M. A. Stewart (Manchester: Manchester Univ. Press, 1979), 213.

26. G.A.J. Rogers has pointed out in conversation that, at one level, the difference is decided on the question of the knowledge of essences.

27. Charles B. Schmitt, *Cicero Scepticus: A Study of the Influence of the "Academica" in the Renaissance* (The Hague: Nijhoff, 1972). Schmitt leaves his study open with the question of why the *Academica* should have faded out as an authoritative text in Italy, and yet continued to have influence in Northern Europe in the seventeenth century (169). Applied to English thought after midcentury, one answer is that the *Academica* fitted a particular reading of scepticism that it found convenient for reasons I discuss.

28. Boyle imagines a hypothetical annihilation of the universe to clarify the question of its essential components: "And if we should conceive all the rest of the universe to be annihilated, save one . . . body—suppose a metal or a stone—it were hard to show that there is physically anything more in it than matter and the accidents we have already named" (*The Origin of Forms and Qualities According to the Corpuscular Philosophy* (1666), in *Selected Papers,* 30). Locke talks of the necessity of clearing ground before beginning with an enquiry into knowledge (*Essay,* bk. 1, chap. 4, sec. 25).

29. See, for example, Walter Charleton discussing the existence and function of vacuum in an atomic universe (*Physiologia,* 30).

30. This metaphor is very clear in John Evelyn, *An Essay on the First Book of T. Lucretius Carus De Rerum Natura Interpreted and Made English Verse* (London, 1656), 170–71, in which Evelyn talks of "this magazine or *Caos* of *Atomes,*" which "fall into that goodly Fabrick and admirable *Architecture* of the *Universe* or World, which with so much *Extasie* and wonder we daily contemplate." Locke consistently refers to the construction of knowledge in architectural tropes—foundations, cabinets, conduits, furniture.

31. Thus Boyle physically attempts "the dissipation and reunion of the parts of common amber" (*The Origin of Forms and Qualities,* in *Selected Papers,* 91). And Charleton writes similarly of "the *Syncritical* and *Diacritical* Experiments of Chymistry, (whereby all Bodies are sensibly dissolved into those *Moleculae,* or First Conventions of Atoms, which carry their specifical seminaries; and the Heterogeneous parts of diverse Concretions, after dissolution, coagmented into one mass, and united *per minimas*)" (*Physiologia,* 109).

32. Jackson Cope quite properly argues that Glanvill's political purposes and

attacks on atheism are served by an emphasis on the method of the Royal Society, rather than the substance or results of its enquiries (*Joseph Glanvill: Anglican Apologist* [St. Louis: Washington Univ. Studies, 1956], 30).

33. The classic statement is Neal W. Gilbert, *Renaissance Concepts of Method* (New York: Columbia Univ. Press, 1960); and Anthony Grafton refines and particularizes the argument in his *Joseph Scaliger: A Study in the History of Classical Scholarship*, vol. 1 of *Textual Criticism and Exegesis*, 2 vols. (Oxford: Clarendon Press, 1983), esp. 6–7. See also Patrick Grant, *Literature and the Discovery of Method in the English Renaissance* (Athens: Univ. of Georgia Press, 1985), esp. 12.

34. Locke, *Essay,* bk. 4, chap. 1, sec. 2. John Wilkins expresses a very similar view in *Of the Principles and Duties of Natural Religion* (London, 1678), 56.

35. See also Rogers, "The Basis of Belief," 20: "In large measure the history of English philosophy in the seventeenth century is the story of the charting of that path which brought unity between the methods of the natural sciences and the claims of the philosophers."

36. See Patey, *Probability and Literary Form;* and Shapiro, *Probability and Certainty*. However, I would argue that neither sufficiently isolates the question of method and its effect on the rhetoric of neoclassical discourse.

37. See J.G.A. Pocock, *Politics, Language and Time: Essays on Political Thought and History* (New York: Atheneum, 1973), esp. 21.

38. See for example, Christopher Hill, *The Century of Revolution, 1603–1714* (New York: Norton, 1961), 160–61; 219–20; 271.

39. John Yolton stresses Locke's commitment to the ideal of natural history, which he also tends to associate with Baconianism. As I shall argue later, Bacon had no defined method that would be useful for the purposes and rhetoric of the Royal Society. Bacon represents more of an authorizing trope than a true philosophical influence. But natural history loosely defined certainly could be a way of describing the organic development of the reader in the *Essay*. See John W. Yolton, *Locke and the Compass of Human Understanding* (Cambridge: Cambridge Univ. Press, 1970), 5ff.

40. See *Dictionary of National Biography*.

41. The dates of Walton's *Biblia Polyglotta* can be somewhat confusing, but the first of the volumes was issued, according to its title page, in 1653, and the final volume, including all the prefatory matter, in 1657.

42. See the biographical sketch in Thomas Stanley, *The Poems and Translations*, ed. Galbraith Miller Crump (Oxford: Clarendon Press, 1962), xxi–xxxiv.

43. Bernard Rochot describes Gassendi's bibliography in some detail in *Les Travaux de Gassendi sur Epicure et sur L'Atomisme, 1619–1658* (Paris: Vrin, 1944), v–xviii.

44. Significantly, Luke is attractive because of the forensic vocabulary of his Gospel and Acts. The other major New Testament source for such a forensic rhetoric is Paul. Both Luke and Boyle address "Theophilus."

45. Robert Boyle, *The Works of the Honourable Robert Boyle,* ed. Thomas Birch, 2d ed., 6 vols. (London, 1772), 1:307.

46. Ibid., 1:306.

47. Ibid., 2:256.

48. Ibid., 2:254.

49. Foucault, Hacking, and Shapiro all suggest the importance of disregarding

the modern divisions between modes of discourse. Shapiro solves the problem of presentation by providing a series of chapters on different disciplines or ur-disciplines in juxtaposition. See Michel Foucault, *The Order of Things: An Archeology of the Human Sciences* (New York: Vintage, 1973); Hacking, *The Emergence of Probability;* and Shapiro, *Probability and Certainty.*

50. The reference to history is deliberate: both Cassirer and Levine argue for the eighteenth century as an age that, contrary to post-Romantic assumptions, did indeed value history as a distinct form of knowledge. See Ernst Cassirer, *The Philosophy of the Enlightenment,* trans. Fritz C. A. Koelln and James P. Pettegrove (Princeton: Princeton Univ. Press, 1951), chap. 5; and Joseph M. Levine, *Dr. Woodward's Shield: History, Science, and Satire in Augustan England* (Berkeley: Univ. of California Press, 1977), esp. chap. 15.

51. By arguing the origin of our ideas in the actual world, for example, Locke seems to want to ensure that our mental behavior evinces a certain form of cognitive, implicitly social responsibility (*Essay*, bk. 4, chap. 4, sec. 12). Foucault also describes how metaphors of origin are prescriptive in thrust (*Order of Things,* 104ff; 114ff.).

52. See, for example, Locke, *Essay*, bk. 2, chap. 1, sec. 24. And also Charleton, *Physiologia,* 18.

53. "But Knowledge began in the Mind, and was founded on particulars; though afterwards, perhaps, no notice be taken thereof: it being natural for the Mind (forward still to enlarge its Knowledge) most attentively to lay up those general Notions, and make the proper use of them, which is to disburden the Memory of the cumbersome load of Particulars" (*Essay*, bk. 4, chap. 12, sec. 3).

54. Thomas Stanley reports that Carneades argued for example that "wherefore as when in Life we enquire concerning some little thing, we examine of Witness; when we enquire into something of greater consequence, we examine more; but when of a thing most necessary, we examine each of the Witnesses by the joint testimony of all." Our knowledge of this life is merely probable (*The History of Philosophy,* 3d ed. [London, 1701], 220–24).

55. *Essay*, bk. 1, chap. 1, sec. 5.

56. See ibid., bk. 2, chap. 23, sec. 12. Glanvill anticipates Locke's suggestions by imagining telescopic sight as signifying forms of essentialist knowledge in *The Vanity of Dogmatizing,* Sigs. B1^v; B2^v-B3^r. He asks whether Adam naming objects denoted his being plunged somehow within a world of essences laid bare. This he doubts.

57. Locke attacks unmediated identifications made by those who unthinkingly deify opinions: They "are apt to reverence them as sacred Things, and not to suffer them to be prophaned, touched, or questioned: They look on them as the *Urim* and *Thummim* set up in their Minds immediately by GOD Himself, to be great and unerring Deciders of Truth and Falsehood, and the Judges to which they are to appeal in all manner of Controversies" (*Essay*, bk. 4, chap. 20, sec. 9). He also denies that God is an innate principle (ibid., bk. 1, chap. 4, sec. 9). Charleton attacks astrology and mysticism in his *Physiologia,* 348, arguing that we must rather "advance to the Consideration of *Particular* instances, that by the Solution of Singulars, we may afford the greater relief to mens Curiosity, and have so many Opportunities of examining the Verisimility of our former Thesis." He also attacks Van Helmont for refusing to supply an explanation for the rainbow from secondary causes. Van Helmont believes

that "the Rainbow, is a *supernatural Meteor*, or *Ens extempore created* by Divinity, as a sensible Symbol of his Promise no more to destroy the inhabitants of the Earth by Water, having no dependence at all on Natural Causes" (58).

58. Charleton attacks precisely the notion of subsumption into the universal and the erosion of identity *"in the selfe same nature and per se"* (*Epicurus's Morals* [London, 1656], Sig. b3ᵛ), which he associates first with the Egyptian priesthood and then with the Stoics (ibid., Sigs. b2ʳ&ᵛ). Stanley describes Carneades's resistance to the Stoics in his *The History of Philosophy*, 220–24.

59. Horace is disturbed precisely by the social connotations of the Stoic sage as a "King" and satirizes the idea in *Sat*. 1.3. See also Glanvill, *The Vanity of Dogmatizing*, 136–37.

60. Stanley, *The History of Philosophy*, 313. See also *Epicurus's Morals. . . . To which is Added, an Essay on Epicurus' Morals. Written by Monsieur St. Evremont*, trans. John Digby (London, 1712), ix. Digby describes the Stoics' dislike of the mild Epicurus.

61. See also Glanvill, *The Vanity of Dogmatizing*, 150–51; also, Locke attacks those who "taking things upon trust, misimploy their power of Assent, by lazily enslaving their Minds, to the Dictates and Dominion of others, in Doctrines, which it is their duty carefully to examine; and not blindly, with an implicit faith, to swallow" (*Essay*, bk. 1, chap. 4, sec. 22).

62. In *Epicurus's Morals*, Charleton writes that "they, who live soberly and Contingently, are said to live honestly, according to Decorum" (105).

63. See Glanvill, *The Vanity of Dogmatizing*, 189: "All knowledge of Causes is *deductive*; for we know none by simple intuition; but through the mediation of its effects."

64. Thus Boyle makes the knowledge of the resurrection solely dependent on the sufficient and explicit evidences afforded by Scripture: "For if God had not in the scripture positively revealed his purpose of raising the dead, I confess I should not have thought of any such thing" (*Some Physico-Theological Considerations about the Possibility of the Resurrection* (1675), in *Selected Papers*, 192–93). Boyle also explains the necessarily contingent nature of the knowledge that God has permitted us in *Discourse of Things above Reason*, in ibid., 239.

65. Boyle recommends a strict phenomenalism—the observation of physical effects as signs—as the means of interpreting nature. See *About the Excellency and Grounds of the Mechanical Hypothesis* (1674), in *Selected Papers*, 144. Locke says that our knowledge of God is infallible, but that the knowledge still comes to us mediated by ideas or notions: "The truest and best Notions Men had of God, were not imprinted, but acquired by thought and meditation" (*Essay*, bk. 1, chap. 4, sec. 15).

66. Charleton, in *Epicurus's Morals*, very self-consciously sees his biography of Epicurus as "my accommodation of him . . . as might be exactly sutable [*sic*] as well to your wishes, as to his owne minde" (Sig. A3ᵛ). See also Glanvill, *The Vanity of Dogmatizing*, 96–97, and also 23: "We cannot conceive any thing, which comes not within the verge of our senses; but either by like experiments which we have made, or at least by some remoter hints which we receive from them."

67. See Robert Hooke, *The Method of Improving Natural Philosophy*, in *The Posthumous Works of Robert Hooke* (London, 1705), 8–9.

68. Locke writes: "Perception is the first Operation of all our intellectual Fac-

ulties, and the inlet of all Knowledge into our Minds" (*Essay*, bk. 2, chap. 10, sec. 15); also "We shall . . . use our Understandings right, when we entertain all Objects in that Way and Proportion, that they are suited to our Faculties" (ibid., bk. 1, chap. 1, sec. 5). Thomas Stanley records Epicurus's first canon of judgment as saying (in Gassendi's redaction): "The Notion (or Idea, and form as it were, which being anticipated is called Praenotion) is begotten in the Mind by *Incursion* . . . By *Proportion* . . . By *Similitude* . . . [and] by *Composition*" (Stanley, *The History of Philosophy*, 552).

69. On proportion, see also Glanvill, *The Vanity of Dogmatizing*, 210; Locke, *Essay*, bk. 1, chap. 1, sec. 5, quoted in the text at p. 61; and Boyle, *Some Physico-Theological Considerations*, in *Selected Papers*, 192–93, quoted in n.65 above.

70. *The Vanity of Dogmatizing*, 67.

71. Leibniz attacks this position precisely because it is "somatic": "Experience is necessary, I admit, if the soul is to be given such and such thoughts, and if it is to take heed of the ideas that are within us. But how could experience and the senses provide the ideas? Does the soul have windows? Is it similar to writing-tablets, or like wax? Clearly, those who take this view of the soul are treating it as fundamentally corporeal" (G. W. Leibniz, *New Essays on Human Understanding*, trans. and ed. Peter Remnant and Jonathan Bennett [Cambridge: Cambridge Univ. Press, 1981], bk. 2, chap. 1, sec. 110).

72. John Yolton usefully summarizes four possible seventeenth-century models of perception: "(1) According to the scholastic interpretation, the *form* of the object exists in corporeal as well as in incorporeal substances. One frequently finds quasi-literal talk of objects penetrating the mind, of the mind assimilating the object, of intimate union. (2) A wildly impossible view . . . is that the object is *literally* present to or in the mind. (3) Another interpretation holds that the object is present in the mind by proxy, by representation. The object cannot be in the mind, but ideas can. Ideas, then, in some way (resemblance is frequently suggested) represent objects. This view, in one strongly stated version, makes ideas third things between knower and object. (4) Finally, it is maintained that to be in the understanding is simply to be understood. This view goes along with treating ideas as identical to perceptions: to have an idea just is to perceive" (*Perceptual Acquaintance from Descartes to Reid* [Minneapolis: Univ. of Minnesota Press, 1984], 38).

73. Charleton, *Physiologia*, 127–28. Glanvill writes: "All Knowledge of Causes is *deductive:* for we know none by simple intuition; but through the mediation of its effects" (*The Vanity of Dogmatizing*, 189).

74. John Herman Randall, Jr., *Aristotle* (New York: Columbia Univ. Press, 1960), 97. This is not to say that Aristotle's account of knowledge is not in some ways "empirical." It is frequently described as such, and there is no reason to object, as long as we understand how different late-seventeenth-century forms of empiricism are, because more consistently sceptical about the role of cognition in depicting the world and the role of language in depicting the mind or world. It is nevertheless probable that Aristotle's account of induction lies behind the late-seventeenth-century account of the derivation of universals from particulars; but what each meant the universal or particular to denote differs based on differing epistemologies. Deborah Modrak usefully describes the self-contradictions in Aristotle's epistemology in *Aristotle: The Power of Perception* (Chicago: Univ. of Chicago Press, 1987), 78.

75. Modrak, *Aristotle*, 82. Richard A. Watson summarizes the Scholastic position,

which deeply influenced Descartes: "The thing itself is known through the intelligible species, which amounts to knowing directly the thing's essential form. . . . The first intention in knowing is the essential form of the thing known; the intelligible species is not a representative being as such, but the known essence. . . . Second, the Scholastic[s contend] that the action of the material thing causes a material image to be conducted through the medium to the sense organs . . . [and] it is clear that no Epicurean material species travels from the thing known to the knower. The Scholastics then require that the phantasm formed by Imagination contain as abstractable the essential form or intelligible species of the thing to be known. For the Scholastics, what is known is not something which belongs to the knower; the intelligible species *is* the essential form of the thing known shared by the knower. . . . Third, on the Scholastic account of perception the significance of the maxim, *Nihil est in intellectu quod non prius fuit in sensu,* is apparent. If material things did not act through a medium upon the sense organs, nothing would be known. But the maxim does not mean that anything sensible or material is found in the Intellect; what is known are immaterial natures" (*The Downfall of Cartesianism, 1673–1712: A Study of Epistemological Issues in Late-Seventeenth-Century Cartesianism* [The Hague: Nijhoff, 1966], 7).

76. Randall, *Aristotle,* 7. Charleton stresses the political consequence of Aristotelian absorption into the universe by stressing the passivity of the human intellect confronted by the "*Intellectus Agens,* which he teacheth to be diffused through the whole world" (*Epicurus's Morals,* Sig. b3ʳ).

77. See Peter Alexander, *Ideas, Qualities and Corpuscles: Locke and Boyle on the External World* (Cambridge: Cambridge Univ. Press, 1985), chap. 4; M. A. Stewart, "Locke's Mental Atomism and the Classification of Ideas: I," *Locke Newsletter* 10 (1979): 53–82; Stewart, "Locke's Mental Atomism and the Classification of Ideas: II," *Locke Newsletter* 11 (1980): 25–62; and Yolton, *Perceptual Acquaintance,* esp. chap. 5.

78. W.K.C. Guthrie captures the chief point in his elegant introduction to Greek philosophy. For all of Aristotle's revolt against Platonic mysticism, he retained the logic of phenomena by two devices that are foreign to late-seventeenth-century scepticism, and these are "(a) the conception of immanent form; (b) the conception of potentiality *(dynamis).*" The two concepts are interrelated, such that "the view of natural creatures as progressing from the potential to the actual by virtue of their own dynamic nature cannot be separated in the mind from the analysis of things taken as they stand which reveals the necessity for an indeterminate substratum capable of being informed to different degrees by qualities which in themselves are untransformable" (*The Greek Philosophers from Thales to Aristotle* [1950; reprint, New York: Harper and Row, 1975], 128; 134).

79. By contrast to Aristotle as a philosophical tyrant, Plato often plays the role of a sceptic. Cope argues that it is Glanvill's sceptical appreciation of Plato that disturbed the late Aristotelian and Catholic Thomas White, who was a radical innatist of sorts (Cope, *Glanvill,* 133).

80. Robert Hooke, *Micrographia: Or Some Physiological Descriptions of Minute Bodies Made by Magnifying Glasses. With Observations and Enquiries Thereupon* (London, 1665), 1.

81. Hooke uses the notion of the labyrinth also in "Lectures of Light," in *Posthumous Works,* 84.

82. Ibid.

83. Glanvill, *The Vanity of Dogmatizing*, 217–23.

84. See Yolton, *John Locke and the Way of Ideas*, 67. Yolton also discusses Locke's representationalism in *Locke and the Compass of Human Understanding*, 133. Locke's emphasis on the "actual view" of objects of consciousness occurs, for example, in the *Essay*, bk. 1, chap. 4, sec. 20.

85. See also Locke, *Essay*, bk. 1, chap. 4, sec. 25.

86. Ian Hacking, *Why Does Language Matter to Philosophy?* (Cambridge: Cambridge Univ. Press, 1975), esp. chap. 2. Peter Alexander suggestively describes Locke's resistance to the purely private nature of signs as a doctrine of "minimal publicity" (*Ideas, Qualities and Corpuscles*, 200).

87. If Hobbes, Locke, and others did not resolve the problem of solipsism to Quine's analytical standards, they attempted nonetheless to avoid or ameliorate it by certain devices for rendering knowledge public, not least by describing their conceptualist economies in public language. One prevailing metaphor consistently stresses the idea of *action,* occurring both within and outside mental space. The distinction between old and new empiricism is not as clear-cut as Quine implies. See W. V. Quine, *The Ways of Paradox and Other Essays* (1966; rev. ed., Cambridge: Harvard Univ. Press, 1976), 58.

88. Of course I am fully aware of the purely conventionalist basis for contract, by which we arbitrarily agree that a certain word will govern a certain form of behavior, regardless of any apparent referential force in the word chosen for the task. When critics refer to Hobbes's and Locke's "nominalism," they usually denote this aspect of their linguistic philosophies. But both thinkers assume that the *original* of our ideas comes from atomic impact on the mind, a very literal model of reference; so it is more apt to think of them as *conceptualists,* for they assume that ordinary language has some anchors in the actual world, even if these are insufficient grounds for political philosophy. I am arguing here that the language used to describe originary signs denotes the influence of contractualist requirements on a wide variety of Hobbesian and Lockean commitments. Locke talks of exchanging signs by definition (*Essay*, bk. 3, chap. 4, sec. 6).

89. Lorraine J. Daston points out some of the analytical difficulties of this position in "Rational Individuals *versus* Laws of Society: From Probability to Statistics," in *Probability since 1800: Interdisciplinary Studies of Scientific Development*, ed. Michael Heidelberger et al. (Bielefeld: Univ. of Bielefeld, 1983), 7–26.

90. The debate is most clearly focussed around the question of transubstantiation.

91. In his *Principles of Philosophy* (1644), Descartes writes that "whenever we perceive something clearly [decreed by an absolute God] we spontaneously give our assent to it and are quite unable to doubt its truth" (*The Philosophical Writings of Descartes,* trans. John Cottingham et al., 2 vols. [Cambridge: Cambridge Univ. Press, 1985], 1:204–7). The Restoration would have treated such an expression of cognitive subjection as the philosophical equivalent to the absolutist French monarchy of Louis XIV, or the claims of Catholic infallibilism. If knowledge is mediated, no assent can be *spontaneous*.

92. Samuel Fisher, the Quaker, even disposes of the mediations of Scripture as a less certain guide to spiritual knowledge than the movements of the Spirit. See *The*

Testimony of Truth Exalted, by the Collected Labours of that Worthy Man, Good Scribe, and Faithful Minister of Jesus Christ, Samuel Fisher (London, 1679), 13–14; 29–30; 49–50. Fisher's book is a collection of tracts published between 1656 and 1662, and it includes violent attacks on John Owen's attachment to the Scriptures as merely "the Outward Transcripts, or Texts of the Scripture" (49). I owe this reference to Richard Popkin.

93. Locke discusses giving up our power of assent (*Essay*, bk. 1, chap. 4, sec. 22).

94. Locke, *Essay*, bk. 4, chap. 19, sec. 9. That is, the enthusiasts seem to employ mere analogies (similes) among the figures of experience (seeing and feeling), but if we inspect the actual claims these appear to illustrate, they collapse these identifications as corollaries to dogmatism and unmediated claims on the lives of others. They are not exemplary in function; only demonstrative. I do not believe that Locke says that we can do without such similes, because most knowledge is based on what he calls "juxtaposition."

95. That is, the exposure of relations as artificial rather than metaphysical denotes a civilizing and socializing activity in itself.

96. I have already mentioned the work of R. F. Jones. Like Jones, Robert Adolph stresses the "utilitarian" value of "plain style," though the Restoration could hardly be described as "utilitarian" without considerable violence to history. See Robert Adolph, *The Rise of Modern Prose Style* (Cambridge: MIT Press, 1968).

97. Boyle shows how synecdoche and convention are two halves of the same formulation. The nominal and conventional terms that divide references to one object from references to another, are themselves derived from necessarily accidental, partial, and limited observations of those objects, and are synecdochic—they *sufficiently* represent the whole (and thus denote genus or species) by adumbrating a part. See *The Origin of Forms and Qualities*, in *Selected Papers*, 38. Glanvill discusses synecdoche in *The Vanity of Dogmatizing*, 67.

98. We only imagine atoms, that is, by looking on the dense and obscure face of macroscopic bodies and by inferring analogies with atomic, submicroscopic behavior. Locke describes the atomic constitution both of matter and ideas in his *Elements of Natural Philosophy*, with which Newton may have assisted (See *The Works of John Locke*, 11th ed., 10 vols. [London: W. Otridge et al., 1812], 3:303–4). For a bibliographical description of the *Elements*, see John C. Attig, *The Works of John Locke: A Comprehensive Bibliography from the Seventeenth Century to the Present* (Westport, Conn.: Greenwood, 1985), 127–28.

99. Locke describes the origins of language in pictorial terms in the *Essay*, bk. 3, chap. 3, sec. 7.

100. See Hobbes, *Leviathan*, 668–69.

101. The power of the myth is precisely what Wittgenstein seeks to exploit in his *Philosophical Investigations;* nor do I believe that he comfortably ironizes it in the course of converting linguistic philosophy into the study of language as social use, as some might believe. In any case, Augustine is already ahead of the game, because his picture of the moment where he learned language by his parents' ostensive gestures presupposes language operating as a complete behavioral system of authority into which he is inducted. Steven Speilberg intuited and exploited the popular power of the myth in his film *E.T.,* in which a lovable alien learns human

language by ostension. Last, W. V. Quine strongly argues for the intuitive power of the notion that language is sporadically attached to the world by ostension and example.

102. Christopher Norris, *Deconstruction* (London: Methuen, 1982), 58.

103. The necessity of language and power is partly what Paul de Man seeks to describe in his characterization of "the resistance to theory." A critique of figuration as the locus of power cannot free us from being implicated in our own forms of representation and power. See Paul de Man, *The Resistance to Theory* (Minneapolis: Univ. of Minnesota Press, 1986), 3–20.

104. Norris, *Deconstruction,* 82. I would indeed suggest that the Quaker attempt to dispose of the mediations of Scripture as *written* text is partly what incited their exclusion from acceptable social practice. Charleton thus figures his pen as the phenomenal point of contact between himself and his reader (*Physiologia,* 60). And Sprat glorifies the invention of printing as the means for the expansion and securing of knowledge, rather than as an unfortunate linguistic compromise (*History of the Royal Society* [London, 1667], 22).

105. On writing, see chapter six below.

106. Richard W. F. Kroll, "*Mise-en-Page,* Biblical Criticism, and Inference during the Restoration," *Studies in Eighteenth-Century Culture,* ed. O. M. Brack, Jr., vol. 16 (Madison: Univ. of Wisconsin Press, 1986), 3–40.

107. This view of Locke's attitude to plain style is even retailed by Paul de Man, "The Epistemology of Metaphor," *Critical Inquiry* 5 (1978): 13–30.

108. For the dating of the drafts of Locke's *Essay,* see *An Early Draft of Locke's Essay, Together with Excerpts from His Journals,* ed R. I. Aaron and Jocelyn Gibb (Oxford: Clarendon Press, 1936), xi–xxviii. Because the Aaron and Gibb transcript of Draft A is not quite as accurate as Nidditch's, I cite both versions below. Thus see also *Draft A of Locke's "Essay concerning Human Understanding": The Earliest Extant Autograph Version,* ed. P. H. Nidditch (Sheffield: Univ. of Sheffield, Department of Philosophy, 1980).

109. Aaron and Gibb, *An Early Draft,* 3; and Nidditch, *Draft A,* 21.

110. Locke recognizes the same problem in the *Essay* proper, for example when he realizes that we can only imagine the "origins" of knowledge or language in the context of what he calls "languages made" (bk. 3, chap. 5, sec. 15). He makes the same point in a different way by stating that we cannot know the original meaning of a word in the mind of another individual (bk. 3, chap. 6, sec. 45).

111. Aaron and Gibb, *An Early Draft,* 45; Nidditch, *Draft A,* 22–23. Glanvill makes a similar point in *The Vanity of Dogmatizing,* Sigs. A6^v-A7^r.

112. Aaron and Gibb, *An Early Draft,* 4–5; Nidditch, *Draft A,* 23, 26.

113. See Locke, *Essay,* bk. 4, chap. 3, sec. 27; and Hobbes, *Leviathan,* 302, which adumbrates a theory of speech acts. Hobbes later writes that "a sign is not a sign to him that giveth it, but to whom it is made; that is, to the spectator" (ibid., 401), which I take to be an expression of the same linguistic argument.

114. See chapter six below.

115. Simon Patrick recommends the necessary forms of the Church of England, which he argues are nevertheless neither idolatrous or fanatical. See *A Brief Account,* 7; 13. See also William Sherlock, *A Preservative Against Popery: Being Some Plain Direc-*

tions to Unlearned Protestants, How to Dispute with Romish Priests. The First Part (London, 1688), 14.

116. Hobbes attacks incantation and enchantment in *Leviathan*, 474–75.

117. Charleton, *Physiologia*, 349–52. See also Glanvill, *The Vanity of Dogmatizing*, Sigs. A6^v-A7^r.

118. Boyle typifies the logic that attacks claims to transubstantiation: "The chief thing that inquisitive naturalists should look after in the explicating of difficult phenomena is not so much what the *agent* is or does, as what changes are made in the *patient* to bring it to exhibit the phenomena that are proposed, and by what means, and after what manner, those changes are affected" (*About the Excellency and Grounds of the Mechanical Hypothesis*, in *Selected Papers*, 145). The movement is emphatically single, from known effect to inferring an unknown cause. This prevents claims for a double negotiation between implicitly known causes to known and predictable effects and vice versa.

119. Charleton, *Physiologia*, 90.

120. See Michael Ketcham, *Transparent Designs: Reading, Performance, and Form in the "Spectator" Papers* (Athens: Univ. of Georgia Press, 1985); also J.G.A. Pocock, who writes that "in England Addisonian sociability to some degree took the place of clerical and academic structures which had lost much of their salience" ("Clergy and Commerce: The Conservative Enlightenment in England," in *L'Eta dei Lumi: Studi Storici sul Settecento Europeo in Onore di Franco Venturi*, ed. R. Ajello et al., 2 vols. [Naples: Jovene Editori, 1985], 546). Pope implies that a serious and elegant woman's intellectual equipment will include "studying Locke" ("Epistle II: To a Lady," l. 23).

121. Charleton, *Physiologia*, 104.

122. Boyle, *An Introduction to the History of Particular Qualities* (1671), in *Selected Papers*, 112. Boyle also deploys a military analogy to depict the arrangement of corpuscles relative to one another in complex bodies (*The Origin of Forms and Qualities*, in *Selected Papers*, 51). And he speaks of the corpuscular hypothesis as more *catholic* (or "fertile and comprehensive") than others (ibid., 51; and *An Introduction to the History of Particular Qualities*, in *Selected Papers*, 103). Locke speaks about groups of ideas as a "Tribe" (*Essay*, bk. 2, chap. 8, sec. 7); and also characterizes disputes by a military metaphor: "It happening in Controversial Discourses, as it does in assaulting of Towns; where, if the ground is but firm, whereon the Batteries are erected, there is no farther enquiry of whom it is borrowed" (*Essay*, bk. 1, chap. 4, sec. 25).

123. This effect is well described by Ketcham, *Transparent Designs*, 94; 97; 113–14; 142; and esp. 143. Ketcham happily relates this representational device not only to the cognitive function of the landscape garden and neoclassical theories of physiognomy but also to the development of family ideology as encouraging the family as the "scene" in which illocutionary symbolism should occur.

124. Plato, *Cratylus, Parmenides, Greater Hippias, Lesser Hippias*, trans. H. N. Fowler (Cambridge: Harvard Univ. Press; London: Heinemann, 1953), 191. Suspending the question of whether knowledge is fixed and unitary, or fluid, Socrates interrupts Cratylus, and concludes "but now go into the country as you have made ready to do; and Hermogenes here will go with you a bit."

125. Early on in the dialogue, Socrates has asked, "And speaking is an action, is it not?" (ibid., 19).

126. Like Locke, Dryden retails the fiction that his essay grew from "loose papers . . . the writing which, in this rude and indigested manner wherein your Lordship now sees it, served as an amusement to me in the country" (John Dryden, *Of Dramatic Poesy and Other Critical Essays*, ed. George Watson, 2 vols. [London: Dent; New York: Dutton, 1962], 1:12−13).

127. Ibid., 1:18−19.

128. Ibid., 1:92. The desire to return to social activity is anticipated by Dryden's preface, which speaks of his exclusion from the urbane life of London by the plague (1:12−13).

129. Ketcham, *Transparent Designs*, chaps. 1 and 2.

130. Simple *perception* is often conceived of in terms of *perspective*, as where Locke speaks of perception as "the *inlet* of all Knowledge into our Minds" (*Essay*, bk. 2, chap. 10, sec. 15; my emphasis); or where he talks of thoughts operating within a "Scene" (bk. 2, chap. 11, sec. 9).

131. Boyle underscores his own act of representing his own argument in *The Origin of Forms and Qualities*, in *Selected Papers*, 32.

132. Locke, however, contrasts the activities of "wit" and "judgment," the former depicting the pure and irresponsible play of forms, the latter acting in response to the mind's apprehension of particulars (*Essay*, bk. 2, chap. 11, sec. 2−4). Although Sprat is often assumed to attack rhetoric, he provides positive grounds for figuration in his description of wit, which should "be founded on such images which are generally known, and are able to bring a strong, and a sensible impression on the *mind*" (*History of the Royal Society*, 413). See also chapter eight below.

133. Speaking of the Interregnum, Burnet records that Whichcote was "disgusted with the dry systematical way of those times" (*History of His Own Time*, 6 vols. [Oxford: Oxford Univ. Press, 1833], 1:339). Simon Patrick writes that the Latitude-men do not "hold any other Doctrine than the Church, since they derive it from the same fountains, not from the *Spinose school-men*, or *Dutch systematicks*, neither from *Rome* nor *Geneva*, the Council of *Trent*, not Synod of *Dort*, but from the Sacred writings of the Apostles and Evangelists . . . " (*A Brief Account*, 9).

134. Boyle attacks systems on very similar grounds. Although he seems also to criticize method, he simply attacks those who apply method indiscriminately in such a way as to create a falsely coherent system. Boyle himself uses *essays* specifically as the sceptical and fragmenting device he inherits from Montaigne. See *Some Considerations Touching Experimental Essays in General* (1661), in *Works*, 1:300−301. Robert Frank makes the argument that the systematic nature of Mayhow's physiological work betrays its isolation from the authority and power of the Oxonian group of which Boyle was a prominent member (*Harvey and the Oxford Physiologists* [Berkeley: Univ. of California Press, 1980], 274).

135. In part two, I shall discuss, among other things, the problem of Descartes as a figure for whom mid-seventeenth-century English thinkers had to account. Even if, for example, Richard Watson's characterization of the late-seventeenth-century downfall of Cartesianism is correct, I do not believe that in England it is primarily for the reasons he describes, namely the failure *logically* to resolve certain analytical implications of the mind-body problem. In Glanvill's *The Vanity of Dogmatizing*, the figure of "Descartes" actually executes epistemological and ethical prescriptions closer

to the historical Gassendi than to Descartes. This tactic constitutes a silent and effective revision of Descartes, while it protects Glanvill from too explicit an alliance with neo-Epicureanism. See Watson, *The Downfall of Cartesianism.*

136. Charleton, *Physiologia,* 84.

137. Locke, *Examination of P. Malebranche,* in *Works,* 9:213.

138. Ibid., 9:217; 212; 214.

139. Ibid., 9:216–217.

140. Boyle, *The Origin of Forms and Qualities,* in *Selected Papers,* 61.

141. See John Wilkins, *Mercury, Or the Secret and Swift Messenger* (London, 1641), 11.

142. Speaking of Descartes's theory of vision, Charleton writes: "The opinion of the excellent *Monsieur Des Cartes,* . . . with a kind of pleasant violence, hath so ravisht the assent of the most of the Students of Physiology, especially such as affect the accommodation of Mechanick Maxims to the sensible operations of Nature; that their minds abhor the embraces of any other" (*Physiologia,* 151).

143. This fear is also registered frequently in an aleatory metaphor, in which the discrimination is destroyed by the hearer being forced to swallow an undigested mass of knowledge. See, for example, Glanvill, *The Vanity of Dogmatizing,* Sig. A3^r; Hobbes, *Leviathan,* 727; and John Dryden, *Absalom and Achitophel,* ll. 108–13.

144. See, for example, John Wilkins's *Mercury,* 1–4; 17–18. For the issue at greater length, see chapter six below.

145. See J.G.A. Pocock, "Verbalizing a Political Act: Toward a Politics of Speech," *Political Theory* 1 (1973): 27–45.

3. The Neo-Epicurean Revival: Method, Atomism, and the Palpable Image

1. Charles E. Ward, *The Life of John Dryden* (Chapel Hill: Univ. of North Carolina Press, 1961), 32.

2. Alan Roper disagrees that the poem makes such an implicit claim, but Charleton's well-publicized association with the neo-Epicurean revival, as well as Epicurus's usefulness as an ally against Aristotle, makes this implication likely, if not inevitable. For a description of Charleton's neo-Epicurean output, see chapter five below.

3. Dryden vigorously dramatizes the exercise of power and displacement in the setting and performance of his *Essay of Dramatic Poesy.* The defeat of the Dutch fleet disrupts visions of European cultural continuity; just as the critical dialogue itself reveals the seams between the various competing points of view, so the French are singled out as a locus to be revised, translated, and displaced.

4. E. A. Burtt, *The Metaphysical Foundations of Modern Science: The Scientific Thinking of Copernicus, Galileo, Newton and Their Contemporaries* (1932; reprint, Atlantic Highlands: Humanities Press, 1980), 134. See also Michel Foucault, *The Order of Things: An Archeology of the Human Sciences* (New York: Vintage, 1970), 70ff., on the classical employment of "genesis," "mathesis," and "taxonomia," which express similar principles of knowledge.

5. John Dryden, Preface to *Ovid's Epistle's, Translated by Several Hands* (1680), in *Of Dramatic Poesy and Other Critical Essays,* ed. George Watson, 2 vols. (London: Dent; New York: Dutton, 1962), 1:262–73.

6. Ibid., 1:269–70.

7. Ibid., 1:271–72.

8. This vision of the fragments of the past is powerfully evoked by Henry More in *An Antidote against Atheism* (1652; 3d ed., 1667), in *Philosophical Writings of Henry More,* ed. Flora Isabel Mackinnon (New York: Oxford Univ. Press, 1925), 6.

9. See "To the Earl of Roscommon," in *The Works of John Dryden,* ed. H. T. Swedenberg, Jr., et al., 15 vols. to date (Berkeley: Univ. of California Press, 1956-), 2:172–74. See the editors' commentary on line 4 ("in *Grecian* Gardens") at 2:381.

10. John M. Wallace, "Dryden and History: A Problem in Allegorical Reading," *ELH* 36 (1969): 265–90; "'Examples are Best Precepts': Readers and Meanings in Seventeenth-Century Poetry," *Critical Inquiry* 1 (1974): 273–90; "John Dryden's Plays and the Conception of a Heroic Society," in *Culture and Politics from Puritanism to the Enlightenment,* ed. Perez Zagorin (Berkeley: Univ. of California Press, 1980), 113–34.

11. See Alasdair MacIntyre, "The Relationship of Philosophy to its Past," in *Philosophy in History,* ed. Richard Rorty et al. (Cambridge: Cambridge Univ. Press, 1984), 31–48, and indeed the entire collection of which it is part; also Bernard Williams, *Descartes: The Project of Pure Enquiry* (Harmondsworth, Eng.: Penguin, 1978). Much of what I say echoes, though is not originally indebted to, Lynn Sumida Joy, *Gassendi the Atomist: Advocate of History in an Age of Science* (Cambridge: Cambridge Univ. Press, 1987). I am grateful to Professor Joy for allowing me to see her manuscript before publication.

12. Descartes, *Discourse on the Method* (1637), in *The Philosophical Writings of Descartes,* trans. John Cottingham et al., 2 vols. (Cambridge: Cambridge Univ. Press, 1985), 1:126. (For the sake of convenience, I use the titles provided by this edition throughout my text.)

13. Ibid.

14. Descartes, *Rules for the Direction of the Mind* (1684), in ibid., 1:9.

15. Descartes, *Principles of Philosophy* (1644), in ibid., 1:185.

16. G. W. Leibniz, *New Essays on Human Understanding,* trans. and ed. Peter Remnant and Jonathan Bennett (Cambridge: Cambridge Univ. Press, 1981), bk. 4, chap. 21, sec. 5.

17. Ibid.

18. Ibid., secs. 523–25.

19. Pierre Gassendi, *Institutio Logica,* ed. and trans. Howard Jones (Assen, Holland: Van Gorcum, 1981), 162. Gassendi has just compared the ostensive method of teaching languages by dividing them into elements, and then recombining them, and "the sciences, where instruction is in matters of observation and research, [where] we find the same procedure applies."

20. In *The Archeology of Knowledge,* Michel Foucault attacks our modern distinctions among different discourses as inapplicable to the seventeenth and eighteenth centuries. See *"The Archeology of Knowledge" and the "Discourse on Language"* (New York: Pantheon, 1972), 22. That the late-seventeenth century is a period when certain forms of specialization are appearing in embryo is the intuition of a number of scholars, among them Peter Alexander, *Ideas, Qualities and Corpuscles: Locke and Boyle on the External World* (Cambridge: Cambridge Univ. Press, 1985), 9; Burtt, *Metaphysical Foundations of Modern Science,* 30; and Joy, *Gassendi the Atomist.*

21. For Gassendi's relationship to Newton and Locke, see Joy, *Gassendi the Atomist,* 203–26. In a letter to the author, Joy points out that those pages discuss "highly specific ways in which Gassendi's physics differed from Newton's and his theory of ideas differed from Locke's."

22. Jackson I. Cope, *Joseph Glanvill: Anglican Apologist* (Saint Louis: Washington Univ. Studies, 1956), 135.

23. D. J. Furley, "Lucretius and the Stoics," *Bulletin of the Institute of Classical Studies* 13 (1966): 31.

24. See Joy, *Gassendi the Atomist;* and Louise Tunick Sarasohn, "The Influence of Epicurean Philosophy on Seventeenth-Century Ethical and Political Thought." Ph.D. diss., Univ. of California, Los Angeles, 1979; see also Sarasohn, "Motion and Morality: Pierre Gassendi, Thomas Hobbes and the Mechanical World View," *Journal of the History of Ideas* 46 (1985): 363–79.

25. A. A. Long, *Hellenistic Philosophy: Stoics, Epicureans, Sceptics,* 2d ed. (Berkeley: Univ. of California Press, 1986), 1.

26. Bernard Frischer, *The Sculpted Word: Epicureanism and Philosophical Recruitment in Ancient Greece* (Berkeley: Univ. of California Press, 1982).

27. Arguably the standard account is still Marie Boas, "The Establishment of the Mechanical Philosophy," *Osiris* 10 (1952): 412–541.

28. E. J. Dijksterhuis, *The Mechanization of the World Picture: Pythagoras to Newton* (Princeton: Princeton Univ. Press, 1986), 434.

29. See Robert Frank, Jr., *Harvey and the Oxford Physiologists: A Study of Scientific Ideas* (Berkeley: Univ. of California Press, 1980), 90.

30. See Rom Harré, *Matter and Method* (London: Macmillan, 1965).

31. See, for example, Richard Westfall, "The Foundations of Newton's Philosophy of Nature," *British Journal for the History of Science* 1 (1962): 171–82.

32. For example, Kargon treats Descartes's and Gassendi's cosmologies as carrying equivalent weight for the Newcastle Circle. As I shall argue in chapter five, if their physics can be treated as equivalent, the implications for method and ethics cannot. See R. H. Kargon, *Atomism in England from Hariot to Newton* (Oxford: Oxford Univ. Press, 1966), 63.

33. J. S. Spink, *French Free Thought from Gassendi to Voltaire* (London: Athlone Press, 1960), 85–132; and Ira O. Wade, *The Intellectual Origins of the French Enlightenment* (Princeton: Princeton Univ. Press, 1971), 207–30.

34. Thomas Franklin Mayo, *Epicurus in England, 1650–1725* (Dallas: Southwest Press, 1934), 148.

35. Samuel I. Mintz, *The Hunting of Leviathan: Seventeenth-Century Reactions to the Materialism and Moral Philosophy of Thomas Hobbes* (Cambridge: Cambridge Univ. Press, 1962), 32.

36. *Selected Philosophical Papers of Robert Boyle,* ed. and intro. M. A. Stewart (Manchester: Manchester Univ. Press, 1979), xxx.

37. Philip Merlan confirms that one can "speak of the philosophy of Epicurus as a philosophy of joy rather than of pleasure" (*Studies in Epicurus and Aristotle,* Klassisch-Philologische Studien, vol. 22 [Wiesbaden: Harasowitz, 1960], 37). Erasmus includes an Epicurean dialogue in his colloquies. See, for example, *The Colloquies, or Familiar Discourses of Desiderius Erasmus of Roterdam, Rendered into English* (London, 1671), as

well as numerous other Restoration editions and translations, such as one translation by Sir Roger L'Estrange (*Twenty Select Colloquies out of Erasmus Roterdamus* [London, 1680]). Erasmus had edited Jerome, one of the chief patristic sources for Christian suspicions of Epicurus. See *Bibliotheca Erasmiana: Répertoire des Oeuvres d'Erasme,* ed. Ferdinand van der Haegen (Gand: Bibliothèque de l'Université de l'Etat, 1893). Valla adopts a refined view of *hēdonē* in *De Voluptate* (1431). See Lorenzo Valla, *De Voluptate: On Pleasure,* trans. A. Kent Hieatt and Maristella Lorch (New York: Albaris Books, 1977). On the Renaissance revision and appropriation of Epicurus, see the papers by Jacques Bailbé, M. Maxwell, and Françoise Jukovsky in *Actes du Congrès Guillaume Budé* (1969); E. Belowski, *Lukrez in der Französischen Literatur* (Berlin: Ebering, 1934); Cosmo Alexander Gordon, *A Bibliography of Lucretius* (London: Hart-Davis, 1962); George Depue Hadzsits, *Lucretius and His Influence* (New York: Longmans, Green, 1935); G. R. Hocke, *Lukrez in Frankreich von der Renaissance bis zur Revolution* (Köln: Kerschgens, 1935); Howard Jones, *Pierre Gassendi, 1592–1655: An Intellectual Biography* (Nieuwkoop: De Graaf, 1981), 214ff.; and B.J.M. Timmermans, "Valla et Erasme, Défenseurs d'Epicure," *Neophilologus* 23 (1937–38): 414–19.

38. See Danton B. Sailor, "Moses and Atomism," *Journal of the History of Ideas* 25 (1964): 3–16; see also Cope, *Glanvill,* 140ff.

39. For a greater discussion of Gale and Creech, see chapter five below. Joseph Glanvill explicitly attacks Hobbes and Epicureanism (*The Vanity of Dogmatizing: Or Confidence in Opinions Manifested in a Discourse of the Shortness and Uncertainty of Our Knowledge and Its Causes* [London, 1661], 43), but at the same time accepts atomism (47) and uses the classic examples of Epicurean hypotheticalism: the round tower and the size of the sun (e.g., 88). He also praises Gassendi as the "*Restorer of Epicurus*" (176–77), and as having demolished Aristotle (156; 184).

40. See A. J. Festugière, *Epicurus and His Gods* (Oxford: Blackwell, 1955), 85; G.E.R. Lloyd, *Greek Science after Aristotle* (New York: Norton, 1973), 21; E. Zeller, *The Stoics, Epicureans, and Sceptics* (1879; reprint, New York: Russell and Russell, 1962), 20; 420–23.

41. Especially well defined by Festugière, *Epicurus,* 9, and Lloyd, *Greek Science after Aristotle,* 2. Long, however, resists the notion that the sense of cultural uncertainty is really new (*Hellenistic Philosophy,* 3).

42. Festugière's classic study argues that Hellenistic philosophy needed to respond to a crisis that had been developing since the last third of the fifth century— namely, a conflict between civic and personal religion (*Epicurus,* 4); see also Zeller, *Stoics, Epicureans, and Sceptics,* 17. Important Epicurean texts or texts vital to its transmission deal with the problem of social collapse and a cultural restructuring by contract. I discuss Lucretius, *De Rerum Natura* 5.1093–1155 in my introduction. See also Cicero, *De Finibus,* trans. H. Rackham (Cambridge: Harvard Univ. Press; London: Heinemann, 1971), 63, which indicts civic and personal discord. Throughout my notes, I follow *The Oxford Classical Dictionary,* 2d ed., in its abbreviations of classical titles ("D.L.," "*Fin.,*" "Lucr.," etc.).

43. Long, *Hellenistic Philosophy,* 11.

44. Zeller, *Stoics, Epicureans, and Sceptics,* 2; Bernard Frischer argues that the gaps in high classical philosophy derived from an inability to articulate the connection between theory and practice; he writes that "the unity of theory and practice in

Epicureanism [is] the formal reason that, unlike Aristotle, Epicurus does not compartmentalize his philosophy but rigorously links part to part" (*Sculpted Word*, 26–33; 37). It is one of the theses of G.R.E. Lloyd's *Magic, Reason, and Experience* that "the Greeks preeminently bring into the open and discuss second-order questions concerning the nature of the inquiry [of mathematics and medicine] itself," but that nevertheless, unlike later Greek science, science up to Aristotle was weak in its rigidity and in its failure to implement systematic experimental programs. See *Magic, Reason, and Experience: Studies in the Origin and Development of Greek Science* (Cambridge: Cambridge Univ. Press, 1979), 232; 266–67.

45. S. Sambursky, *The Physical World of Late Antiquity* (Princeton: Princeton Univ. Press, 1987), 22. Frischer also summarizes the position in three points (*Sculpted Word*, 35–36).

46. On the failure of classical Greek self-criticism, see Lloyd, *Magic, Reason, and Experience*, 234. Frischer writes that Epicureanism "is not only conscious of its own place in the history of philosophy and of the principles of life latent in healthy human beings, it is also conscious of itself as a coherent system" (*Sculpted Word*, 36).

47. I discuss this issue elsewhere in "The Question of Locke's Relation to Gassendi," *Journal of the History of Ideas* 43 (1984): 339–59.

48. See Frischer, *Sculpted Word*, 37.

49. I use Frischer's characterization of the Epicurean community here (*Sculpted Word*, 63). See also Diogenes Laertius, *Lives of Eminent Philosophers*, trans. R. D. Hicks, 2 vols. (Cambridge: Harvard Univ. Press; London: Heinemann, 1925), 10.10: "Friends indeed came to him from all parts and lived with him in his garden." Moreover, Frischer writes that "Epicureanism also makes conscious the transformation of the Greek *polis* by Alexander" (*Sculpted Word*, 41).

50. See Lloyd, *Greek Science after Aristotle*, 3–4.

51. "The Epicurean faces the dilemma of how to retreat from the dominant culture while still bringing a message of salvation to mankind" (Frischer, *Sculpted Word*, xv).

52. See especially Frischer, *Sculpted Word*, chap. 3.

53. See Ibid., xvi.

54. Lloyd, *Greek Science after Aristotle*, 6.

55. See especially Elizabeth Asmis, *Epicurus' Scientific Method* (Ithaca: Cornell Univ. Press, 1984), chap. 10.

56. Ibid., 188–89.

57. Lloyd, *Greek Science after Aristotle*, 89–90.

58. D.L., 10.31.

59. For example, ibid., 10.78.

60. Ibid., 10.32.

61. Asmis writes that Epicurus has "an absolute reliance on sense perception" (*Epicurus' Scientific Method*, 143–44). De Witt argues that Epicurus is an intuitionist and that "anticipations" are innate ideas. See N. W. De Witt, *Epicurus and His Philosophy* (Minneapolis: Univ. of Minnesota Press, 1954).

62. E. de Lacy, "Meaning and Methodology in Hellenistic Philosophy," *Philosophical Review* 47 (1938): 390–409; and J. M. Rist, *Epicurus: An Introduction* (Cambridge: Cambridge Univ. Press, 1972), esp. 19–20. See also Gisela Striker, "Epicurus

on the Truth of Sense Impressions," *Archiv für Geschichte der Philosophie* 59 (1977): 125–42; N. W. De Witt, "Epicurus: All Sensations Are True," *Transactions of the American Philosophical Association* 74 (1943): 19–32; and Asmis, *Epicurus' Scientific Method*, 19–20; also 164.

63. Thomas Stanley, *The History of Philosophy*, 3d ed. (London, 1701), 552.

64. D.L., 10.64. Long also mentions that Pyrrho may have been influenced by an obscure figure, Anaxarchus, who may have been a Democritean, and whose atomism allows for a certain subjectivism (*Hellenistic Philosophy*, 80).

65. Ibid., 10.85–86. It is possible then to interpret the statement that the wise man "will be a dogmatist but not a mere sceptic," especially in the original *[dogmatiein te kai ouk aporēsein]* (ibid., 10.120).

66. See ibid., 10.44; 54.

67. Ibid., 10.33; see also Asmis, *Epicurus' Scientific Method*, 23.

68. Asmis summarizes the cognitive process: "The foundation of all cognition consists in the presentations obtained by the perceptual organs (including the mind acting as a perceptual organ); next are opinions added by the mind and verified directly by presentations of the perceptual organs; and finally, there are scientific opinions, which are verified by the use of reason on the basis of presentations obtained by the perceptual organs" (*Epicurus' Scientific Method*, 164).

69. D.L., 10.31.

70. Ibid., 10.50.

71. Rist, *Epicurus: An Introduction*, 33: "Contacts of the mind are nowhere said to guarantee us the truth of propositions."

72. Cicero, *Fin.*, 1.22; 25; 63–64.

73. See Cicero, *De Natura Deorum; Academica*, trans. H. Rackham (Cambridge: Harvard Univ. Press; London: Heinemann, 1979), *Acad.* 1.40–41; D.L., 6.45–47 on Zeno; and Long, *Hellenistic Philosophy*, 108; 144; 146, on Stoic realism and Stoic *logos*.

74. Stanley, *The History of Philosophy*, 309.

75. See, for example, Lucretius, *De Rerum Natura*, trans. W.H.D. Rouse and M. F. Smith (Cambridge: Harvard Univ. Press; London: Heinemann, 1975), 4.318ff. Lucretius discusses the possibility of the *eidōla* mingling, and Epicurus also permits the problem created by cognitive distance.

76. D.L., 10.146–47; and esp. 10.32: "Hence it is from plain facts that we must start when we draw inferences about the unknown. For all our notions are derived from perceptions, either by actual contact or by analogy, or resemblance, or composition, with some slight aid from reasoning."

77. Ibid., 10.50.

78. Ibid., 10.51. Asmis summarizes the canon very well (*Epicurus' Scientific Method*, 99–100). This is Stanley's rendition of the canons of sense and "praenotion" in his translation of Gassendi's *Philosophiae Epicuri Syntagma*, which constitutes his section on Epicurus in *The History of Philosophy*, 549–53:

CHAP. II.

(a) *Canons of Sense, the first Critery*. . . .

CANON. I.

(b) *Sense is never deceived; and therefore every Sensation, and every Perception, of an Appearance is true...*

CANON. 2.

(n) *Opinion follows Sense, and is superadded to Sensation, and capable of Truth or Falsehood. ...*

CANON. 3.

(r) *All Opinion attested, or not contradicted by the evidence of Sense, is True. ...*

CANON. 4.

(a) *An Opinion, contradicted or not attested by evidence of Sense, is false. ...*

CHAP. III.

Canons of Praenotion or Anticipation; the Second Criterie.

CANON. I.

(A) *All anticipation or Praenotion, which is in the Mind, depends on the Senses, either by Incursion, or Proportion, or Similitude, or Composition, ...*

CANON. 2.

Anticipation is the very notion, and (as it were) Definition of the Thing; without which, we cannot Enquire, Doubt, Think, nor so much as Name any Thing. ...

CANON. 3.

Anticipation is the Principle in all Discourse, as being that to which we have regard, when we infer that one is the same or divers, conjoined with or disjoined from another...

CANON. 4.

That which is Unmanifest ought to be demonstrated out of the Anticipation of a Thing Manifest. ...

79. Literally, "what cannot be perceived" (See Asmis, *Epicurus' Scientific Method*, 351).

80. Cicero, *Fin.* 2.48.

81. Lucr. 4.324–468.

82. Ibid., 4.353–63.

83. Ibid., 4.436–42.

84. D.L., 10.90; also Lucr. 4.478–99. Thomas Creech's pioneering translation presents a graph showing how various different astronomers calculated the size of the sun, by contrast to Epicurus (*T. Lucretius Carus, Of the Nature of Things*, 2 vols. [London, 1714], 2:492). (See p. 104.)

85. D.L., 10.94–95.

86. Ibid., 10.91–93.

87. Ibid., 10.32; and also 80: "When, therefore, we investigate the causes of celestial and atmospheric phenomena, as of all that is known, we must take into account the variety of ways in which analogous occurrences happen within our experience."

88. Ibid., 10.40.

89. Ibid., 10.32; 59.

90. Lucretius contrasts this view with the tradition of elements associated with Anaxagoras (Lucr., 1.830–920).

91. This strategy lies behind the view that the gods are, like the rest of nature, made of atoms, though finer.

92. Lucr., 2.1023–89. The discussion about the plurality of worlds was of major interest in the mid-seventeenth century and after. See, for example, Richard Baxter, *The Reasons of the Christian Religion,* in *The Practical Works of Richard Baxter,* 4 vols. (London, 1845), 2:198; Walter Charleton, *Physiologia Epicuro-Gassendo-Charletoniana* (London, 1654), 11ff.; Christian Huygens, *The Celestial Worlds Discovered* (London, 1698); John Wilkins, *The Discovery of a New World; or, A Discourse Tending to Prove, that it is Probable there may be another Habitable World in the Moon* (London, 1638). Of course, Baxter's attack on the new knowledge causes him to attack the hypothesis that there might be other worlds such as ours, because that erodes his Aristotelian distinctions between the lunary and sublunary spheres.

93. Of this inheritance, the Restoration was evidently well aware. See for example, Joseph Glanvill, *The Vanity of Dogmatizing,* 46–47. Heinrich Gomperz describes the two main Greek traditions of interpreting the elements, stemming from the differences between Anaximenes and Anaximander ("Problems and Methods of Early Greek Science," *Journal of the History of Ideas* 4 [1943]: 169).

94. Asmis offers an excellent contrast between Epicurean and Aristotelian induction (*Epicurus' Scientific Method,* 215–16). On the difference between Stoic essentialism and atomism, see *Nat. D.,* 1.71. It is worth noting that Epicurus still retains some *qualitative* values for the elements by endowing atoms with a variety of shapes, but Lucretius assails Anaxagoras's qualitative view of matter (Lucr., 1.830–920).

95. Rist calls this curious relation *isonomia* (*Epicurus: An Introduction,* 144ff.).

96. D.L., 10.3.

97. The nature of Stoic fatalism or determinism is a complex issue, well described by J. M. Rist, *Stoic Philosophy* (Cambridge: Cambridge Univ. Press, 1969), chap. 7. But as Rist is the first to point out, the interpretation of the Stoics as strict determinists is encouraged by some internal terminological confusions, as well as Cicero's representation of their position (see ibid., 121).

98. Lucr., 1.346–57.

99. Ibid., 2.216–93.

100. *Nat. D.,* 1.65–66.

101. See also the relations between force, the soul of the world, and necessity in the *Acad.,* 1.29.

102. *Nat. D.,* 1.55. See also the voluntarism in D.L., 10.133–34.

103. D.L., 10.41.

104. In translating Gassendi's small *Syntagma* for his *The History of Philosophy,* Stanley combines Lucretius's and Diogenes Laertius's accounts of language and society (*The History of Philosophy,* 591–92).

105. D.L., 10.150.

106. See, for example, Stanley, *The History of Philosophy,* 549–50; 591.

107. D.L., 10.46. See also Robert Boyle, *An Introduction to the History of Particular Qualities* (1671), in *Selected Papers,* 106–7; and Stanley, *The History of Philosophy,* 564–65, 568–69. Stanley's translation of Gassendi's small *Syntagma* runs thus: "For as Letters give a divers representation of themselves, not onely those which are of different figure or form, as *A* and *N,* but even the same Letters, if their position or

order be changed; position, as in *N* and *Z*; order, as in *AN, NA*; So, not onely atomes, which are of divers figures, (as also of different bulk and motion) are naturally apt to affect divers senses" (564). Epicurus calls the images of objects both *tupeis* and *eidōla*, which anticipates Locke's emphasis on the activity of imprinting ("types" as both figural and something almost physical) as the mind receives impressions from without.

108. See *Nat. D.*, 1.50; and 1.103–4, which discuss the grounds of memory.

109. The view is suggested at D.L., 10.62; and 72 concerning time. See also see Lucr., 4.768–76.

110. Long, *Hellenistic Philosophy*, 55.

111. Rist, *Epicurus: An Introduction*, 91.

112. *Acad.*, 1.39–41. As Long points out, there is accordingly no real Stoic account of probability (*Hellenistic Philosophy*, 129).

113. *Nat. D.*, 1.36.

114. This effect within Stoicism is well described in relation to John of Salisbury by Timothy J. Reiss, *The Discourse of Modernism* (Ithaca: Cornell Univ. Press, 1982), 78–79.

115. On the politics of Epicureanism, see *Epicurus's Morals*, trans. John Digby (London, 1712); and also the contrast between the Stoics and Epicureans in François Bernier, *Three Discourses of Happiness, Virtue, and Liberty. Collected from the Works of the Learn'd Gassendi* (London, 1699), 53.

116. Marx was one of the first to make this claim. See Benjamin Farrington, *Science and Politics in the Ancient World* (1939; reprint, New York: Barnes and Noble, 1966).

117. In a powerful critique of Farrington, Arnoldo Momigliano reminds us that "with some, yet not very much exaggeration, it is right to maintain that all Greek and Roman culture after the fifth century B.C. was aristocratic." See Momigliano, *Secondo Contributo alla Storia della Studi Classici* (Rome: Edizione di Storia e Letteratura, 1960), 375–88.

118. Frischer, *Sculpted Word*, 62.

119. See D.L., 10.13, where the context of the discussion is precisely the issue of inherited forms of philosophical authority.

120. To support his reading of Epicurus's radical socialism, Farrington also enlists a reductive and positivistic interpretation of the rejection of magic by "science."

121. See Momigliano, *Secondo Contributo*, 378.

122. Ibid., 381.

123. Frischer, *Sculpted Word*, chap. 3. It is suggestive to contrast this Epicurean view of the icon with the Stoics'. Rist writes that "the [Stoic] wise man possesses the virtues; the ordinary people have only images and likenesses of virtue (*simulacra rerum honestarum et effiges*)" (*Stoic Philosophy*, 225).

124. *Fin.*, 1.65.

125. Frischer, *Sculpted Word*, 96.

126. This distinction becomes loaded for the Restoration. Unless the image serves exclusively as a mental or cognitive token, the *eidōlon* could degenerate into mere idolatry. But if the Epicurean image authorizes a calculated rejection of the mysteriousness of religious imagery, it can provide the grounds for a positive, yet

nonidolatrous, notion of imagistic power. On images, see Stanley, *The History of Philosophy*, 585–86.

127. Walter Charleton, *Epicurus's Morals* (London, 1656), 96.

128. D.L., 10.13.

129. *Fin.*, 1.30–31. The image is also the object of a theory of action because, for example, eros is stimulated by the images of the objects of desire (Lucr., 4.877–97).

130. For clarity, see D.L., 10.13; also 36.

131. D.L., 10.26.

132. Ibid., 10.120.

133. I adopt Frischer's suggestive term.

134. Thus fragmentary texts can serve alternatively sceptical and gnostic purposes, as in the case of Heraclitus's fragmentary utterances about the *logos*. Gassendi apparently associates his activity of reassembling the fragmented textual evidences of Epicureanism with the larger question of Epicurus's own attitude to textualizing the self (see Stanley, *The History of Philosophy*, 539–40).

135. Diogenes Laertius uses the adjective *polugraphōtatos* to describe Epicurus in this relation (D.L., 10.26).

136. As we shall see, the parallel with Lukan and Pauline epistolary strategies is obvious and significant.

137. See the notes to the Loeb edition of Diogenes Laertius's *Lives*, 662.

138. D.L., 10.130.

139. This is not to say that *De Rerum Natura* is not governed by numerous formal symmetries. Part of my point is that the appearance of open-endedness at the end of the poem finds symbolic justification in Lucretius's cosmology and hermeneutic.

140. Cicero expounds the history of the philosophical dialogue in *Fin.*, 2.1–2. He also depicts the tradition of "negative dialectic," which begins with Plato in *Nat. D.*, 1.1; and also 1.11–12.

141. *Acad.*, Prefatory Letter, 1.

142. Ibid., 2.148.

4. Gassendi's Architectonic Method and the Quest for Epicurus's Image

1. Swift also repeats the same intellectual map (though to satiric effect) in book three of *Gulliver's Travels*.

2. On Foucher, see Richard Watson, *The Downfall of Cartesianism, 1673–1712* (The Hague: Nijhoff, 1966), chapter 2.

3. G. W. Leibniz, *New Essays on Human Understanding* trans. and ed. Peter Remnant and Jonathan Bennett (Cambridge: Cambridge Univ. Press, 1981), bk. 4, chap. 2, sec. 14.

4. For Gassendi's predecessors in the history of atomism, see R. H. Kargon, *Atomism in England from Hariot to Newton* (Oxford: Clarendon Press, 1966), chaps. 1–6; Howard Jones, *Pierre Gassendi, 1592–1655* (Nieuwkoop: De Graaf, 1981), 205–25; A.G.M. van Melsen, "Atomism: Antiquity to the Seventeenth Century," in *Dictionary of the History of Ideas* (New York: Scribner's, 1968), 126–31; and Lancelot Law Whyte, *Essay on Atomism: From Democritus to 1960* (Middletown, Conn.: Wesleyan Univ. Press, 1961). See also the articles on the Renaissance adaptations of Epicurus, cited in chapter three above, n.37.

5. Examples include the restriction of discussion about Gassendi to primarily epistemological issues: Henri Berr, *Du Scepticisme de Gassendi,* trans. Bernard Rochot (1898; reprint, Paris: Michel, 1960); Howard T. Egan, *Gassendi's View of Knowledge: A Study of the Epistemological Basis of His Logic* (New York: Univ. Press of America, 1984); Richard Popkin, *The History of Scepticism from Erasmus to Spinoza* (Berkeley: Univ. of California Press, 1979), chap. 5; and the conscription of Gassendi as a forerunner of modern materialist philosophy (O. R. Bloch, *La Philosophie de Gassendi: Nominalisme, Matérialisme et Métaphysique* [The Hague: Nijhoff, 1971]). Edward A. Driscoll argues for the influence of Gassendi on Locke by appealing to the pleasure-pain principle ("The Influence of Gassendi on Locke's Hedonism," *International Philosophical Quarterly* 12 [1972]: 87–110). Edward John Kearns, *Ideas in Seventeenth-Century France: The Most Important Thinkers and the Climate of Ideas in Which They Worked* (Manchester: Manchester Univ. Press, 1979), almost completely ignores Gassendi. An excellent review of Gassendi historiography appears in Lynn Sumida Joy, *Gassendi the Atomist: Advocate of History in an Age of Science* (Cambridge: Cambridge Univ. Press, 1987), 13–19.

6. On Gassendi's immense cultural importance, see Alexandre Koyré, "Gassendi: Le Savant," in *Pierre Gassendi, 1592–1655: Sa Vie et Son Oeuvre* (Paris: Michel, 1955), 60–61. Although Koyré finds Gassendi uninteresting as a 'scientific' figure, he points out how influential Gassendi was as a *cultural* one: "Il n'a rien inventé, rien découvert et . . . il n'existe pas de loi de Gassendi"; but all the same "il a été, effectivement, un rival de Descartes et a exercé sur la deuxième moitié du siècle une influence des plus considérables." A series of arguments has based its claims for Gassendi's importance to early modern science on a rather loose series of analogies between Gassendi's work and the premises of British empiricism. See David Fate Norton, "The Myth of 'British Empiricism,'" *History of European Ideas* 1 (1981): 331–34; R. H. Kargon, *Atomism in England,* passim; Richard W. F. Kroll, "The Question of Locke's Relation to Gassendi," *Journal of the History of Ideas* 45 (1984): 339–59; and J. R. Milton, "Locke and Gassendi: A Reappraisal," *Oxford Studies in the History of Philosophy* 2 (forthcoming).

7. Joy, *Gassendi the Atomist,* 66.

8. Ibid., chap. 9.

9. Ibid., 219–24. Unlike Joy, I am persuaded of the substantial connectedness among Gassendi, Boyle, and Locke. For Boyle's relationship with Locke, see Peter Alexander, *Ideas, Qualities and Corpuscles: Locke and Boyle on the External World* (Cambridge: Cambridge Univ. Press, 1985).

10. Gassendi, *Syntagma Philosophicum,* Physics, bk. 3, chap. 8, sec. 1, in *The Selected Works of Pierre Gassendi,* trans. Craig Brush (New York: Johnson Reprint, 1972), 399; *Opera Omnia* 1:279–82. Future references will appear as "Brush," followed by the reference to the *Opera Omnia* (hereafter referred to as *OO*), 6 vols. (Lyons, 1658).

11. Ibid.

12. Ibid.

13. Against Laurens Laudan's claim that it is primarily Descartes who represents hypothetical method to the later seventeenth century, G.A.J. Rogers argues persuasively that this was not the case. See G.A.J. Rogers, "Descartes and the Method of English Science," *Annals of Science* 29 (1972): 237–55.

14. The debate has hinged on the force we should give to Gassendi's announce-

ment about his commitment to the "middle way" (*Syntagma.*, Logic, bk. 2, chap. 5: Brush, 326; *OO* 1:79). See Jones, *Gassendi*, 136. Popkin seems to imply a swing from an early Pyrrhonism to a more mitigated scepticism (*History of Scepticism*, 99–109).

15. *Exerc.*, bk. 2, exerc. 6, art. 6: Brush, 101; *OO* 3:203; and Reb. to Med. 2, doubt 1, art. 2: Brush, 176; *OO* 3:286.

16. Reb. to Med. 2, doubt 1: Brush, 176; *OO* 3:286. Rebutting Descartes, Gassendi writes that the Sceptics' "way of distinguishing between the acts of daily life and the inquiry after truth resulted in their rejection of indifference in questions about everyday conduct and their endorsement of obeying their country's laws, of passing judgment in cases of necessity, of offering their services, in a word, of doing everything that good men and citizens do, both privately and publicly."

17. *Exerc.*, bk. 2, exerc. 6, art. 6: Brush, 101; *OO* 3:203–6.

18. *Exerc.*, Preface: Brush, 18–21; *OO* 3:100ff.

19. See, for example Reb. to Med. 1, doubt 1: Brush, 168; *OO* 3:281; *Syntagma.*, Logic, bk. 2, chap. 2: Brush, 302–3; *OO* 1:72ff.; and *Syntagma.*, Logic, bk. 2, chap. 1: Brush, 293; *OO* 1:69. Also Pierre Gassendi, *Institutio Logica (1658)*, ed. and trans. Howard Jones (Assen: Van Gorcum, 1981), lxv; and 156ff.: *OO* 1:120. (All references to the latter edition shall appear as *"IL"* and "Jones," followed by references to the *Opera Omnia.*)

20. On ancient notions of probability within the tradition of rhetoric, see Victoria Kahn, *Rhetoric, Prudence, and Skepticism in the Renaissance* (Ithaca: Cornell Univ. Press, 1985); Douglas Lane Patey, *Probability and Literary Form: Philosophic Theory and Literary Practice in the Augustan Age* (Cambridge: Cambridge Univ. Press, 1984), chap. 1; and Victoria A. Silver, "'Sensible and Plausible Elocution': Rhetoric and the Shape of Knowledge in Bacon, Browne, and Hobbes." Ph.D. diss., Univ. of California, Los Angeles, 1984.

21. See especially *Syntagma.*, Logic, bk. 2, chap. 5: Brush, 330–31; *OO* 1:81, where Gassendi discusses Aristotle's *Rhetoric*.

22. *OO* 1:1–30.

23. *OO* 1:35–66.

24. *OO* 1:67–90.

25. Joy describes Gassendi dramatizing the conflict between the Middle Academy and the Stoa in his *Animadversiones in Decimum Librum Diogenis Laertii* (Lyons, 1649) and the *Syntagma Philosophicum* (printed in *OO*). See Joy, *Gassendi the Atomist*, 155.

26. Pierre Gassendi, *Exercitationum Paradoxicarum Adversus Aristoteleos* (Grenoble, 1624).

27. Gassendi, *Disquisitia Metaphysica, seu Dubitationes et Instantiae adversus Renati Cartesii Metaphysicam et Responsa* (Amsterdam, 1644).

28. Gassendi, *Epistolica Exercitatio, in qua Praecipua Principia Philosophiae Roberti Fluddi Medici Reteguntur* (Paris, 1630). See also Joseph Bougerel, *Vie de Pierre Gassendi* (1737; reprint, Geneva: Slatkine Reprints, 1970), 75. Bougerel writes that Gassendi assaulted Fludd for his Cabalistic tendencies, which constituted "la source de toutes ces vaines imaginations, qui sont le fondement de la magie" (77–78).

29. Gassendi, *Ad Librum D. Edoardi Herberti de Veritate Epistola* (completed in 1634, but first published in the *Opera Omnia* of 1658). See also letter to Diodati,

Geneva, 29 August 1634: Brush, 111, where Gassendi attacks Cherbury's instinctualism; and Jones deals particularly well with Gassendi's criticism of Herbert of Cherbury (*Gassendi*, 116–34).

30. Thus Gassendi points out that we cannot truly have degrees of certainty, only, in effect, degrees of uncertainty (Reb. to Med. 2, doubt 1, art. 5: Brush, 178; *OO* 3:289).

31. Reb. to Med., Prefatory Epistle: Brush, 158; *OO* 3:273.

32. This is what Gassendi means when he wishes to retain the "intermediate steps" of knowledge—namely, the continuing operations of inferential activity. See Reb. to Med. 3, doubt 8: Brush, 216; *OO* 3:341.

33. This is the implication of Brett's comment that "the direct material of thought is purely symbolic of the external reality" (G. S. Brett, *The Philosophy of Gassendi* [London: Macmillan, 1908], 133).

34. Reb. to Med. 4, doubt 1: Brush, 237; *OO* 3:362.

35. Reb. to Med. 4, doubt 1: Brush, 235; *OO* 3:361.

36. See *Exerc.*, bk. 2, exerc. 3, art. 11: Brush, 61–64; *OO* 3:171; Reb. to Med. 6, doubt 4: Brush, 271; *OO* 3:399–400.

37. *Exerc.*, bk. 2, exerc. 3, art. 11: Brush, 62; *OO* 3:172. Gassendi insists, however, that he is not questioning matters of "faith alone derived from revelation and God's authority" (*Exerc.*, bk. 2, exerc. 6, art. 1: Brush, 86; *OO* 3:192). On authority, see also *IL,* pt. 2: Jones, 119; *OO* 1:106.

38. *Exerc.*, bk. 2, exerc. 3, art. 11: Brush, 62; *OO* 3:172.

39. *Syntagma.*, Logic, bk. 2, chap. 6: Brush, 364; *OO* 1:90: Because Descartes "concludes that the intellect should find help as it proceeds in its judgment not so much from examining things themselves both in themselves and by themselves as from its thoughts alone examined by itself in solitude, it is obvious that his method is less fitting than Bacon's." See also Gassendi's criticism of epistemological method in the *Meditations* (Reb. to Med., Prefatory Epistle: Brush, 158; *OO* 3:273). Gassendi also writes: "When the whole course of the *Meditations* has been completed, no one knows more certainly that the tower seen up close is smooth or that the rod seen in the air is straight than if he had stayed on his own doorsill" (Reb. to Med. 1, doubt 1: Brush, 169; *OO* 3:281). It is significant that in both instances, Gassendi dispraises Descartes's fugitive and cloistered virtue.

40. *Exerc.*, bk. 2, exerc. 5, art. 5: Brush, 75; *OO* 3:187–88.

41. *Syntagma.*, Logic, bk. 2, chap. 6: Brush, 363; *OO* 1:90.

42. Ibid.

43. Joy, *Gassendi the Atomist*, 61.

44. See, for example, M. M. Slaughter's excellent discussion of Bacon in *Universal Languages and Scientific Taxonomy in the Seventeenth Century* (Cambridge: Cambridge Univ. Press, 1982), 89–97. In his translation of Gassendi's small *Syntagma*, Thomas Stanley uses *"Anticipation"* and *"Praenotion"* interchangeably, but to denote the action of Epicurean *prolēpseis* ("Containing the Epicurean Sect," *The History of Philosophy*, 3d ed. [London, 1701], 552).

45. *Exerc.*, bk. 2, exerc. 5, art. 7: Brush, 84; *OO* 3:191.

46. *Exerc.*, bk. 2, exerc. 1, art. 1: Brush, 30; *OO* 3:149. See also *IL,* pt. 1, canon 4: Jones, 86; *OO* 1:93.

47. Jones, 38: "Syllogismus itaque Nihil aliud est, quam Cogitatio, internave ratio."

48. *Exerc.,* bk. 2, exerc. 3, art. 10: Brush, 59; *OO* 3:171; Reb. to Med. 2, doubt 1: Brush, 184; *OO* 3:290; Reb. to Med. 2, doubt 7: Brush, 198–99; *OO* 3:310; Reb. to Med. 5, doubt 1, [Descartes's] Reply: Brush, 248–49; *OO* 3:375–76; see also *Exerc.,* bk. 2, Exerc. 5, art. 4: Brush, 70; *OO* 3:185.

49. See, for example, Bernard Williams, *Descartes: The Project of Pure Enquiry* (Harmondsworth, Eng.: Penguin, 1978), 216, where Williams describes Descartes's discussion of the properties of wax, whose essence does not lie in its sensible qualities. See also Reb. to Med. 5, doubt 1, [Descartes's] Reply: Brush, 248–49; *OO* 3:375–76.

50. Reb. to Med. 3, doubt 10: Brush, 221; *OO* 3:353.

51. Reb. to Med. 6, doubt 2: Brush, 267; *OO* 3:388.

52. *Exerc.,* bk. 2, exerc. 1, art. 5: Brush, 40; *OO* 3:152; *Exerc.,* bk. 2, Exerc. 6, art. 5: Brush, 87–88; *OO* 3:197; Reb. to Med. 6, doubt 2: Brush, 266; *OO* 3:388.

53. Reb. to Med. 6, doubt 2: Brush, 266–67; *OO* 3:388.

54. *Exerc.,* bk. 2, exerc. 6, art. 5: Brush, 88; *OO* 3:197.

55. Reb. to Med. 2, doubt 8: Brush, 200; *OO* 3:312.

56. Reb. to Med. 2, doubt 6: Brush, 195; *OO* 3:307: "The internal faculty works inside the brain and has within the brain the imprints of external appearances adhering to it, imprints transmitted from the organs and functions of the external senses and engraved there; and in addition to these it has the imprints of its own actions, in a word all that is necessary to reflection." Gassendi's somatic and tactile language is remarkably like that of Locke's.

57. Joy handles the seventeenth-century debate about indivisibles in exemplary fashion. See Joy, *Gassendi the Atomist,* esp. 83–129. One of Joy's chief theses is that Gassendi wanted consistently to preserve the distinction between physical and mathematical approaches to the subject: particles may be mathematically indivisible for provisional purposes, but that does not alter the irreducible quality of physical atoms. However, the power of conception in Descartes, unaided by the senses, leads him to write in the *Principles of Philosophy* (1644) that "we cannot grasp in our thought how . . . indefinite division [of particles] comes about, but we should not therefore doubt that it occurs" (*The Philosophical Writings of Descartes,* trans. John Cottingham et al., 2 vols. [Cambridge: Cambridge Univ. Press, 1985], 1:239).

58. *Exerc.,* bk. 2, exerc. 6, arts. 1–5: Brush, 86–89; *OO* 3:192–98; Reb. to Med. 5, doubt 1: Brush, 257; *OO* 3:358; Reb. to Med. 6, doubt 2: Brush, 267; *OO* 3:388; *IL* pt. 1: Jones, 83; *OO* 1:192.

59. *Exerc.,* bk. 2, exerc. 5, art. 5: Brush, 76–77; *OO* 3:188.

60. Ibid.; see also *Exerc.,* bk. 2, exerc. 6, art. 6: Brush 99; *OO* 3:204.

61. Reb. to Med. 5, doubt 1: Brush 256–57; *OO* 3:378: "In childhood we were not geometers, and we only became geometers through the lessons of our teachers or books or through discovery or study and our own work. Likewise we learned about the triangle formed of lines devoid of width from teachers or the books of Euclid or others; or else we derived it by our own thinking as we reasoned about the triangle and other figures which were present in our senses or that we had formed by putting together, breaking down, or moving about the ones that had been present in the senses." See also Reb. to Med. 5, doubt 3: Brush, 264–65; *OO* 3:384, where Gassendi

describes hypotheses in astronomy as contingent. Significantly for the somatic argument I describe in later chapters, Gassendi at this juncture compares the examination of the heavens to examining someone else's face.

62. The essays on logic in the *Syntagma* appear as "De Logicae Origine," "De Logicae Fine," and "Institutio Logica" in *OO* 1:35–132. The "Institutio Logica" was also published separately.

63. Gassendi also somewhat confusingly distinguishes between logic and method in the preface to the *Institutio Logica* (Jones, 120). But here, Gassendi uses the word "method" to denote a system of ordering rather than analysis.

64. Jones, xix.

65. *IL*, pt. 4: Jones, 156; *OO* 1:120.

66. *IL*, pt. 4: Jones, 158; *OO* 1:121. The strategy also informs Antoine Arnauld's *Logic: or, The Art of Thinking* (1685), as well as Jean Le Clerc's *Logica*, the first London edition of which (1692) was published in two volumes, the first dedicated to Boyle, and the second to Locke.

67. *Exerc.*, bk. 2, exerc. 1, art. 3: Brush, 34–35; *OO* 3:150; *Exerc.*, bk. 2, exerc. 1, art. 5: Brush, 40; *OO* 3:152. Gassendi writes, for example, "and just what routes will logic produce to lead me to the complete knowledge of the nature of a flea, not to mention the sun?" (*Exerc.*, bk. 2, exerc. 1, art. 3: Brush, 33; *OO* 3:150).

68. *IL*, pt. 4: Jones, 159; *OO* 1:121: Gassendi is discussing the method of "resolution" and "composition": "It goes without saying that this is the method employed in connection with all things made up of or constructed from many parts. For we determine whether a machine, shall we say a clock, is in good condition either by removing the mechanism and discovering whether each part separately is functioning properly, or by assembling the individual parts to determine whether they fit together properly and produce the right effect."

69. *IL*, pt. 4: Jones, 156; *OO* 1:120.

70. *IL*, pt. 4: Jones, 158; *OO* 1:121.

71. *IL*, pt. 4: Jones, 159; *OO* 1:121.

72. For example, Gassendi suggests a need to supplement Cicero's probabilism in the *Exercitationes* (*Exerc.*, bk. 2, exerc. 1, art. 2: Brush, 32; *OO* 3:149).

73. See Sextus Empiricus, *Against the Logicians,* in *Sextus Empiricus,* trans. R. G. Bury, 4 vols. (Cambridge: Harvard Univ. Press; London: Heinemann, 1933–35), 2.146ff. Gassendi discusses signs in the *Syntagma,* Logic, bk. 2, chap. 5: Brush 330–32; *OO* 1:80–81.

74. *IL*, pt. 4: Jones, 160; *OO* 1:122; *Syntagma,* Logic, , bk. 2, chap. 5: Brush, 333; *OO* 1:81.

75. *Exerc.*, bk. 2, exerc. 6, art. 5: Brush, 95; *OO* 3:202; Reb. to Med. 1, doubt 1: Brush, 166; *OO* 3:279; Reb. to Med. 1, doubt 1: Brush 168; *OO* 3:281; *IL*, Preface: Jones, 80; *OO* 1:91; *IL*, pt. 1: Jones, 94–95; *OO* 3:96–97; *IL*, pt. 4: Jones, 160; *OO* 1:122.

76. *IL*, pt. 4: Jones, 160; *OO* 1:122. See also *Exerc.*, bk. 2, exerc. 1, art. 5: Brush, 40; *OO* 3:152; *Exerc.*, bk. 2, exerc. 5, art. 5: Brush, 68; *OO* 3:184–85; *Exerc.*, bk. 2, exerc. 6, art. 2: Brush, 87; *OO* 3:92.

77. *IL*, pt. 4: Jones, 160; *OO* 1:122; and on analogy, see *Exerc.*, bk. 2, exerc. 3, art. 3: Brush, 50; *OO* 3:167.

78. *Syntag.*, Logic, bk. 4, chap. 5: Brush, 333; *OO* 1:81; *Syntag.*, Logic, bk. 4, chap.

5: Brush, 345–46; *OO* 1:85; *IL,* Preface: Jones, 80–81; *OO* 1:91. In the *Institutio Logica,* Gassendi provides the image of a yardstick to describe the canon (Jones, 80; *OO* 1:91).

79. *IL,* pt. 4: Jones, 162:

The schoolmaster, whose profession is to teach the proper use of language, first of all divides language into its proper parts, noun, verb, and so on (not to mention such minor elements as syllables and letters), and after pointing out the properties and qualities peculiar to each of these in turn, teaches how to put them together to form suitable expressions and complete sentences. . . . Thus a physicist who is giving instruction in the natural sciences places as a model before our eyes, like the larger and smaller parts of a building, only on an extended scale, the structure of nature or the machine of the world, the sky, the earth, and all that they contain, and analysing them into their smallest possible components takes these as the primary units which go to make up the whole.

Gassendi actually repeats the analogy twice in the same section, applying it also to medical symptomology (Jones, 161–62; *OO* 1:122–23).

80. *IL,* pt. 4: Jones, 163; *OO* 1:123: "It is here, in researching the external world, that wherever possible we call upon anatomy and chemistry and the other sciences to enable us as far as possible to analyse bodies and break them down into their structural units in an attempt to understand the precise nature of their composition and to determine by extrapolation whether the composition of other bodies can be accounted for in the same or in a different way."

81. A striking example occurs in Samuel Hartlib, *The True and Readie Way to Learne the Latine Tongue* (London, 1654), Sig. A3^r.

82. See, for example, *Syntag.,* Physics, bk. 5, chap. 7, sec. 1: Brush, 426–27; *OO* 1:366–67; and Gassendi cites Lucretius in Reb. to Med. 5, doubt 1: Brush, 250; *OO* 3:377.

83. Thus, for example, Gassendi rejects action at a distance (*De Motu,* First Letter, 14: Brush, 133; *OO* 1:493).

84. See *IL,* Preface: Jones, 80; *OO* 1:91; the Latin is *imagines* (Jones, 1).

85. Gassendi is taking issue with a passage in Descartes's second Meditation (see Reb. to Med. 2, doubts 6, 8: Brush, 193–98; *OO* 3:306–10; Brush, 197n.16). See, especially, Reb. to Med. 2, doubt 6: Brush 195; *OO* 3:307: "For the external sense cannot exercise reflection except when an external body reflects the image either of its shape or of its voice. On the other hand the internal faculty works inside the brain and has within the brain the imprints of external appearances adhering to it, imprints transmitted from the organs and functions of the external senses and engraved there; and in addition to these it has the imprints of its own actions, in a word all the things necessary for reflection."

86. "In the first place there are ideas which pass through the senses, and are impressed upon the mind, and these are ideas of things which themselves enter into the senses . . . . Transference, adaptation, analogy, or comparison is when the mind transfers and adapts the idea of a city one has seen to a city one has not yet seen and thus pictures the latter as being like the former" (*IL,* pt. 1: Jones, 85–86; *OO* 1:92–93). See also *IL,* pt. 2: Jones, 102; *OO* 1:99–100.

87. Reb. to Med. 1, doubt 1: Brush, 165; *OO* 3:279.

88. *IL,* pt. 1: Jones, 92; *OO* 1:96.

89. On Gassendi's suspicion of language, see *IL,* pt. 4: Jones, 164; *OO* 1:123. Gassendi says that we may actually perceive opposite effects from the external world, yet must arbitrarily agree to use the same words to perpetuate social intercourse (*Exerc.,* bk. 2, exerc. 6, art. 5: Brush, 92; *OO* 3:199–200).

90. Reb. to Med. 2, doubt 1: Brush, 256–57; *OO* 3:378.

91. Reb. to Med. 3, doubt 7: Brush, 209; *OO* 3:337.

92. Ibid.

93. Descartes at one point attacks "corporeal images" or "images of corporeal things" (Reb. to Med. 4, [Descartes'] Reply: Brush, 228; *OO* 3:359); see also Egan, *Gassendi's View of Knowledge,* 138ff.

94. Gassendi attacks Descartes for implying that a given idea is already whole and complete in itself and therefore closed to modification by subsequent experience (Reb. to Med. 3, doubt 10: Brush, 221–22; *OO* 3:353).

95. Reb. to Med. 3, doubt 8: Brush, 218; *OO* 3:343.

96. Brush, 26: "I thought it best to select just those opinions which were, so to speak, the foundation doctrines of the Aristotelians; for when they cave in, they cause the total collapse of the others at the same time. Therefore, I appear to be imitating those who dig out underneath the foundations when they are besieging a city; when they fall in, the whole defensive system of walls and towers collapses."

97. Gassendi introduces the idea of taxonomy when attacking Aristotle (*Exerc.,* bk. 2, *exerc.* 1, art. 4- Brush, 37; *OO* 3:151) and also when attacking Descartes (Reb. to Med. 2, doubt 6: Brush, 191; *OO* 3:306).

98. *Exerc.,* bk. 2, exerc. 6, arts. 2 and 5: Brush, 87–88; *OO* 3:192; 196: "Since the judgment of different men about the same things as they are first perceived by the senses are so very different, what other conclusion can one draw except that it is legitimate for each man to label things the way he sees them? But it is not legitimate to state that they are such by their nature."

99. *Exerc.,* bk. 2, exerc. 5, art. 4: Brush, 72; *OO* 3:186; Gassendi later uses the same examples in the *Institutio Logica,* pt. 1 (Jones, 99; *OO* 1:98).

100. *Exerc.,* bk. 2, exerc. 5, art. 5: Brush, 81; *OO* 3:189.

101. Reb. to Med. 3, doubt 10: Brush, 223; *OO* 3:353: "Since experience shows that the ideas in our minds are like images of things, and the images are not of a thing's essence, but of its accidents, it follows that just as the image of a certain man reproduced in a picture is all the more perfect if the symmetry, the arrangement, and the representation of a great number of parts is more elaborately worked out, and each of the individual traits which are in the separate parts is more carefully reproduced, so the idea of any thing becomes all the more perfect if it portrays more of its accidents, or more of the things surrounding it, as it were, in a more ordered fashion, with greater skill, and more lifelike."

102. *Exerc.,* bk. 2, exerc. 5, art. 4: Brush, 68; *OO* 3:126: "Because of its difference, every single thing differs from every other thing in some way, either by reason of its specific difference, or by reason of its generic difference. But it is still always true that in every single thing there is something by which it is separated from everything else. Therefore, if we are to know the difference of a thing perfectly, we must know everything else perfectly."

103. Richard Baxter, *The Reasons of the Christian Religion*, in *The Practical Works of Richard Baxter*, 4 vols. (London, 1845), 2:183.

104. Marin Cureau de la Chambre, *Traité de la Conoissance des Animaux* (Paris, 1647), trans. *A Discourse of the Knowledge of Beasts, Wherein all that hath been said for, and against their Ratiocination, is Examined* (London, 1657). La Chambre dislikes the conversion of the probable into the demonstrative (8). This habit he ascribes to Chanet's ontological discontinuities (e.g., 33).

105. Ibid., 4; 13; 18; 23; 25. For example, la Chambre writes that "imagination & the Understanding comprehend all the knowing faculties, as the Appetite and the Will expresse all the motive faculties of the Soul" (18); and later: "Now because Knowledg cannot be otherwise conceived but as a representation of the objects which are made in the mind; If the Sensitive Soul knows, and if to know is to operate; it of necessity must present it self with the objects; and because it cannot otherwise represent a thing but by forming its picture, it follows that in knowing things, it forms pictures and images of them, and that there is no other action which may be attributed unto it proportionable to the perfection and excellency of its Nature" (22–23). La Chambre's view of the mental economy is strikingly like Walter Charleton's in his *Natural History of the Passions* (London, 1674), which I discuss in chapter six below.

106. As la Chambre recognizes, Montaigne had already made a similar point (*A Discourse of the Knowledge of Beasts*, 3; 11).

107. Ibid., 7.

108. See for example, Ibid., Sig. A3ᵛ; also 2–3. "Essences and Properties are known but by effects: It is not more reasonable to conclude that Beasts doing reasonable things, have a reasonable Faculty, then to affirm that the effects are not reasonable, because Beasts have not a reasonable Faculty? the Effects appear, the Power is occult" (Sig. A3ᵛ).

109. La Chambre enlists both the Platonic metaphor of harmony and the Aristotelian figure of the organism.

110. Bougerel, *Vie de Pierre Gassendi*, 163.

111. On the power of intuition, see Descartes, *Rules for the Direction of the Mind* (1684), in *Philosophical Writings*, 1:14; on the opposition between certainty and probability, see ibid., 1:44; 47; and *Meditations*, in ibid., 2:9–10; on the conflict of science and history, see *Rules for the Direction of the Mind*, in ibid., 1:13.

112. In a letter to an unknown friend (dated 23 July 1649), Descartes clearly opposes the skills of the philosopher to those of the rhetor. And in *Rules for the Direction of the Mind*, Descartes treats writing—like rhetoric, a palpable art—solely as a mnemonic, in order to allow "the imagination to devote itself freely and completely to the ideas immediately before it." See *Philosophical Writings*, 1:327; 67.

113. Descartes clearly devalues the function of analogical reasoning in *Rules for the Direction of the Mind*, in *Philosophical Writings*, 1:29; 40. Analogy does not constitute the necessary mode by which we apprehend experience; at best it is a tool to be used, then discarded in the face of true, immediate knowledge.

114. Descartes assumes a complete contrast between the apprehensions of the intellect *tout seule*, and the imagination. See, for example, *Rules for the Direction of the Mind*, in *Philosophical Writings*, 1:58–59. He holds to the belief that we can rationally penetrate through cryptic figures, such as the riddle of the Sphinx itself, by distin-

guishing between their literal and metaphorical functions, or use the charm of fables as a preface to some fuller knowledge (ibid., 1:55; and also *Discourse on the Method* (1637), in *Philosophical Writings*, 1:112; 113.

115. On the conflict of intuition and vision, see Descartes, *Rules for the Direction of the Mind*, in *Philosophical Writings*, 1:33; and on the difference between truth and the outer garment, see ibid., 1:17. By contrast, Charleton celebrates the activity of his pen as a form of contingent mediation between himself and his reader: "And now at length having run over these six stages, in as direct a course, and with as much celerity, as the intricacy and roughness of the way could tolerate; hath our Pen attained to the end of our *Digression:* wherein, whether we have gratified our Reader with so much either of satisfaction, or Delight, as may compensate his time and patience; we may not praesume to determine" (*Physiologia Epicuro-Gassendo-Charletoniana* [London, 1654], 60).

116. See for example, *IL*, bk. 1, chap. 14: Jones, 96; *OO* 1:97.

117. *Syntag.*, Logic, bk. 2, chap. 6: Brush, 359; *OO* 3:89. This clarity Gassendi also sees to be an aim of Bacon's (ibid., Brush 362).

118. *Exerc.*, Preface: Brush, 27; *OO,* 3:103.

119. *Exerc.*, Preface: Brush, 20; *OO,* 3:100.

120. *Syntag.*, Logic, bk. 2, chap. 5: Brush, 329; *OO* 1:80.

121. By operationalism, I mean in this context the notion that knowledge is constructed by the manipulation of externalized, phenomenal counters, in a way that reflects the original definition of operationalism in the philosophy of science. Scientific knowledge is interpreted as the sum of the laboratory operations the scientist orchestrates, not as some essential epistemic property. For a description and criticism of this view, see Rom Harré, *The Philosophies of Science: An Introductory Survey* (Oxford: Oxford Univ. Press, 1985), 161–63.

122. *Exerc.*, bk. 2, exerc. 6, art. 7: Brush, 104; *OO* 3:207: "It may well be that the basis for knowledge does exist, but for a knowledge of experience and, I may say, of appearances; for our intellect knows or learns through its experience of numerous appearances. As for 'demonstration,' that can be accomplished in various ways, either by pointing with the finger, or by teaching in a lesson, or by some other method. But the intellect does not know anything in Aristotelian fashion, nor does there exist any demonstration such as Aristotle describes it."

123. La Chambre, *Discourse,* 36.

124. *Exerc.*, bk. 2, exerc. 1, art. 5: Brush, 38–39; *OO* 3:151–52.

125. *Exerc.*, bk. 2, exerc. 6, art. 7: Brush, 102; *OO* 3:206. There are other similar strategic uses of language-as-use (*Exerc.*, bk. 3, exerc. 5, art. 4: Brush, 74; *OO* 3:186; *Exerc.*, bk. 2, exec. 4, art. 4: Brush, 67; *OO* 3:178).

126. *Syntag.*, Logic, bk. 2, chap. 5: Brush, 337; *OO* 1:83.

127. Margaret J. Osler, "Voluntarism and Latitudinarianism in the Thought of Robert Boyle," in *Philosophy, Science, and Religion in England, 1640–1700,* ed. Richard W. F. Kroll et al. (Cambridge: Cambridge Univ. Press, 1991). J. E. McGuire shows how Descartes is also a voluntarist in this theological sense. See "Boyle's Conception of Nature," *Journal of the History of Ideas* 33 (1972): 530.

128. For Descartes's impatience with the notion of *in partem utremque,* see *Meditations on First Philosophy* (1641), in *Philosophical Writings*, 2:5.

129. See Descartes's *Discourse on the Method,* in *Philosophical Writings,* 1:122. Significantly, Descartes sees the edifice of knowledge as constructed by a single architect or builder (ibid., 1:116).

130. *Exerc.,* bk. 2, exerc. 5, art. 5: Brush, 76−77; *OO* 3:188.

131. Marjorie Grene makes a similar argument to what follows, which is also partly indebted to Joy, and presents a sympathetic view of Gassendi's objections to Cartesianism: *Descartes* (Minneapolis: Univ. of Minnesota Press, 1985), chap. 6. Reb. to Med. 1, doubt 1: Brush, 169; *OO* 3:281; and Gassendi levels the same accusation against Aristotle (*Exerc.,* bk. 2, exerc. 1, art. 3: Brush, 33; *OO* 3:150).

132. Chapelain to Gassendi, 20 October 1640, in *Lettres de Jean Chapelain,* ed. Philippe Tamizey de Larroque, 2 vols. (Paris: Impr. Nationale, 1880−83), 1:706: "Je vous avoue que je ne souhaitte guère rien plus que la publication de cette solide physique qui se preuve par des exemples palpables et qui ne suppose rien qu'on puisse raisonnablement disputer" (cited by Joy, *Gassendi the Atomist,* 127n.85).

133. Williams, *Descartes,* 19.

134. *Discourse on the Method,* in *Philosophical Writings,* 1:112−13.

135. See Descartes's description of the use of writing in the *Discourse on the Method,* in *Philosophical Writings,* 1:144. He argues also that words may fade but we remember what they signify (*The World, or Treatise on Light* [1664], 1:81). He contrasts words with the Real Idea (*Rules for the Direction of the Mind,* 1:61.); see also ibid., 1:43; and ibid., 1:17: Descartes privileges the spark in the mind over illustration. I have already mentioned how Descartes sees writing as a disposable instrument, a proleptic to the pure communion of mind and idea (ibid., 1:67ff.). In the *Discourse,* too, he doubts the usefulness of writing (1:142).

136. See, for example, Descartes's prefatory letters to *The Passions of the Soul* (1649), in *Philosophical Writings,* 1:326ff. See also his dedication to Elizabeth of Bohemia, prefacing the *Principles of Philosophy,* in ibid., 1:190ff. Admittedly, one must expect a degree of hyperbole in such dedications, but even then, Descartes's language seems excessive.

137. Joy handles the biography of Peiresc especially well (*Gassendi the Atomist,* chap. 3).

138. *Exerc.,* Preface: Brush, 16ff.; *OO* 3:98ff.

139. *Exerc.,* Preface: Brush, 22−23; *OO* 3:101. Interestingly, Descartes also speaks of Theseus and the labyrinth (*Rules for the Direction of the Mind,* in *Philosophical Writings,* 1:20), but for him, following the clue of method leads to certainty (ibid., 1:16).

140. *IL,* pt. 4: Jones, 165; *OO* 1:123. On the Royal Society method of "cooperative compilation" of natural histories, see P. B. Wood, "Methodology and Apologetics: Thomas Sprat's *History of the Royal Society,*" *British Journal for the History of Science* 13 (1980): 1−26.

141. Descartes speaks of an absolute control over one's thoughts (*Discourse on the Method,* in *Philosophical Writings,* 1:124).

142. Descartes rejects majority opinion in *Discourse on the Method,* in *Philosophical Writings,* 1:119.

143. Descartes behaves as lord and master of nature (*Discourse on the Method,* in *Philosophical Writings,* 1:142−43) and as a military commander (ibid., 1:145).

144. Descartes, *Discourse on the Method*, in *Philosophical Writings*, 1:148.

145. This is precisely the view of Gassendi that Seth Ward holds in *Vindiciae Academiarum* (Oxford, 1654), 28.

146. See Alexandre Koyré, *From the Closed World to the Infinite Universe* (Baltimore: Johns Hopkins Univ. Press, 1968). Koyré writes that "the Epicurean tradition was not a scientific one," and his note elaborating that statement argues that the revival of Epicureanism by Gassendi "remained perfectly sterile" (5; 5n.7). See also Richard Westfall, *The Construction of Modern Science: Mechanisms and Mechanics* (1971; reprint, Cambridge: Cambridge Univ. Press, 1977). Westfall writes that "in a word, Gassendi was the original scissors and paste man, and his book [the *Syntagma Philosophicum*] contains all the inconsistencies of eclectic compilations" (39). I hope that my argument can confirm Joy's defense of Gassendi as deserving a less narrowly scientistic and more truly historical cultural commentary.

147. Koyré, "Gassendi: Le Savant," 61. See also Koyré, "Gassendi et la Science de Son Temps," in *Etudes d'Histoire de la Pensée Scientifique* (Paris: Presses Universitaires de France, 1966), 284–96. Koyré writes: "Si, *pour nous,* Gassendi n'est pas un grand savant, pour ses contemporains c'en était un, et même un très grand, l'égal et le rival de Descartes" (284–85).

148. Craig Brush, Introduction to Gassendi, *De Motu*, Brush, 116; see also Bougerel, *Vie de Pierre Gassendi*, 11; and Joy, *Gassendi the Atomist*, 127–29.

149. Brush, Commentary on Gassendi, *De Motu*, Brush, 132.

150. Georges Mongrédien describes how, owing to their length, complexity, and Latin vehicle, Gassendi's ideas did not immediately penetrate into the world of letters in the way Descartes's did; but at the same time, Gassendi established in the years 1641–42 a circle in Paris one can only describe as Epicurean in its intellectual and social ethos. See Georges Mongrédien, "Gassendi: L'Influence Immédiate," in *Pierre Gassendi, 1592–1655: Sa Vie et Son Oeuvre* (1955), 119ff. "Mais il y eût pour Gassendi un autre mode de diffusion de sa pensée, c'est l'action, d'une part de ses élèves, d'autre part, de ses amis" (120). The group included Luillier, at whose home Gassendi lived, Chapelle, Bernier, La Mothe Le Vayer, Dassoucy, Cyrano de Bergerac, and perhaps Molière.

151. See Antoine Adam, *Les Libertins au XVIIᵉ Siècle* (Paris: Buchet/Chastel, 1964), esp. intro.; Joan DeJean, *Libertine Strategies: Freedom and the Novel in Seventeenth-Century France* (Columbus: Ohio State Univ. Press, 1981), chap. 1; René Pintard, *La Mothe le Vayer, Gassendi, Guy Patin* (Paris: Boivin, n.d.); Pintard, *Le Libertinage Erudit dans la Première Moitié du XVIIᵉ Siècle*, 2 vols. (Paris: Boivin, 1943); and Popkin, *History of Scepticism*, chaps. 5 and 7.

152. Popkin, *History of Scepticism*, 88. Popkin cites a contemporary letter from Gui Patin, *Lettres de Gui Patin*, ed. Paul Triaire (Paris, 1907), 616–17.

153. The next chapter discusses the tenor of Gassendi's ethic as it was received by the English émigré group in the Paris of the 1640s.

154. See James Orchard Halliwell-Phillips, *A Collection of Letters Illustrative of the Progress of Science in England, from the Reign of Queen Elizabeth to that of Charles the Second* (London: Historical Society of Science, 1841), 86–87: "I perceive Mr. Hobbes esteems neither of [Reita's] glass nor beleevs his discoveries, for he is joined in a great friendship with Gassendes" (Sir Charles Cavendish to John Pell, 10/20 December 1644).

155. See, for example, Pierre Gassendi, *Lettres Familières de Gassendi à François Lullier Pendant l'Hiver 1632-1633*, ed. and intro. Bernard Rochot (Paris: Vrin, 1944).

156. Mongrédien, "Gassendi: L'Influence Immédiate," 137.

157. In this preface, Sorbière treats Descartes as a dogmatist (Joy, *Gassendi the Atomist*, 211). See also Bougerel, *Vie de Pierre Gassendi*, 222–28. About Gassendi's concern about the ordering of his texts, including the *Animadversiones* and the *Opera Omnia*, see Bernard Rochot, "Gassendi: Vie et Charactère," in *Pierre Gassendi: Vie et Oeuvre*, 46–47.

158. See Joy, *Gassendi the Atomist*, chap. 3. This biography was translated into English by William Rand as *The Mirrour of True Nobility and Gentility* (London, 1657). Locke frequently refers to this book in his notebooks from the period 1655–65 (see Bodleian MS Locke f. 14).

159. Gassendi published *De Vita et Moribus Epicuri* in 1647; this was followed by the *Animadversiones in Decimum Librum Diogenis Laertii* (1649) and the *Philosophiae Epicuri Syntagma* (1649), and the synthetic *Syntagma Philosophicum*, posthumously published in the *Opera Omnia* of 1658.

160. See, for example, Bougerel, *Vie de Pierre Gassendi*, 155 on Gassendi's antiquarianism. See also ibid., 292–93; 324–25. Walter Charleton was to translate Lady Margaret Cavendish's famous biography of her husband; and in an early notebook, Locke records his reading in Gassendi primarily by reference to Gassendi's biography of Peiresc. See Bodleian MS Locke f. 14, passim.

161. Bougerel, *Vie de Pierre Gassendi*, 67–68.

162. Ibid., 292–93. Bougerel elsewhere discusses Gassendi attacking astrology and forms of gnostic and hermetic knowledge; Bougerel also describes his presenting a history of astronomy in the preface to his life of Tycho Brahe. All these Bougerel believes, and I argue, must be seen as expressions of a consistent epistemologico-ethical program.

163. Ibid., Sig. āiijᵛ.

164. Ibid., 24–25; 382.

165. Ibid., 129.

166. Ibid., 290.

167. See chapter three above.

168. Bougerel, *Vie de Pierre Gassendi*, 104; and also Gassendi, *OO* 6:46; 48.

169. Bougerel, *Vie de Pierre Gassendi*, 130–31.

170. *Lettres Familières à François Lullier*, 24n.46.

171. Ibid., 52.

172. It is also possible that the roll suggests to Gassendi the openness of the Epicurean approach to knowledge, a commitment to the linearity of experience and language that Achitophel will attack in *Absalom and Achitophel* as the "mouldy rolls" of history (l. 302), whereas the book here represents the containment of knowledge in peculiarly commodified and entrapped forms.

173. On the wise man's "Sepultre," see Charleton, *Epicurus's Morals* (London, 1656), 97.

5. "Living and Speaking Statues": Domesticating Epicurus

1. Lucy Hutchinson had already completed a translation of Lucretius in manuscript (see BM Add. MS 19.333). She refers to making the translation while attending to her young children, which probably places the translation in the 1640s, taking a cue from her *Memoirs of the Life of Colonel Hutchinson,* ed. James Sutherland (London: Oxford Univ. Press, 1973), 33–34.

2. John Evelyn, *An Essay on the First Book of T. Lucretius Carus De Rerum Natura Interpreted and Made English Verse* (London, 1656), 109. Sixteen hundred and fifty-six was a year of wonders, in that it also saw the publication of Walter Charleton's *Epicurus's Morals,* following the publication of his *Physiologia Epicuro-Gassendo-Charletoniana* (London, 1654).

3. I adopt Joy's argument that Gassendi's *Animadversiones,* never printed entire in the *Opera Omnia,* represents Gassendi's most synthetic philosophical oeuvre prior to the publication of the large *Syntagma Philosophicum* (1658), which Evelyn could not have known in 1656. Although she refers to Evelyn's translation of Lucretius, Joy does not seem to notice that it adumbrates a comprehensive grasp of Gassendi's published work and therefore indicates a knowledge of Gassendi in circles that were profoundly to influence Restoration culture. Evelyn cites many of Gassendi's works, including the *Animadversiones* in his *Essay* at 109; 110; 123; 131; 135; 136; 138 *[Animadversiones]*; 147; 169; 172 *[Animadversiones]*. See Lynn Sumida Joy, *Gassendi the Atomist: Advocate of History in an Age of Science* (Cambridge: Cambridge Univ. Press, 1987), 70. The specificity of relations between Gassendi and English cultural figures is suggested by the striking fact that the figure of Epicurus on the title page of Gassendi's *De Vita et Moribus Epicuri* (1647) and his *Animadversiones* (1649) is virtually identical to the frontispiece of Walter Charleton's *Epicurus' Morals* (1656) (see pp. 153–54 above). The image of Epicurus is almost literally and physically the vehicle of cultural transmission.

4. Writing to Jeremy Taylor on 27 April 1656, Evelyn says that "my Essay upon Lucretius, which I told you was engaged, is now printing, and (as I understand) near finished: my animadversions upon it will I hope provide against all the ill consequences, and totally acquit me either of glory or impiety" (*Diary and Correspondence of John Evelyn, F.R.S.,* 4 vols. [London: Bohn, 1859], 3:73). References to Evelyn's letters are to this edition and will appear as *Corres.*

5. Evelyn, *Essay,* Sig. A6^v.

6. William Rand, trans., *The Mirrour of True Nobility and Gentility. Being the Life of the Renowned Nicolaus Claudius Fabricius Lord of Peiresk, Senator of the Parliament at Aix. Written by the Learned Petrus Gassendus . . .* (London, 1657), Sig. A3^v.

7. Ibid., Sig. A6^r.

8. Ibid., 6:202. The book has odd pagination, so my references may appear slightly misleading.

9. Ibid., 6:203.

10. Ibid., 6:204.

11. Ibid.

12. A classic case occurs in Marie Boas's monograph "The Establishment of the Mechanical Philosophy," *Osiris* 10 (1952): 412–541, a canonical text in the historiography of midcentury natural philosophy. For Boas, Bacon and Descartes are the two

"heroes" of the story. I am proposing that, in contrast to the attention lavished on these two hugely authoritative figures, we also admire less epic—and perhaps more enduring—values for the narrative of cultural history.

13. Evelyn, *Essay,* Sig. A3^r.

14. Ibid., Sig. A5^r.

15. See Richard Westfall, "Some Unpublished Boyle Papers Relating to Scientific Method," *Annals of Science* 12 (1956): 63–73; 103–17.

16. I refer to Evelyn's *Essay on . . . Lucretius* (1656) and to Thomas Creech's translation of *De Rerum Natura,* which appeared first in 1682, but reappeared regularly thereafter. The "third edition" of Creech's translation, published in 1683, includes a series of poems to Creech by such authors as Evelyn, Nahum Tate, Thomas Otway, Aphra Behn, and E[dmund] W[aller]. Dryden translated parts of Lucretius in *Sylvae* (1685).

17. A careful assessment of relations between Descartes and More is to be found in Alan Gabbey, "Philosophia Cartesiana Triumphata: Henry More (1646–1671)," in *Problems of Cartesianism,* ed. Thomas H. Lennon et al. (Kingston, Montreal: McGill-Queen's Univ. Press, 1982), 171–250.

18. See, for example, Joseph Glanvill, *The Vanity of Dogmatizing* (London, 1661), 146, and the commentary on Sprat in Charles Webster, "The Origins of the Royal Society," *History of Science* 6 (1967): 116–19.

19. R. H. Kargon describes how William Boswell, who inherited Bacon's manuscripts and in response to the emergence of the mechanical hypothesis, arranged to have his atomistic works, *inter alia,* published in 1653, under the title *Scripta in Naturalia et Universalia Philosophia* (*Atomism in England from Hariot to Newton* [Oxford: Clarendon Press, 1966], 52).

20. Brian Vickers, for example, shows that the polemics surrounding the nature of language in the Restoration had less to do with substance than the institutional position of the combatants: the appropriation of Bacon was primarily symbolic ("The Royal Society and English Prose Style: A Reassessment," in *Rhetoric and the Pursuit of Truth: Language Change in the Seventeenth and Eighteenth Centuries* [Los Angeles: William Andrews Clark Memorial Library, 1985], 3–76).

21. See, variously, Robert G. Frank, *Harvey and the Oxford Physiologists: A Study of Scientific Ideas* (Berkeley: Univ. of California Press, 1980), chap. 4; A. R. Hall, *The Scientific Revolution, 1500–1800: The Formation of the Modern Scientific Attitude,* 2d ed. (Boston: Beacon Press, 1962), 166–68; Michael Hunter, *Science and Society in Restoration England* (Cambridge: Cambridge Univ. Press, 1981), passim; M. M. Slaughter, *Universal Languages and Scientific Taxonomy in the Seventeenth Century* (Cambridge: Cambridge Univ. Press, 1982), 90–100; and Richard S. Westfall, *The Construction of Modern Science: Mechanisms and Mechanics* (1971; reprint, Cambridge: Cambridge Univ. Press, 1977), 114.

22. See, for example, John W. Yolton, *Locke and the Compass of Human Understanding* (Cambridge: Cambridge Univ. Press, 1970), 7, which stresses Locke's Baconianism.

23. This is the distinction that Evelyn communicates between Boyle's critical method and Bacon's less discriminate inductivism. See *Corres.,* 3:348: Talking of Boyle, Evelyn writes that "never did stubborn matter come under his inquisition but

he extorted a confession of all that lay in her most intimate recesses; and what he discovered he as faithfully registered, and frankly communicated; in this exceeding my Lord Verulam, who (though never to be mentioned without honour and admiration) was used to tell all that came to hand without much examination."

24. See Thomas Sprat, *Observations on Monsieur Sorbière's Voyage into England* (London, 1665), 233–34: "I scarce know two men in the World, that have more different colors of Speech, than these two great Witts: the Lord *Bacon* short, allusive, and abounding with Metaphors: Mr. *Hobbs* round, close, sparing of similitudes: but ever extraordinary decent in them. The one's way of reas'ning, proceeds on particulars, and pleasant images, only suggesting new ways of experimenting, without any pretence to the *Mathematicks*. The other's bold, resolv'd, setled upon general conclusions, and in them, if we will believe his *Friend, Dogmatical.*"

25. Samuel Sorbière, *Relation d'un Voyage en Angleterre, Ou sont Touchées Plusieurs Choses, qui Regardent l'Estat des Sciences, et de la Religion, et Autres Matières Curieuses* (Paris, 1664).

26. Sprat, *Observations*, 110–11.

27. Ibid., 180.

28. Sorbière, *Relation*, 91; 93.

29. Ibid., 92.

30. Ibid., 94; 82–83.

31. Sprat, *Observations*, 241–42.

32. See Thomas Franklin Mayo, *Epicurus in England, 1650–1725* (Dallas: Southwest Press, 1934), 170.

33. The *National Union Catalogue* and *Short Title Catalogue* record the following publications for Gassendi: *Institutio Astronomica* (1653; anr. ed., 1653; 1674; 1675; 1683; 1702); *Institutio Logica et Philosophiae Epicuri Syntagma* (1660; 1668); *The Mirrour of True Nobility and Gentility* (1657); *Three Discourses of Happiness, Virtue, and Liberty* (1699); and *The Vanity of Judiciary Astrology* (1659; anr. ed., 1659). I have also shown that the section on Epicurus in volume three of Thomas Stanley's popular *History of Philosophy* (1655–62; vol. 3: 1659) is a translation of Gassendi's *Philosophiae Epicuri Syntagma*. And, finally, Walter Charleton's *Physiologia Epicuro-Gassendo-Charletoniana* (1654) is often treated as a redaction of Gassendist views.

34. The *Short Title Catalogue* and the *Gallery of Ghosts* record the following titles for Descartes: *A Discourse of Method* (1649); *Renati Descartes Epistolae* (1668; 1683); *Ethice* (1685); *Renatus Descartes Excellent Compendium of Music* (1653); *Exercitationes* (1685); *R. des Cartes Meditationes* (1664; anr. ed., 1664); *The Passions of the Soule* (1650); *Principia Philosophiae* (1664); *Six Metaphysical Meditations* (1680); *Specrmene Philosophiae* (1667); and *The Use of the Geometrical Playing Cards* (1697).

35. See C. T. Harrison, "The Ancient Atomists and English Literature of the Seventeenth Century," *Harvard Studies in Classical Philology* 45 (1934): 1–79; and "Bacon, Hobbes, Boyle, and the Ancient Atomists," *Harvard University Studies and Notes in Philology and Literature* 15 (1933): 191–218.

36. Harrison, "Ancient Atomists," 23.

37. Kargon, *Atomism in England*, chap. 8; Harrison, "Ancient Atomists," 56ff. A particularly vivid example of the degree to which influential writers were acquainted with neo-Epicureanism is Edward Stillingfleet's *Origines Sacrae: Or a Rational Ac-*

count of the Grounds of the Christian Faith (1662; 3d ed., Cambridge, 1701). Already in 1662, Stillingfleet records "the *Atomical* or *Epicurean Hypothesis*" as "that which makes most noise in the World" (301), and, though he attacks its materialist implications, he actually seeks to subordinate the atomic hypothesis to providence. One device Stillingfleet uses is to attack the potential dogmatism of Epicurean physics by resorting to Epicurus's own probabilistic criteria for knowledge in his canon (303). Stillingfleet displays a considerable acquaintance with Gassendi's *Opera Omnia* (e.g., 307; 309).

38. Cudworth pushes Greek atomism back to Empedocles, Pythagoras, and Anaxagoras, accusing Democritus and Leucippus of being "the first atheizers of this ancient Atomic physiology" (*The True Intellectual System of the Universe,* ed. Thomas Birch, 4 vols. [London: R. Priestley, 1820], 1:53); and John Smith, attacking Epicurus in great detail, reminds his readers that Democritus was "the first Author" of the atomic thesis (*Select Discourses* [London, 1660], 47).

39. See for example, Kargon's comment on *The Origin of Forms and Qualities* in *Atomism in England,* 99.

40. Slaughter writes, however, that "for the most part, the early Royal Society was firm in asserting its opposition to hypothetical physics. . . . The 'empirics' rejected all theories and asserted the primacy of natural history—of the minute observation of phenomena and the recording of data" (*Universal Languages,* 190). She sees Locke as a hypotheticalist and Boyle and Hooke as "empirics." These dichotomies seem too absolute.

41. M. A. Stewart, ed. and intro., *Selected Philosophical Papers of Robert Boyle* (Manchester: Manchester Univ. Press, 1979), xxx.

42. Richard S. Westfall, "Some Unpublished Boyle Papers Relating to Scientific Method," *Annals of Science* 12 (1956): 63–73; 103–17.

43. Cudworth, *True Intellectual System,* 1:53.

44. Danton B. Sailor, "Moses and Atomism," *Journal of the History of Ideas* 25 (1964): 3–16; see also E. A. Burtt, *The Metaphysical Foundations of Modern Science: The Scientific Thinking of Copernicus, Galileo, Newton, and Their Contemporaries* (1924; reprint, Atlantic Highlands, N.J.: Humanities Press, 1980), 149.

45. Cudworth, *True Intellectual System,* 1:20.

46. Ibid., 2:123.

47. Cudworth must be one of the last people to have defended the authenticity of the hermetic corpus against Isaac Casaubon's devastating criticisms of it (*True Intellectual System,* 2:124–30). For Isaac Casaubon's effect on hermeticism, see Anthony Grafton, "Protestant versus Prophet: Isaac Casaubon on Hermes Trismegistus," *Journal of the Warburg and Courtauld Institutes* 46 (1983): 78–93; Grafton is elaborating in part the suggestion of Frances A. Yates, *Giordano Bruno and the Hermetic Tradition* (New York: Vintage, 1964), 423–37.

48. Henry More also shares something of this peculiar midcentury ambivalence toward atomism and method. For a discussion of the difference between More and Stillingfleet on these and related issues, see Alison Coudert, "Limits of Latitudinarianism: Henry More's Reaction to the Kabbala and Quakerism"; and Sarah Hutton, "Neoplatonism and Latitudinarianism: Henry More, Edward Stillingfleet and the Decline of *Moses Atticus,*" in *Philosophy, Science, and Religion in England, 1640–*

1700 (Cambridge: Cambridge Univ. Press, 1991), ed. Richard W. F. Kroll et al. John Tulloch provides a critique of Cudworth's uncritical method: see *Rational Theology and Christian Philosophy in England in the Seventeenth Century*, 2 vols. (Edinburgh: Blackwood, 1872), 2:479–80; and Joseph M. Levine refers to More's "hopelessly unhistorical" use of the ancient wisdom ("Latitudinarians, Neoplatonists, and the Ancient Wisdom," in *Philosophy, Science, and Religion*).

49. *True Intellectual System*, 2:64.

50. Ibid., 4:211.

51. Ibid., 2:328.

52. Theophilus Gale, *The Court of the Gentiles: Or A Discourse Touching the Original of Human Literature, both Philologie and Philosophie, from the Scriptures, and Jewish Church* (London, 1669), Sig. π3ʳ; italics reversed.

53. Ibid., Sig π2ᵛ.

54. Ibid., Sig. π3ʳ; italics reversed.

55. Ibid., 14.

56. See Thomas Harmon Jobe, "The Devil in Restoration Science," *Isis* 72 (1981): 343–56.

57. Richard Bentley, *The Folly and Unreasonableness of Atheism* (1692; 5th ed. entitled *Eight Sermons Preach'd at the Honourable Robert Boyle's Lecture* [London, 1724]).

58. Ibid., 125.

59. Ibid., 61.

60. Mayo, *Epicurus in England*, 191–92.

61. Thomas Creech, trans., *T. Lucretius Carus, Of the Nature of Things* (London, 1715). Creech died in 1700. Cosmo Alexander Gordon points out that the '1715' edition is a state of the 1714 edition (*A Bibliography of Lucretius* [London: Hart-Davis, 1962], 178–79). He also suggest that the additional reflections are by John Digby, the translator of *Epicurus' Morals* (ibid., 171).

62. See chapter four above, n.6.

63. Joy, *Gassendi the Atomist*, chap. 9.

64. See Kargon, *Atomism in England*, chaps. 8 and 9.

65. J. B. van Helmont, *Deliramenta Catarrhi*, trans. Walter Charleton (London, 1650); *A Ternary of Paradoxes*, trans. Walter Charleton (London, 1650).

66. Kargon, *Atomism in England*, 86.

67. See Richard W. F. Kroll, "The Question of Locke's Relation to Gassendi," *Journal of the History of Ideas* 45 (1984): 339–59. Although I demonstrate this fact, I mistake the 'small' *Syntagma* (1649)—which Stanley translated—for Gassendi's 'large,' final *Syntagma Philosophicum* (1658).

68. See "An Account of the Life and Writings of *Thomas Stanley, Esq.*," in Thomas Stanley, *The History of Philosophy*, 3d ed. (London, 1701), Sig. d1ᵛ.

69. The *National Union Catalogue* records the following: *The History of Chaldaic Philosophy* (1662; 1687; 1701); and *The Life of Socrates* (1701).

70. See *The Evelyn Library*, 4 vols. (London: Christie's, 1977–78), 3, item #1409; John Harrison and Peter Laslett, eds., *The Library of John Locke*, 2d ed. (Oxford: Clarendon Press, 1971), item ##758; 2755; John Harrison, ed., *The Library of Isaac Newton* (Cambridge: Cambridge Univ. Press, 1978), item ##1551–1552.

71. Jackson I. Cope, *Joseph Glanvill: Anglican Apologist* (Saint Louis: Washington Univ. Studies, 1956), 133–39.

72. Stanley writes that "the Learned *Gassendus* was my precedent" (*The History of Philosophy*, Sig. $\pi2^r$).

73. Ibid., Sig. $\pi2^v$ (italics reversed).

74. Additionally, Bernier's important *Abrégé de la Philosophie de Mr. Gassendi* (Paris, 1674) was issued five times in the first ten years of its existence.

75. Margaret C. Jacob, *The Newtonians and the English Revolution, 1689–1720* (Ithaca: Cornell University Press, 1976), 33.

76. For details of Evelyn's life, see the introduction to E. S. de Beer, ed., *The Diary of John Evelyn*, 6 vols. (Oxford: Clarendon Press, 1955), 1:1–43.

77. Thomas Stanley, *Historia Philosophiae* (Leipzig, 1711). In the section devoted to Epicurus (pt. 12, 924–1110), there are sixty-seven references to the *Animadversiones* in the marginalia, almost exactly half of them in the section on ethics.

78. *The Autobiography of Giambattista Vico*, ed. Max Harold Fisch and Thomas Goddard Bergin (1944; reprint, Ithaca: Cornell Univ. Press, 1963), 126; 128.

79. *The Works of the Honourable Robert Boyle*, ed. Thomas Birch, 2d ed., 6 vols. (London, 1772), 6:724.

80. Ibid., 1:194.

81. Ibid., 1:222.

82. Kargon, *Atomism in England*, 63; and Frank, *Harvey and the Oxford Physiologists*, 90–93.

83. Helen Hervey, "Hobbes and Descartes in the Light of Some Unpublished Letters of the Correspondence between Sir Charles Cavendish and Dr. John Pell," *Osiris*, 10 (1952): 67–90.

84. In the dedication to *The Mirrour of True Nobility and Gentility*, Rand mentions his friendship with Hartlib (*"Harlib"*), who had ten years previously recommended Gassendi's life of Peiresc to him (Sig. A3^r).

85. Robert Vaughan, D.D., ed., *The Protectorate of Oliver Cromwell, and the State of Europe during the Early Part of the Reign of Louis XIV*, 2 vols. (London: Henry Colburn, 1838), 2:367–68.

86. Ibid., 2:370.

87. Hervey, "Hobbes and Descartes," 78.

88. Ibid., 73.

89. James Orchard Halliwell-Phillips, *A Collection of Letters Illustrative of the Progress of Science in England, from the Reign of Queen Elizabeth to that of Charles the Second* (London: London Historical Society of Science, 1841), 86.

90. Ibid., 87.

91. Vaughan, *Protectorate*, 2:371–72.

92. Hervey, "Hobbes and Descartes," 73.

93. Ibid., 85.

94. Halliwell-Phillips, *Collection of Letters*, 80.

95. Ibid.

96. Hervey, "Hobbes and Descartes," 78.

97. Ibid.

98. Ibid.

99. Ibid., 80.

100. Boyle, *Works*, 1:xli.

101. Ibid., 6:76.

102. Ibid., 1:xxxvii.

103. Ibid., 1:xli.

104. Ibid., 1:xxxviii.

105. Ibid., 1:xxxix.

106. Ibid., 1:xl.

107. Ibid. This metaphor of coinage also occurs in Rand's translation of Gassendi's life of Peiresc.

108. On the role of corresponding societies and learned colleges, see Charles Webster, ed., *Samuel Hartlib and the Advancement of Learning* (Cambridge: Cambridge Univ. Press, 1970), 30.

109. Gassendi, *De Vita et Moribus Epicuri* (Lyon, 1647), Sigs. II2^v-II3^r. It was approved on 5 August 1647.

110. Boyle, *Works*, 6:77.

111. Ibid.

112. *The Correspondence of Henry Oldenburg*, ed. A. Rupert Hall and Marie Boas Hall, 9 vols. (Madison: Univ. of Wisconsin Press, 1965–73), 2:42. In *Some Considerations touching the Usefulness of Experimental Natural Philosophy*, Boyle writes in praise of Epicurus: "And as confident as those we speak of use to be, of knowing the true and adequate causes of things, yet *Epicurus* himself, as appears by ancient testimony, and by his own writings, was more modest, not only contenting himself, on many occasions, to propose several possible ways, whereby a phaenomenon may be accounted for, but sometimes seeming to dislike the so pitching upon any one explication, as to exclude and reject all others: and some modern philosophers, that much favour his doctrine, do likewise imitate his example, in pretending to assign not precisely the true, but possible causes of the phaenomenon they endeavour to explain" (*Works*, 2:45).

113. See E. S. de Beer, introduction to *The Diary of John Evelyn*, 1:10. And also Evelyn's own dedication to Sir Richard Browne in *Publick Employment and an Active Life Prefer'd to Solitude* (London, 1667), Sigs. A4^v-A5^r: "I might here mention the constant *Asylum* which the Persecuted *Clergy* found within your *walls* upon all occasions. . . . When your *Chappel* was the *Church* of *England* in her most *glorious estate*." For a description of the state of the church in exile during the Interregnum, see R. S. Bosher, *The Making of the Restoration Settlement: The Influence of the Laudians, 1649–1662* (Westminster: Dacre Press, 1951), chap. 2.

114. Taylor to Evelyn, 16 April 1656, *Corres.*, 3:71. See also Seth Lerer, *Boethius and Dialogue: Literary Method in the Consolation of Philosophy* (Princeton: Princeton Univ. Press, 1985), 32ff., for a commentary on the epistemological and literary significance of the Ciceronian dialogue.

115. Like *De Rerum Natura*, the *Tusculanian Disputations* occur in five movements.

116. For example, Evelyn's correspondents include Wilkins, Sprat, Boyle, Hartlib, Jeremy Taylor, Pepys, Clifford, Creech, Meric Casaubon, Lady Margaret Cavendish, Wotton, Sir Thomas Browne, and Glanvill.

117. Charleton predicts a relationship between reading and friendship in *Epicurus's Morals,* when he writes to his reader that "if the Rule hold, that Similitude of Opinions, is an argument of Similitude in Affections, and Similitude of Affections the ground of Love and friendship, certainly I am not altogether destitute of support for my conjectures, and consequently that you will soone admitt him [Epicurus] into your bosome" (Sig. A4ʳ).

118. On the Taylor-Evelyn friendship, see Tulloch, *Rational Theology,* 1:366–67. Jeremy Taylor's *A Discourse of the Nature, Offices and Measures of Friendship with Rules of Conducting it. Written in answer to a Letter from the Most Ingenious and Vertuous M.[rs] K.[atharine] P.[hilips]* (London, 1657; reprint, London: Chapman and Hall, 1920) includes an appendix consisting of two exemplary letters.

119. Taylor to Evelyn, *Corres.,* 3:94.

120. Ibid., 3:97.

121. Evelyn records in his diary that he began planting for his garden on 17 January 1653: "This was the beginning of all the succceeding *Gardens, Walkes, Groves, Enclosures* & *Plantations* there." See John Evelyn, *Diary,* ed. E. S. De Beer, 6 vols. (London: Oxford Univ. Press, 1955), 3:80.

122. In his diary, Evelyn records a number of visits to Sayes Court, mostly by royalists, including King Charles II himself. But the entry for 1 May 1657 reads: "There had ben at my house this afternoone *Laurence* president of *Olivers* Council, & some other of his Court Lords to see my Garden and plantations."

123. Taylor, *Discourse,* 58.

124. Ibid., 59.

125. Rand, *Mirrour of True Nobility and Gentility,* Sig. A6ʳ.

126. For bibliographic commentary, as well as illustrations of the Jansson and Marolles frontispieces, see Cosmo Alexander Gordon, *A Bibliography of Lucretius* (London: Hart-Davis, 1962), 135–36; 154–55; and 172–75.

127. Thomas P. Roche, Jr., has suggested in conversation that Mary Evelyn's early training in Renaissance iconology could have come to her in France, through the second school of Fontainebleau.

128. For a reading of this icon, see Thomas P. Roche, Jr., *The Kindly Flame: A Study of the Third and Fourth Books of Spencer's "Faerie Queene"* (Princeton: Princeton Univ. Press, 1964), 23–26.

129. Interestingly, Evelyn himself describes the revision or rendering orthodox of cultural figures in terms of the activity of denuding a female image (Evelyn to Taylor, 27 April 1656, *Corres.,* 3:73–74).

130. Evelyn was himself to design the famous frontispiece to Sprat's *History of the Royal Society.*

131. See John Wilkins to Evelyn, 16 August 1656, *Corres.,* 3:76; and Evelyn to Meric Casaubon, 15 July 1674, *Corres.,* 3:246–47.

132. Taylor to Evelyn, 9 October 1656, *Corres.,* 3:78n.

133. Evelyn to William Wotton, 30 March 1696, *Corres.,* 3:349.

134. Taylor to Evelyn, 9 October 1656, *Corres.,* 3:72.

135. Taylor to Evelyn, 29 August 1657, *Corres.,* 3:98ff.

136. Taylor to Evelyn, 9 October 1656, *Corres.,* 3:73.

137. Evelyn to Wotton, 12 September 1703, *Corres.,* 3:391.

138. Evelyn to Mr. Maddox, 10 January 1656–7, *Corres.*, 3:85; see also Evelyn to Wotton, 30 March 1696, *Corres.*, 3:346.

139. Evelyn to Wotton, 12 September 1703, *Corres.*, 3:395–96. The myth demonstrates by an almost parabolic narrative that the two families are allied by blood.

140. *Diary*, 10 July 1654.

141. See Evelyn to Wotton, 12 September 1703, *Corres.*, 3:391.

142. Evelyn to Robert Boyle, 9 August 1659, *Corres.*, 3:114.

143. Ibid., 3:115.

144. Evelyn to Lord Viscount Cornbury, 9 September 1665, *Corres.*, 3:167. Later, we discover in a letter to Pepys that Durdans is also one of those loci in which cultural artifacts are being gathered.

145. Evelyn to Boyle, 3 September 1659, *Corres.*, 3:116.

146. Ibid., 3:117.

147. Ibid.

148. Ibid., 3:119.

149. Ibid., 116.

150. Evelyn to Samuel Pepys, 12 August 1689, *Corres.*, 3:295.

151. Ibid., 3:304; 308.

152. Ibid., 3:295.

153. Ibid., 3:302.

154. Evelyn mentions that Prince Henry's collection of ten thousand medals was dispersed by the Civil War (ibid., 3:305–6); he also fears that Ashmole's collection may have been destroyed by fire (ibid., 3:299).

155. Ibid., 3:300.

156. Ibid., 3:302.

157. See Evelyn, *Instructions concerning Erecting of a Library* (London, 1661); and *Corres.*, 3:303: "Yes, he was a great lover at least of books, and furnished a very ample library, writ himself an elegant style, favoured and promoted the design of the Royal Society; and it was for this, and in particular, for his being very kind to me both abroad and at home, that I sent *Naudaeus* to him in a dedicatory address, of which I am not so much ashamed as of the translation."

158. Evelyn uses an extended image of dismemberment (*Corres.*, 3:309) and also refers to the new mode of writing as embodying "nervous, natural strength, and beauty, genuine and of our own growth" (ibid., 3:311).

159. Evelyn refers to Wren's "sumptuous structure" (*Corres.*, 3:306).

160. *Corres.*, 3:311.

161. Ibid., 3:310.

162. Ibid., 3:297.

163. Ibid.

164. Ibid., 3:304.

165. For example, Evelyn refers us to "sundry more of that fair sex who ruled the world" (ibid., 3:298).

166. *Corres.*, 3:298.

167. Ibid., 3:296.

168. Ibid., 3:299.

169. Evelyn to Lord Godolphin, 16 June 1696, *Corres.*, 3:354ff.

170. Ibid., 3:354.

171. Ibid., 3:355.

172. Evelyn to Pepys, 12 August 1689, *Corres.*, 3:297.

173. Sir Geoffrey Keynes, *John Evelyn: A Study in Bibliophily with a Bibliography of His Writing* (Oxford: Clarendon Press, 1968), 231.

174. Ibid.

175. Evelyn to Pepys, 12 August 1689, *Corres.*, 3:303-4.

176. Ibid., 3:304.

6. "Somaticall Science": Neoclassical Linguistics, Action, and Writing

1. For discussions of language theory and language schemes in the seventeenth and eighteenth centuries, see Hans Aarsleff, *From Locke to Saussure: Essays on the Study of Language and Intellectual History* (Minneapolis: Univ. of Minnesota Press, 1982); "Language and Knowledge in the Sixteenth and Seventeenth Centuries" (1964); also *The Study of Language in England, 1780-1860* (1967; reprint, Minneapolis: Univ. of Minnesota Press, 1983); E. N. da C. Andrade, "The Real Character of Bishop Wilkins," *Annals of Science* 1 (1936): 4-12; Sidonie Clauss, "John Wilkins' Essay Toward a Real Character: Its Place in the Seventeenth-Century Episteme," *Journal of the History of Ideas* 43 (1982): 531-53; Jonathan Cohen, "On the Project of a Universal Character," *Mind* 63 (1954): 49-63; Murray Cohen, *Sensible Words: Linguistic Practice in England, 1640-1785* (Baltimore: Johns Hopkins Univ. Press, 1977); Paul Cornelius, *Languages in Seventeenth- and Early Eighteenth-Century Imaginary Voyages* (Geneva: Droz, 1965); Benjamin DeMott, "Science versus Mnemonics: Notes on John Ray and on John Wilkins' *Essay toward a Real Character, and a Philosophical Language*," *Isis* 48 (1957): 3-12; R. F. Jones, *The Triumph of the English Language: A Survey of Opinions Concerning the Vernacular from the Introduction of Printing to the Restoration* (1953; reprint, Stanford: Stanford Univ. Press, 1966); James Knowlson, *Universal Language Schemes in England and France, 1600-1800* (Toronto: Univ. of Toronto Press, 1975); Stephen K. Land, *The Philosophy of Language in Britain: Major Theories from Hobbes to Thomas Reid* (New York: AMS Press, 1986); *From Signs to Propositions: The Concept of Form in Eighteenth-Century Semantic Theory* (London: Longman, 1974); Vivian Salmon, *The Study of Language in Seventeenth-Century England* (Amsterdam: Benjamins, 1979); M. M. Slaughter, *Universal Languages and Scientific Taxonomy in the Seventeenth Century* (Cambridge: Cambridge Univ. Press, 1982); and James Thompson, *Language in Wycherley's Plays: Seventeenth-Century Language Theory and Drama* (University: Univ. of Alabama Press, 1984).

2. See, for example, Cohen, *Sensible Words,* xxiv.

3. See Slaughter, *Universal Languages,* chap. 9. I disagree with Slaughter's persistent assumption that taxonomy and printing must prejudice scientific description in favor of an essentialist taxonomy. Indeed, one purpose of my argument is to show that printing and taxonomy came to serve as metaphors for the *anti*-essentialist ethic I describe.

4. See Land, *From Signs to Propositions,* 184ff.

5. For this point in relation to Condillac, see Aarsleff, *From Locke to Saussure,* 30; 210-24.

6. See Jayne E. Lewis, "Reinventing the Neoclassical Fable." Ph.D. diss., Princeton Univ., 1988. I owe much to this dissertation for helping me formulate parts of the argument that follows.

7. Daniel Defoe, *An Essay upon Literature: Or, An Enquiry into the Antiquity and Original of Letters* (London, 1726), 12.

8. See, for example, Aarsleff, *From Locke to Saussure*, 278–92.

9. René Descartes to Marin Mersenne, 20 November 1629, in *Correspondance du P. Marin Mersenne*, ed. C. de Waard, 16 vols. (Paris: Presses Universitaires de France, 1937), 2:323–28.

10. Physiognomy naturally provides a means to talk about the inferential nature of human knowledge, but there is also a strong tradition, extending back to Aristotle and especially Galen, in which facial and bodily signs are also thought of as an exact means by which to mark character. As we shall see below, both attitudes inform John Bulwer.

11. See, for example, Edward Stillingfleet, *Origines Sacrae: Or a Rational Account of the Grounds of the Christian Faith, as to the Truth and Divine Authority of the Scriptures* (1662; 3d ed., Cambridge, 1701), 13.

12. The recognition of the authority embedded in the acquisition of language also informs the Lucretian accounts of the origins of speech. See, for example, Walter Charleton, *Epicurus's Morals* (London, 1656), in *"Of the Originall of Right and Justice"*; and also Thomas Stanley, *The History of Philosophy,* 3d ed. (London, 1701), 591–92.

13. See Samuel Hartlib, *The True and Readie Way to Learne the Latine Tongue* (London, 1654); and Robert Hooke, "Dr. Hook's Method of Making Experiments," in *Philosophical Experiments and Observations of the Late Dr. Robert Hooke, S.R.S.* (London, 1736), 26–28; and William Petty, *The Advice of W.P. to Mr. Samuel Hartlib, for the Advancement of Some Particular Parts of Learning.* (London, 1648), in *Harleian Miscellany,* 8 vols. (London, 1744–46), 6:1–13.

14. John Wilkins, *An Essay towards a Real Character and a Philosophical Language* (London, 1668), 2.

15. Ibid.

16. Ibid., 2; 3–4; 4; 6.

17. "Now spoken sounds are symbols of affections in the soul, and written marks symbols of spoken sounds. And just as written marks are not the same for all men, neither are spoken sounds. But what these are in the first place signs of—affections of the soul—are the same for all; and what these affections are likenesses of—actual things—are also the same" (Aristotle, *Categories and De Interpretatione,* trans. J. L. Ackrill [Oxford: Clarendon Press, 1963], 43).

18. Wilkins, *Essay,* Sig. a3^v.

19. Ibid., Sig. a2^r.

20. Ibid., 21; 20; 21; 20.

21. "That *conceit* which men have in their minds concerning a Horse or Tree, is the Notion or *mental image* of that Beast, or natural thing, of such a nature, shape and use. The *Names* given to these in several Languages, are such arbitrary *sounds* or *words,* as Nations of men have agreed upon, either casually or designedly, to express their Mental notions of them. The *Written word* is the figure or picture of that Sound" (ibid., 20).

22. Ibid., 355.

23. Ibid., 385: "*Writing* is but the figure of *Articulate sound,* and therefore subsequent to it; yet in order of *Nature* there is no priority between these: But *voice* and *sounds* may be as well assigned to Figure, as *Figures* may be to *Sounds.*"

24. Ibid., Sig. a3^r.

25. Ibid., 414; and passim.

26. Ibid.

27. Ibid., 385-86.

28. Ibid.

29. Ibid., 354.

30. Ibid., 452.

31. For a very similar point, see also John Bulwer, *Philocophus: Or, the Deafe and Dumbe Mans Friend* (London, 1648), Sigs. A4^r-A5^r and chap. 2., in which the mouth represents the visible point of language production. Wilkins clearly does not want to abolish metaphor from philosophical discourse (*Essay,* 354).

32. *Essay,* 357. Wilkins says that there are thirty-four such simple sounds (383).

33. Ibid., 359.

34. Ibid., 355.

35. See especially, John Locke, *An Essay concerning Human Understanding,* ed. Peter H. Nidditch (Oxford: Clarendon Press, 1975), bk. 3, chap. 6, secs. 7ff.

36. Ibid., bk. 3, chap. 6, sec. 30.

37. *T. Lucretius Carus the Epicurean Philosopher, His Six Books De Natura Rerum Done into English Verse with Notes,* trans. Thomas Creech (Oxford, 1682), 171. Cyril Bailey translates the passage as follows: "But the diverse sounds of the tongue nature constrained men to utter, and use shaped the names of things, in a manner not far other than the very speechlessness of their tongue is seen to lead children on to gesture, when it makes them point out with the finger the things that are before their eyes." See *Lucretius on the Nature of Things,* trans. Cyril Bailey (1910; reprint, Oxford: Clarendon Press, 1926), 220.

38. More recent discussions of the Webster-Ward debate appear in P. B. Wood, "Methodology and Apologetics: Thomas Sprat's *History of the Royal Society,*" *History of Science* 13 (1980): 17; and Slaughter, *Universal Languages,* 35-40.

39. R. F. Jones, *Ancients and Moderns: A Study of the Rise of the Scientific Movement in Seventeenth-Century England,* 2d ed. (Gloucester: Peter Smith, 1961); and "Science and English Prose Style in the Third Quarter of the Seventeenth Century," "The Attack on Pulpit Eloquence in the Restoration: An Episode in the Development of the Neo-Classical Standard for Prose," and "Science and Language in England of the Mid-Seventeenth-Century," in R. F. Jones et al., *The Seventeenth Century: Studies in the History of English Thought and Literature from Bacon to Pope* (Stanford: Stanford Univ. Press, 1951), 75-110; 111-42; 143-60.

40. See Allen G. Debus, *Science and Education in the Seventeenth Century: The Webster-Ward Debate* (London: Macdonald, 1970), esp. 37-43; and Charles Webster, ed. and intro., *Samuel Hartlib and the Advancement of Learning* (Cambridge: Cambridge Univ. Press, 1970), 1-72.

41. H. R. Trevor-Roper, "Three Foreigners: The Philosophers of the Puritan Revolution," in *Religion, the Reformation and Social Change* (London: Macmillan,

1967), 237–93. Although Trevor-Roper's is a seminal essay of its kind, I think it still confuses the content of the argument with the methods involved. This is not a mistake that Richard H. Popkin makes in relation to the millenarian views of William Whiston, in which calculations about the Second Coming of Christ depended upon an entirely probabilist, conjectural epistemology. See Richard H. Popkin, "Preface," in James E. Force, *William Whiston: Honest Newtonian* (Cambridge: Cambridge Univ. Press, 1985), xii-xiii.

42. Joseph Webster, *Academiarum Examen* (London, 1654), 85.

43. Seth Ward, *Vindiciae Academiarum* (Oxford, 1654), 39.

44. Ibid., 6.

45. Ibid., 7.

46. Ibid., 49.

47. Ibid., 21.

48. *Academiarum Examen*, Sig. A2^r.

49. Ibid., 91. Or, alternatively, a "dictator" (ibid., 66).

50. *Academiarum Examen*, 54.

51. Ibid., 68.

52. Ibid., 11.

53. Ibid., 34.

54. Ibid., 38.

55. Ibid., 76.

56. See also ibid., 32.

57. Ibid., 75.

58. *Vindiciae Academiarum*, 46.

59. Ibid., 22. For example: "The Paradoxicall Protoplast, being Characteristically bound to the Ideal Matrix of Magicall contrition, by the Symphoniacall inspeaking of *Aleph tenebrosum*, and limited by *Shem hamphorash* to the central Idees, in-blowne by the ten numerations of *Belimah,* which are ten and not nine, ten and not eleaven; and consequently being altogether absorpt in decyphering the signatures of *Ensoph,* beyond the sagacity of either a Peritrochiall, or an Isoperimetrall expansion."

60. *The Works of Sir Thomas Browne,* ed. Sir Geoffrey Keynes, 4 vols. (Chicago: Univ. of Chicago Press, 1964), 3:245.

61. *Academiarum Examen*, 99–100.

62. Ibid., 99.

63. Ibid., 101.

64. Ibid., 85.

65. Ibid.

66. Ibid., 99.

67. Johan Amos Comenius, *Orbis Sensualium Pictus,* trans. Charles Hoole (London, 1659), Sig. A3^v.

68. Antoine Arnauld, *The Art of Thinking,* trans. James Dickoff and Patricia James (New York: Bobbs-Merrill, 1964), 36n.4. Pierre Clair and Françoise Girbal, however, refer their reader to earlier scholastic sources. See Antoine Arnauld and Pierre Nicole, *La Logique ou l'Art de Penser,* ed. Clair and Girbal (Paris: Presses Universitaires de France, 1965), 43n.42.

69. *Academiarum Examen*, 97.

70. Ibid., 7; 9.

71. Ibid., 6.

72. *Vindiciae Academiarum*, 4; 13; 5; 14—15; 29; 30; 36.

73. Ibid., 21; 25.

74. Ibid., 41.

75. Ibid., 30.

76. Ibid., 39.

77. Ibid., 45.

78. *Academiarum Examen*, 25. Throughout this chapter, I use the phrase "deaf and dumb" simply to reflect seventeenth-century usage.

79. Ibid., 26.

80. *Vindiciae Academiarum*, 37.

81. Ibid., 44.

82. *Academiarum Examen*, 28.

83. For physiognomy, see Alan T. McKenzie, "The Countenance You Show Me: Reading the Passions in the Eighteenth Century," *Georgia Review* 32 (1978): 758—73; and F. Price, "Imagining Faces: The Later Eighteenth-Century Sentimental Heroine and the Legible, Universal Language of Physiognomy," *British Journal for Eighteenth-Century Studies* 6 (1983): 1—16. For references to Aesop in this relation, see Richard West's dedicatory poem to John Wilkins's *Mercury, Or the Secret and Swift Messenger* (London, 1641), "To his honour'd Friend I. W. on his learned Tract, *The Secret and Swift Messenger*," Sig. A8r; John Bulwer, *Chirologia: Or the Natural Language of the Hand Composed of the Speaking Motions, and Discoursing Gestures thereof. Wherunto is Added Chironomia: Or, the Art of Manuall Rhetoricke* (London, 1644), 20; and George Dalgarno, *Didascalocophus: Or the Deaf and Dumb Mans Tutor* (Oxford, 1680), 72.

84. See René Descartes, *The Passions of the Soul* (1649), in *The Philosophical Writings of Descartes,* trans. John Cottingham et al., 2 vols. (Cambridge: Cambridge Univ. Press, 1985), 1:328.

85. On *actio*, see Bulwer, *Chironomia*, Sig. A8v. One of the pathological texts most often cited by the language theorists is John Willis, *De Anima Brutorum* (Oxford, 1672).

86. John Bulwer, *Anthropometamorphosis: Man Transform'd: Or, the Artificiall Changeling* (London, 1653).

87. Charles Lebrun, *A Method to Learn to Design the Passions* (1734; reprint, Los Angeles: Augustan Reprint Society, 1980), 53. An earlier, somewhat fuller translation of the *Conference of Monsieur Le Brun* (London, 1701) elaborates: "The Nature of every Animal being described by its external Form, the Physiognomists say, that if a Man happens to have any part of his Body resembling that of a Brute, we may from such part, draw Conjectures of his Inclinations, this is what they call Physiognomy" (40).

88. The mysterious relations between shapes of the head and matters of character and social sympathy is of prime concern in Johann Caspar Lavater, *Essays on Physiognomy, Designed to Promote the Knowledge and Love of Mankind,* trans. Henry Hunter, 5 vols. (London, 1789—98).

89. William Holder, *Elements of Speech: An Inquiry into the Natural Production of Letters: With an Appendix concerning Persons Deaf and Dumb* (London, 1669).

90. Ibid., 7.

91. Wilkins's *Essay* appeared a year before Holder's piece, but Holder had already delivered his thesis before the Royal Society, as is suggested by an appendix to his publication.

92. Holder, *Elements of Speech*, 9–10.

93. Ibid., 32. Elsewhere, Holder writes that "these Letters have their *Material* and their *Formal* Causes, and *Organs* proper to each" (ibid., 64). And he sums up the position: "*Language* is a Connexion of Audible signs, the most apt and excellent in whole nature for Communication of our Thoughts and Notions by Speaking. *Written Language* is a description of the said Audible Signes, by Signes Visible. The *Elements* of Language are Letters, *viz*. Simple discriminations of Breath or Voice, Articulated by the Organs of Speech" (ibid., 63).

94. Ibid., 111.

95. Bulwer, *Chironomia*, Sig. A8v.

96. Wilkins, *Mercury*, 11.

97. For a commentary on the significance of Hermes, see Ralph Cudworth's comparison between Hermes and Thoth in *The True Intellectual System of the Universe*, 4 vols. (London: R. Priestley, 1820), 2:130–31.

98. Wilkins, *Mercury*, 6; 42; 53.

99. Ibid., 86–87.

100. Ibid., 4.

101. Defoe records that Gutenberg had likewise to steal his printing tools from Coster (*An Essay upon Literature*, 121).

102. Wilkins, *Mercury*, 1.

103. Ibid., 2–3.

104. Ibid., 7.

105. Ibid., 169.

106. Ibid., 169–70.

107. Ibid., 5.

108. Ibid., 5–6.

109. Ibid., 19.

110. Ibid., 33.

111. Ibid., 37.

112. Ibid., 126; 31. Elsewhere, Wilkins writes: "Those living bodies, that are most observable for their speed, and celerity in messages, are either Men, Beast, Birds" (ibid., 124).

113. Ibid., 26. Wilkins also denies the pentagram mystical power and indicts what he calls "superstitious women" (ibid., 98).

114. Ibid., 22.

115. Ibid., 25.

116. Ibid., 22. This aural danger Wilkins contrasts with God's insertion of a single significant letter *(h)* into the names of Abram and Sara, as well as the naming of Christ as alpha and omega (ibid., 84–85).

117. Ibid., 104.

118. Ibid., 8.

119. Ibid., 115.

120. Ibid., 112.

121. Ibid., 115.

122. Thus Wilkins writes of "compact" (ibid., 44; 73) and *"invented Characters"* (ibid., 87).

123. Ibid., 101–2.

124. Ibid., 69. See also Wilkins's discussion of changing the "places" and "powers" of letters in some linguistic grid (ibid., 65).

125. Ibid., 106ff. Thus Wilkins attacks using a single letter as itself a principle of knowledge (ibid., 84).

126. See also ibid., 92–93; and 96: "It is easie to apprehend . . . how a man may contrive any private saying in the forme of a Landskip or other picture."

127. Ibid., 16.

128. Ibid.

129. Ibid., 19–20.

130. John Bulwer, *Pathomyotomia, or a Dissection of the Significative Muscles of the Minde* (London, 1649), 24.

131. See also Bulwer, *Chirologia*, Sig. A6ᵛ-A7ʳ: "I shall lay claime to all metaphors, proverbiall translations or usurpations, and all kinde of symbolicall Elegancies taken and borrowed from Gestures of the Body, with the depredations the subtiler Arts of Speech have made upon them for the advancement and exaltation of their particular inventions and designes. All these . . . being but as so many severall lines that meet in an angle, and touch in this point; I intend to reduce and bring home to their fountaine and common parent the Body of man." See also *Chironomia*, 8: it is a "Rhetoricall mystery" that God's spirit should be represented as his *"Finger."*

132. John Bulwer, *Philocophus: Or, the Deafe and Dumbe Mans Friend. Exhibiting the Philosophicall Verity of that Subtile Art, which may Inable one with an Observant Eie, to Heare what any Man Speaks by the Moving of his Lips* (London, 1648).

133. *Pathomyotomia*, Sig. A2ᵛ.

134. Ibid., Sig. A7ʳ.

135. *Chironomia*, Sig. A7ʳ; 20.

136. *Pathomyotomia*, 4.

137. See, for example, *Chirologia*, Sigs. A2ʳ-A4ᵛ; and also 3; 7.

138. *Pathomyotomia*, 55.

139. *Chironomia*, Sig. A6ᵛ.

140. Ibid., Sig. A7ʳ.

141. Ibid., Sig. A8ʳ.

142. Ibid., Sig. A7ᵛ.

143. Ibid., Sig. A8ʳ.

144. *Pathomyotomia*, 15. See also ibid., 16; and 22–23.

145. Ibid., 37.

146. *Chironomia*, Sig. A8ᵛ.

147. Ibid., 4.

148. *Pathomyotomia*, Sig. A9ʳ; 25.

149. See ibid., Sig. A2ᵛ; 40.

150. *Chirologia*, 2.

151. *Chironomia*, 4.

152. Ibid., 7.

153. *Pathomyotomia*, Sig. A10ᵛ.

154. Ibid., Sig. A8ʳ.

155. Ibid., Sig. A4ᵛ.

156. *Chirologia*, 184–85: "All men use to count forwards till they come to that number of their *Fingers*, and being come to that number, prompted as it were by nature to returne at this bound or But of numericall immensity, (about which all numbers are reflected and driven round) they repeat againe the same numbers returning into unity from whence their account began, which we must not account as an accident, but a thing propagated from the fountaine of nature, since it is ever done and that by all Nations."

157. *Philocophus*, 17; *Pathomyotomia*, 42.

158. *Philocophus*, 20.

159. In *Philocophus*, Bulwer writes: "And verily children at first, no otherwise then Brutes, doe expresse their *Appetitions*, being not able to pronounce Letters" (4).

160. *Pathomyotomia*, 2; In *Chironomia*, Bulwer writes: "Man could [not] have enjoyed the honor of an articulate voice had not nature planted this magazine of speech in the body and stored it with native ammunition for the defense and arming of oral reason" (6).

161. Ibid., 22; See also *Chironomia*, 6.

162. *Chironomia*, 4.

163. Ibid., 4–5. Bulwer talks similarly of *"the scheme or outward figure of each Affection in the Countenance"* (*Pathomyotomia*, Sig. A8ʳ).

164. Nieuhof and Defoe discuss the directionality of reading conventions in different cultures. See Jan Nieuhof, *An Embassy Sent by the East-India Company of the United Provinces to the Grand Tartar Cham or Emperour of China*, trans. John Ogilby (London, 1669), 160. See also Defoe, *An Essay upon Literature*, 78.

165. *Pathomyotomia*, Sig. A8ᵛ.

166. Ibid., 27.

167. *Chironomia*, 8.

168. Ibid., 19.

169. Ibid., 12. Bulwer also records Pylades developing a universal gestural language during the reign of Nero (ibid.).

170. Ibid., 10; 11.

171. *Chirologia*, Sig. A6ᵛ (italics reversed).

172. Henry, Earl of Monmouth, trans., *The Use of Passions. Written in French by J. F. Senault* (London, 1671).

173. See Jean François Senault, in *Biographie Universelle, Ancienne et Moderne* (Paris: Michaud, 1825); and also Voukossava Miloyevitch, *La Théorie des Passions du P. Senault et la Morale Chrétienne en France au XVIIᵉ Siècle* (Paris: Rodstein, 1935), esp. pt. 4.

174. Senault writes: "Pride hath made them eloquent in their Invectives, and Ambition hath furnished them with Reasons, which are fairly entertained by such men, who are offended that they have a Body, and afflicted that they are not Angels" (*Use of Passions*, 4).

175. Ibid., 42.

176. Ibid., 48.

177. Christ's bodily existence is also central to seeing the power of his example: *"Thy Actions, since thou hast vouchsafed to become Man, serve us for Instructions;* and we find *examples* in *thy life,* which we may securely imitate. Before *thy* temporal *Birth,* we had no *model* which was not *imperfect"* (ibid., Sig. a5^r).

178. Ibid., 48–49.

179. Ibid., 48; 51.

180. Ibid., 11.

181. Ibid.

182. Ibid., Sig. b2^v.

183. Ibid., 76.

184. Ibid., 5–6.

185. Ibid., 12.

186. Ibid., 13.

187. Ibid., 13–14.

188. Ibid., 14.

189. Ibid. Senault writes of the soul in this condition: "She treats of Angels."

190. Ibid., 15.

191. Ibid., 15–16.

192. Walter Charleton, *Natural History of the Passions* (London, 1674).

193. Ibid., 3; see also Sig. bb5^v.

194. Thus Charleton speaks of clocks and engines (ibid., 34–35) and a watch (170–71) to represent the necessity of inference.

195. Descartes, *Passions of the Soul,* in *Philosophical Writings,* 1:339. This is exactly the dualistic Cartesian principle that also disturbs Glanvill and that leads him to argue, like Charleton, for some method of mediating between incorporeal spirit and gross body. Glanvill finds this capacity in the senses: "We cannot conceive any thing, which comes not within the verge of our senses" (Joseph Glanvill, *The Vanity of Dogmatizing* [London, 1661], 23).

196. Descartes, *Passions of the Soul,* in *Philosophical Writings,* 1:340.

197. For Charleton's debts to Bacon, see *Natural History of the Passions,* Sigs. bb4^v; cc1^r; to Willis's *De Anima Brutorum,* see ibid., Sigs. bb5^r; bb5^v; cc1^r; 41; to "the *immortal Gassendus,"* see ibid., Sig. bb5^r; and to Gassendi's *Animadversiones,* see ibid., Sig. bb7^r; to Descartes, *Passions of the Soul,* see ibid., 41; to Hobbes, see ibid., 41; to "those three excellent Men, *Gassendus, Descartes,* and our *Mr. Hobbes,"* see ibid., Sig. cc1^v; to Digby, see ibid., 3; 41; and, of course, to "our *Oracle, Epicurus,"* see ibid., Sig. cc1^v.

198. *Natural History of the Passions,* Sig. bb1^v.

199. Ibid., Sig. bb2^v.

200. Ibid., 53; also Sig. A5^v.

201. Ibid., Sigs. A6^r-A6^v.

202. Ibid., 52–53.

203. Ibid., Sig. bb5^r.

204. Ibid., Sig. cc1^v.

205. Ibid., Sig. bb7^r; also 10.

206. Ibid., 9. On the sensible soul intertexed with the body, see ibid., 14.

207. For a précis of this view, see Walter Charleton, *The Ephesian Matron* (1668; reprint, Los Angeles: Augustan Reprint Society, 1975), 22ff.

208. Charleton, *Natural History of the Passions*, 20.

209. Ibid., 52.

210. Ibid. Charleton also writes: "To me (I confess) it seems Unintelligible, how an incorporeal Agent, not infinite, can physically act in, and upon a gross body *immediately,* or without the intervention of a third thing; which though corporeal too, is yet notwithstanding of parts so spirituous, and of a constitution so subtil, as to approach somwhat neerer to the nature of a pure *Spirit,* than solid and ponderous body doth" (ibid., 51).

211. Ibid., 38.

212. Ibid., 14.

213. See also ibid., 72; 92.

214. Ibid., 28.

215. See, for example, ibid., 84; 92. Charleton also attaches his catalogue to an ethical notion of balancing various passions, which he aligns with Epicurus (ibid., 187–88).

216. Ibid., 31.

217. Ibid., 33. Charleton admits the possibility of cognitive disjunction in this process. On the imagination, see ibid., 40; 47; 61; 182–83.

218. Ibid., 32.

219. Ibid., 65.

220. Ibid., 39.

221. Ibid., 48.

222. Ibid., 49.

223. Ibid., 64.

224. Ibid., Sig. A2ᵛ.

225. Ibid., 187.

226. Dalgarno, *Didascalocophus*, 2. Dalgarno goes on to write: "Neither is there any reason in Nature, why the mind should more easily apprehend, the images of things imprest upon Sounds, than upon Characters."

227. Ibid., 20–21.

228. See, for example, ibid., 32ff., esp. 36: "For when dumb people make it appear, that they understand many things that pass in discourse . . . the truth is, what they understand, is from a concurrence of circumstances, many of which are often as material, as the motion of the speakers lips; such as, his eyes, countenance, time, place, persons, &c."

229. Ibid., 8ff.

230. Ibid., 9.

231. Ibid., 8.

232. Ibid., 1.

233. Ibid., 20.

234. Ibid., 19.

235. Ibid., 8.

236. Ibid., 16–17.

237. Ibid., 22.

238. Ibid.

239. Ibid., 17.

240. Ibid., 10.

241. Ibid., 72.

242. Ibid., Sig. A3^r.

243. Ibid., 62.

244. Ibid., 47.

245. Ibid., 22.

246. Ibid., Sigs. A4^v-A5^r.

247. Ibid., Sig. A5^r.

248. Ibid., Sigs. A3^r-A3^v.

249. Ibid., 73.

250. Ibid., Sigs. A3^r-A3^v.

251. Ibid., 81.

252. Ibid., 27.

253. Ibid.

254. Ibid., 29.

255. Ibid., 30.

256. Ibid., 30–31.

257. Erik Iversen, *The Myth of Egypt and Its Hieroglyphs* (Copenhagen: Gec Gad, 1961), 88.

258. See P. Conor Reilly, S.J., *Athanasius Kircher: Master of a Hundred Arts, 1602–1680* (Rome: Edizioni del Mondo, 1974), which includes a bibliography of Kircher's publications. See also Baleslaw Sczesniak, "Athanasius Kircher's *China Illustrata,*" *Osiris* 10 (1952): 385–411. There are frequent allusions to Kircher in the materials I discuss in this book; for example, in Cudworth, *True Intellectual System,* 2:120ff.; and in the appendix to Gassendi's life of Peiresc *(The Mirrour of True Nobility. Being the Life of the Renowned Nicolaus Claudius Fabricius Lord of Peiresk,* trans. William Rand [London, 1657]).

259. See, for example, William Warburton, *The Divine Legation of Moses Demonstrated,* 2 vols. (1738–41; reprint, London: Tegg, 1837), 2:42. See also Cornelius, *Languages,* chap. 4.

260. Gabriel de Magalhães, *A New History of China* (London, 1688), 70.

261. Stillingfleet, *Origines Sacrae,* 3.

262. Ibid., 13.

263. Pierre Gautruche, *The Poetical History: Being a Compleat Collection of all the Stories Necessary for a Perfect Understanding of the Greek and Latine Poets and other Ancient Authors* (1669; 6th Eng. ed., London, 1693), 420; 422.

264. Nieuhof, *An Embassy,* 159.

265. Warburton, *Divine Legation,* 61.

266. Gautruche, *Poetical History,* 418.

267. Nieuhof, *An Embassy,* 158.

268. Magalhães, *New History,* 69.

269. Nieuhof, *An Embassy,* 157.

270. Warburton, *Divine Legation,* 23; 24; 25.

271. Ibid.

272. Magalhães, *New History*, 68–69.

273. Defoe, *Essay upon Literature*, 80.

274. Warburton, *Divine Legation*, 68.

275. Descartes, *Rules for the Direction of the Mind*, in *Philosophical Writings*, 1:43.

276. Ibid.

277. Dalgarno, *A Discourse of the Nature and Number of Double Consonants*, appended to *Didascalocophus*, 99.

278. Magalhães, *New History*, 71.

279. On Warburton, see Ian Balfour, "Hurd, Warburton, and the Hieroglyphic Style," in "The Rhetoric of Romantic Prophecy." Ph.D. diss., Yale Univ., 1985; Jacques Derrida, "Scribble (writing-power)," *Yale French Studies* 58 (1979): 117–47; A. W. Evans, *Warburton and the Warburtonians: A Study in Some Eighteenth-Century Controversies* (London: Oxford Univ. Press, 1932); Robert M. Ryley, *William Warburton* (Boston: Twayne, 1984); Leslie Stephen, "Warburton," in *Essays in Freethinking and Plainspeaking* (London: Smith, Elder/Duckworth, 1907), 317–68.

280. Warburton, *Divine Legation*, 33.

281. Ibid., 32.

282. Ibid., 33.

283. Ibid.

284. Ibid., 34.

285. Ibid.

286. "How nearly the *apologue* and *instruction by action* are related, may be seen in the account of Jeremiah's adventure with the Rechabites; an instruction partaking of the joint nature of *action* and *apologue*.

This was the birth of the FABLE; a kind of speech which corresponds, in all respects, to *writing by hieroglyphs*, each being the symbol of something else understood. And, as it sometimes happened, when an hieroglyphic became famous, it lost its particular signification, and assumed a general one; as the *caduceus*, for instance, which was, at first, painted only to denote the pacific office of Hermes, became, in time, to be the common symbol of league and amity" (ibid., 37).

287. Ibid.

288. Ibid., 38.

289. Ibid.

7. Text and Action in Biblical Criticism

1. Hans Frei, *The Eclipse of Biblical Narrative: A Study in Eighteenth- and Nineteenth-Century Hermeneutics* (New Haven: Yale Univ. Press, 1974).

2. This process is also described in different terms by Richard H. Popkin, "Cartesianism and Biblical Criticism," in *Problems of Cartesianism*, ed. Thomas M. Lennon et al. (Kingston, Montreal: McGill-Queen's Univ. Press, 1982), 61–81.

3. William Warburton, *The Divine Legation of Moses Demonstrated*, 2 vols. (1738–41; reprint, London: Tegg, 1837), 1:63.

4. John Owen, *The Works of John Owen, D.D.*, ed. Rev. William H. Goold, 16 vols. (New York: Carter, 1853), 16:395–96.

5. See Richard Simon, *A Critical History of the Old Testament* (London, 1682), bk. 1, chaps. 14 and 15.

6. Gerard Reedy, S.J., *The Bible and Reason: Anglicans and Scripture in Late Seventeenth-Century England* (Philadelphia: Univ. of Pennsylvania Press, 1985), 62.

7. On the view that the Anglican divines largely ignored the possibilities of the new textual criticism, see ibid., 102–3.

8. The principle also applies to a prophetic agent whose purpose is to orchestrate a series of publicly constituted symbols as a means to prophetic teaching.

9. We have seen how even Gassendi is driven by his phenomenalism to question our ability to account for the process of transubstantiation, even if he does not challenge the dogma (see chapter five above). See also Edward Stillingfleet, *The Doctrine of the Trinity and Transubstantiation Compared, as to Scripture, Reason, and Tradition, in a New Dialogue between a Protestant and a Papist, the Second Part* (London, 1687), 33.

10. We could say that this inferential argument provides a purely historical justification for a vigorously formalist approach to the text.

11. See, for example, Hobbes's demand that the reader attend to "the main Designe" of the Scriptural text to avoid becoming distracted with "atomes of Scripture" (Thomas Hobbes, *Leviathan*, ed. C. B. Macpherson [Harmondsworth, Eng.: Penguin, 1968], 626).

12. See *The Works of John Locke*, 11th ed., 10 vols. (London: W. Otridge et al., 1812), 8:vi-vii.

13. See William Chillingworth, *The Religion of Protestants a Safe Way to Salvation*, in *The Works of William Chillingworth, M.A.* (Philadelphia: Davis, 1840): "Probability is no sufficient ground for an infallible assent of faith" (91). Edward Knott was the alias of Matthias Wilson.

14. Lucius Cary, Viscount Falkland also contributed to the assault on infallibility in his own *Discourse of Infallibility* (London, 1651), which was attacked in turn by Thomas White, against which Falkland issued a defense.

15. Laud's anti-Catholic tract reads in many ways like his godson's, cast as it is in a dialogue with Father Fisher. See *A Relation of the Conference betweene William Lawd . . . And Mr. Fisher the Jesuite* (1639), in *The Works of the Most Reverend Father in God, William Laud, D.D.*, 3 vols. (1847–60; reprint, New York: AMS Press, 1975), vol. 2.

16. Chillingworth, *Religion of Protestants*, 429.

17. Significantly, Chillingworth also attacks Stoic gnosticism and arrogance (ibid., iv).

18. Ibid., 481. Chillingworth discusses the material objects of our faith in ibid., 109.

19. Ibid., 477, where Chillingworth also introduces Grotius.

20. On the relation of visibility to assent, see ibid., 433: "That power which infuseth into the understanding assent, which bears analogy to sight in the eye, must also infuse evidence, that is, visibility, into the object: and look what degree of assent is infused into the understanding, at least the same degree of assent must be infused into the object."

21. See H. R. Trevor-Roper, *Archbishop Laud, 1573–1645* (Hamden, Conn.: Archon, 1962); and also Edward Stillingfleet, *An Answer to Several Late Treatises, Occasioned*

by a Book Entituled a Discourse concerning the Idolatry Practiced in the Church of Rome, 2d ed. (London, 1674), 340: "Our Question in the Resolution of Faith, [does] not relate to the workings of the divine Spirit on our minds of which no satisfactory account can be given to others; but to the external motives and grounds of faith, whether they must be infallible or not?" W. K. Jordan comments on Laud's formalism (*The Development of Religious Toleration in England: From the Accession of James I to the Convention of the Long Parliament (1603–1640)* [Cambridge: Harvard Univ. Press, 1936], 130).

22. On Christ as a divine representative, who yet avoids becoming an idol, see William Sherlock, *The Second Part of the Preservative against Popery* (London, 1688), 5; 12.

23. See, for example, Stillingfleet, *An Answer*, 55.

24. For the importance of the visibility of the church in the Laudian tradition, see R. S. Bosher, *The Making of the Restoration Settlement: The Influence of the Laudians, 1649–1662* (London: Black, 1951), 33. On the formal conditions of the church, see John Tulloch, *Rational Theology and Christian Philosophy in England*, 2 vols., 2d ed. (Edinburgh: Blackwell, 1874), 1:457, where Tulloch discusses Stillingfleet's *Irenicum* (1659). See also Edward Fowler, *A Defence of the Resolution of this Case* (London, 1684). The Catholics did attack the notion of privacy I describe. See *Dr. Stillingfleet's Principles* (Paris, 1671), in *A Collection of Several Treatises in Answer to Dr. Stillingfleet* (n.p., 1672), 66.

25. Stillingfleet, *An Answer*, 237; the Roman Catholics did mount a defense of what amounts to the literal. See *Fanaticism Fanatically Imputed to the Catholick Church by Dr. Stillingfleet* (n.d.), in *A Collection of Several Treatises*, 155. A literal interpretation of *Hoc est Corpus meum* is also defended by the author of *Dr. Stillingfleet's Principles*, 20. In *The Roman Church's Devotions Vindicated from Dr. Stillingfleet's Mis-Representation* (1672), in *A Collection of Several Treatises*, 83–84, the author (O.N.) defends the view that "in . . . supernaturall communications, *The Soul knows*, or contemplates *without any thoughts*, discursive; *sees in darkness*; or in the obscurity of Faith, not clearly."

26. See Bosher, *The Making*, 265.

27. See for example, Edward Stillingfleet, *Origines Sacrae: Or a Rational Account of the Grounds of the Christian Faith, as to the Truth and Divine Authority of the Scriptures* (1662; 3d ed., Cambridge, 1701). Stillingfleet's entire thrust is expressed symbolically by his opening dedication to Sir Roger Bourgoine: "It was the early felicity of *Moses*, when expos'd in an Ark of *Nilotic papyre*, to be adopted into the favor of so great a Personage as the daughter of *Pharaoh:* Such another Ark is this Vindication of the Writings of that Divine and Excellent Person expos'd to the World in" (Sig. a2r). Moses is always carried by scribal vehicles, like the papyrus of his little boat.

28. See Phillip Harth, *Contexts of Dryden's Thought* (Chicago: Univ. of Chicago Press, 1968), 201–6. Citing Belarmine, Harth points out that the Protestant equation between the merely oral and the nonwritten was a technical mistake, because the "nonwritten" simply referred to traditional doctrines not written by the first apostles. However, Harth also admits that the mistake was not only the consequence of an anti-Catholic polemic, because many Catholics themselves were not clear on the distinction (204).

29. See, for example, William Sherlock, *A Preservative against Popery: Being Some Plain Directions to Unlearned Protestants, How to Dispute with Romish Priests, the First Part* (London, 1688), 56.

30. Ibid., 75.

31. One might also include Erasmus and Scaliger as vital heralds of what Casaubon and Grotius came to represent. See my essay *"Mise-en-Page,* Biblical Criticism, and Inference during the Restoration," *Studies in Eighteenth-Century Culture,* ed. O. M. Brack, Jr., vol. 16 (Madison: Univ. of Wisconsin Press, 1986), 3–40; and Anthony Grafton's ongoing study of Scaliger, of which volume one has appeared: *Joseph Scaliger: A Study in the History of Classical Scholarship,* vol. 1, *Textual Criticism and Exegesis* (Oxford: Clarendon Press, 1983). Certainly, in John Pearson's variorum commentary on the Bible, *Critici Sacri* (London, 1660), Scaliger, Grotius, and Casaubon share about equal billing. On Grotius's visit to England and his meeting with Overall, Andrewes, and Casaubon, see Jordan, *Development,* 344.

32. See Mark Pattison, *Isaac Casaubon, 1559–1614* (London: Longmans, 1875), 327, where Pattison speaks of the nature of textual criticism before Casaubon and Andrewes.

33. Anthony Grafton, "Protestant versus Prophet: Isaac Casaubon on Hermes Trismegistus," *Journal of the Warburg and Courtauld Institutes* 46 (1983): 78–93.

34. Frances Yates, *Giordano Bruno and the Hermetic Tradition* (New York: Vintage, 1964), chap. 21.

35. See Harry Carter, *A History of the Oxford University Press,* 1 vol. to date (Oxford: Clarendon Press, 1975), 1:41–42; Basil Hall, "Biblical Scholarship: Editions and Commentaries," in *The Cambridge History of the Bible,* vol. 3, *The West from the Reformation to the Present Day,* ed. S. L. Greenslade (1933; reprint, Cambridge: Cambridge Univ. Press, 1968), 63–64.

36. Kroll, *"Mise-en-Page,* Biblical Criticism, and Inference in the Restoration," 20–26.

37. Simon, *A Critical History of the Old Testament,* bk. 3, chaps. 21–24.

38. This statement is not quite exact if we take into account Hammond's prescriptions for comparative and implicitly interlinear methods of textual scholarship, which anticipate the *Biblia Polyglotta* by some three or four years, and which I describe below. But it is true if we compare the *Biblia Polyglotta* to earlier interlinear editions of the Bible, whose organization of the text tended toward the allegorical, rather than the philological.

39. Walton's *Prolegomena* and *Appendix* to the Polyglot were often published separately from the Bible proper; it is with these in particular that Simon takes issue.

40. See Owen, *Works,* 16:319.

41. Ibid., 16:326; 330ff.

42. See ibid., 16:355.

43. See ibid., 16:357.

44. See ibid., 16:365; also 16:362.

45. See R. F. Jones, "Science and English Prose Style in the Third Quarter of the Seventeenth Century" and "The Attack on Pulpit Eloquence in the Restoration: An Episode in the Development of the Neo-Classical Standard for Prose," in R. F. Jones et al., *The Seventeenth Century: Studies in the History of English Thought and Literature from Bacon to Pope* (Stanford: Stanford Univ. Press, 1951), 75–110; 111–142; and Reedy, *Bible and Reason,* 15.

46. See especially Owen, *Works,* 4:7ff.

47. Ibid., 4:59.

48. Ibid., 4:70.

49. John Owen, *[Theomachia Autexoustiastikē] or, A Display of Arminianism* (1642), in *Works*, 10:53; 10:78.

50. See Owen, *A Review of the Annotations of Hugo Grotius* (1656), in *Works*, 12:619–39.

51. Some striking connections with the Gassendi circle are suggested by the papers of Guy Patin under the rubric "Grotiana," in which Patin's dealings with a number of significant figures in the world of textual editing are recorded. He records meeting Grotius on 1 June 1643, at a time when the English émigrés are also in Paris. See René Pintard, *La Mothe le Mayer, Gassendi, Guy Patin: Études de Bibliographie et de Critique Suivies de Textes Inédits de Guy Patin* (Paris: Boivin, n.d.), 69.

52. Hugo Grotius, *The Truth of Christian Religion*, trans. Simon Patrick (London, 1680), 280–81; 277–78; 293.

53. The issue of Socinianism chronically plagued Grotius. He himself issued a tract that enjoyed much of the success of *De Veritate Religionis Christianae*, entitled *Defensio Fidei Catholicae de Satisfactione Christi, adversus F. Socinum* (Amsterdam, 1617). Both Patrick and Grotius's biographer defend him from charges of Socinianism. See Grotius, *The Truth*, Sig. a1ʳ; and Grotius, *The Rights of War and Peace* (London, 1715), xivff.

54. Grotius, *The Truth*, 25.

55. Ibid., 219.

56. Ibid., 21.

57. Ibid., 155.

58. Ibid., 48.

59. Ibid., 5off.

60. Ibid., 55–62.

61. Ibid., 64.

62. Ibid., 48.

63. Ibid., 102–3.

64. Ibid., 117. Grotius continues: "Nay this very thing ought to vindicate and free these *Writers* from all suspicion of *falshood;* it being usual with those that would have lies and untruths credited, to relate all *circumstances* by compact and agreement, so as there shall not appear any colour or shew of *difference.* Or if it be so, that any small *difference,* which cannot so exactly be reconciled, a whole Book shall lose its credit; then we must believe no *Books* at all, specially those of history."

65. Ibid., 120; 116–17.

66. In a useful note in his edition of *The Correspondence of John Locke*, E. S. de Beer summarizes the Remonstrants' emphasis on the *vita activa*: "The Remonstrants regarded Erasmus as a precursor. With him they sought the source of theology in the New Testament and especially in the Gospels. Christianity was interpreted mainly as a pious and virtuous life; with this went a large tolerance for those who differed in their opinions" (*The Correspondence of John Locke*, ed. E. S. de Beer, 8 vols. [Oxford: Clarendon Press, 1976–89], 2:648).

67. Grotius, *The Truth*, 291; 293.

68. Owen's excellent, if somewhat overly sympathetic, editor describes the

course of the debate between Owen and Hammond in the 1650s. Owen had accused Hammond of being overly influenced by Grotius, whom he suspected of Socinianism, ironically because of Grotius's putatively anti-Socinian tract, *Defensio Fidei Catholicae* (1617), described above. See Owen, *Works*, 12:619. See also Henry Hammond, *A Second Defence of the Learned Hugo Grotius* (London, 1655); and *A Continuation of the Defence of Hugo Grotius* (London, 1657).

69. See John W. Packer, *The Transformation of Anglicanism, 1643–1660: With Special Reference to Henry Hammond* (Manchester: Manchester Univ. Press, 1969).

70. Thus Burnet mourns the passing of Hammond on the eve of a new age. See Edward Burnet, *History of His Own Time*, 6 vols. (Oxford: Oxford Univ. Press, 1833), 1:322.

71. In addition to defending Grotius against Owen, Hammond defended another hero of Restoration theological moderation, namely Lucius Cary, in *A View of Some Exceptions which have been Made by a Romanist to the Lord Viscount Falkland's Discourse of the Infallibility of the Church of Rome* (London, 1646).

72. Henry Hammond, "A Postscript concerning New Light, or Divine Illumination," in *A Paraphrase and Annotations upon all the Books of the New Testament*, 4 vols. (1639; reprint, Oxford: Oxford Univ. Press, 1845), 1:xix. (I use a short title in the following notes.)

73. Ibid., 1:x-xi.

74. Werner Schwarz, *Principles and Problems of Biblical Translation: Some Reformation Controversies and Their Background* (Cambridge: Cambridge Univ. Press, 1955), esp. chaps. 5 and 6.

75. Hammond, "Postscript," in *Paraphrase . . . of the New Testament*, 1:xi.

76. See, for example, Hammond, "Advertisement," in ibid.; and "Preface" in *A Paraphrase and Annotations upon the Books of the Psalms*, 2 vols. (1653; reprint, Oxford: Oxford Univ. Press, 1850), 1:xi. (I use a short title in the following notes.)

77. Hammond, "Postscript," in *Paraphrase . . . of the New Testament*, 1:xi, v.

78. Ibid., 1:xviii.

79. Hammond, "Preface," in *Paraphrase . . . of the Psalms*, 1:vi.

80. Hammond, "Advertisement," in *Paraphrase . . . of the New Testament*, 1:viii.

81. Ibid.

82. Hammond, "Postscript," in *Paraphrase . . . of the New Testament*, 1:xxv.

83. Hammond, "Preface," in *Paraphrase . . . of the Psalms*, 1:x-xi.

84. Ibid., 1:xi.

85. Hammond, "Postscript," in *Paraphrase . . . of the New Testament*, 1:xiii.

86. Ibid., 1:xiii-xiv.

87. Ibid., 1:xiv.

88. Hammond, "Preface," in *Paraphrase . . . of the Psalms*, 1:vii.

89. Ibid., 1:viii.

90. Hammond, "Annotations" on the title of "The New Testament," in *Paraphrase . . . of the New Testament*, 2:v.

91. Henry Hammond, *Of the Reasonableness of the Christian Religion* (1650), in *The Miscellaneous Works of Henry Hammond, D.D.*, 3 vols., 3d ed. (Oxford: John Henry Parker, 1849), 2:20.

92. See ibid., 2:22.

93. Ibid., 2:7.

94. Ibid., 2:8.

95. "The miracles wrought by Christ and his Apostles . . . are another kind of God's speaking to us in men, and upon earth, particularly that of raising the dead, and are by the Apostles styled, what in reason they are, demonstrations and testifications of God Himself. But above all His own resurrection out of the grave, after He had been crucified by them. God by thus raising Him is said, most truly according to the dictates of reason, to have given all men faith, i.e. an argument of full conviction, that He was what he pretended to be, and so set Him out as the person to be believed on, being powerfully and determinately pointed out by that great act to be the Son of God" (ibid., 2:9).

96. Ibid., 2:9–11; 2:13.

97. A competent description of Le Clerc is Samuel A. Golden, *Jean Le Clerc* (New York: Twayne, 1972), though Golden devotes most attention to the *Bibliothèques,* which is not our present concern.

98. Le Clerc was also Locke's earliest biographer. See Jean Le Clerc, *The Life and Character of Mr. John Locke* (London, 1706), a translation of the original article on Locke in the *Bibliothèque Choisie.*

99. See, for example, *The Correspondence of John Locke,* 3:36n. See also Annie Barnes, *Jean le Clerc (1657–1736) et la République de Lettres* (Paris: Droz, 1938); and Rosalie Colie, *Light and Enlightenment: A Study of the Cambridge Platonists and Dutch Arminians* (Cambridge: Cambridge Univ. Press, 1957), esp. chap. 2.

100. For example, the translator of *Twelve Dissertations out of Monsieur Le Clerk's Genesis* (London, 1696) is probably Thomas Brown (1663–1704), who, having offended Hammond's biographer, Dr. John Fell, while at Oxford, compensated by writing Fell's epitaph. Brown was later to preface Creech's translation of Lucretius (1682) with some verses. Le Clerc himself translated the oriental portion of Stanley's *History of Philosophy,* which we can safely assume he read.

101. [Thomas Brown], "Preface," in *Twelve Dissertations,* Sig. A2ᵛ.

102. Le Clerc, "Preface" in *An Historical Vindication of the Naked Gospel* (London, 1690), Sig. A2ʳ.

103. Ibid.

104. Le Clerc, *Twelve Dissertations,* 102–3.

105. For example, Le Clerc writes: "But since these different Hypotheses are supported by no competent Witnesses, that is to say, such as flourished in the same Times, or such as might have learn'd the Truth out of the Memoirs of their Contemporaries, they may be as easily rejected, as they are brought upon the Stage" (ibid., 129–30). The sense in which the postures of the mind achieve almost a reified quality is suggested, of course, by the theatrical metaphor examined in chapter six above.

106. Ibid., 2.

107. Ibid., 46.

108. Ibid., 47.

109. Ibid., 59–60.

110. Ibid., 61; 80.

111. Ibid., 96; 98.

112. Ibid., 92; 54.

113. Ibid., 94; 130.

114. Ibid., 99.

115. Ibid., 237; 40.

116. "A Philosophical Ear . . . is not to be imposed upon by [the] miserable Rhetoric" of "oratorical . . . argumentation. . . , [which] may serve well enough for the Pulpit, or a popular Harangue" (ibid., 245).

117. Ibid., 4; 5; 10; 28.

118. Ibid., 32.

119. Ibid., 29–30.

120. Ibid., 32–33.

121. Ibid., 11.

122. Like Clifford Geertz, Le Clerc seems to hold that language is not only a defining feature of human culture but also that it responds to an almost biological necessity for manipulating our environment by the use of symbols: if we read the Genesis account as a cultural myth, Moses suggests "that the Invention of a Language, which is of such absolute necessity to all the affairs of humane Life, was one of the first cares of our first Parents" (ibid., 288). See Clifford Geertz, *The Interpretation of Cultures* (New York: Basic Books, 1973), 61ff.

123. Le Clerc, *Twelve Dissertations*, 288; 289.

124. Ibid., 39. Greek and Latin avoid such figures as *"to break the Staff of Bread,"* or the statement *"God was a War-like Man,* That *he was roused up like a Sleeper,"* because, as Le Clerc points out, Cicero says: *"the chief Excellence of a word figuratively applied, consists in making a greater Impression upon the Sense; therefore all gross sordid Images are carefully to be avoided, that may nauseate the Hearer."*

125. Ibid., 276. In *A Supplement to Dr. Hammond's Paraphrase and Annotations on the New Testament* (London, 1699), Le Clerc also elaborates something akin to Wittgenstein's family resemblances, which like Wittgenstein's must presuppose the palpability of symbolic relations and negotiations among them. If we suppress the constituent elements of a figure of speech, we mystify it. For example, he takes up *diathēkē,* a word that has teased both Grotius and Hammond: "The word . . . , in whatever sense it be taken, is metaphorical, and borrowed from the Customs of Men; for Covenants and Testaments properly so called, are only made amongst Men. Now Metaphorical Terms are seldom grounded upon a perfect Similitude between those things, to which they are indifferently applied; and therefore they cannot always be scrued up to the whole Latitude of their natural signification. It is sufficient if there be any Agreement, tho but small, between the thing, of which any word is used in a metaphorical sense, and that which it properly signifies. So that all that can be inferred from the bare word is, that several things expressed by it, have some affinity with one another. And in order to determin wherein that similitude lies, we must carefully consider both things themselves: Which being done, we may argue from the thing to the signification of the word, but not from the word to the thing" (xxiii-xxiv).

126. Ibid., 69.

127. Ibid., 40–41.

128. Ibid., 53–54.

129. Ibid., 24.

130. Ibid., 136.

131. Ibid., 131.

132. Ibid., 234.

133. Ibid., 143. The rabbis betook "themselves to Allegory" in ignoring Moses' purpose in representing the serpent speaking in Eden.

134. Ibid., 30; 45.

135. "Fables don't merely arise from nothing, as elsewhere it happens, but have truth to their foundation" (ibid., 271), though not "all the Fables of the *Grecians* are derived from Histories in the Bible, changed and corrupted" (ibid., 234).

136. Ibid., 234; 267.

137. Ibid., 57; 38.

138. Ibid., 85; 88.

139. Samuel Craddock, *The Harmony of the Four Evangelists* (London, 1668), title page.

140. See *Dictionary of National Biography*.

141. John Lightfoot, *The Harmony of the Foure Evangelists* (London, 1644), Sig. A1ᵛ.

142. John Lightfoot, *The Harmony, Chronicle and Order of the Old Testament* (London, 1647), 1.

143. John Lightfoot, *The Harmony, Chronicle and Order of the New Testament* (London, 1655), Sig. A1ʳ.

144. Bodleian MS Locke f.1., 303ff.; 470ff.

145. Jean Le Clerc to John Locke, 7 June 1698, in *The Correspondence of John Locke*, 6:423.

146. Jean Le Clerc, *The Harmony of the Evangelists* (London, 1701), 584.

147. Ibid., 596.

148. Ibid., Sig. A4ʳ.

8. Method, Image, and Action in Literary Criticism

1. On neoclassical criticism, see Walter Jackson Bate, *From Classic to Romantic: Premises of Taste in Eighteenth-Century England* (Cambridge: Harvard Univ. Press, 1946), esp. 25, where Bate points to the "essentially unclassical interest in 'method' itself" during the Restoration. See also William Edinger, *Samuel Johnson and Poetic Style* (Chicago: Univ. of Chicago Press, 1977), 31; Jean Hagstrum, *Samuel Johnson's Literary Criticism* (1952; reprint, Chicago: Univ. of Chicago Press, 1967), esp. chap. 1; *The Sister Arts: The Tradition of Literary Pictorialism and English Poetry from Dryden to Gray* (Chicago: Univ. of Chicago Press, 1958); Robert D. Hume, *Dryden's Criticism* (Ithaca: Cornell Univ. Press, 1970); Emerson R. Marks, *The Poetics of Reason: English Neoclassical Criticism* (New York: Random House, 1968); *Relativist and Absolutist: The Early Neoclassical Debate in England* (New Brunswick, N.J.: Rutgers Univ. Press, 1955); Robert Marsh, *Four Dialectical Theories of Poetry: An Aspect of English Neoclassical Criticism* (Chicago: Univ. of Chicago Press, 1965); and Irène Simon, ed. and intro., *Neo-Classical Criticism, 1660–1800* (Columbia: Univ. of South Carolina Press, 1971). Spingarn's essay, which prefaces his invaluable edition of seventeenth-century criticism, remains an incisive piece of criticism. See J. E. Spingarn, ed. and intro., *Critical Essays of the Seventeenth Century,* 3 vols. (Bloomington: Indiana Univ. Press, 1957), 1:ix-cvi. More recent work includes John L. Mahoney, *The Whole Internal Universe: Imita-*

tion and the New Defense of Poetry in British Criticism, 1660–1830 (New York: Fordham Univ. Press, 1985); Douglas Lane Patey, *Probability and Literary Form: Philosophic Theory and Literary Practice in the Augustan Age* (Cambridge: Cambridge Univ. Press, 1984); and Rose A. Zimbardo, *A Mirror to Nature: Transformations in Drama and Aesthetics, 1660–1732* (Lexington: Univ. Press of Kentucky, 1986). Although not derived from it, my argument receives support from Patey's. I depart from Patey in (among other things) my emphasis on the literary methods of the critical texts I examine and in my greater focus on the specific forces at play within Restoration criticism. (All references to Spingarn's *Critical Essays* appear as "Spingarn" below.)

2. Marks, *Poetics of Reason,* 45.

3. For a similar point, see Patey, *Probability and Literary Form,* 175.

4. Sir Robert Howard, Preface to *The Great Favourite* (1668), in Spingarn, 2:110.

5. Thomas Rymer, Preface to the translation of René Rapin's *Reflections on Aristotle's Treatise of Poesie* (1674), in *The Critical Works of Thomas Rymer,* ed. Curt A. Zimansky (New Haven: Yale Univ. Press, 1956), 16.

6. John Dennis, *The Impartial Critick, or Some Observations upon a Late Book, Entituled a Short View of Tragedy Written by Mr. Rymer* (1693), in *The Critical Works of John Dennis,* ed. Edward Niles Hooker, 2 vols. (Baltimore: Johns Hopkins Univ. Press, 1939), 1:11.

7. Sir William Davenant, "The Author's Preface to His Much Honor'd Friend, M. Hobbes," in *Sir William Davenant's Gondibert,* ed. David F. Glandish (Oxford: Clarendon Press, 1971), 44.

8. For discussion of Hobbes's critical theory, see James Engell, *The Creative Imagination: Enlightenment to Romanticism* (Cambridge: Harvard Univ. Press, 1981), esp. chap. 2. The Hobbes-Davenant debate raised contemporary interest among the group I have discussed in chapter 3 above, and it is curiously linked with Gassendi's neo-Epicureanism. On March 1649, Cavendish reports to Pell that "I have not yet Mr: Gassendes his Epicurean philosophie; nor have heard from Mr: Hobbes a long time, but Sr: William Davenant latelie sent my Brother a Preface to an intended Poem of his not yet printed; but the preface printed and directed to Mr: Hobbes, with Mr: Hobbes his answear to it, likewise printed and bound together." See Helen Hervey, "Hobbes and Descartes in the Light of Some Unpublished Letters of the Correspondence between Sir Charles Cavendish and Dr. John Pell," *Osiris* 10 (1952): 87.

9. For a 'psychological' view, see Clarence De Witt Thorpe, *The Aesthetic Theory of Thomas Hobbes* (Ann Arbor: Univ. of Michigan Press, 1940), esp. chap. 3.

10. Thomas Sprat, *The History of the Royal Society of London,* ed. Jackson I. Cope and Harold Whitmore Jones (Saint Louis: Washington Univ. Studies, 1959), 111–12.

11. On Epicurean accounts of the relation between sense data and the operations of judgment and reason, see Benjamin Farrington, *The Faith of Epicurus* (London: Weidenfield and Nicholson, 1967), 109; and J. M. Rist, *Epicurus: An Introduction* (Cambridge: Cambridge Univ. Press, 1972), 89.

12. Davenant, Preface to *Gondibert,* in *Gondibert,* 21.

13. On wit, see Thomas Hobbes, *Leviathan,* ed. C. B. Macpherson (Harmondsworth, Eng.: Penguin, 1968), 134–35; and Sprat, *History of the Royal Society,* 413–16.

14. Davenant, Preface to *Gondibert,* in *Gondibert,* 19–20.

15. Ibid., 38.

16. Thomas Hobbes, *The Answer of Mr Hobbes to Sr Will. Davenant's Preface Before Gondibert* (1650), in *Gondibert*, 49.

17. Thomas Hobbes, *De Corpore*, in *The English Works of Thomas Hobbes*, ed. Sir William Molesworth, 11 vols. (London: Bohn, 1839–45), 1:66.

18. Ibid.

19. Ibid., 1:17. Hobbes had already articulated the view in *Leviathan*, 101: "The generall use of Speech, is to transferre our Mentall Discourse, into Verball; or the Trayne of our Thoughts, into a Trayne of Words; and that for two commodities; whereof one is, the Registring of the Consequences of our Thoughts; which being apt to slip out of our memory, and put us to a new labour, may again be recalled, by such words as they were marked by."

20. See J.W.N. Watkins, *Hobbes's System of Ideas: A Study in the Political Significance of Philosophical Theories* (London: Hutchinson, 1965), esp. 144–50.

21. See Richard Peters, *Hobbes* (Harmondsworth, Eng.: Pelican, 1956), 82.

22. "For seeing all names are imposed to signifie our conceptions; and all our affections are but conceptions; when we conceive the same things differently, we can hardly avoyd different naming of them" (*Leviathan*, 109).

23. Hobbes, *English Works*, 1:15; 1:13.

24. Hobbes, Answer to Davenant, in *Gondibert*, 52.

25. Hobbes, *Leviathan*, 106.

26. Hobbes, *English Works*, 1:14.

27. Ibid., 1:14–15.

28. Hobbes, Answer to Davenant, in *Gondibert*, 53.

29. Ibid., 51.

30. For the revision of Aristotelian notions of probability in seventeenth-century critical theory, see Joan C. Grace, *Tragic Theory in the Critical Works of Thomas Rymer, John Dennis, and John Dryden* (Rutherford, N.J.: Fairleigh Dickinson Univ. Press, 1975), 19ff.

31. Hobbes, *Preface to Homer's Odysses, Translated by Tho. Hobbes of Malmesbury* (1675), in Spingarn, 2:71.

32. Alan Roper has pointed out to me that Horace himself discusses the balance between standing far off and standing too near in the same passage in which he describes his principle of *ut pictura poesis*.

33. See, for example, Hobbes, *Leviathan*, 690–91. Hobbes also writes against Aristotelian essentialism in *Decameron Physiologicum* by concentrating on the verb "to be": "For having said in themselves (for example): *a tree is a plant*, and conceiving well enough what is the signification of those names, knew not what to make of the word *is*, that couples those names; nor daring to call it a body, they called it by a new name (derived from the word *est*), *essentia*, and *substantia*, deceived by the idiom of their own language. For in many other tongues, and namely in the Hebrew, there is no such copulative. They thought the names of things sufficiently connected, when they are placed in their natural consequence; and were therefore never troubled with essences, nor other fallacy from the copulative *est*" (*English Works*, 7:81).

34. Sir Robert Howard, *Preface to Four New Plays* (1665), in Spingarn, 2:101–2.

35. John Evelyn, Letter to Sir Peter Wyche (1665), in Spingarn, 2:310.

36. Sir William Temple, *An Essay upon the Ancient and Modern Learning* (1690), in Spingarn, 3:64.

37. William Wotton, *Reflections upon Ancient and Modern Learning* (1694), in Spingarn, 3:206–7.

38. Alan Roper has pointed out that the Horation motto from the Renaissance to Addison tended to take the prescriptive form, *"ut pictura poesis erit."* Here I focus on the descriptive possibilities of the Horatian maxim.

39. George Granville, Lord Landsdowne, *An Essay upon Unnatural Flights in Poetry* (1701), in Spingarn, 3:292.

40. R. F. Jones, *Ancients and Moderns: A Study in the Rise of the Scientific Movement in Seventeenth-Century England,* 2d ed. (Gloucester, Mass.: Peter Smith, 1961), esp. chap. 2. Jones characteristically tends to think of all figuration as 'unscientific.' See also *Samuel Johnson: Selected Poetry and Prose,* ed. Frank Brady and W. K. Wimsatt (Berkeley: Univ. of California Press, 1977), 280.

41. Wotton, *Reflections,* in Spingarn, 3:219.

42. Evelyn to Wyche, in Spingarn, 2:310.

43. Temple, *Of Poetry,* in Spingarn, 3:88.

44. Wotton, *Reflections,* in Spingarn, 3:218.

45. Temple, *Of Poetry,* in Spingarn, 3:75ff. Temple holds to the runic origins of languages, but he attacks the magical properties ascribed to them by the Romance tradition (ibid., 79).

46. Temple, *Of Poetry,* in Spingarn, 3:78.

47. Walter Charleton, *Physiologia Epicuro-Gassendo-Charletoniana* (London, 1654), 369.

48. Ibid., 373. Here Charleton describes not sound, but the powers of "invisible Emanations" on snakes, which a trickster releases to overwhelm his audience. The principle applies obviously to the invisible powers of music, which he has just discussed.

49. Howard, Preface to *The Great Favourite,* in Spingarn, 2:108.

50. See Brian Vickers, "The Royal Society and English Prose Style: A Reassessment," in *Rhetoric and the Pursuit of Truth: Language Change in the Seventeenth and Eighteenth Centuries* (Los Angeles: William Andrews Clark Memorial Library, 1985), 6–9.

51. Granville, *Essay upon Unnatural Flights,* in Spingarn, 3:293.

52. Granville, "Explanatory Annotations on the Foregoing Poem," in ibid., 3:295–96.

53. Dennis, *Impartial Critick,* in *Critical Works,* 1:24.

54. As a qualification to my argument, Patey presents a caveat against treating the dialogue form as always expressing an inferential model of literary apprehension. See Patey, *Probability and Literary Form,* 173–74.

55. Marks, *Poetics of Reason,* 27.

56. John Ogilby, *The Fables of Aesop, Paraphrased in Verse, and Adorn'd with Sculpture* (London, 1651), frontispiece.

57. Davenant, Preface to *Gondibert,* in *Gondibert,* 7.

58. Ibid., 7; 9; 13; 15–16.

59. Ibid., 31.

60. Ibid., 17.

61. Hobbes, Answer to Davenant, in *Gondibert,* 49.

62. Ibid., 50.

63. Sir Robert Howard, Preface to *Four New Plays,* in Spingarn, 2:100.

64. Temple, *Essay,* in Spingarn, 3:32.

65. A locus classicus of neoclassical discussions of fables is, of course, Bacon's *De Sapientia Veterum,* in which Bacon describes a *dämmerung* of obscure historical knowledge. See *The Works of Francis Bacon,* ed. James Spedding, Robert Leslie Ellis, and Douglas Denon Heath, 14 vols. (London: Longman, 1857–74), 6:342. According to the logic of my argument conducted here and in relation to neoclassical linguistics, Thomas Noel makes a false distinction between "the animal or Aesopoian fable" and "literary plot, story, or narrative in general," because it is precisely their common cognitive and somatic roots that unite them. See Thomas Noel, *Theories of the Fable in the Eighteenth Century* (New York: Columbia Univ. Press, 1975), 1.

66. Dennis, *Impartial Critick,* in *Critical Works,* 1:35.

67. Davenant, Preface to *Gondibert,* in *Gondibert,* 30.

68. Ibid., 40–41: "And as Poesy is the best Expositor of Nature (Nature being misterious to such as use not to consider) so Nature is the best Interpreter of God, and more cannot be said of Religion." Patey diagrams this relation in *Probability and Literary Form,* 129.

69. Ibid., 41.

70. Frank Kermode, *The Genesis of Secrecy: On the Interpretation of Narrative* (Cambridge: Harvard Univ. Press, 1979), esp. chap. 2.

71. Temple, *Essay,* in Spingarn, 3:35–36.

72. Temple, "Of Poetry," in Spingarn, 3:81.

73. Exactly the same relationship between figure or image and fable informs Sir Roger L'Estrange's advertisement for his *Fables.* Beginning with the premise that "children *are but* Blank Paper, *ready Indifferently for any Impression,*" he argues that we can instruct them by a *"Natural Direction,"* because they manifest a universal human fascination with fables. See Sir Roger L'Estrange, *Fables* (London, 1692), Sig. A1ᵛ.

74. Temple, "Of Poetry," in Spingarn, 3:88; 3:89; 3:90.

75. Davenant, Preface to *Gondibert,* in *Gondibert,* 10–11.

76. Ibid., 16.

77. Eric Rothstein, *George Farquhar* (New York: Twayne, 1967), 121–22.

78. George Farquhar, "A Discourse upon Comedy, in Reference to the English Stage. In a Letter to a Friend" (1702), in *Eighteenth-Century Critical Essays,* ed. Scott Elledge (Ithaca: Cornell Univ. Press, 1961), 80–99, esp. 92.

79. Hobbes, Answer to Davenant, in *Gondibert,* 52–53; Preface to *Homer's Odysses,* in Spingarn, 2:67ff.

80. See Patey, *Probability and Literary Form,* 102–3.

81. Hobbes, Answer to Davenant, in *Gondibert,* 51.

82. Edward Phillips, Preface to *Theatrum Poetarum* (1675), in Spingarn, 2:267–68.

83. Ibid., 2:268.

84. Dennis, *The Impartial Critick,* in *Critical Works,* 1:39.

85. Ibid.

86. Wotton, *Reflections,* in Spingarn, 3:219.

87. Grace, *Tragic Theory,* 38.

88. Rymer, "Preface to Rapin," in *Critical Works*, 2–3.

89. Rymer, *A Short View of Tragedy, Its Original, Excellency, and Corruption, with Some Reflections on Shakespear and Other Practitioners for the Stage* (1693), in *Works*, 112ff. For extracts of King Francis I's legislation, see Thomas Rymer, *A Short View of Tragedy* (1693; facsimile reprint, Menston, Eng.: Scolar Press, 1970), 169–82. Zimansky's standard edition omits this material.

90. Rymer, *The Tragedies of the Last Age Consider'd and Examin'd by the Practice of the Ancients and by the Common Sense of All Ages* (1678), in *Critical Works*, 2–3.

91. Rymer, "Preface to Rapin," in *Critical Works*, 8. Elsewhere, Rymer writes: "Therefore *Aristotle* is always telling us that Poetry is *[spoudaioteron kai philosophōteron]*, is more general and abstracted, is led more by Philosophy, the reason and nature of things, than History: which only records things higlety, piglety, right or wrong as they happen" (*Critical Works*, 163).

92. "Nothing is more odious in Nature than an improbable lye; And, certainly, never was any Play fraught, like this of *Othello*, with improbabilities" (Rymer, *A Short View*, in *Critical Works*, 134).

93. Rymer, *A Short View*, in *Critical Works*, 165.

94. For example, Rymer objects to the language put in Brutus's mouth (ibid., 166).

95. Rymer, *A Short View*, in *Critical Works*, 148–49; see especially ibid., 84–85; 110–11.

96. Ibid., 88.

97. Ibid., 117.

98. Ibid., 108.

99. Ibid., 44–45.

100. Rymer, *Tragedies of the Last Age*, in *Critical Works*, 19; Rymer, *A Short View*, in *Critical Works*, 85. Here, of course, Rymer is referring to *actio*, or "acting," in the common seventeenth-century sense, but the argument still connects with my wider discussion of "action" as an ideal.

101. Rymer, *A Short View*, in *Critical Works*, 87.

102. Ibid., 112.

103. Ibid., 111.

104. Davenant, Preface to *Gondibert*, in *Gondibert*, 39.

9. The Nod of God in *Absalom and Achitophel*: Dryden's Process of Speech

1. Samuel Johnson, *Lives of the Poets: A Selection*, ed. J. P. Hardy (Oxford: Clarendon Press, 1971), p. 179.

2. See Phillip Harth's salutary article, in which he warns against reading the poem's influence on political events: "Legends no Histories: The Case of *Absalom and Achitophel*," in *Studies in Eighteenth-Century Culture*, ed. Harold E. Pagliaro, vol. 4 (Madison: Univ. of Wisconsin Press, 1975), 13–29.

3. Johnson, *Lives*, p. 178.

4. The classic statement on David's final speech is Godfrey Davis, "The Conclusion of *Absalom and Achitophel*," reprinted in *Essential Articles for the Study of John Dryden*, ed. H. T. Swedenberg (Hamden, Conn.: Archon, 1966), 210–24. That the speech closely parallels King Charles II's constitutionally important speech at Oxford

does not necessarily mean that it constitutes a sufficient *epistemological* answer to the verbal corruption that David has initiated early in the poem. Bernard Schilling also fails to see that the poem is beset with linguistic problems from the outset; he writes that "in the end the king needs only to speak in order to prevail" (*Dryden and the Conservative Myth: A Reading of Absalom and Achitophel* [New Haven: Yale Univ. Press, 1961], 147). Other works with a political reading include: Michael J. Conlon, "The Passage on Government in Dryden's *Absalom and Achitophel*," *Journal of English and Germanic Philology* 78 (1979): 17–32; James Kinsley, "Historical Allusions in *Absalom and Achitophel*," *Review of English Studies*, n.s. 6 (1955): 291–97; Thomas E. Maresca, "The Context of Dryden's *Absalom and Achitophel*," *ELH* 41 (1974): 340–58.

5. William Myers, *Dryden* (London: Hutchinson, 1973), 93.

6. John Dryden, *Absalom and Achitophel*, in *The Works of John Dryden*, ed. Edward Niles Hooker and H. T. Swedenberg, Jr., 15 vols. to date (Berkeley: Univ. of California Press, 1956-), 2:3 (italics reversed); 2:4; 2:3; 5.

7. Dryden, *Life of Plutarch*, in *Works*, 17:272.

8. Dryden, *Absalom and Achitophel*, in *Works*, 2:4 (italics reversed); 2:3.

9. Dryden, *Life of Plutarch*, in *Works*, 17:271.

10. In *Astraea Redux*, Dryden compresses the ideas of method, language, analogy, experience, and rule into a few lines describing King Charles II's sufferings abroad:

> Nor is he onely by afflictions shown
> To conquer others Realms but rule his own:
> Recov'ring hardly what he lost before,
> His right indears it much, his purchase more.
> Inur'd to suffer ere he came to raigne
> No rash procedure will his actions stain.
> To bus'ness ripened by digestive thought
> His future rule is into Method brought:
> As they who first Proportion understand
> With easie Practice reach a Masters hand.
>
> (*Works*, 1:24, ll. 83–92)

Method is the product of experience, or "purchase," which is King Charles II's greater of two claims to rule, the other being "right."

11. Dryden, *Absalom and Achitophel*, in *Works*, 2:5 (italics reversed).

12. John Dryden and Sir William Soames, trans., *The Art of Poetry. Written in French by the Sieur de Boileau, Made English* (1683), in Dryden, *Works*, 2:124–56, ll. 151–55.

13. Dryden, *Life of Plutarch*, in *Works*, 17:271.

14. The hollow spewing of words is associated with David's licentiousness, as I shall argue, but also with the notion of the force and abuse of the "pen" in its double entendre, as where Dryden tells MacFlecknoe to "stretch [thy] Pen" (l. 143) and pictures "Venom" touching "thy *Irish* pen" (ll. 201–2), an image of sexual and verbal failure. True writing is thus associated with the propagation of true works, of true heirs; false writing—in both *Mac Flecknoe* and *Absalom and Achitophel*—is associated with incontinence and orality.

15. It is interesting to remember that "motion" frequently carries a satanic resonance in *Paradise Lost*.

16. The "force" applied in this case is an exact equivalent to Dryden's wider criticism of "force" and rape.

17. Worsley defends the "Oracle" of Catholic tradition by distinguishing two senses in which language can be viewed: "external Language" "is twofold, First *Private* and *Immediate*. 2. *Publick* and *Mediate*." Against the somatic tradition I describe, Worsley takes these two ways of seeing language as two different means of approaching knowledge, the first representing the possibility of penetrating the space of God's mind ("his interiour mind"). Moses represents both modes of apprehension: at the burning bush, he experiences "Gods private and immediate way of speaking"; but when he becomes a prophet to the Israelites, he must use public and mediated forms of persuasion, such as miracles. By enforcing this distinction, Worsley, a Catholic, is attempting to erode Anglican and certain Presbyterian attempts to forge a single hermeneutic for all modes of experience, as well as to preserve the Catholic prerogative to police certain "religious" issues. See Edward Worsley, *Reason and Religion. Or the Certain Rule of Faith* (Antwerp, 1672), 545–49.

18. Thomas Hobbes, *Leviathan*, ed. C. B. Macpherson (Harmondsworth, Eng.: Penguin, 1968), 410.

19. Ibid., 411; 466.

20. It is precisely the misleading appearance of self-evidence in maxims that most disturbs Locke. In failing to expose the processes by which they have customarily been raised from particulars, maxims offer a chimera of innate truths that disturbs Locke and Dryden for similar empirical and political (though not party-political) motives. See, for example John Locke, *An Essay concerning Human Understanding*, ed. Peter H. Nidditch (Oxford: Clarendon Press, 1975), bk. 4, chap. 7, sec. 14.

21. Earl Miner, *Dryden's Poetry* (Bloomington: Indiana Univ. Press, 1967), 118.

22. See, for example, l. 115. The poem's engagement with *Paradise Lost* is instructive at this juncture: Dryden wants us to see that the poem opens *in medias res* in the realm of satanic chaos, as if we had begun our reading of Milton's poem without the corrective and proleptic entry through the invocation to book one. The narrator has absorbed those fallen values and only in the process of the poem learns to exercise discrimination. The best explication of the rhetorical relation between Milton and Dryden is Anne Davidson Ferry, *Milton and the Miltonic Dryden* (Cambridge: Harvard Univ. Press, 1968).

23. Gen. 38:9.

24. Gal. 4:25–26.

25. Rom. 7:12.

26. Gal. 3:24.

27. Juliet Mitchell comments on narcissism: "It is a question of finding the self-image in the image of another, and of constituting the self in that discovered image. This first rooting of the self is remote from any notions we might have of 'reality'—it is, and it must be, an imaginary construct." See *Psychoanalysis and Feminism: Freud, Reich, Laing and Women* (New York: Vintage, 1975), 39.

28. Interestingly, Locke uses the phrase "promiscuous use" to describe the collapsing of "three several distinct *Ideas*" into "so doubtful a term" as "*Substance*." Significantly,

this word conflates ideas referring to God, the soul, and the body, which Locke says leads to "Confusion and Error." See *Essay,* bk. 2, chap. 8, sec. 18.

29. The spatialization, the accommodation of divine discourse in inscription, is graphically conveyed in the story of Moses having to reascend Mount Sinai to obtain a second copy of the tablets of the law, which are then placed in the ark. This idea informs Matthew Poole's attack on Catholic oral or nonwritten tradition. He writes: "So little did God trust this (now supposed infallible) way of orall Tradition, that he would not venture the Decalogue upon it . . . but write *[sic]* it with his own finger once and againe after the breaking of the first Tables" (*The Nullity of the Roman Church* [London, 1666], 140).

30. Deut. 31:26–27a.

31. 2 Sam. 6:6–7.

32. Dryden, *Absalom and Achitophel,* in *Works,* 2:4.

33. This problem is established by *Absalom and Achitophel.* There are other Dryden poems less interested in interrogating the grounds of the poet's speech.

34. *Foot-steps* is a favorite term both with Locke and Le Clerc.

35. John Locke, *The Reasonableness of Christianity,* in *The Works of John Locke,* 10 vols., 11th ed. (London: W. Otridge et al., 1812), 7:135.

36. R. B. Onians, *The Origins of European Thought about the Body, the Mind, the Soul, the World, Time, and Fate* (1951; reprint, Cambridge: Cambridge Univ. Press, 1988), 97–99; 138ff.

Index

Designed by Martha Farlow

Composed by The Composing Room of Michigan, Inc., in Galliard

Printed by Princeton University Press on 50-lb. Glatfelter Supple Offset
and bound in Joanna Arrestox A with Rainbow Colonial endsheets